By the same author

EASTERN EUROPE BETWEEN THE WARS, 1918–1941
THE EAST EUROPEAN REVOLUTION
THE PATTERN OF COMMUNIST REVOLUTION
FROM LENIN TO KRUSHCHEV
NEITHER WAR NOR PEACE
NATIONALISM AND COMMUNISM

THE DECLINE OF IMPERIAL RUSSIA
1855–1914

The Decline
of Imperial Russia
1855—1914

by

HUGH SETON-WATSON

METHUEN & CO LTD
11 NEW FETTER LANE EC4

First published October 1952
Reprinted three times
Reprinted in this size 1964
Printed and bound in Great Britain by
Butler & Tanner Ltd, Frome
1.5

CONTENTS

v

PART III

THE LAST CHANCES 1905–1914

MAPS

Drawn by Denys R. Baker

MAPS

INTRODUCTION

THE purpose of this work is to describe and explain the stages of the Decline of the Russian Empire between the Crimean War and the First World War. The Empire's Fall, in revolution and civil war, lies outside its scope, though reference is made to it in the Epilogue. The Fall forms the subject of a vast literature of unequal merit in Russia, Europe and America: the Decline has received far less attention. There are excellent studies of special aspects, but few attempts to survey the whole half-century from the emancipation of the serfs to the catastrophe of 1914. The complexity of the issues, and the varying quality of the sources, forbid the historian to set himself too high an aim. I have tried to pursue accuracy and clarity rather than literary effect. If this work is of practical use to any who wish to understand the background of contemporary Russia it will have served a purpose.

Though Russian history is little known in Europe, there is no subject on which European writers, informed or less informed, are more willing to theorise. From the numerous enthusiastic champions of the various ready-made theories I can expect little patience. There are the various theories about the Slav soul, Dostoevski, the mystics and the noble mujik; and the Polish theories about the inward wickedness and "differentness" of all Russians, which only Poles are able to understand. There are numerous variations on the themes of a happy country of happy people destroyed by the wicked Bolsheviks, or of a vast torture-chamber from which the oppressed people was liberated—if a little roughly—by the glorious—or at least "progressive"—Bolsheviks. There is the version put forward by the infallible author(s) of the *Short History of the CPSU(b)*. Then there are the familiar theories about Russia's role within Europe. To some she is the generous protector and liberator of the poor little oppressed Slav peoples; to others the noble defender of Europe against the Germanic hordes; to others again the impious enemy of the noble Germanic defenders of Europe. This does not exhaust the list. Most of the ready-made theories contain bits—in most cases small bits—of truth. I hope that these bits are to be found within my account, but I am unable to support any of these theories, and both unable and unwilling to produce a rival of my own. This does not mean any general objection to theory as such, or a belief that history should be a mere list of "facts". On the contrary, theoretical analysis and generalisations are an essential part of the historian's task, and in few periods more than in the last decades of Imperial Russia. But I do not see the need for an all-embracing dogmatic explanation or for a quasi-scientific "system". That Russian history in this period is too little known is due to the difficulty of access to material, not to the need for any mysterious key for its understanding.

Most students of history have special interests within their period or subject. It may be well to state my own. Russia first interested me as a great country which in certain respects resembled, and always greatly influenced, the small countries of Eastern Europe, with which I have had some acquaintance during the last decade. Secondly, Russia interested me as a country with a revolutionary tradition of its own, which in recent times has produced the world Communist movement that to-day has made an impact on most countries of the world. Thirdly Imperial Russia, the country within which Leninism was born, provides the first example of a phenomenon which has since repeated itself elsewhere—the impact of western ideas and western economy on a backward social and political structure. The rise of an intelligentsia in rebellion against society and state, and the formation from its ranks of sects of professional revolutionaries, are less specifically Russian phenomena than historians of Russia have considered them. Of these three aspects of Russia it was the first that drew me to the study of the period, but it is the second and third that have most interested me during my work. It is the third aspect whose further study seems to me to offer the most valuable lessons for our own time.

The period falls into three sections—the reign of Alexander II (1855–81), the period of reaction (1881–1905) and the "Revolution" of 1905 and its aftermath (1905–14). Of these three the first has received more and better treatment in Western Europe than the other two. Because it is relatively well known, I have here devoted relatively less space to it. In particular, the sixties, a period of development of political ideas, have received less attention than the seventies, a period of revolutionary action. This is partly because the ideas of the sixties are in some sense a culmination of an earlier period, which cannot be treated within the limits of this

work, and partly because in general this work is concerned more
with action than with ideas. The second and third periods have
been neglected by Western, and even by Russian, writers, with the
exception of the important but restricted field of Leninist scholastics.
The nine years from 1905 to 1914 are as full of important trends
and events as the two preceding periods of twenty-four and
twenty-six years.

The subject also falls into three sections, which may be called
the structure of state and society, political movements and foreign
relations. The book is therefore divided into three Parts which
correspond to the three periods, and each Part into three chapters
which correspond approximately to the three subdivisions of subject. Each Part has a chapter on foreign relations. Within each
Part also the balance between the other two sections of the subject
—structure of state and society and political movements—has been
as far as possible preserved, though this may not at first sight be
obvious owing to the different forms which these took within the
three chronological periods. Thus in Part I the division is between
the basic structure on the accession of Alexander and the reforms
which he introduced; in Part II between economic and political
development; in Part III between the forces set in motion in
1905–6 and the attempt made to repress and to canalise these forces
after 1907. As the chronological subdivisions do not in all cases
correspond to the subdivisions by subject, and as some important
problems belong to more than one of the subdivisions, there has
inevitably been some overlapping between the Parts. This is
especially the case in foreign relations, somewhat less so in economic
affairs. The following are the main examples. The section in
Part I on Russian expansion in Asia is brought down to 1885
though Part I in general ends in 1881. The development of agriculture and industry after 1861 are discussed in Part II, though in
general Part II begins with the reign of Alexander III. The brief
discussions of the Church and of the armed forces in Part I are
there taken down to the end of the century, and these questions
are not again mentioned until after 1905. The Polish Question is
treated in Parts I and II as a matter of foreign policy, in Part III
mainly as a matter of internal policy, in the sections on The
Nationalities in and after 1905. The Ukrainian problem is treated
in the same manner, owing to its close relationship with the Polish.
It is hoped that the reader will be helped rather than hindered by
this arrangement. The special Subjects Index should also facilitate
his task.

It may be well to state here which aspects of Russian development in the period are stressed, and which are underemphasised or omitted. A work of these dimensions cannot describe everything, and it should help the prospective reader to know what he can and cannot expect.

In the sections on "structure of state and society", little attention has been given to personalities. This is partly because relatively more is known to the British reading public of Russian personalities (for instance, Alexander II or Witte or Lenin), than of the problems with which they were connected, and partly because for several outstanding personalities (for instance, Dmitri Tolstoy or Stolypin) very little material is available. Nevertheless I have tried to indicate the part played by personalities at decisive moments in the period.

An important part of these sections concerns economic development. It is a curious phenomenon that at a time when the self-styled prophets of Marxism show by word and by deed that for them political factors have absolute priority over economic, a kind of quasi-Marxist snobbery should be prevalent among non-Marxists and even anti-Marxists in the West. In such circles it is considered almost indecent not to pay lip service to an imagined universal primacy of economic over political factors. During the period of Russian history under review, discussion as to whether the causes of events were principally political or economic has as much value as a discussion as to whether the egg preceded the hen or the hen the egg. That economic changes of great importance took place in Russia at this time cannot be denied. I have tried to put these changes in their historical perspective. My approach to them is of course not that of the specialised economic historian, still less of the economic analyst. I have attempted only to show the general economic background and to discuss certain economic controversies that were vital issues of Russian social and political life. In agriculture the main points are the legal position of the peasantry, the distribution of land, the problems of overpopulation and subsidiary employment, and the standard of living. In the other sectors of the economy they are the growth of the main industries, foreign trade and tariff policy, taxation, the rise of business and working classes and their relations with each other and with the government.

Another essential part of the same section is the question of nationalities. Russia was as much a multi-national empire as was Austria-Hungary. This has not been adequately appreciated in the West, partly because the nations concerned live still further from our shores than do those once ruled by the Habsburgs, and partly because the collapse of the Russian Empire proved in the end less complete than that of Austria-Hungary. This in turn is due principally to the fact that the Russians, though forming less than half the population of the Empire, still dominated the other nations, numerically or culturally or in both respects, more thoroughly than did the German Austrians and Hungarians their Slav or Roumanian subjects. Russian history is usually written as the history of the Russian 44 per cent of the Empire's population. On the other hand writers belonging to one of the nationalities tend to exaggerate their own people's importance and to underrate the Russians. I shall satisfy neither. The limits both of space and of accessible material have prevented as complete a survey as the subject deserves. An attempt has however been made to present the main features of the political and social development of Poles, Ukrainians, Finns, Jews, Balts, Caucasians and Tatars, besides occasional reference to the peoples of Central Asia and the Russian Far East.

The political movements are not considered from the special point of view of the historian of ideas, still less of the political philosopher. I have tried to summarise the ideas of the sixties sufficiently to explain the events of the seventies and later decades. This has made it necessary to dismiss in a few words such a great figure as Herzen, who belongs, I think, essentially to the period preceding the Emancipation. Unsatisfactory though this is, there seemed no other way, within the limits that I have had to impose on myself, of presenting the political development of the last decades of Imperial Russia. This work is also no place for an analysis of the basic ideas of Marx. It is assumed that the reader either has some elementary knowledge of these, or will seek it in one of the many works explaining them, or best of all in the works of Marx himself. Leninism however consists essentially of theory about revolutionary tactics. Leninist doctrines are therefore to some extent analysed, in connection with specific historical events and problems. But it is important to remember that Lenin's greatest successes were achieved after the end of the period here described. This book is not primarily intended to be a study of Lenin. It is a study of a period of Russian history, towards the end of which Lenin played an important but not yet a dominant role. It is also necessary to warn the reader that the limits of space have prevented detailed treatment of all the subtleties of revolutionary controversy.

The complex combination of serious theoretical argument, crude personal insult and ingenious intrigue which characterised the disputes between Mensheviks and Bolsheviks and between different factions even within these two factions require one or more large volumes to themselves. All that has here been attempted is to show the most important causes of the split, and to trace the growth of the most important differences of doctrine which emerged from it. The pious scholiasts of the Marxist faith will be duly disgusted but it is hoped that the infidel reader will be able to find his way and will not be grossly misled. Another problem of revolutionary doctrine, so complex as to defy an attempt at brief treatment, is the question to what extent the Populists and Socialist Revolutionaries considered it possible for Russia to bypass capitalism. The usual generalisations on this subject are not sufficient. I have tried, in the text and in footnotes, to give a picture that is not too misleading. I am by no means satisfied that I have succeeded.

Still more serious, but intentional, is the absence of any survey of Russian literature during the period. During the reign of Nicholas I (1825–1855) literature and literary criticism were the only means by which political ideas could be expressed inside Russia. In the period with which this work deals, this was no longer the case. Nevertheless political discussion still largely took the form of discussion about the characters of the great—and not only the great—works of literature; writers continued to have political influence; and the obsession of most writers with "social issues" had a far-reaching influence on the attitude of the intelligentsia as a whole. Yet it is clear to me that this work is no place to summarise the achievement of Russian nineteenth-century literature. The great writers must speak for themselves. Readers of this work who feel a deeper interest in Russia must go to the great writers for enlightenment. They may also more quickly acquaint themselves with the broad issues raised in literature by reading one or more of the numerous histories of Russian literature.

In the sections devoted to foreign relations I have tried to deal with Russian foreign policy rather than with the details of diplomacy. These sections are of course based on considerable study of diplomatic documents and of the work of diplomatic historians. But as the diplomatic negotiations of this period have been fairly thoroughly studied elsewhere there seemed to be no advantage in describing them once again. The exceptions are a few cases in which I have referred mainly to Russian documents which are somewhat less well known to western readers. Such are the

Björkö treaty of 1905, the French loan to Russia of 1906 and the Russian attitude to the formation of the Balkan alliances in 1911–12. Some space has also been devoted to the negotiations preceding the Franco-Russian Alliance and the Russo-Japanese War. These negotiations are of course very well known to historians, but they are of such importance that they cannot be hastily passed over even in a general survey such as this. In general the emphasis in this work is on the substance of the various international disputes rather than on the manner in which they were treated. In some cases an account of the substance has required a brief explanation of the internal political background in countries other than Russia (Austria-Hungary and the Balkan States). Though this exceeds the limits of Russian history in the narrow sense, it should help rather than confuse the reader.

The western historian of Russia is inevitably dissatisfied with his sources. My own circumstances have confined me to those which can be found in this country, and these I have by no means exhausted. I am well aware of the handicap of having never visited Russia. My generation has been deprived of the opportunities enjoyed by that of the late Sir Bernard Pares, the founder of Russian historical studies in Britain. The feel of the plains and forests and cities of Russia, the personal experience of Russian hospitality and friendship, hostility and obstruction, are absent from my pages. The few contacts that I have had with Russians, and the glimpses that I have had of them at work in other lands, are an insufficient substitute. I can only hope that the detachment of an outsider may have compensating advantages.

Certain subjects within the period have already been thoroughly studied by western writers, to pursue whose footsteps would be almost impertinent, and would in most cases be made impossible by the inaccessibility of the sources. For my sections on agriculture I have relied principally on the masterly work of Professor G. T. Robinson, *Rural Russia under the Old Regime*. For the diplomacy of 1875–8 and the various influences on Russian foreign policy at that time I have relied principally on the late B. H. Sumner's no less masterly work *Russia and the Balkans 1870–1880*.

The problem of spelling defies satisfactory solution. I have followed the usual practice with Russian names, with a few minor exceptions. The Russian aspirate, usually rendered "kh"—which is meaningless to British readers—I have written throughout as "h"—which is near enough to the Russian sound.[1] Thus, Harkov

---

[1] Exceptions are the Asiatic words Khan, Bokhara and Khiva and the Austrian name Khevenhüller, all of which are so written in Latin alphabet, and are not due to transliteration from Cyrillic.

not Kharkov. Family names ending in "iy", which in the West are sometimes rendered with the ending "y" and sometimes "i", are here throughout spelt "i". Thus, Chernyshevski and Trotski. In reproducing Russian phrases or book titles, in cases where "e" is pronounced "yo" or "g" is pronounced "v", they are so spelt. Polish, Czech, Serbo-Croatian, Roumanian and Turkish names are written in the slightly modified Latin spelling used in those languages. In the spelling of Swedish and Finnish names the only unfamiliar letter is "å", which is pronounced approximately as a long "o" in German.

Dates of the month are complicated by the prevalence in Russia until the Revolution of the Julian calendar, as opposed to the Gregorian calendar of Europe. In the chapters on internal policy I have throughout given both dates—e.g. 19th February/4th March 1861. In the chapters on foreign relations, where events occur which are frequently referred to in non-Russian works of diplomatic history, to which the reader may wish to refer or with which he may already be familiar, I have given only the European (Gregorian) dates.

I must acknowledge my great debt to the late Warden of All Souls, Mr. B. H. Sumner. He encouraged me in my work from an early stage, advised me on sources, lent me books, and read the greater part of the MS. No less great has been my debt to Mr. I. Berlin, Fellow of New College, whose vast knowledge of the intellectual life of Russia has been of immense help to me. I have to thank him for many suggestions and for many kinds of help, including the reading of the whole MS. He is of course not responsible for my opinions. Finally I must thank my wife for help of all kinds at all stages of the enterprise.

Oxford,
April 1952.

PART ONE
THE TSAR LIBERATOR 1855-1881

Chapter I

THE BACKGROUND

The Country and the People

THE name Russia at once calls to mind the notion of vastness. It is a land of long broad rivers, of deep dark forests, of sultry heat and extreme cold, of limitless plains. From central Russia the flat land spreads out towards the four points of the compass. Far to the north are the Arctic ices, far to the south the great mountain ranges and the closed sea. To the east the land rolls on, barely broken by the low-lying Urals, until it reaches the Pacific, separated at its northern corner by only seventy miles from America. To the west it rolls into Europe, and meets no important physical barrier before the shores of the Channel.

The most important natural division within European Russia is between the forest and the steppe. In the extreme north is the tundra. From the Arctic Circle until about latitude 57° N. stretch forests of pine and birch. South of this comes the zone of mixed forests, which includes oak and ash as well as conifers. It is a triangular area with its apex in the east near Kazan and stretching in the west roughly between Kiev and St. Petersburg.[1] At the beginning of the nineteenth century a large part of this area was of course under cultivation. To the south of the mixed forest zone comes a transitional region known as the woodland-steppe belt. The northern boundary of the steppe proper corresponds approximately to a line drawn from Kiev through Orel to Kazan. The greater part of the region between this line, the Black Sea and the Caucasus consists of rich agricultural soil, the famous black earth. The exceptions are the Crimean peninsula and the north coast of the Sea of Azov. Further east, the Caspian Sea is surrounded by a belt, some hundred miles broad, of poor pasture land and salt marshes.

---

[1] For a convenient recent description of the geography of Russia, see Jorre, *The Soviet Union* (Longmans, 1950). There is an excellent brief account in Sumner, *Survey of Russian History* (London, 1947), 2nd edition, chapter 1.

I

East of the Ural river the steppe continues into Siberia. To its south are deserts, and beyond them the fertile valleys of Oxus and Jaxartes and the mountain roof of Asia.

Already in the Middle Ages the furs of the northern forests were a source of wealth. They formed an important part of the trade of the Hansa cities.[1] Timber was exported to Britain from the eighteenth century. The typical cereal crop of the northern and central provinces in the middle of the nineteenth century was rye, of the black earth region wheat and maize. The south-western provinces specialised in sugar beet. Central Asia was well suited for cotton. By 1850 the mineral wealth of Russia was beginning to be known. The iron ore of the Urals had been exploited on a small scale since the seventeenth century. The iron of Krivoi Rog, the coal of the Donets basin and the petrol of the Caucasus were discoveries of the nineteenth.

The first Russian state in history was based on the rivers flowing into the Black Sea.[2] Its centre was Kiev, its culture largely Byzantine. It traded with Constantinople, the Moslem world, Central Europe and Scandinavia. In the twelfth century Kiev lost its supremacy, and became no more than the first among several Russian principalities which stretched to the upper Volga and the Dvina. The quarrels between the principalities, and the raids of various nomad races from the east, weakened Russia. In the thirteenth century came complete disaster when the Tatar hosts of Djingiz Khan and his successors overran the country and poured westwards into Europe.

When after a few years the flood receded, little was left of the old Russia. In the south-west, the Dnieper region, with Kiev itself, was conquered by the Grand Duchy of Lithuania, which in 1386 became united with the Kingdom of Poland. In the north-west the city of Novgorod, while paying tribute to the Tatars, became a powerful and prosperous community, growing rich on the Baltic trade and successfully resisting the attacks of the Swedish conquerors of Finland and the German conquerors of Esthonia. The Tatar state, known as the Golden Horde, had its centre at Sarai on the lower Volga and controlled the steppes and the Black Sea coast

---

[1] This subject is fully treated by Goetz, *Deutsch-russische Handelsgeschichte des Mittelalters* (Lubeck, 1922).

[2] For the general course of Russian history, the classic Russian work is V. O. Klyuchevsky, *Kurs russkoy istorii* (5 volumes), of which there is an English translation. S. F. Platonov, *History of Russia* (English translation, New York, 1925), is also an excellent work. Among foreign authors the outstanding works are Stählin, *Geschichte Russlands* (Berlin, 1939), 4 volumes; Milyukov, Seignobos and Eisenmann, *Histoire de Russie* (Paris, 1933), 3 volumes, and Sumner, *op. cit.*

as far west as the Dniester. The central Russian principalities remained as tributaries of the Horde. During the fourteenth century Moscow became the most important of them. It owed much to its geographical position, situated between the upper courses of the Volga and Oka, and not far from the sources of the Dvina and Dnieper. It owed something also to the cunning of its princes, who made themselves the trusted servants of the Tatar Khan by collecting his taxes from their neighbours.

At the end of the fourteenth century Moscow was strong enough to withstand the Tatars in battle, and in 1480 its ruler Ivan III finally repudiated any form of subordination to the Tatars. His grandson Ivan IV, "The Terrible" (1533–84), began the task of conquering the steppe. In 1552 he captured Kazan, and in 1556 Astrahan. Though the population of the Volga valley continued to consist largely of Tatars and other Asiatic races, it has been a part of Russia since then. At the end of the century Russian expansion beyond the Urals began. There was some resistance from the Tatars and Bashkirs of the steppes, but little from the primitive tribes of the forests. The demand for furs was an incentive to pioneers, and by the seventeenth century Russian weapons were greatly superior to those of the people whom they met. By the middle of the seventeenth century Russians had reached the Pacific. In the valley of the Amur river they met the organised power of the Chinese Empire, with which at last a frontier was settled by the Treaty of Nerchinsk in 1689.

Expansion towards the north-west also began in the fifteenth century. Ivan III subdued Novgorod in 1478. Ivan the Terrible began the long series of wars with Poland for the possession of the Baltic coast. At the end of his reign Muscovy had failed: Livonia was held by the Poles, Esthonia by the Swedes. Civil war early in the next century nearly led to the disintegration of Muscovy. But as Russia recovered, Poland declined. The chief rival to Russia in the north-west was now Sweden. The defeat of Sweden in the Great Northern War (1700–21) gave Russia the Baltic coast as far west as Riga, and enabled Peter the Great (1689–1725) to build his new capital at St. Petersburg.

Kiev was recovered from Poland in 1667, and from the middle of the seventeenth century the Cossacks[1] east of the Dnieper had for the most part recognised the authority of the Tsar. After the Great Northern War the Tsar's rule extended approximately to a line drawn between the Dnieper and the Donets rivers at the point where

[1] See below, pp. 32–3.

they are nearest to each other. It was Catherine II (1763-96) who brought under Russian rule the land lying between this line and the Black Sea. The last free Cossacks were subdued by 1775, the Crimea conquered from the Tatars in 1783, and the coast between Dnieper and Dniester taken from the Ottoman Empire in 1792. It was on this piece of coast that was founded in 1794 Odessa, which in the nineteenth century became the principal grain port of the empire. In 1812 the acquisition of Bessarabia brought Russia to the mouth of the Danube. In the west the First Partition of Poland (1772) added a strip of White Russia up to the Dvina and down both sides of the upper Dnieper, while the Second Partition (1793) brought a broad belt from the Dvina to Podolia.

The lands described above were for the most part inhabited either by Russians (including White Russians and Ukrainians) or by minor nationalities, or else were thinly populated and had no organised state authority. But from the end of the eighteenth century Russia began to take territory that was in no way Russian, and had belonged to well-established states. The third partition of Poland (1795) gave her some purely Polish areas, and by the peace settlement of 1815 she acquired the greater part of ethnic Poland.[1] In 1809 Finland, which had been for 600 years a part of Sweden, was united by personal union with Russia. In the first three decades of the nineteenth century Transcaucasia, including Armenia and Georgia, lands of ancient civilisation, were annexed, and both Turkey and Persia were obliged to recognise the conquest.

Russia's advance to the south, and the decline of Turkish power, caused the Russian leaders to take a growing interest in the western coast of the Black Sea, the mouth of the Danube and the Balkan peninsula. These lands were the home of peoples akin to the Russians in religion or language, or both, and formed the hinterland to the Straits of Bosphorus and Dardanelles, the back door to Russia. The problems of these lands will take much space in the following pages. Here it suffices to say that our period opens with a Russian reverse. From 1854 to 1856 Russia was at war with Britain, France and Turkey. In June 1854 the two Danubian principalities of Moldavia and Wallachia were occupied by Austrian troops, which thus prevented the Western Powers and Russia from fighting each other in European Turkey. Instead the war was fought in the Crimea. The Russian defence of Sevastopol was both brave and able, but the Western Powers dominated the Black Sea with their fleets. The war showed the Russians some of the weaknesses

[1] See map facing p. 74.

of their political and economic organisation, and also increased their appreciation of the importance of the Straits. The war was concluded by the Congress of Paris of February–March 1856. Russia ceded a portion of Bessarabia to the principality of Moldavia —which three years later became united with Wallachia to form Roumania—but otherwise lost no territory. The Sultan of Turkey undertook to close the Straits to warships in either direction in time of war. The navigation of the Danube was placed under international control. The Black Sea was neutralised, and no Power was to have a navy in it.

Russia emerged from the Crimean War internally weakened and with her international prestige diminished. But none of the essential factors and resources on which her greatness as a state depended had been affected.

Social Classes

Russia in the middle of the nineteenth century was an overwhelmingly agricultural country. The peasants formed more than three-quarters of its total population of about sixty million. Almost all of them lived in personal bondage, or serfdom.[1]

The serfs were divided into two main categories, State peasants and landowners' peasants. The State peasants were those who lived on lands owned by the State. There were rather less than twenty million of them, including their families. The landowners' peasants lived on private estates belonging to the hereditary nobility. They numbered rather more than twenty million. In addition to these two main groups about ten million more people lived on the land. Some belonged to various minor categories of serfs, and some were free peasant smallholders.

Thus the State owned the land on which lived two-fifths of the peasant population. The State lands were much bigger in the north, including the sparsely populated forest areas, than in the south. In some parts of Russia, the properties of the State and of noble landlords were closely intermingled. In the Urals the State also owned mines and metallurgical works which employed serf labour.

In 1850 there were about 250,000 serf-owning noble landlords in

---

[1] Far the best work available in English on the land question is G. T. Robinson, *Rural Russia under the Old Regime* (Macmillan, 1932). A short popular treatment is Sir John Maynard, *The Russian Peasant* (Gollancz, 1942). An important Russian work is P. Maslov, *Agrarny vopros v Rossii* (SPB, 1908). The period before the reforms is covered by V. Semevski, *Krestyanskii vopros v Rossii vo vtoroy polovine XVIII i pervoy polovine XIX veka* (SPB, 1888).

Russia. More than half of these owned less than ten male serfs each. More than four-fifths of the total number of landlords' serfs however belonged to landlords who owned more than a hundred each. Some of these great landlords owned many thousands of serfs.

Government and society in Russia were founded on the three factors of Crown, nobility and serfs. In practice the Crown denied the nobility any independent political power, but gave them a fairly free hand in dealing with the serfs. The ambition of the Tsars was completely to subject the nobility to themselves. Some were more successful than others. Peter the Great, at the beginning of the eighteenth century, created a hierarchy of state service, which became more important than the hierarchy of birth. The nobles were obliged to serve the State either as soldiers or as civil officials. In return, Peter recognised the full hereditary rights of the nobles over the land they held, which had been limited in the past by certain traditional restrictions. But in 1762 Peter III made the nobles free to choose whether they would enter the state service except in special national emergency, but maintained their power over their serfs.

At the beginning of the nineteenth century, part of the land of the village was cultivated by the serfs for their own use, and part was directly managed by the landowner, or by the local administrator of State property. For the land which they used, the serfs were obliged to pay the owner (private or State) in cash or in labour. Cash payments were called *obrok*, and payment in labour *barshchina*. When paying in labour the serfs in some cases brought their own draught animals and tools to work on the landlord's estate: in other cases they provided only the labour of their hands, while the landowner supplied the means of production.

The serfs had their own social organisation, the village commune (*obshchina*), an institution whose origins derive at least from the sixteenth century, before the system of serfdom was fully developed.[1]

It was the village commune that decided what crops were to be grown on the lands used by the serfs, and all members were bound by its rules on the rotation of crops. From time to time the commune redistributed land between serf households, in accordance with their needs, when the number of mouths in some families had grown and in others had diminished. The commune was responsible for the payment of poll-tax by its members. It also issued

[1] The origins of the commune are a subject of controversy among historians of the pre-Petrine period. For a brief discussion, see Robinson, *op. cit.*, pp. 11-12.

passports, which were needed in order to obtain employment outside the commune's territory. These were only granted if the local landlord agreed.

From the government's point of view, the task of the landlord was to make sure that the peasants paid their taxes and provided recruits for the army. In order that they should perform these two important functions, they had large powers. The landlord could interfere in the redistribution of land between households by the commune, and could increase or reduce the amount of land allotted to a village or to an individual householder. He could confiscate a peasant's movable goods. He could restrict the right of one of his serfs to make a contract with any person living beyond the boundaries of his own estate—for instance, to earn wages by working for such a person, or borrow money, or rent land. Up till the first years of the nineteenth century, he could command or prevent a marriage, sell a serf to another landlord, with or without land, and with or without other members of the serf's family. The *barshchina* at this time was usually three days' labour every week on the landlord's estate, but was sometimes four or five. In periods of labour shortage a serf might be compelled to work continuously for the landlord while his own plot was neglected. The landlord's judicial powers were not clearly defined, but covered most offences other than brigandage and murder. He could impose sentences of flogging and of forced labour in Siberia. The landlord's most important obligations were to feed his serfs in famine and to give them seed in case of crop failure. There was also a general obligation "not to ruin them or deal cruelly with them." In practice these safeguards were far from effective.

State serfs in most cases paid an *obrok* rather than a *barshchina*. Its amount was usually lower than that paid by landlords' serfs, but it increased towards the end of the eighteenth century.[1]

Under Tsar Nicholas I (1825-55) some important reforms were carried out. In 1837 was created a Ministry of State Domains. It was entrusted to General Kiselev, an enlightened man who had the Tsar's personal confidence. In the following year a new system of administration was created. A "Chamber of State Property" was set up in each province, with district and canton authorities under it, to protect the interests of the peasants. State peasants were freed from personal serfdom, and declared to be free citizens in occupation of State land. The State began to buy land from private landlords for the use of the peasants, and made the first steps towards the

[1] Robinson, *op. cit.*, p. 29.

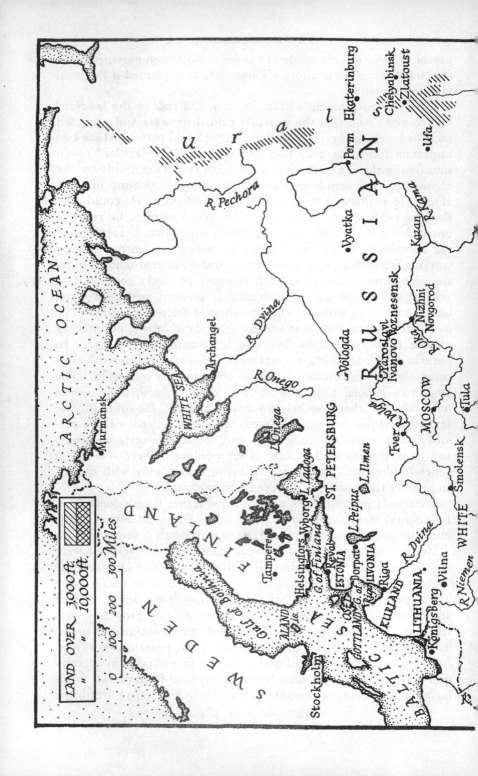

PERSIA

CASPIAN SEA

Baku

R. Ural

Samara

Penza

E M P I R E

Tambov

R. Volga

Tsaritsyn

Astrahan

R. Terek

Vladikavkaz

CAUCASUS

Tiflis

OTTOMAN

Orel

Kursk

R. Don

Harkov

R. Donets

Ekaterinoslav

Yuzovka

Taganrog

Rostov

SEA OF AZOV

Kuban

Stavropol

Ekaterinodar

Novorossiisk

Batum

E M P I R E

Poltava

Kiev

R. Dniepr

Nikolaev

Herson

Sevastopol

Yalta

B L A C K   S E A

CONSTANTINOPLE

SEA OF MARMARA

MINSK

RUSSIA

R. Bug

R. Dniestr

BESSARABIA

R. Prut

Kishinyov

Odessa

Bialystok

Warsaw

Lwow

MOLDAVIA

Carpathians

TRAN-SYLVANIA

ROUMANIA

Bucharest

R. Danube

BULGARIA

GREECE

AEGEAN SEA

Vistula

Łódź

Cracow

P O L A N D

Budapest

Belgrade

SERBIA

U K R A I N E

organisation of credit and of protection from fire and disease. By 1842 this system had been extended to State properties in all the provinces of European Russia.

Kiselev also attempted to improve the lot of the landlords' serfs. But a Committee appointed by the Tsar to examine the question, in which the landlords were strongly represented, could not reach agreement. It whittled down Kiselev's proposals, and finally made even these dependent on voluntary agreement between landlord and serf. When the Decree was published, it was at once followed by a circular from the Minister of the Interior addressed to provincial authorities. This emphasised that there was absolutely no obligation on a landlord to make any contract with his serfs. Consequently Kiselev's plans were not carried out. Serfdom remained in force on the private estates. A few concrete improvements were, however, made. For instance, in 1841 it was forbidden to sell serfs without the whole of their families, and in 1848 serfs were allowed, with their landlords' approval, to acquire immovable property. The categories of persons to whom serfs might be sold were also limited by several decrees.

.   .   .   .   .

The town population of Russia was small at the beginning of our period, but it had been growing rapidly for some time past. In 1724 there were 328,000 people in the towns, in 1796 1,300,000 and in 1851 3,480,000.[1]

The demand for manufactured goods in the old Russia was not large, and was of two kinds. The peasants needed coarse cloth and various metal and wooden tools. The government needed arms for its troops and cloth for their uniforms. The demand of the upper class for luxury goods was satisfied by imports from abroad. Peasant needs were supplied by craft industry. Especially in central and northern Russia, where the soil was not rich and the winter nights were long, many peasants made a large part of their living by making cloth, sacking, nails, buckets or other household objects in their own homes and selling them to merchants, who disposed of them over a wide area. In this way some measure of regional specialisation was achieved, certain districts producing their special product for the greater part of the country. The needs of the government could not, however, be supplied in this manner. Peter the Great was the first Tsar who deliberately encouraged the

[1] P. Milyukov, *Ocherki po istorii russkoy kultury* (5th edition, SPB, 1904), Vol. I, p. 82.

creation of large factories. These were for the most part entrusted to members of the merchant class, which had been of some importance in Moscow at least since the sixteenth century. Others were directly founded by the government. The factory owners received various monopolistic privileges. They were also allowed to employ serfs from the lands of the State or the nobility. This was fiercely resented by the nobility, which regarded it as a breach of its own rights. During the eighteenth century the factory owners met with much criticism both from the nobles and from the lesser merchants, who envied the wealth of their more fortunate fellows. Members of the nobility themselves founded factories on their estates, and could of course freely employ their own serfs in them. The nobles also defended the rights of the peasant craftsmen, if only because they themselves received in feudal money dues a share of their earnings. Whereas Peter had definitely backed the factory owners, Catherine II inclined rather to the nobility. But competition between factories and crafts was not bitter, as they supplied different types of consumer.[1]

At the beginning of the nineteenth century there were three types of factory in Russia. The "possession factories" were those based on the special privileges mentioned. The State had certain rights—which it seldom exercised—to interfere in their management. Their labour force was assigned not to the individual owner but to the factory.[2] Secondly, there were the noble factories, employing nobles' serfs. Third, there were factories employing free wage labour. These gained ground rapidly during the century at the expense of the other types. Wage labour was especially important in the cotton industry, which made great progress in the Moscow region. The industries in which serf labour still predominated were wool, paper and metallurgy. In 1804 the number of workers in factories in Russia was 95,000, of whom 45,000 were free wage earners. At this time 7 per cent of the factory labour force was employed in the cotton industry. In 1825 there were 210,000 workers, of whom 114,000 were wage earners. By 1836 the total number of factory workers had risen to 324,000, of whom 32 per cent were in the cotton industry.[3] During these years Western economic theories were becoming known in Russia, and the view, based on both theory and experience, that free labour was more efficient than serf, was winning support. In 1840 a government

[1] M. Tugan-Baranovski, *Geschichte der russischen Fabrik* (Berlin, 1900), pp. 47–62.
[2] Ibid., *op. cit.*, chapter 3.   [3] Ibid., *op. cit.*, pp. 98, 102, 103.

decree provided a procedure by which owners of "possession factories" could voluntarily emancipate their serfs. Under this decree and by the initiative of individual noble factory owners it is estimated that in the last decades before 1861 about half the factory serfs had been emancipated.

The legal position of the town population was regulated by the Charter of Catherine II of 1785. Townsmen were divided into six classes.[1] Municipal councils were created, consisting of a six-member executive board (with one representative of each class) and a larger assembly. Both were elected, under a franchise which strongly favoured the propertied citizens. The councils were in practice completely overawed by the provincial governors. It was not until 1870 that genuine municipal government began in Russia.[2] Under Catherine II the middle class was divided into separate categories. The merchants were divided between three "guilds", according to their property. The first guild consisted of those who had a capital of more than 10,000 roubles, the second guild of 5,000 to 10,000, and the third guild of 1,000 to 5,000. Those with less than 1,000 roubles capital were reckoned as "lower middle class" (*meshchane*).[3] Each category had its specific rights and obligations towards the State. Below the merchants were the artisans enrolled in corporations (*tsehi*). They were free to engage in their trade and were not bound by serfdom.

This legal framework remained in force during the nineteenth century, but soon ceased to correspond to economic realities. The development of capitalism in the industrial centres, and the rise of business and working classes, deprived it of significance long before it ceased nominally to exist.

Emperor and Bureaucracy

The Russian State was, as its official spokesmen proudly repeated, an autocracy. At its head was the absolute Tsar, who owed his position to God alone, and was responsible to none but Him. This concept derives from the Byzantine "autokrator", whose descendant the Tsar felt himself to be. In practice the Tsar's power had varied through the centuries. But Peter the Great at the beginning of the eighteenth, broke the power of the aristocracy and set up a

[1] These were (a) the richest citizens; (b) citizens who owned a house in the city; (c) merchants belonging to a guild; (d) artisans belonging to a corporation; (e) foreigners and visitors from another city; (f) unskilled workers possessing no immovable property in the city. Klyuchevski, *Kurs russkoy istorii*, Vol. V, p. 100.

[2] See below, p. 51.

[3] Klyuchevski, *loc. cit.* The word "meshchane" defies translation. It has something of the sense of "bourgeois" when used with contempt.

centralised machine. Though at the end of the century Catherine II made important concessions to the nobility, there was no question of a challenge to the autocratic power. In the first half of the nine-teenth century it was maintained, despite certain liberal inclina-tions, by Alexander I, and reinforced by Nicholas I.

Ministers were appointed by the Tsar. They were not a cabinet and never acted as a body. There was no Prime Minister. A body called the "Committee of Ministers" was supposed to co-ordinate policy, but in practice played a very small part. Its President was little more than an honorary figure. The individual ministers per-sonally discussed their business with the Tsar, whose confidence was all that mattered to them. The most important ministries in our period were the Interior and Finance. The former was respon-sible for public order, in its very wide aspects. The latter was not only concerned with State revenue and expenditure, but had close links with the growing business class. It supervised, to some extent even directed, the development of industry and trade, in a sense unknown in Western Europe at this time. Only the Tsar himself was in a position effectively to co-ordinate the policy of the different ministries. As the tasks of government grew more com-plicated during the nineteenth century, the duties of the Tsar became immensely difficult. Only a man of exceptional political understanding could hope to perform them. When the Tsar had not the necessary qualities, the individual ministries went their own ways, sometimes pursuing contradictory policies. In the reign of Nicholas II this became the normal practice. But the situation could not be remedied without challenging the sacred dogma of the Emperor's autocratic power.

Alexander I had founded in 1810 a body called the Council of State. Its function was to prepare and examine legislation. Its members were appointed by the Tsar from the bureaucracy, and numbered thirty-five to sixty persons. They were not able to initiate legislation but merely produced drafts for the Tsar at his request. He was not obliged to accept their recommendations. He frequently disregarded the views of their majority and associated himself with a minority. The Council was in no sense a legislature. Important measures also often took the form of decrees (*ukazy*) or instructions (*povelenia*), which never came before the Council of State at all.

In 1711 Peter the Great had founded the Governing Senate. It was originally a general supervisory authority. It watched over both the administration and the law courts. Its members were appointed by the Tsar from senior State officials, very often from the higher aristocracy. The Senate was reorganised by Alexander I a hundred years later, and its administrative and judicial duties were more clearly separated from each other. Under Nicholas I its powers of control over the administration fell into disuse, but it remained important as the supreme court of appeal of the judicial system. This function was exercised by its two Cassation Departments, one for civil and one for criminal cases.

Immediately subordinate to the Tsar was the "Personal Chancellery of His Imperial Majesty". This was divided into Sections, whose number varied from time to time. The most important were the first three. The First Section dealt with the Tsar's personal papers and was a sort of private secretariat. The Second was concerned with the codification of laws. The Third was in charge of political police. Nicholas I concentrated a great deal of the business of State in his Chancellery. Under his successors it lost some of its importance. But the Third Section continued to be powerful until the end of the reign of Alexander II, when it was merged in the Department of Police.[1]

The Third Section was created in 1826 by Nicholas I and based on a project of General Benckendorff, who became its first head. In 1836 the two offices of Chief of Gendarmes and Head of the Third Section of the Chancellery, which had previously been united in the person of Benckendorff, were formally fused. By its original statute the Third Section was responsible for obtaining information and taking action in regard to religious sects and schismatics. It dealt with all cases of forgery of money or of documents. It issued instructions relating to persons subjected to police supervision, banishment of suspicious persons, and control of all places where persons guilty of "crimes against the State" were detained. It was responsible for all regulations concerning foreigners resident in Russia. Finally a general clause authorised it to produce "reports on all events".[2] The Third Section in fact controlled when it so wished all the lower ranks of the ordinary police. The gendarmerie was organised by regions, into which the country was divided—at first five, then eight from 1843 onwards. The gendarmes executed the orders of the Third Section, and it was they who arrested persons guilty of political offences. A special department of the gendarmerie was responsible for the security of the railways.

---

[1] See below, pp. 71–2.
[2] The decree which created the Third Section is summarised in M. Lemke, *Nikolaevskie zhandarmy i literatura 1826–55 godov* (SPB, 1909), p. 14.

Provincial governors were instructed, when reporting on matters coming under the headings listed, to address their reports directly to the Third Section.

The duties of the Section's employees were supposed to include the commendation of honest but modest officials in all branches of the administration. They were to ensure that such people received reward from higher authority, and to protect the people from abuses.[1] In practice the Third Section paid less attention to this than to the discovery and uprooting of political offences. Persons guilty of offences could be arrested, tried and condemned by the regular courts to exile or prison. But the Head of the Third Section also had authority to order "administrative arrest" of persons whom he considered dangerous to State security. This power was used in an arbitrary, and often in an incompetent, manner. Sometimes the wrong person would be arrested, and the authorities fail or refuse to investigate the mistake. There was no effective appeal against the system. Its victims were sent to "administrative exile" in distant provinces of European Russia or of Siberia without trial. The distinction between exile and imprisonment is important. Exiled persons did not necessarily suffer great material hardship, at any rate by Russian standards. They were forbidden to leave the place of exile, but within it they could live as they wished. Their families could accompany them, they could meet whom they wished, and they could spend money on food, clothes, lodgings and personal possessions. Very poor persons would of course suffer. But this form of punishment was usually inflicted on members of the educated class, who usually had enough means to ensure a minimum of comfort. They were not prevented from earning money in the place of exile, or acquiring and cultivating plots of land. Life in exile was full of frustration and mental unrest, but it was not a life of acute misery. Those imprisoned in a fortress or a penal settlement had a very different lot. The Russian word for the latter (*katorga*) means "the galleys", and derives from the time when slaves were condemned to the oars. A description of these conditions by an eyewitness, which is also a great piece of literature, is *Notes from the House of the Dead* by Dostoevski. Revolting though the whole system must seem by Western standards, with its waste of human ability and its opportunities for petty tyranny, it is still worth pointing out, when the horrors of the Tsarist regime are used as a justification for later horrors in Russia or elsewhere, that

[1] Instructions by Benckendorff to this effect are quoted in Lemke, *op. cit.*, pp. 17–19.

the numbers sent to prison for long terms for political offences were very small by twentieth-century standards.[1]

In the local administration, the most important figure was the provincial governor (*Gubernator*), and in the big cities the town commandant (*Gradonachalnik*). These officials were the executors of the decrees of all the central ministries in their province or city, but were especially responsible to the Ministry of Interior. This Ministry through them controlled the ordinary police. Their hierarchy was largely modelled on the Prussian. The chief of police in towns bore the title *Polizeimeister*. In certain frontier regions (Poland, Lithuania, the Caucasus) and in the two capitals, there were governors-general, who had greater powers and easier access to the Tsar than the ordinary provincial governors.

The old Russia was rigidly based on specified classes. Of these the most important was the nobility. Nicholas I had wished to subordinate the nobles completely to the State power, to make them a class of reliable *Polizeimeister*. In this he was following the example of Peter the Great. Under the "Table of Ranks" introduced by Peter, salaries, grants of land and titles attached to different State functions. A man of non-noble birth who reached a certain level as an army officer or in the civil administration became a noble. A still higher level made his noble status hereditary. A member of one of the leading aristocratic families would of course be favoured in a public career by wealth and personal influence, but he would still have to begin on a comparatively low rung of the ladder.

The nobles had their own assemblies in province and district, each of which elected its leader, who held the title of "marshal of the nobility". These assemblies won greater freedom from the government under Catherine II, but in 1831 a decree of Nicholas I again reduced their powers. The essence of the decree was to create within the noble class a hierarchy of ranks corresponding to that of the State service. It confined the powers of the assemblies to matters affecting only the internal organisation of the noble class, and restricted according to rank and wealth the numbers of those who could elect and be elected to offices within the class.

The most obvious defect of the whole regime was the low quality of its bureaucracy. Some of the great Russian writers have painted a picture of the corrupt, incompetent and arrogant State official.

---

[1] An interesting description of conditions of exiles and prisoners in Siberia in the mid-80's by an American liberal is Kennan, *Siberia and the Exile System* (London, 1891).

The bureaucratic machine was a heavy drain on Russia's resources, and the results of its work hardly seem to have justified the expense. But it must be remembered that the Russian people were accustomed to the machine. The Russian political tradition was paternalist. Changes in the life of the people were expected to come from above, by the action of the officials who were the executive arm of the Tsar. Western and even Russian liberal historians have perhaps been too severe in their judgment on Russian officials. They have been inclined to blame them for not being what they could not possibly have been. Their incompetence was a result of the general economic and cultural backwardness of the country. Their corruption was a result of their poor pay. It was difficult to support a family on the salary of a minor State employee.

Loyalty to wife and children conflicted with loyalty to the State, and it is not surprising if the first usually prevailed. The laws were so cumbrous and obscure that their interpretation in a common-sense manner, in return for a pecuniary consideration, often caused small harm to the public interest. Undoubtedly many officials made a substantial part of their living from such interpretation. This was especially true of the restrictions against schismatics, members of religious sects and Jews. It may even be argued that to some extent such corruption was socially desirable. It would have been better to abolish the unjust or outmoded laws. But if the supreme power was implacably opposed to repeal, the next best thing was corruption. Of course those who could not afford to give bribes suffered the full severity of the machine. And it was to the poor that the bureaucrats showed their most unlovable characteristic—their arrogance. More perhaps than in any other country, officials in Russia considered themselves a superior species, appointed to drive the herds of human cattle. Obedience and patience were required of the cattle, willingness to wait for hours and days for a decision, and acceptance of the decision when given.

The most arrogant and oppressive branch of the bureaucracy was the police. Its oppressiveness was probably increased by its duplication. There were three separate hierarchies, independent of each other—the ordinary police, subject to the provincial governors or town commandants; the gendarmerie, organised by eight regional commands throughout the empire; and the Third Section or its successors with its informers and agents scattered all over the empire. Under such a system a large number of people had a permanent vested interest in the maintenance of fear—fear by the people and fear by the Tsar. The small informer could obtain rewards and honours from his superiors only by providing them with frequent reports on the "political unreliability" of the population of his area. Therefore evidence of sedition had to be found, if necessary had to be manufactured. The senior police officers could rise to the highest posts only by convincing the Minister and the Tsar that sedition was brewing under the surface. This notably contributed to persuade the Tsar that all political reforms were dangerous, and continued repression increased popular discontent to such an extent that the exaggerated statements of the police eventually became a reality.

The Intelligentsia

The formation of a professional class, overlapping with yet distinct from the bureaucracy, merchants and landed nobility, was an inevitable result of the modernisation of Russia, as of other countries. The growth of cities, industries, trade and communications created a need for doctors, engineers, teachers, lawyers and other professional people. The State encouraged their growth. But the cultural backwardness, obsolete class structure and political despotism of Russia made the formation of a professional class an artificial process, little linked with Russian society as a whole. While the Russian masses remained plunged in a swamp of ignorance and poverty, a small crust of well-educated persons, with a nineteenth-century Europeam outlook, came into being. The chasm which separated these modern intellectuals from the bulk of the Russian people was one of the decisive factors in the development of Russia in the nineteenth and early twentieth centuries.

Modern education made its first steps in the time of Peter the Great, who sent selected young Russians to acquire special skills and knowledge in Western Europe. Moscow university was founded in 1755. Catherine II in 1786 founded the first State schools, and in 1787 issued a university statute, based on the Austrian model. But the beginning of a serious system of education dates from the Schools Statute of Alexander I, issued in 1804.[1] This laid down the outlines of a regular system of parish and district elementary schools, secondary schools (or "gymnasia") and universities. Members of all classes, not excluding serfs, were to be admitted. Teaching was at first to be free, but small

---

[1] N. Hans, *History of Russian Educational Policy* (P. S. King & Son, 1931), pp. 45–60. See also *Ministerstvo narodnovo prosveshchenia 1802–1902* (SPB, 1902).

fees were introduced in St. Petersburg in 1819. State scholarships were granted to poor pupils of ability. The poverty of the
country and the lack of teachers of course reduced to very small
proportions the practical achievements under the new Statute.
Nevertheless in the following years some thousands of Russians
obtained an education, and the proportion of non-noble scholars
was high.

The accession of Nicholas I brought in education as in other
fields of public life a marked reaction from the liberal tendencies of
the preceding reign. In December 1828 a new Statute was introduced.[1] The different stages of education were clearly defined.
At the bottom of the pyramid were the Parish Schools, "open also
to the people of the lowest groups". Above them were the District
Schools, open to all classes but "especially designed for merchants
and other townspeople". Then came the secondary schools, whose
purpose was to give "a decent education for children of the gentry
and of civil officials". Serfs were prohibited from access to the
secondary schools. Their curriculum was so arranged that it was
not possible for a pupil of a District School to pass on into them.
All taught Latin from the first year. Some taught Greek, and others
instead taught longer periods of French and mathematics. These
secondary schools (Gymnasia) gave access to the universities.
Parallel with them were "Real Schools", which gave secondary
education of a non-classical type, and from which pupils could not
go to the university but were admitted to other higher educational
institutions.[2]

The most important of Nicholas I's Ministers of Education was
Count Uvarov, who expressed in his report of November the
dominant ideas on the subject. It laid down that the basis of all
education in Russia must be the three principles of autocracy,
orthodoxy and nationality. These had been regrettably weakened in
the preceding reign by "superficial education and visionary and
abortive experiments". During the reign of Nicholas I efforts were
made to discourage middle-class persons from entering the secondary schools. Fees were raised. The poorer families of the gentry
were assisted by the erection of residential "hostels of the nobility"
attached to some of the Gymnasia. Nothing similar was done to
help non-noble middle-class families. During the reign the government also tightened its control over the universities. The country

[1] Hans, *op. cit.*, pp. 67–75.
[2] Among these may be mentioned the St. Petersburg Technological Institute,
the Agricultural Institute and the Building School (for architecture and civil
engineering).

was divided into educational regions, whose centres were university towns.[1] The chief representative of the Minister in each region was a Curator, to whom were subordinated a number of Inspectors. Their duties were not only to ensure educational standards, but to see that no undesirable political views were expressed by teachers or students. Under the university statute of 1835, though the right of the University Councils to elect their own Rector, Deans of faculties and professors was recognised, vacant chairs could be filled by the Minister of Education. In 1839 fees were introduced for university students, and shortly afterwards raised. A decree of October 1849 stated that Rectors would be appointed by the Tsar, and in January 1850 the appointment of professors was entrusted to the Minister, who was to choose them not only for learning but also for "loyalty, moral qualities and way of thinking". The efforts to increase the proportion of children of the nobility among university students also achieved some success.

Despite the interference of the authorities, and the odious atmosphere of petty spying, the quality of university teaching in Russia was high. Those who graduated from Russian universities belonged to the nineteenth century. They were more or less familiar with the material progress of nineteenth-century Europe, and had learned some at least of the modern political and philosophical ideas of the West. The decision of Uvarov's successor, Shirinski-Shihmatov, in 1850 to abolish all lectures on philosophy and to entrust the teaching of logic to professors of theology, was not able to keep modern ideas out of young people's minds. The government's methods were crude and ineffective. It was not ruthless by mid-twentieth century standards. Young Russians, including women—who could not get a university education in Russia—were able to study abroad. Ideas could not in those days be kept out by frontiers. The Russian educated class was aware of the gulf between Russia and Europe. It saw the contrast between its own life and that of the Russian people. It was living, materially and intellectually, in the nineteenth century, the people in the seventeenth or earlier. It saw the poverty and social injustice, the dead weight of a bureaucracy opposed to any constructive initiative, the wealth and indifference of the upper class, the inferiority of Russia

---

[1] The Russian universities were Moscow (founded in 1755), Harkov (1805), Kazan (1805), St. Petersburg (1819), Kiev (1833) and Odessa (1865). The universities of Vilna and Dorpat were older foundations, of German and Polish origin respectively. Vilna was russified after the Polish revolt of 1863, Dorpat in the 1880's. See below pp. 77, 161. Additional educational regions created in later years were Orenburg (1874), Caucasus (1883) and Western Siberia (1885).

to Western Europe—shown in Napoleon's time and more recently in the Crimean War. The intellectuals' own position tormented them. They could not establish contact with the people. The Russian peasant lived in another world and another century. They could not understand his mind, nor he theirs. They were equally cut off from the State machine. There was little room in the bureaucracy for men with reforming or modernising ideas. It was idle to hope that by entering the machine they could themselves improve it. Isolated from both government and people, they pursued their thoughts to their logical conclusions, unaffected by experience of power. This abstract and frustrated atmosphere was well suited to the growth of revolutionary ideas.

The contrast between Russia and Europe, between the nineteenth and the seventeenth centuries inside Russia, and the frustration of educated men and women excluded alike from the chance of power and the trust of the suffering Russian people, form the background to the rise of the Russian revolutionary intelligentsia. Some care must be shown in the use of this word. In the first instance, it means the educated class as a whole, and of course overlaps with the aristocracy and the highest ranks of army and civil service. Obviously, not all members of the intelligentsia in this wider sense were bitterly dissatisfied. Some highly educated Russians of great ability devoted themselves to their tasks in government service, medicine, science or economic life, enjoying the good things of a nineteenth-century life and also, for the most part at least, believing that their use of their special skills would benefit their country or improve the welfare of their people. But it was difficult for any intelligent educated Russian not to feel some frustration. The stupid obscurantism and heavy brutality of the machine, the wretched poverty and ignorance of the people, forced themselves on his attention. The majority of educated people in Russia were against the regime. The word "intelligentsia" in the Russian language was inseparable from the notion of opposition. Thus the majority of educated people, though not necessarily sympathetic to revolutionary ideas, were unwilling to help the authorities to defeat the revolutionaries. They felt that they were on the same side of the barricade as the revolutionaries, in the battle against "them". And the active revolutionaries themselves were a minority formed from their ranks.[1]

[1] In the following pages I shall try to distinguish, when speaking of the intelligentsia, between these three categories—the professional class, the oppositional intelligentsia and the revolutionaries.

In the middle of the century the Russian intelligentsia was divided into two main groups, usually known as the Westernisers and the Slavophiles.

The Westernisers were ashamed of Russia's past and present, and sought deliverance by imitation of the West. One of the most remarkable of them, Chaadaev, declared that Russia had contributed nothing at all to human thought or human progress, yet her people possessed great inner forces and was capable of a great human mission. At present, Russia "constitutes a gap in the moral order of the world". Yet Russia had a vocation to "answer questions of great importance with which mankind is concerned". But this vocation would be fulfilled only by advancing further on the road of westernisation on which Peter the Great had set out a century earlier. The Westernisers were all to some extent attracted by the ideas of the French Revolution. The first who had tried to carry them out were the Decembrists, a small group of idealists whose naïf and unprepared conspiracy had been easily crushed in 1825 by a few of Tsar Nicholas I's troops. In the thirties and forties the ideas of the Westernisers were expressed in the drawing-rooms of St. Petersburg and Moscow but had no effect on political life. These ideas included of course political freedom and constitutional government. Some Westernisers went further, and inclined to some sort of socialism, or were influenced by some of the ideas of Saint Simon. The Westernisers as a whole were less interested in economics than in politics, but they admired the economic progress of the West. Those who inclined to a cautious liberalism were more enthusiastic about following the Western model than the utopian socialists, who were aware of the criticisms made of capitalism in the West. But in the forties disagreements on these points were not essential. Russia's need of modernisation and education, the citizen's need for freedom of expression and a voice in government, and the peasant's need for personal emancipation were more urgent. The liberal Granovski, the romantic revolutionary Herzen, and the radical realist Belinski were united in their belief that Russia must follow the West.

The Slavophiles were no less discontented with the regime of Nicholas I. They were not reactionaries in the sense that they wished to preserve the autocracy exactly as it was. They were well aware of the backwardness and ignorance of the Russian people, the wrongs of the serfs and the absence of civil liberties. They wished, like the Westernisers, to remedy these things. But they sought salvation, not in the imitation of Europe but in a return to what they believed to be the true traditions of Russia. The civilisation of the West was based on rationalism and individualism, which they believed to be dissolving and disintegrating forces. The strength of Russia lay in the faith of her people, and in the sense of belonging to a community (*sobornost*), which they claimed was an essential part of Orthodoxy and of the consciousness of the Russian peasant. The economic and cultural progress of the West had only created terrible social problems with which individualism was unable to deal. Russian faith and Russian *sobornost* would be able to cure these problems. By doing so, Russia would point the way for the West. It was Russia's mission, not to learn from the West but to teach it. The defects of Russia as she was were due to the mistakes of Peter the Great. In his hurry to imitate the West he had perverted the social and political structure of Russia. In particular, he had set up a bureaucracy based on German models and largely staffed at the top level by Germans, and he had subjected the Orthodox Church to the State machine that he had created. Thus people and Tsar had been separated, the Tsar no longer knew what his subjects felt, and the subjects regarded government as a foreign and oppressive force. The Slavophiles were opposed to parliamentary government as a Western institution, but they believed that the views of the people should be expressed to the sovereign through some regular channel. To this end they proposed the revival of the popular consultative assemblies (*Zemskii Sobor*) which had occasionally been held in the sixteenth and seventeenth centuries.[1]

Both Westernisers and Slavophiles were utopians. The real Western Europe was very different from the ideal, as Russian exiles in the West found out for themselves. The most striking example of disillusionment is Herzen, who in 1847 entered Paris "with reverence, as men used to enter Jerusalem and Rome",[2] yet by the end of the following year was thoroughly disgusted with bourgeois Europe, its ideas and its methods. But the happy past of Russia for which the Slavophiles longed was just as unreal as the happy contemporary West. This happy past had never existed. The real Russia of Ivan the Terrible or Alexei Romanov bore little relation to the idealisations of Slavophile theorists.

[1] The *Zemskii Sobor* ("assembly of the land") played a part in Russian history from the mid-sixteenth to the mid-seventeenth century. It included not only spokesmen of the aristocracy and high clergy, but also elected representatives of the provincial gentry and townsmen, and even some peasants. For a brief discussion of its role, see Sumner, *op. cit.*, pp. 80 ff.

[2] E. H. Carr, *The Romantic Exiles* (London, 1933), Penguin edition, p. 32.

The practical political outlook of Slavophiles and Westernisers did not differ so sharply as might be expected. The early Slavophiles were educated Europeans. They did not hate Europe or reject European culture. They wished to reform Russia, above all to emancipate the serfs. On the other hand such Westernisers as Chaadaev and Herzen believed strongly in the mission of Russia in the world. But the fundamental difference remained, and was important. It was the difference between those who regarded the experience of Western Europe as an example to follow and those who felt it was a warning of what to avoid. The controversy between Westernisers and Slavophiles is the first stage in our period of a division which reappeared in other forms, which later split Russian socialism between Populists and Marxists, and Russian Marxism between Bolsheviks and Mensheviks, and which in our own day has split Bolshevism between the followers and opponents of Stalin.

We shall often be concerned in the following pages with the ideas, factions and activities of the intelligentsia in general and of its revolutionary minority in particular. It is essential to bear in mind the peculiar relationship of the intelligentsia to the government machine and to the people, the contrast between Russia and Europe, and the position of the intelligentsia with its head in the nineteenth or twentieth century and its feet in the seventeenth.

Church and Religion

The official Church of the Russian Empire was Orthodox or Eastern Christianity. The extension of the Empire had brought within its frontiers considerable numbers of Catholics (Poles and Lithuanians), Protestants (Letts, Esthonians and Finns), Moslems (Turks and Iranians), and even a few Buddhists (Mongols and Kalmyks). There was also a large Jewish population. But the Russians themselves, and the great majority of Ukrainians, were Orthodox. The non-Orthodox religious groups suffered from various forms of discrimination, or even persecution. These were essentially, at any rate within our period, a reflection of the Greater Russian nationalism of the ruling bureaucracy. They will therefore be mentioned in connection with the problem of Nationalities in the Empire. Here we are concerned only with the Orthodox Church.

Christianity was introduced into Russia when Grand Prince Vladimir of Kiev was converted in 988. The breach between the Churches of Rome and Constantinople was formally completed in 1054, and the Russian Church followed the Greek. In the following centuries the Patriarch of Constantinople was the nominal Head of the Eastern Church. Though the Tatar conquest cut off Russia from Constantinople, the Patriarch's authority was not theoretically challenged by the Russian Church. But the rise of Muscovy, far less influenced by Byzantium than had been the old Kiev state, and the decline of the Eastern empire itself, changed the situation. In 1439, in a last desperate attempt to enlist the help of the West against the Turkish menace, the Patriarch consented at the Council of Florence to reunion with Rome. This was regarded in Moscow as treason, and the Metropolitan of Moscow, Isidore, who had supported the Patriarch at the Council, was driven from his country. When Constantinople fell to the Turks in 1453, the authority of the Patriarch, undermined by the Florence betrayal, was effectively destroyed. The Russian Church was thenceforth independent in practice. In 1589 this state of affairs was formally recognised when Tsar Fyodor created a Patriarchate of Moscow.

During the sixteenth century the Orthodox hierarchy received the support of the Tsar in several important controversies. In its struggles with Constantinople, in its defence of the right of the monasteries to own large landed properties, and in its fight against heretics, the secular power was on its side. In its turn the hierarchy supported the government. The connection became still closer in the seventeenth century, when the reform of the texts of the Scriptures by Patriarch Nikon (1652–66), with the help of Greek monks, led to a schism in the Church. Those who rejected the reforms became known as the Old Believers. The hierarchy, the government and the ruling class accepted the new versions and obeyed Nikon and his successors. But among the peasants and the poorer townspeople the Old Believers retained a large following. They maintained that the government and the official Church were in the hands of Antichrist, and that true Orthodoxy was expressed only in the old ritual. The immediate points in dispute seem incredibly trivial. But beneath the arguments about words and motions of worship was the deep distrust of the Russian masses for innovations associated with foreigners. The Church needed the Tsar's support to defeat the Old Believers, and thenceforth became more than ever dependent on the goodwill of the secular authority. The process reached its culmination under Peter the Great. The great moderniser was able to overrule the opposition of the weakened Church to his drastic reforms. He did not hesitate to seize for secular purposes funds and lands of the monasteries. In 1721 he abolished the office of Patriarch, and placed the Church under a body called the Holy Synod, whose head, the Senior Procurator, was a civil official nominated by the Tsar. This system was in force at the beginning of our period.[1]

The Metropolitans of Moscow, Kiev and St. Petersburg were members of the Synod *ex officio*. The same status was conferred on the Exarch of Georgia after its incorporation in Russia.[2] A further eight or nine bishops were appointed to the Synod for fixed periods by the Tsar on the advice of the Procurator. The Synod was nominally responsible for a large bureaucracy, which in fact took its orders from the Procurator and resembled the permanent staff of a Ministry. Its most important sections were the Economic and Educational Administrations, which dealt with Church property and Church schools. They were staffed mainly by lay officials with a few senior priests. Their inspectors and auditors travelled over the country on behalf of the Procurator.[3]

The priesthood was divided into "black clergy" and "secular clergy". The first were monks, and it was from their ranks only that bishops were recruited. The second were the parish priests, who were obliged to marry before they could be ordained. A member of the secular clergy could enter the black clergy if his wife died or consented to enter a convent. Bishops were chosen by the Tsar from a list of three candidates submitted to him by the Synod. They were liable to be transferred from one diocese to another at the wish of the Procurator, sometimes at short intervals. They were assisted in their dioceses by a consistory of four or five priests, itself dependent on its chancery. The chief figure in the chancery was the secretary, a lay bureaucrat who was responsible both to his bishop and to the Procurator. In practice bishops were over-burdened with routine papers and hampered by antiquated procedure. The Procurator's control, exercised through the chancery secretary, and the mass of formal business, deprived them of independence. Between the bishops and the parish priests were the district priests (*blagochinnie*), who supervised ten to thirty parishes, and were themselves appointed by the bishops.

---

[1] For the history of the Orthodox Church, schismatics and sectarians up to the nineteenth century, the work of Milyukov, *Ocherki po istorii russkoy kultury*, is of great value. A less thorough but useful and readable work is Anatole Leroy-Beaulieu, *L'empire des Tsars et les russes* (Paris, 1881), Vol. III. A recent valuable publication is Albert Ammann, *Abriss der ostslawischen Kirchengeschichte* (Vienna, 1950).

[2] See below, p. 36.

[3] A good summary of the administration, finances and educational system of the Orthodox Church at the turn of the nineteenth–twentieth centuries is given in Curtiss, *Church and State in Russia* (Columbia University Press, 1940), chapters 2–4.

Children of priests received free education in seminaries of the Church. But as secular higher education developed in Russia during the nineteenth century, it attracted away to a secular career the most able pupils of the seminaries. A large part of the non-noble intelligentsia of the second half of the century consisted of sons of priests.[1] Thus the priesthood tended not only to be a hereditary class, but to recruit itself only from its least intelligent members. Priests were often treated by the lay authorities as part of the government machine. They were expected to put up proclamations and decrees in their churches, and to provide statistical information on their parishes to the police. There was even a rule that they must inform against persons who in confession had shown "evil intent towards the sovereign" and had not repented of it.[2] The picture made familiar by revolutionary propaganda, that priests were police spies and ignorant brutes, is of course greatly exaggerated. Many were sincerely devoted to their parishioners, and beloved by them. But their attitude to the civil power often verged on the servile, and their culture was seldom high. Even among the black clergy there was not much sign of profound spiritual life. The most original religious thought of the period came from laymen, such as Homyakov or Solovyov.

The revenues of the Church came from three main sources. The first was the State budget. This provided 23,000,000 roubles in 1900. The second was the property of the monasteries. In 1890 this amounted to 793,777 desyatin of land, of an estimated value of 26,600,000 roubles. The third source consisted of payments from the faithful for candles, communion loaves, ikons, pilgrimages to sacred places and similar objects. This probably yielded a larger yearly income than the Church land.

After the seventeenth-century schism, the Old Believers were divided into two groups.[3] The first believed in the necessity of priests. They persuaded or bribed priests of the official Church to perform the sacraments for them according to the old ritual, and to enter them in the official records as married or christened according to the official rites. In 1847 a prelate of the Orthodox Church of Bosnia, the Metropolitan Ambrose, consented to consecrate three Russian Old Believers as bishops on Austrian soil, at Bela Krinica

[1] Eminent examples are the radicals Chernyshevski and Dobrolyubov (see below, pp. 59, 61, 64–5). For another seminarist (though not a priest's son) who has recently acquired some notoriety, see below, pp. 130 n., 293–4.
[2] Curtiss, *op. cit.*, p. 25, which quotes from Verhovski, *Uchrezhdenie duhovnoy kollegii i duhovny reglament* (Rostov-on-Don, 1916). I have not seen this work.
[3] For a fuller account of schismatics and sectarians, see, in addition to works already quoted, Conybeare, *Russian Dissenters* (Cambridge (Maas.), 1921).

in the Bukovina. These men later appointed further bishops. In 1859 there were ten such bishops in Russia, with their own Council which appointed bishops. The "priestly" Old Believers were then divided between those who recognised an Austrian prelate as their Head, and those who acknowledged the Council.

The more radical Old Believers, the "priestless", believing the official Church to be the instrument of Antichrist, refused to make any use of its services. At first they expected the end of the world. In the first years of the schism there were mass suicides. Rather than live in a godless world, the faithful shut themselves in a house or fortress, set it alight and perished together. Others formed settlements of hermits in the far north. Towards the end of the eighteenth century some of the priestless compromised with the world to the extent that they allowed their members to marry by the rites of the official Church. The more radical broke into various sectarian groups, of whom the most important were the Wanderers (*Stranniki*). These believed in poverty and vagrancy, but in later times some of them acquired property and regular places of rest.

There were many religious sects in Russia, with a considerable following. Some owed their origin to Protestant influences from the West, others to the doubts and spiritual needs of the uneducated masses. Russian writers divide them accordingly into "Evangelical sects" and sects of "Spiritual Christianity". The first stressed the need to base faith not on the instructions of priests but on the words of Scripture. The second held that even the Scriptures were superfluous, and that the faithful could commune directly with God. In the eighteenth century was founded the sect of the Duhobor ("fighters by the Spirit"). They rejected the Church and sacraments, interpreted the Scriptures allegorically, and refused to pay taxes or perform military service. A more moderate and more numerous sect, which held similar beliefs but was more tolerant of the civil power, were the Molokane, so called because they drank milk (*moloko*) on fast days. Both sects had a considerable following in the Volga valley. More extreme were the Hlysts, whose leaders called themselves Christs and had female companions who called themselves Mothers of God (*bogoroditsy*). At their meetings there were wild songs and dances. The faithful, led by their "Prophets" and "Prophetesses", worked themselves into a frenzy. The Hlysts despised the material world. They could mortify the flesh either by denying or by gratifying its lusts. The most extreme faction of the Hlysts were the Skoptsy (eunuchs), who

held that the temptations of the flesh could only be finally overcome by self-castration. Their founder was a certain Selivanov, who
at one time claimed to be the murdered husband of Catherine II,
Tsar Peter III. He was banished to Siberia from 1775 to 1796,
but was then allowed to return to St. Petersburg, where he enjoyed
a reputation as a prophet and holy man in the fashionable society of
the capital. He survived until 1832.

The most important Evangelical sect were the Stundists. Their
name is taken from the German word *Stunde* (hour), which was
given to hymn-meetings held by some German Protestant sects.
Stundism spread from German villages in Bessarabia and in
Ekaterinoslav province to the neighbouring Ukrainian population.
It made good use of the comparative tolerance of the 1860's, but
was persecuted towards the end of the century. Among the
Stundists some of the ideas of "spiritual Christianity" were found,
but on the whole the evangelical trend prevailed. The doctrines of
the Stundists were very close to those of the Baptists. When their
own worship was restricted by the authorities they were able to
make use of such freedom as the government allowed to Baptists,
who had the advantage of international connections.

Proselytism of the Orthodox by members of schismatic groups,
sects or other Christian Churches was forbidden by Russian law.
No one legally christened in the Orthodox Church could be recognised by law as having become a member of another religious
group. A law of 1883 gave various important civil rights, previously
denied to them, to Old Believers and to members of sects other than
the Skoptsy. These included the right to receive passports, to
engage in trade or industry, and to hold minor posts in the bureaucracy. They were also allowed to hold religious services, but with
restrictions which greatly reduced the value of the concession. The
authorities in practice constantly obstructed the opening of new
prayer-houses for schismatics. Children born of marriages conducted by the Old Believers' rites were illegitimate unless the
parents had formally registered under the 1883 law. In general the
authorities became more severe during the last years of the century.
A decree of 1894 proclaimed the Stundists "especially pernicious".
The authorities were told to forbid their prayer-meetings, and to
take steps to prevent them from camouflaging themselves as Baptists. It was stated that the tolerance granted to Baptists applied
only to persons of German origin, whose ancestors had never been
Orthodox. The conflict with the State on military service and
taxes caused many Duhobors to emigrate in 1899 to Canada.

The numbers of schismatics and sectarians cannot be estimated with certainty. The figures based on the declarations of the 1897 census showed only 1,000,000 Old Believers, 176,000 sectarians and 969,000 persons of unspecified beliefs other than recognised religions. The Ministry of the Interior in 1863 had admitted that there were 8,000,000 Old Believers and 220,000 sectarians. This figure was smaller than the truth, especially in the case of the sectarians, and in the following decades there is no reason to suppose that the numbers decreased. An Old Believer bishop, Iuzov, in 1880 estimated 3,600,000 priestly Old Believers, 7,000,000 priestless, 65,000 Hlysts, 1,000,000 "spiritual Christians", and a further 1,000,000 miscellaneous. It seems likely that by 1914 the number of schismatics and sectarians was not much short of 20,000,000.

Undoubtedly schismatics and sectarians were an important element in Russian society. Both Old Believers and Stundists had something of the traditional Puritan virtues. They were sober, hard-working, literate and argumentative. Many were successful in business. The success of the more fantastic doctrines on the other hand reflected the ancient and widespread antagonism to authority, the primitive anarchism that is one, if only one, of the permanent factors in Russian history. Generalisations about the "Russian soul", and discussions as to whether official Church or sects were more "truly Russian", should be treated with reserve. But there can be no doubt that for many Russian peasants, crushed by poverty and tyranny, the schism and the sects seemed to offer an escape into a better world.

The Nationalities

Russia was a multinational state. The Great Russians, speaking the Russian language, formed less than half its population. It was not until the end of the century that reasonably accurate information became available. At that time considerable territory had been acquired in Central Asia which was not part of Russia at the beginning of our period. The population of all parts of the empire had of course also greatly increased. It is nevertheless convenient to begin this survey of the problem of nationalities by setting out the later figures, based on the census of 1897.[1] The following are the main national groups.

[1] Based on the table in O. Hoetzsch, *Russland* (Berlin 1913) pp. 437–8, itself derived from a survey of the results of the 1897 census, published by N. A. Troinitski (SPB, 1905).

	Numbers (to nearest 50,000)	Percentage of total population
Russians	55,650,000	44·3
Ukrainians	22,400,000	17·8
White Russians	5,900,000	4·7
Poles	7,900,000	6·3
Lithuanians	1,650,000	1·4
Letts	1,400,000	1·1
Esthonians	1,000,000	·8
Other Finnish groups[1]	2,500,000	2
Germans	1,800,000	1·4
Roumanians	1,100,000	·9
Jews	5,000,000	4
Georgians	1,350,000	1
Armenians	1,150,000	·9
Caucasian mountaineers	1,000,000	·8
Iranians	1,000,000	·8
Tatars[2]	3,700,000	3
Kirghiz[3]	4,000,000	3·2
Other Turkish peoples	5,750,000	4·7
Mongols	500,000	·4
Miscellaneous others	200,000	·2

These figures are for the Russian Empire. The Grand Duchy of Finland, which was united with Russia only in the person of the monarch, had at the end of the century a population of 3,000,000. Of these, some 2,600,000 were Finns and 400,000 Swedes.

From the political point of view the most important of the nationalities were the Poles. By the partitions of the end of the eighteenth century the greater part of the once powerful and extensive Polish state became part of the Russian Empire. In 1772 Poland had reached the Dnieper in the Ukraine and crossed it in White Russia. It included the towns of Zhitomir, Vitebsk and Minsk, and just fell short of Kiev and Smolensk.[4] This Polish state in fact stretched far to the east of the ethnic limits of the Polish nation. By the peace settlement which followed the Napoleonic wars, Russia's share of Poland was substantially increased beyond that acquired

[1] The most important of these were the Mordvins, numbering over one million.
[2] This includes people from very diverse areas—e.g. the Volga valley, Crimea and Azerbaidjan.
[3] This and the following heading include a number of peoples such as Uzbeks, Turkmens and Kazah, not separately entered. The Kirghiz properly so called were less numerous.   [4] See map facing p. 74.

by the three partitions of 1772, 1793 and 1795. It now included Warsaw and Łódź.

Tsar Alexander I divided his gains from Poland into two parts. The lands of predominantly Polish population were formed into the so-called "Congress Kingdom", and enjoyed for some years a measure of autonomy. The provinces whose population was mainly Ukrainian, White Russian or Lithuanian were incorporated directly into Russia. In these "western provinces" the Ukrainians, White Russians and Lithuanians were the peasants, the townsmen were mostly Jews, while the Poles were landowners and administrators. Under Russian rule, the national and social structure was further modified by the introduction of a Russian bureaucracy. The Poles thus lost their control of the administration but kept their social position as landowners.

The importance of Poland to Russia was strategic and economic. The Polish provinces formed the central part of Russia's western frontier on land, with the German Empire and with Austria-Hungary. Poland was also one of the first areas of the Russian Empire to become industrialised. There were three main industrial areas. The first was the textile centre of Łódź. The second was the Sosnowice area in the south-west, which produced coal, iron and some textiles. The third was Warsaw, which played an increasing part in Russia's sugar production and was also an important centre of agricultural machinery.

The Ukraine is the southern part of Russia, stretching from the Don and the Kuban steppe in the east to the Austrian and Roumainian frontiers in the west. Its history had for many centuries been different from that of central Russia. The first Russian state in history had been based on Kiev, whose civilisation owed much to Byzantine influence. In the Middle Ages, Tatar and Turkish invasions had submerged the whole south. But when the Moslem hordes began to weaken, there had grown up around the Dnieper a state of Cossacks, turbulent and lawless horsemen whose ranks were filled by peasants fleeing from serfdom in Poland or in Muscovy.[1] The Cossacks had maintained their independence by a series of wars and alliances in turn with Poland, Muscovy, the Ottoman Empire and the Crimean Tatars. At the end of the seventeenth

---

[1] A convenient summary of the earlier history of the Ukraine may be found in W. E. D. Allen, *The Ukraine* (Cambridge, 1940). For the period of the present work the most useful surveys are *Velika istoria Ukrainy* (ed. Doroshenko), (Winnipeg, 1948); Krupnyckyj, *Geschichte der Ukraine* (Leipzig, 1943); *Narys istorii Ukrainy* (Academy of Sciences of Ukrainian S.S.R., Kiev, 1942); and Hrushevski, *Abrégé de l'histoire de l'Ukraine* (Paris, 1920).

century they had accepted the rule of the Tsar, but had continued to enjoy special privileges. It is impossible to say how many of the inhabitants of the Ukraine at this time were immigrant Cossacks, and how many were peasants whose ancestors had lived there from the earliest times. The subsequent claim of Ukrainian nationalist historians that the Cossack state was a national Ukrainian state, must be treated with some reserve.

The majority of the Ukrainians were, like the Russians, members of the Orthodox Church, but in the West the Uniate Church had a large following.[1] The language spoken by the Ukrainians was nearer to Russian than was Polish, and had not a substantial body of literature. Therefore the governments in St. Petersburg regarded the people of the Cossack provinces as Little Russians, a slightly different branch of the Russian nation, and their language as a dialect of the Russian language.

In the nineteenth century however began a Ukrainian literary movement. Its first work was the *Aeneid* of Kotlyarevski (1769–1838). The new universities of Harkov (founded 1805) and Kiev (1833) became centres of research into the history of the Ukraine. The greatest Ukrainian poet was Taras Shevchenko, whose *Kobzar* appeared in 1840. The development of literature stimulated the growth of Ukrainian national feeling. Its effect reached beyond the borders of Russia. In Eastern Galicia and Bukovina, provinces of Austria, there were Ukrainian populations, which formed majorities in the areas nearest the frontier with Russia and mingled with Poles in the west and Roumanians in the south. The people of Carpathian Ruthenia, the north-east corner of Hungary, were also akin to the Ukrainians. At this point, on the Danubian side of the Carpathian range, Ukrainians came into contact with Slovaks and Hungarians.

The five million Jews of Russia had lived since the Middle Ages in the eastern provinces of Poland, and had been brought under Russian rule by the partitions. When in 1812 Russia acquired northern Bessarabia, Jews from the Polish borderlands spread there also in large numbers. Throughout the great belt of land from the Baltic to the Black Sea, the towns were filled with Jewish merchants, shopkeepers and artisans, some prosperous but most

---

[1] The Uniate Church was founded at the end of the sixteenth century. It owed allegiance to the Pope, but its priests were allowed to marry and its services were conducted in the language of the country. It was encouraged by the kings of Poland, who hoped through it to win over the peoples of the Polish-Russian borderlands. In practice however the Uniate Church became a centre of Ukrainian nationalism, directed against both the Orthodox Russians and the Roman Catholic Poles.

living in poverty and squalor. The Russian government imposed rigid restrictions on their movement and employment. They were in effect excluded from professions other than trade and artisan crafts, and they were not allowed to live outside the border region, which became known as "the Pale of Settlement".

The reign of Alexander II brought a series of reforms in the position of the Jews.[1] The most irksome of all their burdens, the conscription of adolescents, was repealed by a decree of 1856. In the next two years the Pale was slightly extended by permitting Jews to live in the Polish and Roumanian frontier zones, residence in which had previously been narrowly restricted. Then the obligation to live within the Pale was removed for various categories. In 1859 Jews who were merchants of the first guild and all foreign Jews were allowed to reside and trade throughout the empire. In 1860 this right was extended to Jews who had served in Guards regiments, and in 1867 to all Jews who had been soldiers. In 1861 Jewish graduates of higher institutions of learning were made eligible for government service, and were allowed to trade and reside throughout the empire. In 1861 the city of Kiev was opened for Jewish merchants of the first and second guilds. In 1865 the Pale was abolished for all Jewish artisans and their families, and in the same year restrictions on residence and on purchase of land or urban property within the Kingdom of Poland were abolished.

All these reforms created optimism and loyalty among Russian Jews. Educated Jews began to consider themselves Russian patriots. In the Jewish schools, established since 1840 with government support, interest in purely Jewish subjects declined in favour of Russian language and a generally wider curriculum. Within Russian Jewry the dominant traditional orthodoxy was challenged by a minority of assimilationists. At the same time however anti-Jewish prejudice remained strong among Russian officials. The Tsar himself refused the proposal, made by his ministers Lanskoy and Reutern and by Vasilchikov the Governor-General of Harkov, that the Pale be altogether abolished. Official suspicion of the Jews was also increased by the 1863 revolt in Poland.[2]

The Germans in Russia were divided between a number of separate regions. There were 400,000 in "Congress" Poland and 240,000 in the western borderlands. Nearly 400,000 were settled on the middle Volga, between Samara and Saratov. Another 340,000

---

[1] See Greenberg, *The Jews in Russia* (Newhaven (U.S.), 1944).
[2] See below, p. 78.

were in the Black Sea region, including the Crimea and a colony at the mouth of the Dniester in Bessarabia (acquired by Russia in 1878). Finally, there were some 165,000 Germans in the Baltic provinces. In the compact colonies, the Germans were peasants and townsmen. But owing to their better education and skill, Germans found good employment also in parts of Russia where there were no German settlements. Russian landowners often employed Germans as managers of their estates. In Russian towns there were many German craftsmen and shopkeepers. For instance, Moscow's bakers were very largely Germans. In the bureaucracy and in the armed forces Germans had long played a large part. Many generals had been Germans from the Baltic. But though clearly distinguishable from their Russian fellow-citizens, the Germans of Russia had in the past been loyal servants of the empire.

The Baltic Germans form a special category. The medieval German religious order, the Knights of the Sword, had long ruled the Lettish and Esthonian provinces. They had been replaced for a time by Swedish conquest, but the land had remained the property of German landowners, the secularised descendants of the knights. When the Baltic coast passed under Russian rule, the dominant class of the region remained German. In the nineteenth century, medieval German traditions were still strong. The German landowning nobility (the "Baltic barons") had their provincial diets, which may be compared with the assemblies of the nobility in Russian provinces. The Russian administration, with its provincial governors, was superimposed on German Baltic self-government, but did not greatly interfere with it until the last decades of the century. In the towns, the German burghers had their guilds and municipal institutions. The well-developed school system was essentially German, and there was a German university at Dorpat. The courts administered a German system of law.[1]

The great majority of the population in the area between the Prussian frontier and the Gulf of Finland belonged to the three Baltic nationalities—Lithuanians, Latvians and Esthonians. The Latvians and Lithuanians have very similar languages, quite distinct from the Slav, Teutonic or Finnish languages of the surrounding nations, but differ in religion. The Lithuanians, who formed part of Poland for nearly four hundred years, are Catholics, while the Latvians, who were subjects of Germans or Swedes, are Lutherans. The Latvians share their religion with the Esthonians,

---

[1] For a brief summary of the position of the Germans in Russia, see Hoetzsch, *op. cit.*, pp. 487–9.

but differ widely from them in language. The Esthonian language closely resembles the Finnish.

National feeling developed among the three Baltic nations from the middle of the nineteenth century. In Latvia and Esthonia the pioneers were the Lutheran pastors. The high level of education and comparative prosperity of the people were an advantage. The emancipation of the peasants from serfdom in the sixties made them more accessible to new ideas. The Riga Latvian Society, founded in 1868, was the centre from which Latvian nationalism spread among the educated class, and in time reached the rest of the people. A similar landmark in Esthonian history is the year 1870, when the Esthonian Students' Society was formed, and a committee was created to collect funds for the foundation of a secondary school in which teaching was to be in the Esthonian language. In Lithuania, a poorer country with fewer opportunities of education, the movement began later. The Lithuanians at first followed the leadership of the Polish national movement, and supported the revolt of 1863. It was not till the eighties that a Lithuanian cultural and national movement began. Its first expression was a paper published in Tilsit, across the Prussian border, entitled *Auszra* ("The Dawn").[1]

The Caucasus is the home of a large number of small nationalities. The two most advanced were the Georgians and the Armenians, both of whom had been Christian for many centuries. Georgia had been Russian since 1802. Its church was placed under an Exarch, who was a member of the Most Holy Synod in St. Petersburg, in 1838. The tendency of the Russian government to subject their Church, and the oppressive agrarian conditions, which were partly relieved by the Emancipation of 1861,[2] caused discontent among the Georgian people, but during the reign of Alexander II it had not acquired political form. The Armenians had a Church of their own, which taught a monophysite form of Christianity. The centre of the Armenian religion was the city of Echmiadzin, the residence of the Head of the Church, the Catholicos. It had been under Russian rule since 1828. The Church was supported by the voluntary contributions of the Armenians themselves, including those who were subjects of Turkey or Persia and the many Armenians scattered in other parts of the world. The Church hierarchy was reorganised in the seventies. Thenceforth the priests were elected by the parishioners, and the higher clergy

[1] For an introduction to the history of the Baltic nations, see Hampden Jackson, *Estonia* (London, 1941); Villecourt, *L'Estonie* (Paris, 1932); Segreste, *La Lettonie* (Paris, 1930); Bossin, *La Lithuanie* (Paris, 1933).
[2] See below, pp. 41-7.

LAND OVER 6,000ft.
"   "   10,000ft.

Rostov

RUSSIAN

Astrahan

CASPIAN

R.Kuban

Novorossiisk

Ekaterinodar   Stavropol

KUBAN

DAGHESTAN

BLACK

Sochi   Elbruz
18,493ft.

R.Terek   Vladikavkaz
Kasbek   Grozny
16,550ft.

SEA

Kutais   GEORGIA

Batum   Tiflis

EMPIRE

Kars   Echmiadzin   Elizavetpol

ARMENIA   Erivan   Baku

OTTOMAN   Erzurum   Ararat
16920ft.   AZERBAIDJAN   R.Araxes

L.Van   Tabriz
KURDISTAN   L.Urmia

CASPIAN SEA

Aleppo   Mosul

EMPIRE   MESOPO   PERSIA

R.Tigris

Damascus   R.Euphrates   Baghdad   MIA

Jerusalem

ARABIA   Basra

0   100   200   300 Miles

2. THE CAUCASUS AND MIDDLE EAST

by the priests. The Armenian Church was thus a democratic organisation, and formed the core of Armenian national feeling. Until the end of the century the Russian authorities did not interfere with it.[1]

The Moslem subjects of the Russian Empire were extremely diverse. The most advanced, both in education and in national feeling, were the Tatars of the Volga, whose centre was Kazan. In the 18th century the Russian State authorities backed the efforts of the Orthodox Church forcibly to convert them. After the Pugachov rebellion of 1773–5, in which considerable numbers of Tatars were involved, proselytism was stopped. A "Moslem spiritual assembly" was set up, with official approval, in Orenburg in 1788, and the office of Mufti of Orenburg, created in 1840, became the centre of Islamic life in Russia. The Tatar traders were allowed by Catherine II to create their own self-governing merchant organisation, with rights of trade with Central Asia, Persia and China. One result of this was growing cultural contact between Kazan and Buhara. In the first half of the 19th century Kazan university was a meeting-ground of western and eastern culture. Relations between its Russian and Tatar teachers were good. But in the 1850's the direction of Russian oriental studies was moved to St. Petersburg, and Kazan once more became a centre of Orthodox proselytism. The leading figure in this period was the Russian professor Ilminski, a friend of Pobedonstsev.[2] Ilminski encouraged the study of the Turkish dialects and languages of the Volga-Ural area, and encouraged every element of diversity. His aim was to remove the smaller ethnic and linguistic groups from Tatar cultural influence. He encouraged the use of the Cyrillic, rather than the Arabic alphabet for publications in their languages. There was a keen competition between Russian and Tatar missionaries for the conversion of the small Finno-Ugrian language groups, and of the Chuvash, whose language belongs to the Turkish group. Though the Orthodox had State backing, the Tatars held their own in the cultural battle.[3]

A special Moslem community were the Tatars of the Crimea. Another were the Turks of Azerbaidjan, beyond the Caucasus. Immediate neighbours of Turkey, they were liable to be influenced

---

[1] For the history of Georgia before the Russian conquest, see W. E. D. Allen, *History of the Georgian People* (London, 1932). For an Armenian nationalist account of Armenian history, see Pasdermadjian, *Histoire de l'Arménie* (Paris, 1949).
[2] See below, pp. 131–2.
[3] The best account that I have found of this subject is G. von Mende, *Der nationale Kampf der Russlandtürken* Berlin 1936.

by developments in Turkey, such as the Panislamic movement encouraged by Sultan Abdul Hamid in the last decades of the century. The growth of an oil industry in Baku also increased their importance. The Moslem mountaineers of the Caucasus range, extremely various in race and language, kept up guerrilla resistance for the first half of the century. Their last leader, the chieftain Shamil, was defeated by the Russian forces in 1859. Of the Moslems of Central Asia more will be said later.[1]

There were two national groups of Buddhist religion in the Russian Empire. One were the Kalmyks, who lived in the steppes around the northern shore of the Caspian Sea. The other were the Buryat Mongols, who lived beyond Lake Baikal, on the frontier with China. The Buryats were akin to the Mongols living within the Chinese Empire. Discontented with rule from Peking, the Mongols at times regarded Russia as a protector. Finally in the Siberian Far North were small numbers of primitive pagan tribes.

Finland occupied a special position. It was not part of the Russian Empire, but a separate Grand Duchy, united with Russia only by the person of the Tsar, who was Grand Duke. This situation had existed since 1809, when Finland was taken from Sweden, of which it had been a part for most of its recorded history. Alexander I had called a Diet in 1809 at Borgå (Porvoo), based, like the parliament of Sweden, on four Estates elected by a restricted franchise. He had set up a Government Council, modelled on the Council of State in Sweden. This body, which was the effective government of Finland, was divided into a Department of Economy and a Department of Justice. The first handled general administration, the second the judiciary. In 1816 the title of the Council was changed to Senate, and this name was kept until the collapse of the Russian Empire. The highest official in Finland was a Governor-General, appointed by the Tsar. In 1811 was created a State Secretariat for Finland in St. Petersburg, headed by a Secretary with the rank of Minister, who was normally a native of Finland.

Alexander I and Nicholas I ruled Finland autocratically, by decree. During their reigns the Diet was not again summoned. But the laws and administration of the country were not those of Russia, but those which had existed in Finland under Swedish rule. In the first half of the century the main political issue in Finland was the language question. The official language of the Grand Duchy was Swedish, but the language of the great majority of the

[1] See below, pp. 84–7.

people was Finnish. The Swedes, forming some 12 per cent of the population, included people of all social classes, but in the upper class they predominated. Higher education, commerce, government business and court proceedings were conducted in Swedish. From the 1840's the movement for equal status for the Finnish language made rapid progress.[1]

With the accession of Alexander II concessions were made to Finnish national feeling. In 1856 and 1859 some provision was made for the use of the Finnish language in public business. In 1863 the Tsar summoned the Diet, and after this it met at regular intervals. It was however still the old corporative and unrepresentative Diet. On 1st August 1863 an important decree on the languages was issued. It declared that Swedish was still the official language of the Grand Duchy, but that Finnish was to be equal to it in all matters directly affecting the Finnish-speaking part of the population. Documents and records in Finnish were to be accepted in all law-courts and administrative offices in the country. Within twenty years, complete practical equality of the two languages was to be achieved in all public business. In 1865 a supplementary law provided that from 1872 all judges and officials were to be required to use Finnish in the discharge of their duties in areas of Finnish population.

Throughout the reign of Alexander II the political and cultural position of the Finns grew stronger and the traditional institutions of the Grand Duchy were not attacked from St. Petersburg. In the first half of the century, social contact between the Swedish aristocracy of Finland and the Russian aristocracy had ensured the prevalence of Swedish influence at the court of the Tsar. The Russian bureaucracy was however less sympathetic to the Swedes, and supported the Finnish nationalists against them. For a time the Finns, whose main political organisation was the Old Finnish Party, regarded the Russians as friends in their struggle against the Swedes. It was not till the end of the century that the Russian bureaucrats, by directing their russifying zeal against the Finns as well, reunited Finns and Swedes in common resistance to their aims.

[1] For the history of Finland between 1809 and 1914, see Schybergson, *Geschichte Finnlands* (Gotha, 1926); Wuorinen, *Nationalism in Modern Finland* (New York, 1931); von Törne, *Finland under hundra trettio år* (Stockholm, 1943); Hampden Jackson, *Finland* (London, 1940).

Chapter II

FROM REFORM TO ASSASSINATION

The Emancipation of the Serfs

Russia's defeat in the Crimean War exposed to the whole world the rottenness of the Russian State. Even before the war Nicholas had been partly aware of it, and in his way had striven for reform. But the European revolutions of 1848 had been a shock to him, and after that he had obstinately opposed change. In 1855 he was succeeded by Alexander II, who decided to reconsider the problem of serfdom. Apart from the person of the monarch, two further factors contributed to the change of attitude at the top. One was that the big landowners of the south, whose crops were beginning to enter into international trade and to bring good returns, were beginning to find that wage labour was more efficient than serfs. The second was the striking growth of minor outbreaks of violence by the peasants. There were 400 cases in the ten years 1845–55 and 400 more in the five years 1855–60. Two hundred and thirty serf-owners or bailiffs had been killed by peasants between 1835 and 1854, and fifty-three between 1858 and 1861.[1]

The first public indication of impending reform was a manifesto issued in 1856 by Alexander II on the conclusion of peace. In it he spoke of the need for "laws equally just for all, equally protecting for all". At the request of the Governor-General of Moscow, the Tsar made a speech to the Moscow nobility, in which he used the startling and famous phrase: "It is better to abolish serfdom from above than to wait until the serfs begin to liberate themselves from below." The Tsar had now committed himself. But he wished the initiative to come from the nobles themselves. Their response was disappointing. A high official of the Ministry of Interior was instructed to begin discussions with them, but those whom he sounded were hostile. They especially opposed any granting of land to the liberated serfs, which was an essential part of the Tsar's intention. After months of hesitation by the nobles, the Tsar lost

[1] Sumner, *op. cit.*, p. 141.

his patience, and ordered the Minister of the Interior to produce a draft within three days. This was published on 20th November/3rd December 1857 as an Imperial Rescript addressed to the Governor-General of Lithuania.[1]

The Rescript proclaimed the liberation of landowners' peasants from personal serfdom and the principle that they should be enabled to buy land from the landlords. It directed that the details should be considered by committees of the nobility in each province. These were to be composed of two delegates elected by the nobility of each district in each province, and the chairman was to be in each case the provincial marshal of the nobility. Some time before this the Tsar had appointed a Secret State Committee to examine the whole question. One of its leading figures was General Rostovtsev, who had previously been Director of Military Schools and was the Tsar's trusted and intimate friend.

For a year after the publication of the Rescript discussions were held all over the country. Political and social issues were debated by the gentry and the educated class with greater freedom and eagerness than ever before in Russia's history. In March 1859 the Tsar appointed "drafting commissions" to examine the proposals put forward by the provincial committees. Rostovtsev was appointed Head of the Commissions, and his closest collaborators were men of enlightened views.[2] After studying the proposals, they summoned delegates from the provincial committees in two groups. The first group, representing nineteen provinces, came in the autumn of 1859, were admitted three or four at a time to the Commissions, and gave their opinions orally. The members of this group were on the whole favourable to the Government's principles. They wished the peasants to be free and to receive land. Their objections were to the manner in which the Reform was being carried out. They wished its execution to be entrusted not to the governmental bureaucracy but to local organs of self-government. The second group of delegates came in early 1860. They were more hostile to the Reform in itself, and spoke in defence of the landlords' traditional rights over the peasants. They tried to influence the Tsar against the Commissions by accusing their members of liberal sympathies.

---

[1] The preparations leading to the emancipation, and the personalities concerned, are described in A. A. Kornilov, *Obshchestvennoe dvizhenie pri Alexandre II* (Moscow, 1909). The emancipation is treated in greater detail by the same author's *Krestyanskaya reforma* (SPB, 1905).

[2] The most important of these were the Assistant Minister of Interior, N. A. Milyutin, the Slavophile intellectual Samarin and Prince Cherkasski.

At this point Rostovtsev died and was succeeded by Panin, known as a man of reactionary sympathies. The appointment was considered to be the result of conservative pressure on the Court. But in fact it had little influence on the result. The work of the drafting commissions came to an end in October 1860, and their proposals went before the main Secret Committee and then the Council of State. The Tsar was himself present at the later sessions of both bodies, and supported the drafting commissions' plans. In the end these were only very slightly modified. Finally the Archbishop of Moscow was requested to write the text of the Imperial decree, which was published on 19th February/4th March 1861.

The essential points of the Reform were the following. All personal serfdom was abolished, and the peasants now became free citizens. The peasants were to receive land from the landlords' estates, and were to pay the landlords for it. The State advanced the money to the landlords, and recovered from the peasants fixed annual sums. These became known as "redemption payments". The land holdings received by the peasants were controlled, as before, by the village commune. The commune was in most cases collectively responsible for the payment of redemption debts and, as previously, of taxes. Finally a system of peasant self-government was set up. Each village had its assembly of householders, at the head of which was an elected official known as the "Elder" (*starosta*). Several communes together formed a "canton" (*volost*), which had its Elder and its court. The canton court was empowered to judge minor civil disputes which did not involve any person who was not a peasant. It was guided rather by peasant custom than by written law. Thus, though the peasants were emancipated from the disabilities of serfdom, justice was administered to them separately from other classes, and on different principles.

Two features of the new system call for more careful explanation —the nature of the redemption payments and the place of the village commune in the Reform.

The amount of compensation to landlords was fixed at a rate considerably higher than the prices of land prevailing at the time of the Reform. An estimate by a Russian authority in 1906 gives the following figures for three regions of Russia.[1] The sums paid to the landlords are compared with the value of the land at average land prices for 1863-72.

[1] Lositski, *Vykupnaya operatsia* (SPB, 1906), quoted by Robinson, *op. cit.*, p. 88.

	Redemption cost	Land value
	(in millions of roubles)	
Black-soil provinces	341	284
Non-black-soil provinces	340	180
Western provinces	183	184

The redemption price was low in the western provinces because for political reasons the Government favoured the peasants against the Polish landlords, who were the mainstay of the Polish national movement. But the difference between black-soil and non-black-soil provinces is of great importance.

In the non-black-soil region, the northern part of European Russia, the crop yield was not high, and many serfs were engaged in industrial occupations either in their homes or in factories. In these areas a large part of the landowners' wealth came from their share in the peasants' industrial earnings, in the form of the *obrok* which the peasants paid in cash. The loss of land was not so heavy a blow to them as the loss of the persons of the serfs. It had been solemnly laid down in government statements that redemption was to be paid only for land, and on no account for human beings. But in fact the landlords of the northern provinces succeeded in obtaining sums so greatly in excess of the land's value as to compensate them for the loss of their serfs' earnings.

On the other hand, in the black-soil provinces of the south, the land was of more value than were the serfs. The landlords in this region were developing their estates on modern capitalist lines, and their crops were competing in the great European markets. They were finding wage labour more useful than serf. They had no objection to the personal liberation of the serfs, but wished to prevent them from obtaining more than the absolute minimum of land. The result of their efforts was that in the end the serfs in the south received by the redemption process an area considerably smaller than had been the land which under serfdom they had cultivated for their families. In other words, the landlords cut off a part of what had been, not legally but in practice, the serfs' land. The total area cultivated by landlords' peasants in 43 provinces of European Russia before the Reform was about 35 million *desyatin*,[1] in 1877 it was 33·75 million. But in the southern provinces the difference was proportionately much higher. In the best black-soil area it amounted to about one-quarter.[2] The lands thus appropriated by the landlords were called in Russian *otrezki* ("cut-off bits").

---

[1] One *desyatin* is equal to 2.7 acres.   [2] Robinson, *op. cit.*, p. 87.

Thus the general effect was that the landlords succeeded in passing most of the burden of the emancipation from themselves on to the peasants, by charging excessive prices in the north, or by keeping an undue proportion of the land in the south. In the north, the peasant in practice had to pay a personal ransom, in the south he got less than what he considered his rightful share of land.

The land which became the property of peasants was administered by the village commune. There were two types of commune —the "hereditary" (*podyornoe*), in which the peasant's holding could be transmitted to his heir without any external interference, and the "repartitional" (*obshchinnoe*), in which land was subject to periodic redistribution.

The repartitional type was the more widespread of the two, especially in north and central Russia. All communes, of either type, controlled three types of land. These were the house and garden allotments in which the families lived; the open fields under plough, in which was applied a crop cycle determined by the village; and the meadow-lands, pastures and forests. In both types of commune the first type of land belonged to the individual peasants, and the third type of land to the commune. In the hereditary type of commune, the second type of land belonged definitely to the individual household. In the repartitional type of commune however the second type of land only belonged to the household as long as this was justified by its needs. It was liable to redistribution if these should change. That is to say, if the members of the household increased, it would become entitled to more land, and if they diminished it might be expected to give up some land to another household suffereing from land shortage. These redistributions took place at irregular intervals, and often not for very many years at a time.

In many villages land differed in quality. In order to avoid unjust distribution it was often necessary for households each to have portions of land of each quality. Moreover, as the children set up households of their own, each wanted to have land of different qualities. In this way, holdings became more and more divided into small strips, often separated from each other by considerable distances. This of course made for inefficient cultivation. The more prosperous and successful peasants wished to consolidate their holdings, to exchange their scattered strips for others concentrated in one place. If they could manage this, they could make themselves independent of the village crop cycle. Under the hereditary tenure, this was only possible with the consent of every householder whose land would be displaced by the consolidation. Under the repartitional tenure, a householder who paid up the full sum of his redemption debt could compel the commune to give him, in exchange for his scattered strips, a holding of similar size and quality consolidated "as far as possible" in one place, or failing this to pay him an indemnity. Few peasants were however able to avail themselves of either of these provisions.

It was also very difficult for a peasant to separate himself personally from the commune, even if he was prepared to do without land. Under the hereditary tenure, he could only do this if he transferred the allotment assigned to him to someone else who was willing to accept the outstanding redemption debt on it, or himself paid the whole debt. Under the repartitional tenure, he could do so if he himself paid half the outstanding redemption debt and induced the commune to pay the other half. This the commune was entitled to refuse.

Some confusion was caused by obscurity in the definition of administrative units. The difference was not made clear between the "village community", which was recognised by the new laws, and to which the powers above mentioned were assigned, and the "peasant commune", the traditional organisation described earlier. In the case of large villages belonging to one landowner, there was no trouble, because the "community" and the "commune" were identical. But it often happened that different settlements of peasants were associated with each other for different purposes— for instance, for common use of forests or pastures. The new laws treated as a unit the peasants settled on one landlord's estate. Where old-standing connections existed with land belonging to another owner, confusion resulted. The Senate, the highest court of appeal in Russia, gave conflicting verdicts during the next thirty years. It was never made absolutely clear what powers belonged to which units.[1]

The laws provided that a transitional stage should exist before redemption came into effect. This was known as the period of "temporary obligation". During it the peasants held the allotments allocated to them by the Reform, and paid for them either an *obrok* or a fixed labour obligation (*otrabotok*). The size of the allotment was settled by appointed officials known as "arbitrators of the peace". These men enjoyed a secure status, as they could only be dismissed by the Senate. They were to mediate in

[1] This rather complicated administrative question is discussed in Robinson, *op. cit.*, pp. 67-71.

disputes between landlords and peasants. On the whole they did their job in an enlightened manner. The laws also provided that if landlord and peasant both agreed, the landlord could give, free of payment, an area one-quarter the prescribed size, and thereby fulfil all obligations on either side. This provision was in fact used by a number of poorer peasants. The condition of "temporary obligation" dragged on in some areas for twenty years. It was not until December 1881 that the payment of redemption annuities and the transfer of allotments to the legal possession of peasants, was made universally compulsory.[1]

The position of the State peasants was regulated in 1866. They had been freed from personal serfdom by Nicholas I.[2] Now they received as permanent allotments all the land, except forests, which they had previously held. For the first twenty years they paid an *obrok*, at a rate slightly higher than they had previously paid but appreciably lower than the average *obrok* on landlords' estates. In 1886 the *obrok* was replaced by annual redemption payments, also considerably lower than the redemption payments paid by landlords' peasants. The organisation of the villages in communes, repartitional or hereditary, did not substantially differ in the case of State peasants from that described above for landlords' peasants.

Political Reforms and Opposition

The emancipation was bound to be followed by administrative reforms. The structure of local government, the army and the judicial system, all of which had been based on serfdom, needed to be radically changed. In 1859, when the first group of deputies from the provincial committees were being consulted by Rostovtsev's drafting commissions, various proposals for representative institutions were put forward. The boldest came from the nobility of Tver province. The marshal of nobility of Tver, A. M. Unkovski, drew up, with seventeen others who attended the drafting commissions, an address to the Tsar with requests for liberal reforms. He was also responsible for a more radical address, signed besides himself by two deputies from Yaroslavl and two from Harkov. This asked for an elected authority to deal with economic affairs, an independent judiciary, and some machinery through which any failures or abuses by the local bureaucracy could be regularly brought to the notice of the supreme authority. The

[1] In Georgia the conditions of emancipation were especially unfavourable to the peasants. Georgian landlords continued to enjoy quasi-feudal privileges until 1905 and even later.
[2] See above, p. 7.

Tsar's reply was to order a formal and public rebuke to be administered to the signatories of both addresses. Alexander's view of public discussion of national issues was shown by his instruction to the Minister of Interior to send out a circular forbidding assemblies of the nobility to hold debates on the peasant question. The assemblies of Tver and Vladimir disobeyed the circular, the former directly and the latter by keeping just within the letter of the instruction. The Tsar then ordered the banishment of Unkovski to Vyatka province in the east of European Russia.[1] These events caused a considerable stir among the noble class. The hostility of a large part of the gentry towards the bureaucracy could not be doubted.

In February 1862 the nobility of Tver passed a resolution in favour of financial and judicial reforms, publicity in administration, and an elected assembly. Thirteen "arbitrators of the peace" from Tver province passed a more radical resolution. They declared that their action would be guided not by the government but by "the people's wishes". One of the thirteen was Alexei Bakunin, the younger brother of the anarchist.[2] The thirteen were arrested by order of the Minister of the Interior and imprisoned in the Peter-Paul fortress in St. Petersburg.[3] They were sentenced to two years' prison but were set free before the full term had expired.

It was clear by now that the Tsar was not willing to consider the creation of a nation-wide representative body. His refusal, and the repressive action taken against those who proposed such action, mark a turning-point in Russian history. This was the moment, if ever there was one, when the foundations of a Russian parliamentary democracy might have been laid. Russia was, it is true, economically and culturally far behind Europe. But the Russian masses were so inarticulate, and so accustomed to obedience, that their discontents need not have shaken the structure of the State. There was a group of men, small if compared to the whole population of the empire yet not insignificant in number, which was accessible to enlightened ideas derived from the European liberal tradition. Within a parliament, based on a restricted franchise, reactionaries and liberals, Slavophiles and Westernisers, could have argued out their views, and their deliberations would have benefited Russia. Useful reforms could have been achieved. The gentry and the business class could have won political experience. The growth of the bourgeoisie and the increase in prosperity of at least a section

---

[1] Kornilov, *Obshchestvennoe dvizhenie pri Alexandre II*, pp. 58–9 and 64–6.
[2] See below, p. 63.   [3] Kornilov, *op. cit.*, pp. 113–17.

of the peasantry would in the course of time have made possible some extension of the franchise. By 1900 Russia might have reached a stage where a bolder advance towards democracy could have been achieved by peaceful means.

This prospect was cut off by the Tsar's refusal. The dogma of autocracy, the dead weight of bureaucracy, and the influence of the most reactionary section of the aristocracy, sufficed to prevent action. The peasant riots, the "seditious" attitude of the Tver nobility, the Polish revolt and the leaflets of the radical intellectuals[1] were used to persuade Alexander that further progress would bring Russia to the brink of revolution. And so the task was left uncompleted. It was not to be resumed until the period of Stolypin (1906–11), when forces had already been released with which moderate measures could not deal. If Stolypin's policy had been carried out in the 1860's, by such men as Milyutin and Korf, the whole history of modern Europe might have been different.

The most important administrative reform that Alexander was prepared to consider was in local government. A commission was set up in 1861, under P. A. Valuyev, who had succeeded the more liberal Count Lanskoy as Minister of Interior in April of that year. The Commission's task was to prepare proposals on the composition and powers of assemblies which were to be set up in provinces and districts in European Russia.[2] The main subject of discussion was whether the assemblies were to represent all classes of the population in each province and district, or only the nobility. The Commission met at irregular intervals, and prolonged its discussions until November 1863, when the Tsar intervened with a sharp order to finish the job by 1st January 1864. The proposals were discussed in the Council of State in December 1863. The decree was duly published on 1st/14th January 1864. It was a compromise between the views of the reactionaries and the liberals.

All classes were to be represented, but each class was to elect its deputies separately. The district assemblies were elected in three electoral colleges (*Curiae*)—nobility, townsmen and peasants. The peasant representatives were indirectly chosen. The peasants who finally sat in the district assemblies were chosen by peasant "electors", themselves elected by *starosty* of communes and cantons, who were elected by the householders' assemblies of the communes. The proportion of seats in the assemblies allotted to the three

[1] See below, pp. 59–60.
[2] I have used throughout the words "province" for the Russian *gubernia* and "district" for the Russian *uyezd*.

electoral colleges varied according to local conditions. The property qualification for membership of the townsmen's college was also not the same in all areas. The members of the provincial assemblies were elected by the district assemblies of each province. Both district and provincial assemblies, henceforth mentioned by their Russian name of "zemstvo", elected from their midst an administrative board (*uprava*), which exercised the executive powers entrusted to the zemstvos by the law.[1]

These were the result of a struggle between the opposing factions in the Commission and in the Council of State. The reactionaries had tried to reduce the zemstvos' competence, but in the end the proposal of the liberal Councillor of State, E. P. Kovalevski, to entrust to them public health, administration of local prisons, and part of the financing of local education, was accepted. The zemstvos were however required to carry out, at their own expense, certain local functions of the central government. Valuyev himself bitterly and successfully opposed the proposals of the liberals that the expense of these functions should be borne by the central government, and that the zemstvos should have some say in the assessment of taxes raised in their area by the central government. A victory for the reactionaries was the decision, opposed by Baron Korf and the liberals, that the office of chairman of the assemblies should not be held by a person elected by the members, but should be given in all cases to the district and provincial marshals of the nobility.

In 1865-6 zemstvo institutions were introduced in twenty-seven provinces of European Russia, and soon afterwards into seven more. They were never extended to the non-Russian frontier areas. A calculation made in the seventies estimated that 40-45 per cent of the seats in district assemblies were held by landowners or by government officials. With regard to the zemstvos' revenue, figures for 1871 show that the average rate of taxation on land owned by peasants was almost twice as high as on land owned by the nobility. By 1895 this relationship had not appreciably changed.[2] Nevertheless, despite the predominance of the noble class, the zemstvos did

[1] The discussions and preparations leading to the creation of the zemstvos are discussed in G. A. Dzhanshiev, *Epoha velikih reform* (Moscow, 1900).

[2] Peasants in 1871 paid 10·6 kopeks per desyatin of land, nobles 5·6. In 1895 peasants paid 21·6 kopeks and nobles 11. *Obshchestvennoe dvizhenie v Rossii v nachale XX veka* (ed. Martov, Maslov and Potresov) (SPB, 1908-11), Vol. I, p. 164. This enormous work, by a group of Menshevik writers, containing a survey of political, social and economic conditions in Russia before, during and after 1905, will frequently be quoted hereafter. It will be referred to as *O.D.* For a survey of the work of the zemstvos in the following decades, the best work is Veselovski, *Istoria zemstva za sorok let* (SPB, 1909).

work of real value to the whole community, especially in road-building, public health and famine relief, and to a lesser extent in education. The zemstvos employed growing numbers of secretaries, doctors, schoolteachers, agricultural engineers, statisticians, and other experts. These men and women were recruited from the expanding intelligentsia. Most were of non-noble origin and many held radical political views. The work of the zemstvos was thus based on a sort of semi-conscious collaboration between the mild liberalism of the more enlightened landlords and the radicalism of the professional class, for which at that time this was almost the only field of legal activity open.

The establishment of local government in the cities came later. Municipal councils (*gorodskaya duma*) were set up in 1870. Eight cities were given status of provinces, and had a town commandant whose rank was equal to that of governor. The remainder were incorporated in the provinces with the status of districts. The franchise for the councils was based on a census of house property or of payments of trade tax. As there was no income tax in Russia citizens who were not householders and did not pay trade tax were not enfranchised. This meant that a large part of the professional class was excluded from city government. The city councils were fairly large bodies. The bulk of their business was transacted by the city board (*uprava*), chosen from their number, at whose head was the mayor or "city head". The mayor was elected by the municipal voters, but his appointment had to be confirmed by the Minister of the Interior. In the case of the mayors of St. Petersburg and Moscow, two names were submitted by the Council to the Tsar, who chose one of them. The decisions of the Council and its executive organs were subject to the confirmation of the governor or town commandant, and their regulations had to be executed by the police, which took its orders not from them but from the Polizeimeister who was responsible to the Minister of Interior.

The task of preparing judicial reforms was entrusted to a Commission headed by Zarudny, an official of the Ministry of Justice, who made a study of foreign systems during journeys abroad from 1858 onwards. The Commission reported in October 1862, and received the Tsar's approval. The new system was not officially decreed until December 1864. It was put into practice in St. Petersburg and Moscow in 1865, and slowly extended to other parts of European Russia. It created for the first time a modern machinery of justice, based on West European, especially French, experience. The basis of the new system was the regional court (*okruzhny sud*), of which there was one in each province for civil and criminal cases. Trial was by jury in criminal but not in civil cases. Above the regional court was the "Chamber of Justice" (*Sudebnaya palata*), of which there were ten in Russia. The final court of appeal remained the Cassation Departments of the Senate. Judges were irremovable. Court proceedings were public. The procedure of justice was greatly accelerated. Judges received a decent salary—an important and effective safeguard against corruption. They were appointed by the government, but were obliged to have professional qualifications. Juries were selected in turn from lists prepared by commissions of the zemstvos and municipal councils. There was a small property qualification. An important weakness in the system was that a government official might only be prosecuted with the consent of his administrative superior. More important was the fact that in the following decades, as a result of the struggle with the revolutionary movement, a number of offences were removed altogether from the jurisdiction of juries and entrusted to special tribunals. Administrative arrest[1] was not abolished.

The judicial reform brought into being a new profession—the bar. This soon attracted many of the most brilliant Russian intellectuals. The efficiency, integrity and eloquence of Russian barristers could stand comparison with those of any other European country. The freedom of expression in the court-room, and the publicity given to trials. were of great importance for the formation of Russian public opinion. To some small extent they compensated for the absence of a parliament and the restrictions on the press.[2]

In the countryside, the cantonal court for purely peasant disputes[3] remained, despite the opposition of those who wished to remove all class differentiation from Russian justice. But the reform introduced "Justices of the Peace", who could try minor offences, and whose jurisdiction extended to all classes in country districts. They were elected by zemstvo assemblies, and there was one for about 40,000 inhabitants. Appeal could be made from their decisions to an Assembly of Justices of the Peace at provincial level. On the whole the Justices of the Peace did their work well, and won the confidence of the people.

Reform of the army was carried out by D. A. Milyutin, who

---

[1] See above p. 15.

[2] For subsequent restrictions on the powers of the courts, see below, pp. 71, 134, 136. There is a brief discussion of the legal profession in Russia in Sliozberg, *Dorevolutsionny stroy Rossii* (Paris 1935). Another valuable source are the memoirs of A. F. Koni, *Na zhiznennom puti* (SPB, 1914).

[3] See above, p. 43.

was appointed Minister of War in 1861 and held the office for twenty years. Hitherto there had been no regular conscription. All serfs and the lower category of townsmen were liable to service. Those on whom fell the haphazard choice of the authorities were obliged to serve for twenty-five years, during most of which they were separated from their families. Milyutin began his term as minister by reducing the period of service to sixteen years. He then modernised the system and procedure of military law and reduced the severity of punishments. He reorganised the officers' training institutions, laying less emphasis on drill and paying greater attention to professional skill.

The next important change was to reduce the personnel of the War Ministry, and to enable it to devote itself to the most important tasks, by decentralising the command of the troops. In 1862 regional (*okrug*) commands were created in Warsaw, Vilna, Kiev and Odessa. In 1864 further regional commands were set up in Riga, St. Petersburg, Moscow, Harkov, Kazan and Finland. In 1865 the system was extended to the Caucasus, Orenburg, Western and Eastern Siberia. During the following decades new commands were created, and reorganised, in Central Asia and the Far East. These regional commands relieved the central ministry of much detailed work which had formerly been a crushing burden.

Milyutin also increased the importance of the General Staff, which received a status equal to that of the main administrative divisions of the War Ministry. In 1865 the post of Chief of General Staff was created for the first time. Though this was an important step forward, much still remained to be done. In the following years the General Staff was loaded with various ill-assorted tasks, and the need for a systematic organisation became ever more clear. A number of reforms were proposed, and commissions of investigation appointed, but it was not until March 1900 that action was taken. The Tsar then gave his consent to a new scheme which clearly defined the duties of the General Staff, and laid down that the Chief of General Staff should normally hold the position of deputy War Minister. But this system had not yet come into operation when war with Japan began.[1]

Milyutin's most important reform was the introduction of conscription. By the law of 13th/26th January 1874 military service was made compulsory for all male Russian subjects aged 20 years who were passed as medically fit. Exemption was granted to only sons

[1] The reform of the General Staff is summarised in *Stoletie Voennovo Ministerstva* (SPB, 1902–11), Vol. III, section vi, pp. 247–8 and 284–6.

or only grandsons who supported their parents or grandparents; to persons who supported a brother or a sister who was a minor; and to those who had a brother serving in the army at the time. The normal period of service was six years, followed by nine years in the reserve and five more years in the militia. Those who had received primary education had to serve for only four years. Partial secondary education reduced the term to three years, complete secondary education to two years, and university education to six months.

These reforms laid the foundation of a modern Russian army. The quality of training and command, and the relations between officers and men, remained for long inferior to those prevailing in Western armies. They could only improve as general education improved and social and political conditions were modernised. Abuses were not at once removed. It was for instance not unusual for wealthier persons to bribe army doctors to declare them unfit for service. Nevertheless the improvement was substantial, and was already visible in the Russo-Turkish war of 1877-8.

The navy received little attention in the reign of Alexander II. The removal in 1870 of the disarmament clause of the Paris Treaty of 1856[1] was not followed by serious naval building, as the war with Turkey fully occupied the available resources. It was not until the nineties that naval expansion became rapid, and this was a result of developments not in Europe, but in the Far East. The Black Sea fleet was also greatly strengthened in the nineties. At the beginning of the reign of Alexander III Russia had only one battleship, in 1902 she had twenty-six, as well as thirty-nine cruisers. Some indication of the growth of the navy can be given by the sums allocated to it under the budget. These were:[2]

1855	..	..	19 million roubles
1865	..	..	21 ,,
1875	..	..	26 ,,
1885	..	..	38 ,,
1895	..	..	55 ,,
1900	..	..	86 ,,
1902	..	..	98 ,,

Education and Radicalism.

From the beginning of the reign, the application of the censorship had been less severe than under Nicholas I. During the preparations for emancipation, the Press had discussed the peasant question

[1] See below, pp. 94, 96.   [2] *Ministerstvo Morskoe 1802–1902* (SPB, 1902).

with comparative freedom. After the appointment of Valuyev as Minister of Interior, the system had again become stricter. But the machinery had not been formally changed. The Ministry of Interior was responsible for supervision of books, the book trade, printing, and all printed notices and placards. The Ministry of Education also had a more general right of censorship. The Press was regulated by various committees of censors set up by the Censorship Statutes of 1804, 1826 and 1828. During the sixties some attempt was made to co-ordinate these different authorities.

A decree of January 1863 entrusted the direction of all censorship to the Ministry of Interior. The general line of policy was to be laid down by the Council of the Ministry, while its detailed execution was the task of the Chairman of the St. Petersburg Censorship Committee. Book publication was to be supervised by a separate Committee. On 6th/19th April 1865 a new decree dealt with the censorship of the Press. For the first time, discussion of legislation and of government policy was specifically permitted. The Press was freed from preventive censorship: editors no longer had to submit their texts to the censor before publication. Penalties could however still be imposed after publication for articles which offended existing regulations. These were entrusted to a special office within the Ministry of Interior—the Chief Administration for Press Affairs.[1]

In practice the censorship remained strict. In 1866 the great radical journal *Sovremennik* ("The Contemporary"), in which the Socialists Chernyshevski and Dobrolyubov wrote, was suppressed. At the end of the year jurisdiction over Press offences was transferred from the regional courts to the chambers of justice. In June 1867 the publication in the Press of accounts of meetings of societies and class organisations was made subject to special permission by provincial governors. At the same time the supervision of public libraries was transferred from the Ministry of Justice to the Ministry of Interior. In July 1873 the Ministry of Interior was empowered to inform editors of papers exempt from preventive censorship that for certain periods discussion in their columns of certain subjects of "State significance" was "unsuitable". As the revolutionary movement grew at the end of the seventies, censorship became increasingly severe.

In education the first years of the reign were marked by continued severity. In 1861 Putyatin was appointed Minister of Education. In May he produced some new rules for university

---

[1] *Ministerstvo Vnutrennih Dyel, istoricheskii ocherk, 1802–1902* (SPB, 1902), pp. 149–52.

administration, which reduced the assistance given to poor students and banned the corporative organisations of the students. Examination rules were also made stricter. In September students rioted in St. Petersburg. Some were arrested and some were expelled. The riots continued in October, and there were also disorders at Moscow university. In December the Tsar replaced Putyatin by the liberal-minded Golovnin, but at the same time several liberal professors were forced to resign their chairs. One of them, K. D. Kavelin, was then sent abroad by Golovnin to study European university systems. With his advice and the help of other more or less liberal experts, Golovnin produced a new University Statute, published on 18th June/1st July 1863. Rectors were to be chosen for four years by the Council of Professors, and the appointment subject to confirmation by the Tsar. Deans were elected by their faculties for three years, subject to the approval of the Minister of Education. Professors were chosen by the Council and confirmed by the Minister. Teaching, especially of law, was made much freer. Whereas in the past the curriculum had been laid down within rigid limits by the authorities, professors were now able to present their subject as they wished. The Curators still kept general discretionary powers over the universities, but for the next years these were sparingly used. The universities in practice ran themselves. The main point of disagreement among the authors of the Statute had concerned the right of students to set up their own organisations. The more conservative advisers had opposed this, and their view prevailed.

Golovnin was replaced by Count Dmitri Tolstoy on 14th/27th April 1866. The change was a result of the attempt on the Tsar's life, on 4th/17th April, by the student Karakozov. A commission of enquiry, appointed immediately after the crime, attributed it to the growth of radical ideas as a result of the more liberal educational policy. The new minister had been Procurator of the Holy Synod since 1856. He was undoubtedly a strong conservative and a champion of Orthodoxy. His autocratic manner of dealing with criticism soon made him hated by liberals. In the first years of the following reign, as Minister of Interior, he was responsible for a series of repressive and reactionary measures. But his tenure of the Ministry of Education (1866–80), though it marked a turn to the right, cannot fairly be described as a period of unrelieved obscurantism.[1]

---

[1] Tolstoy's record as Minister is discussed, and his measures are described, in Hans, *op. cit.*, pp. 110 *ff.* On his policy as Minister of Interior, see below pp. 134–6.

The most important change introduced by Tolstoy was in the curriculum of secondary schools. By a law of 31st July/13th August 1871 the hours devoted to Greek in those classical schools (Gymnasia) which already taught Greek were considerably increased, while in the classical schools where no Greek was taught there was a similar increase in the hours devoted to Latin, mathematics and modern languages. The same law also deprived the local educational authorities of the right to vary curricula within their districts: the directives of the Ministry were to be uniformly applied in all areas. Tolstoy at the same time increased the number of the modern secondary schools (Real Schools), and regulated their curricula by a law of 15th/28th May 1872. The hours of natural science were diminished in favour of mathematics and drawing. This change was defended on the ground that science was too difficult for children of this age—a view for which in the Russian cultural conditions of the seventies there was much to be said. The law was however interpreted by Russian liberal opinion as a reactionary manœuvre to deprive children of modern knowledge. Tolstoy was a strong supporter of religious education, and restored to the Orthodox Church schools a government grant which had been abolished in 1818. The amount of the grant rose from 1866 to 1871 to the sum of 1,500,000 roubles yearly, at which it was then stabilised.

Tolstoy also made changes in other sectors of education. A law of May 1872 reorganised the District Schools. Tolstoy had proposed to give them a curriculum which would enable their pupils to pass on into the gymnasia, and so eventually to the universities, but this was prevented by the Council of State. It was however made possible to pass from them to a Real School, and so to a higher technological institute. Elementary education continued to be subject to the Ministry's Inspectors. The zemstvos made grants—greatly varying from one locality to another—to cover part of their expenses, but had only a small say in their administration. The local Pedagogical Councils, which supervised them, were so composed that bureaucrats were always in a majority. From 1874, marshals of nobility were made *ex officio* chairmen of the Councils in both provinces and districts. Tolstoy in May 1871 closed the existing teachers' training colleges and produced a new Statute to cover this field. Under his new system the number both of training colleges and of teachers considerably increased.

Women's education made progress during the seventies, tolerated rather than aided by the Minister. In 1872 Higher Courses of lectures for women were organised by Moscow university. The

Military Medical Academy of St. Petersburg admitted women to its courses, and the Minister of War provided a grant for the purpose. In 1876 an imperial Statute for Women's Higher Courses was issued. Use was made of it not only in the two capitals, but also in Kazan, Kiev and Odessa. By 1881 there were some 2,000 women students of a university standard in Russia.

Thus the reign of Alexander II brought a substantial growth of Russian education. Even the period of Tolstoy's ministry saw a great increase in the number of teachers and pupils, both male and female. But the positive achievements were almost entirely forgotten by later generations in their rage at Tolstoy's changes in the school's curriculum.

Tolstoy's policy confirmed the Russian progressive intelligentsia in its belief that only scientific education is progressive and that an education based on the humanities is essentially reactionary. This view had been gaining ground under the influence of some German philosophers, especially Feuerbach. It was passionately proclaimed by the radicals of the sixties. The fact that Tolstoy, who in his general policy was certainly a reactionary, should as Minister of Education favour the classics and neglect or discourage the natural sciences, seemed to be further proof of the view. Tolstoy thus without doubt contributed by his measures to reinforce the naïf enthusiasm for science, and no less naïf contempt for the humanities and for all disinterested learning, which characterised the progressive intelligentsia of Russia throughout our period, and had important effects also in the Soviet period.

During the sixties were formulated the radical ideas from which later emerged the revolutionary movement. Most Russian writers lay stress on the fact that several of the prominent radicals of this generation were persons of non-noble origin (*raznochintsy*). This gradual change in the social origin of the intellectuals is perhaps less important for the ideas held—the children of the Russian nobility were quite as capable of extreme revolutionary thought as their social inferiors—than for the personal attitude to the world. The intellectuals from the nobility had a certain urbanity, a certain belief in good manners that the *raznochintsy* lacked. The former were aware with their minds of the poverty and suffering of the Russian masses: the latter had lived in the midst of it, were not only aware of it but felt it. There is a venom and fanaticism in the language of the *raznochintsy* which is not found in their gentlemen predecessors, and which became and has remained an essential part of the Russian revolutionary tradition. This intolerant and savage attitude to the world is to some extent responsible for the growing indifference of the new intellectual generation to merely political reforms, for its insistence that it is more important to increase the material welfare of the people than to give Russia constitutional liberties. It was Belinski, the first of the radical *raznochintsy*, who said, "The people have a need for potatoes, but not the least for a constitution".[1] Twenty years later this view was widespread among the intelligentsia.

The leader of the radicalism of the 1860's was the editor of the periodical *Sovremennik* ("The Contemporary"), the socialist N. G. Chernyshevski. He distinguished clearly between liberalism and democracy. Liberalism, concerned with freedom of speech and constitutional liberties, was essentially a matter for the educated class, but democracy was concerned with the material welfare of the masses. Chernyshevski considered himself a democrat but not a liberal. If the welfare of the people could be served by despotic methods, he would not hesitate to support them. Both Chernyshevski and Herzen in 1857–8 praised the Tsar when he announced his intention of abolishing serfdom. Both were disillusioned by the events of the following years, and were bitterly critical of the final terms of emancipation. But the political conclusions which they drew from the new situation were not the same. Herzen did not give up all hope in the reforming zeal of the Tsar, or in the ability of the enlightened section of the gentry to persuade him to carry reform further. Chernyshevski and the radicals concluded that the Tsar had come down on the side of the socially reactionary forces, and that social progress was now dependent on the overthrow of the autocracy.

During 1861 a number of illegal leaflets were printed by the radicals. The first, called *Velikoruss* ("The Great Russian") appeared in July. It was an appeal to the educated classes to take over power from the incompetent government, whose mistakes were rousing the hatred of the peasants and leading the country to a repetition of the terrible Pugachov rebellion of the previous century.[2] The second number of *Velikoruss* appeared early in September, repeated the same warning, and asked the educated classes to demand from the Tsar, not a ready-made constitution but an elected Constituent Assembly, which should itself choose a Constitution for Russia. The third number, which appeared two weeks

[1] Quoted by F. Dan, *Proiz'hozhdenie bolshevizma* (New York, 1946), p. 36.
[2] Pugachov led a revolt in 1773–5, claiming to be the Tsar Peter III, who had been murdered eleven years earlier. The centre of the revolt was the Ural region, but it spread westward to Kazan and across the Volga before it was crushed.

later, contained a proposed text of an address to be presented to the Tsar.[1] In the same month appeared an appeal *To the Young Generation*, written by the poet M. Mihailov, which called for both a constitution and a transformation of society. In May 1862 appeared the most revolutionary leaflet of all, entitled *Young Russia*, and written by P. Zaichnevski. It demanded elective national and provincial assemblies, elective judges, the formation of publicly owned factories and shops, universal education, the abolition of monasteries and of the institution of marriage. The aim was to be a revolution which would "radically change all, without exception, of the foundations of contemporary society". The ruling class would of course resist, and so the people must strike down their enemies pitilessly wherever they might find them.

These leaflets were of small importance, for few persons read them. But they alarmed the authorities, and gave powerful arguments to the reactionaries who wished to hold Alexander back from further reforms. When some fires broke out in St. Petersburg, a panic rumour spread that they had been started by revolutionary incendiaries. The police arrested a number of radicals, including Chernyshevski himself. That he had some sympathy for the ideas expressed in the leaflets is certain, but that he was actually concerned in their preparation is not sure. The main evidence against him at his trial, which was supposed to show that he was the author of an appeal "To the landlords' peasants", is suspect. Nevertheless he was condemned to prison and exile in Siberia. Arrested in July 1862, he was sentenced in May 1864, and remained in Siberia until 1883. He was not allowed to return to his home town Saratov until 1889, and died a few months later.[2]

One of the most important points in the socialism of Chernyshevski and the radicals of the 1860's was their faith in the Russian peasant commune. The importance of this institution had first been pointed out by the German traveller Baron von Haxthausen in the forties.[3] The baron had regarded it as a bulwark of tradition against any radical ideas, such as he saw to his distaste were gaining ground in his own country. But Herzen had drawn from the baron's observations the conclusion that the commune might be made into an organ of a socialist society, for which Russia would have greater aptitude than the Western countries where capitalism and the

[1] The *Velikoruss* group is described in M. Lemke, *Ocherki osvoboditelnovo dvizhenia 60-h godov* (SPB, 1908), pp. 59 ff.

[2] Chernyshevski's imprisonment is described in M. Gernet, *Istoria tsarskoy tyurmy* (Moscow, 1946), Vol. II, pp. 236–77.

[3] An English translation of the baron's work, entitled *The Russian Empire, its People, Institutions and Resources*, appeared in London in 1856.

bourgeoisie had struck deep roots. Chernyshevski adopted the idea. He believed that the commune could train the Russian peasants in the habit of productive association. Chernyshevski's ideas of the future socialist state were not unlike those of the utopian socialist Fourier. He wrote a long novel, *What is to be done?*, whose heroes organised associations similar to the *phalanstères* of the French theorist. The task of Russian socialists must be to introduce into the peasant commune, the craftsmen's *artels*,[1] or any other suitable institutions, the true spirit of association, and to convert these associations into true organs of socialism. This task was more important than the task of political reform. Chernyshevski differed from Herzen in his belief that the desired end could not be attained without force. Herzen towards the end of his life hoped increasingly that peaceful transformation was possible. But both Chernyshevski and Herzen believed that Russia might be able to avoid the stage of capitalism which had brought so much suffering in the West, and go straight from the existing semi-feudal society to a socialist society. The same idea is found in Mihailov's leaflet *To the Young Generation*: "Europe does not, and cannot, understand our social aspirations. She is not our teacher in economic questions. We believe that we are called to contribute to history a new principle, to say a word of our own, and not to repeat the traces of Europe." This belief, which in its confidence in Russia's special mission recalls the views of the Slavophiles, was to become the central doctrine of the Populist branch of Russian socialism in the following years.

The arrests of 1862, the conflict with the liberal nobility and the Polish revolt of 1863[2] caused a marked swing towards reaction. In 1866 *Sovremennik* was finally suppressed. In the same year occurred the first violent expression of the hatred of the radical intelligentsia for the government, when the student Karakozov fired a shot at the Tsar. This act, as we have seen, led to the replacement of the liberal Minister of Education Golovnin by the conservative Count Dmitrii Tolstoy.

Another important radical writer of the 1860's was D. I. Pisarev. Born of a poor noble family, on leaving the university at the age of 20 in 1860 he became a regular contributor to the journal *Russkoe Slovo* ("Russian Word"), which was a rival to *Sovremennik* for the support of the younger generation of radicals.[3] Pisarev was himself involved in the illegal propaganda activity of 1861–2. Arrested

---

[1] See below, p. 117.   [2] See below, p. 78.
[3] The life, doctrines and influence of Pisarev are exhaustively described in A. Coquart, *Dmitri Pisarev et l'idéologie du nihilisme russe* (Paris, 1946).

in July 1862, he remained in prison until November 1866. It was during his imprisonment that most of his work was written. Two years after his release he was drowned when bathing on the Latvian coast. If Chernyshevski was a pupil of Fourier, Pisarev owed something to Saint-Simon, whose emphasis on leadership and on the development of personality he shared. Pisarev was sceptical about the chances of mass risings or revolution in Russia. He held that the main task for the present was for the intellectuals to perfect themselves, to make themselves fit for leadership in the future. "Consciousness" was more important than mere enthusiasm. The "thinking realist" was the leader whom the times required. This realist must be ruthlessly critical, and must accept nothing from the past or from the older generation without severe examination. Pisarev welcomed the character of Bazarov, in Turgenev's *Fathers and Sons*, which most radicals had denounced as an unfair caricature. To Pisarev, Bazarov was a model to be imitated, and the name "Nihilist", invented by Turgenev for those who would "accept nothing", a proud title. Education should be based on science. The humanities were a waste of time, except for history, which should only be studied from a materialist point of view and as a means of finding arguments to support materialist theories. Pisarev was especially hostile to all forms of aestheticism, theories of art for art's sake and treatment of beauty as an end in itself. The product of art is "socially negligible". Talented persons who become artists are wasting abilities which could be placed at the service of the people. Pisarev also denounced traditional forms of morality, and substituted enlightened self-interest. Gratification of one's desires would not, he argued, lead to mere sensualism. The "consistent realist" must understand that his own abilities belong to society, and cannot be cast away on "various pleasant follies". The only real gratification is the "clear consciousness that you are of real use to people, that you are paying in some small way the accumulated mass of your debts". The purpose of "all thinking and all activity of every man" is "to solve for ever the unavoidable question of hungry and naked people; apart from this question there is definitely nothing about which it would be worth while to worry, think and fuss". Pisarev made no contribution to the political programme, tactics or organisation of revolution in Russia. But he formulated more clearly than anyone the Puritan utilitarianism which became the accepted morality of the Russian revolutionary movement. The testimony of the revolutionaries of the next generation shows how great was his influence.

After 1866 political ideas could not be freely discussed in Russia. It was therefore among the Russian exiles that theories were formulated. Herzen, whose exiled paper *Kolokol* ("The Bell") had had many readers in Russia, even in government circles, in the first years of the reign, was losing his influence among the young generation. He died in 1870.[1] Michael Bakunin (1814–76), the founder of Anarchism, enjoyed prestige in his native land, but his doctrines—a curious mixture of Panslavism, federalism and anarchy—had more followers in Italy and Spain than in Russia. His influence on Russian youth was due to his romantic appearance, his stormy career and his sufferings. His childlike enthusiasm for violence and uprisings, regardless of circumstances, and his famous phrase—"The passion for destruction is also a constructive passion"—won him much admiration. To the more extreme and impatient of the Russian radicals Bakunin was a symbol, but hardly a political teacher.[2]

More important as a theorist was P. L. Lavrov (1823–1900). Lavrov was an instructor at the Artillery School, and joined the abortive revolutionary society "Land and Liberty", founded in 1862 by N. Serno-Solovievich.[3] After the Karakozov attempt, Lavrov was banished to Vologda province, where he wrote under the pseudonym Mirtov a work entitled *Historical Letters*, which had a great influence. In 1870 he escaped to Switzerland, where he began to publish a periodical *Vperyod* ("Forward"). Lavrov stressed, like Pisarev, but in less provocative terms, the importance of the moral and intellectual development of the individual. He always made clear that the purpose of this development was to be social revolution. He was against premature violence, or mass risings at a time when success was not possible. Meanwhile a long period of peaceful propaganda was necessary. The intellectuals should get to know the people, and should educate them. In particular, use should be made of such communal organisations as existed in Russia—the village commune and the *artel*. Lavrov was a friend and admirer of Karl Marx. He was aware that capitalism was making headway in Russia. He did not commit himself to the view that Russia could bypass capitalism and go straight to a form of socialism of her own. In Lavrov are to be found some of the views

---

[1] Herzen, whose life belongs essentially to the period before 1855, is only briefly mentioned in this work. To treat him with the attention which he deserves would unduly extend its scope.

[2] For the life of this remarkable man, see E. H. Carr, *Bakunin* (Macmillan, 1937).

[3] The activities of Serno-Solovevich are described in Lemke, *op. cit.*, pp. 39–66, 143–55, 183–224.

of both the Populist and the Marxist branches of socialism, which did not become clearly divided until the 1880's.

Mention should also be made of P. N. Tkachev (1844–85). A friend of Pisarev, he was arrested with him in 1862, and condemned to a few months in prison. He contributed after his release to *Russkoe Slovo*, was arrested again in 1869 in connection with the Nechaev affair,[1] was sent into administrative exile, and escaped abroad in 1871. From 1875 to 1877 he published in Switzerland a journal *Nabat* ("The Alarm"). He argued that revolutions are made not by the masses but by small groups of determined men. The revolutionaries in Russia must become such a group of leaders. Their aim must be to seize the State machine, not to destroy it. They must "convert the given, conservative state into a revolutionary state". It has been rightly said that Tkachev was applying the principles of Pisarev not in Pisarev's own field of psychology and economics, but in the field of politics, which Pisarev had ignored. His attitude to the State machine influenced later revolutionaries, not least among them Lenin.

Though literary history lies outside the scope of this work, it would be absurd not to refer to the role of literature and of literary criticism in spreading revolutionary ideas and a revolutionary state of mind. Ideas that could not be expressed in the form of straightforward political commentary could appear disguised and diluted in the form of characters in novels and in essays of literary criticism. This loophole in the censorship was so well used by the radical writers of the second half of the century, that true literary criticism was swamped by political doctrines. Literary works were judged not by their literary merits but by their help or damage to the revolutionary cause. In the forties Belinski had started this school of criticism. He was followed in the first years of Alexander's reign by N. A. Dobrolyubov, who collaborated with Chernyshevski in *Sovremennik*. Dobrolyubov used the outstanding works of the time as occasions for denunciations of aspects of the old Russia, and especially of the ineffectiveness of the educated class.[2] Of the great writers of the following period, Leo Tolstoy stood outside the current of political radicalism, while Dostoevski opposed it. But many eminent figures belonged to it—the poet Nekrasov, the satirist Saltykov, the populist novelists Gleb Uspenski and Korolenko. In their works may be found a picture of Russian

---

[1] See below, p. 65.
[2] Especially important were his famous reviews of Turgeniev's *On the Eve*, Goncharov's *Oblomov* and Ostrovski's *Menace*.

society, and of the aspirations of those who wished to change it. The revolutionary utilitarianism of Dobrolyubov and his successors has remained the standard by which Russian literature is judged in the Soviet period.

The Revolutionary Movement

Though it made a great impression on Russian opinion and on the Tsar himself, Karakozov's attempt on the life of Alexander II was the isolated act of an idealist, without clear aims or any systematic following. The first attempt to create an organisation of revolutionary conspirators was made by Sergei Nechaev. As a schoolteacher in St. Petersburg, he agitated among his colleagues, urging them to lead a peasant revolt, for which he maintained that conditions were already ripe. He escaped to Switzerland, and met Bakunin. In 1871 he returned to Russia, representing himself as the delegate of a non-existent revolutionary committee. In its name he tried to organise real conspiratorial groups. He had the original idea that the best way to tie the conspirators to each other was to compromise them together in crime. With this aim he accused one member of a group as a spy and persuaded the others to murder him. The affair was discovered by the police, and Nechaev, who had fled once more to Switzerland, was extradited as a common criminal. He was imprisoned in the Peter-Paul fortress, where he died after some years. He managed to keep up a correspondence from prison with revolutionaries outside, and refused an offer from them to rescue him on the ground that this would be a diversion of effort from the true goal. His case made a profound impression. His unscrupulous methods caused horror, but his undoubted devotion and courage won a certain reluctant admiration.[1]

In the years 1869–72 there was formed a group of young revolutionaries in St. Petersburg who became known, after the name of one of their members, as the "Chaikovsky Circle". Their leading figure was M. A. Natanson, a student of the Medical-Surgical Academy. Natanson disagreed with Nechaev's view that the peasants were ready for a rising. He favoured only propaganda. The circle's first aim was political education among university students. It organised the sale at half-price of selected books on political and economic problems which were permitted by the

[1] Carr, *Bakunin*, chapter 28, contains a brief account of the Nechaev case. Documents relating to his trial are published in a collection issued by the Soviet Central Archieves, entitled *Nechaev i Nechaevtsy*, ed. B. P. Kozmin (Moscow, 1931). The figure of the younger Verhovenski in Dostoevski's *Possessed* is of course modelled on Nechaev.

censor but were considered by the organisers to provide good background knowledge for future revolutionaries. Although there was nothing illegal in this, the authorities found it suspicious, and dissolved the bookselling organisation. The members of the circle then began secretly to sell banned books, founded a secret press in St. Petersburg, distributed a few pamphlets, and started discussion groups among workers in the capital and among intellectuals in some big provincial cities. Another circle was founded about the same time by one Dolgushin, and also published and distributed secret pamphlets.[1]

These groups were the pioneers of what came to be called the "Populist" (*Narodnik*) movement. In 1873–4 began the first big student "movement to the people" (*hozhdenie v narod*). Students went out into the countryside and preached socialism to the peasants. They did win some converts, more among town workers than among peasants, but on the whole the movement was a failure. The peasants for the most part could understand nothing of what they said, and in some cases assaulted them or handed them over to the police. The authorities however took the movement very seriously. Many students were arrested, banished or imprisoned. In 1875 those who had escaped arrest began seriously to consider the lessons of these two years. They agreed that their failure was due to too little study and preparation, to the desire to do too much at once, lack of security precautions and lack of a central disciplined organisation. In 1877 these lessons were taken into account in the formation of the secret society "Land and Liberty". The title was that used fifteen years earlier by the unsuccessful Serno-Solovyevich, Chernyshevski's friend. But it was an entirely new, and much more effective, organisation.

The founders of "Land and Liberty" were Natanson, who had by now returned from his banishment, and A. D. Mihailov. It was formed of revolutionaries from St. Petersburg and from the southern cities (Odessa, Kiev and Harkov). All were agreed that political issues must come after social and economic. Agitation for a constitution did not interest them. This they left with contempt to the liberal landowners and the bourgeoisie: their own task was to organise the social revolution. But mere peaceful propaganda was not enough. Active preparations must be made for a peasant uprising. And as the authorities had no scruples of humanity in dealing with them, but pitilessly sent them to years of prison, they

[1] The activities of these "circles" are described in Aptekman, *Obshchestvo Zemlya i Volya* (Moscow, 1919).

need not be squeamish about their means. Terrorism was to be a weapon of self-defence. Policemen and bureaucrats would be "executed" as a reprisal when a revolutionary was unjustly treated. Here there was a difference between the northerners and southerners. The latter laid greater stress on terrorism, but all accepted it in principle.

The society was more centralised than its predecessors. The directing body was called the "basic group" (*osnovnoy kruzhok*). New members could be admitted to it on the recommendation of three existing members. New groups were to be organised throughout the country. They were to have autonomy in their own internal affairs, but their chief organisers were obliged to give an account of their activity to the "basic group". The "basic group" was divided into sections. The first and most important was the "administrative section", located in St. Petersburg. It was responsible for providing false documents, and gave general political directives. It summoned from time to time the "council" of "Land and Liberty", which consisted of all members of the society who happened to be in St. Petersburg at the time, and gave approval to the administrative section's decisions. Three special sections existed for activities among the intelligentsia, the factory workers and the peasants. Finally there was the "disorganising section", which had three main duties—the rescue of arrested comrades from prison; measures of protection against government oppression (assassination of prominent officials); and "protection of revolutionary honour" (assassination of renegades and police spies within the society's ranks). The society had a clandestine press, bought abroad by a member named Zundelevich, brought back to St. Petersburg, and successfully operated in great secrecy for four years.

In 1876 a new "movement to the people" was organised. In contrast to the earlier movement of 1873–4, when individuals simply went out and preached to the peasants, the new wave was based on "settlements" (*poselenia*). Groups of revolutionaries went to live among the people, practising a normal trade or profession and so getting themselves accepted by those among whom they lived. Once thus accepted, their task of propaganda would be much easier. Some learned manual trades, others went as medical orderlies or as midwives serving under the zemstvos. Young women played a prominent part in the movement. The best "settlements" were in the provinces of Saratov on the Volga and of Rostov on the Don. These regions were chosen because it was thought that the members of religious sects, who were especially numerous there, would be promising material for revolutionary agitation. The revolutionaries took a lot of trouble about the sects. For instance, A. D. Mihailov made himself so familiar with their doctrines that he engaged in public theological debates on their behalf with priests of the Orthodox Church who had been specially chosen for their skill in expounding official dogma.[1]

Their most successful action was the organisation of a secret league of peasants in the Chigirin district of Kiev province. The leader, Stefanovich, produced a forged imperial edict to the peasants to prepare an armed rising on behalf of the Tsar against the nobles, bureaucrats and priests. Over 900 peasants took an oath, and were organised and drilled in groups of twenty-five. Eventually the affair was revealed by a drunken indiscretion, and mass arrests were carried out in August 1877. In the following May however Stefanovich and his chief assistants Bochanovski and Deutsch were rescued from Kiev prison by the "disorganising section".

In 1877 two mass trials of arrested revolutionaries were held, known as the Trial of the 50 (February to March, in Moscow) and the Trial of the 193 (from October 1877 until January 1878, in St. Petersburg). The accused took the opportunity of their legal defence to make long denunciations of the regime and to preach their ideas. Great excitement was aroused, and much sympathy was felt for the revolutionaries among the educated public, including people who were far from sharing their views. On 24th January, /6th February, the day after sentence was passed in the trial of the 193, Vera Zasulich fired a revolver at the police commandant of St. Petersburg, General Trepov, who had given orders for an imprisoned student to be flogged. She was duly brought to trial, but the jury acquitted her. Orders were given for her "administrative arrest" as soon as she should be released, but she escaped. A decree then transferred from civil to military courts all matters of "resistance to the authorities, rebellion, assassination or attempts on the lives of officials". But during the year 1875 acts of terrorism increased. The victims were individual officials, gendarmes, spies and renegades. In the summer political prisoners in the Peter-Paul

---

[1] For the life of Mihailov, see Pribyleva-Korba and Figner, *A. D. Mihailov* (Moscow, 1925). On the activities of the revolutionaries in the seventies, see Aptekman, *op. cit.*; D. Footman, *Red Prelude* (London, 1944); Stepnyak, *Underground Russia* (London, 1883); Thun, *Geschichte der revolutionären Bewegung in Russland* (Leipzig, 1883); Debogorii-Mokrievich, *Vospominania* (SPB., 1906); *Materialy dlya biografii A. I. Zhelyabova* (Moscow, 1930) (containing a sketch written by L. Tihomirov and first published anonymously in London in 1882); Figner, *Zapechatlyonny trud* (Moscow, 1921); Akselrod, *Perezhitoe i peredumannoe* (Berlin, 1923).

fortress made a hunger-strike, and some died. As a reprisal for these "martyrs" the Head of the Third Section, General Mezentsev, was assassinated by Kravchinski (Stepnyak). "Land and Liberty" published a pamphlet justifying the action and entitled *A Death for a Death*. In September several leading figures of the society were arrested, including both Natanson and his wife. During the autumn however it was reorganised by A. D. Mihailov, who returned from Rostov for the purpose. In February 1879 the governor of Harkov was assassinated, and in March there was an unsuccessful attempt on the new Head of the Third Section, General Drenteln. In April an attempt was made on the Tsar himself by one Solovyov. This led to more savage reprisals by the authorities, including executions of men who had not committed any violent crimes—for instance Osinski, the rescuer of the Chigirin conspirators, and Lisogub, a rich landowner who from sympathy had given his fortune to the revolutionaries.

The development of terrorism and repression led to serious disagreements within the ranks of "Land and Liberty". It was decided to hold a secret congress with as many delegates as possible, to reconsider the society's position. There were three main issues. Firstly, was propaganda or terrorism the more important method? Secondly, were the peasants or the city workers the more useful material for the revolutionary movement? Thirdly, should the society concern itself with political objectives or not? The congress was fixed to meet in Voronezh at the end of June.

A few days beforehand, a group of politically minded members assembled at the nearby watering-place, Lipetsk. In their debates a specially clear and strong line was taken by Zhelyabov, from the southern town of Odessa. He argued that though the ultimate aim was indeed social revolution, this was impossible to achieve until after a long period of preparatory propaganda, and this in turn was impossible without political liberty. Therefore agitation for a constitutional assembly must be of interest to revolutionaries. The liberal gentry had shown themselves incapable of producing results in this direction. New forces must agitate with new methods for this aim. The new methods must be systematic terrorism, which must not be confined to acts of reprisals for fallen comrades but must be directed at the highest target in Russia—the Tsar himself. The execution of the Tsar would force the regime to capitulate. Civil liberties would be granted, and the work of preparing the revolution could then seriously begin. Meanwhile, in order to achieve the execution of the Tsar, a much more centralised and conspiratorial organisation must be set up. These views were supported by A. D. Mihailov.

At the Voronezh congress a formal split was avoided, but it was clear that those who put politics first and counted on the town workers were widely separated from those who wished to devote themselves entirely to propaganda among the peasants. And a month later, at a meeting in St. Petersburg, the final breach occurred. "Land and Liberty" was dissolved, and in its place appeared two organisations—"Black Partition" and "The People's Will". Each had two illegal papers, one general and one specially for the workers. In practice "Black Partition", which stood for propaganda and a non-political attitude, was ineffective. Its main leaders, G. V. Plehanov and P. B. Akselrod, left Russia, and later created in Switzerland the first group of Russian Marxist theorists.[1] The rest of their lives was spent in the Social Democratic movement. Meanwhile the organisation in Russia petered out. But the "People's Will," had a brief but sensational career. It devoted all its energies to the assassination of the Tsar, and though it lost all its best people in the process, it brought off its plan on 1st/14th March 1881.

Among the remarkable personalities who led "People's Will", perhaps the most interesting is A. D. Mihailov, the party's best organiser and security expert. Though he had achieved considerable success in his propaganda work among sectarian peasants on the Volga and in disaffected Cossack villages in the Don valley, he decided on his return to St. Petersburg in the autumn of 1878 that work must in future be concentrated on town workers and students. In the following year he did some propaganda among them himself. But his main tasks were the supervision of members' security, editing and distribution of the illegal paper, secret correspondence with the provinces, and the production of false passports. He was known to his colleagues as "The hall-porter" and "Cato the censor". He insisted on strict discipline, and on the duty of a member always to accept and carry out the majority view, even when he disagreed with it personally. Mihailov was an expert at shaking off police trailers. There were few connecting passages, or houses with two exits, in St. Petersburg that he had not explored and mapped. One of his greatest triumphs was to place one of his own men, Kletochnikov, in the Third Section's Headquarters. This led to the discovery of a police spy within the revolutionaries' ranks, who was then "executed". It was Mihailov more than any-

[1] See below, pp. 139–140.

one else who put the organisation on its feet again after the arrests of 1878. It is extraordinary in view of his conspiratorial technique that in the end he walked into a police trap in a photographer's shop, although he had already noticed something suspicious about this shop on an earlier occasion.[1] He died in prison in 1880.

Another striking figure was Stephen Halturin, a Petersburg workman, who founded in 1878 the North Russian Workers' Union, the first attempt at a Russian trade union. It was of course an illegal organisation, as workers had no right of combination. In contrast to "Land and Liberty"'s official policy, the Union strongly favoured the political struggle. It played a part in the organisation of strikes in the cotton mills of St. Petersburg in 1878 and 1879. It was betrayed to the police by the informer Reinstein (the same whose identity was later discovered by Kletochnikov, Mihailov's man). Many of its members were arrested, but Halturin escaped. Halturin then planned to assassinate the Tsar in the Winter Palace. He obtained employment in the palace as a workman, and hid in his bed the dynamite with which the organisation supplied him. The fumes gave him frightful headaches, but he kept the dynamite under his pillow every night. The supplier of the explosives was arrested by the police, who also learned that a plot was being prepared against the Tsar. But a search at the palace discovered nothing. At last everything was ready, and on 5th/18th February 1880 the explosion took place. The Tsar was not in the room at the time. Halturin escaped detection, and was arrested only after the assassination of Strelnikov, the military prosecutor of Odessa, in 1882.[2] He died on the gallows.

As the wave of assassinations grew, the government passed various measures strengthening the powers of the police and of military courts. It also issued vague appeals to the public, asking for co-operation against "sedition". As however not even the most moderate claims of the constitutionalists were granted, the appeals fell on deaf ears. After the February 1880 explosion, it was felt that more drastic action was required. The Tsar appointed a Supreme Commission, under General Loris-Melikov, with full powers both for the repression of revolutionary activities and for examining means of removing their causes. All administrative authorities, including ministers, were placed under it. One of its first actions was the suppression of the Third Section, and its transfer to the Police Department of the Ministry of the Interior. The aim of this

---

[1] This episode is described in Footman, *op. cit.*, pp. 159–60.
[2] Halturin's activity as a labour organiser is described in Plehanov, *Russkii abochii v revolyutsionnom dvizhenii* (Geneva, 1892), pp. 65–70, 78–88.

change was of course not to diminish, but to concentrate repression. Loris-Melikov was however reputed to be a man of relatively liberal views. His appointment was greeted by the Tver zemstvo.

Hitherto the zemstvo liberals had been so strongly opposed to the government's reactionary policy that they had refused their co-operation against "sedition", arguing that the methods used for repression so infringed the rights of peaceful citizens that the zemstvos, as representatives of Russian society, were unable to give assistance. A section of the liberals had even had some contact with a wing of "Land and Liberty", especially with Osinski. The antipathy of the revolutionaries to the constitutionalists, and of the latter to the use of violence, had prevented agreement. However, the zemstvos sometimes used quite strong language. In 1878 the Tver zemstvo had passed a resolution expressing the hope that the Tsar, who had found it necessary to grant the liberated Bulgars a constitution,[1] might grant the Russian people, "who had borne all the burdens of war with such readiness, and with such unreserved love for their Tsar-liberator, the same benefits, which alone will enable them, in the words of the Tsar, to 'enter on the path of gradual peaceful and legitimate development'".

With the appointment of Loris-Melikov, the official attitude to the zemstvos became more friendly. He showed more understanding in matters of taxation and in peasant affairs, and somewhat relaxed the Press censorship. Above all, he made some new ministerial appointments, including the replacement of Count D. Tolstoy as Minister of Education by the liberal Saburov. After six months, the Commission was abolished and Loris-Melikov became Minister of the Interior. He then began plans for the creation of an elected body to take some part in legislation. He proposed to create three "provisional preparatory commissions"—administrative, financial and general. The members of the first two were to be appointed. Their proposals were to come in due course before the third, which was to consist of their united membership together with an unstated number of local experts, elected by zemstvos and city councils. From the "general commission" the proposals were to pass to the Council of State, to which for this purpose were to be added fifteen persons elected by "public opinion". If these proposals had ever been put into effect, a step would have been taken towards representative institutions. But they were very far from being a "Constitution", which they have sometimes been called.

[1] See below, p. 169.

Meanwhile the plans of "The People's Will" went ahead. Arrests made serious gaps in their ranks. Goldenberg, who had murdered the Governor of Harkov in 1879, was caught, and was persuaded by the interrogating gendarme officer to disclose the names of several of his colleagues. The officer appears to have convinced him that the government were anxious to get into touch with the revolutionaries in order to discuss with them the reforms which the Tsar had decided to carry out. When at a later interview another official made it clear that this had been no more than a clever manœuvre, Goldenberg was horrified by what he had done, and later hanged himself in his cell.[1] The information provided by him was of use to the police, but as all the main revolutionaries were living under false names it was not so easy to find them. In February 1881 Zhelyabov, the chief organiser of the assassination, was arrested. A. D. Mihailov had already been caught some months earlier, and since then the organisation's security methods had considerably deteriorated. But the remnant continued their preparations, led by Zhelyabov's mistress Sophia Perovskaya, the daughter of a general, and a member of the "Chaikovsky circle" as a student ten years before.

On 1st/14th March 1881 the Tsar rode through St. Petersburg on his way back from a military parade. The first bomb thrown wrecked his carriage but did not harm Alexander. As he was walking beside it another bomb was thrown from close quarters. He was horribly wounded, and died an hour later.

The assassination did not, as the revolutionaries had hoped, smash the autocracy. The remaining leaders of "The People's Will" were rounded up and the organisation ceased to exist. Six persons implicated in the crime, including Perovskaya and Zhelyabov, were publicly hanged. After seventy years, the most striking feature of the whole story seems the fact that a few dozen brave and ruthless people were able to defy the largest police force in the world and to kill the most powerful and best-guarded autocrat. The exploits of "The People's Will" made a deep impression on later Russian revolutionaries. Lenin himself, who disagreed with their ideas, admired and followed their methods of organisation.

Thus the reign of Alexander II, which began with bright promise, and changed to dreary stagnation, ended in tragedy. The Tsar-liberator was a victim of the unsolved conflict between social reform and the dogma of political autocracy. His death was followed by a return to unrelieved reaction.

[1] On Goldenberg, see *Krasny Arhiv XXX*, pp. 117-53.

Chapter III

FOREIGN RELATIONS

The Polish Question

THE Polish nation was never reconciled to Russian rule. Eight centuries of independent statehood, and at least two hundred years as a Great Power, had created a powerful Polish national feeling. Poles would never become Russians, and would never cease to believe in Poland's right to independence. National antagonism was increased by religious antagonism. Orthodox Russians saw in Catholicism the hated Western schism. Catholic Poles despised Orthodoxy as the expression of "oriental barbarism". It was a matter not only of religious dogma, but of two ways of life.

The autonomy granted by Alexander I to Poland in 1815 had been withdrawn by Nicholas I after the unsuccessful revolt of 1830. The new situation had been formally established by the Organic Statute of 1832. During Nicholas' reign Poland had no separate political institutions. Existing Polish schools met with official obstruction, and the extension of the school system was in practice impossible.

The accession of Alexander II brought new hopes. The hostility of the authorities to Polish initiatives was appreciably reduced. Ideas of reform began to be discussed. Their most important forum was the Agricultural Society, founded in 1857 and representing liberal landlords. The society considered ways of improving the situation of the Polish peasant, its more moderate members recommending no more than the replacement of feudal labour dues by money rents, the more progressive wishing to transfer land into peasant ownership. The society was also a centre of Polish nationalism. It was pressed by the radical nationalists, especially among the students, to place Poland's claim for national self-government boldly before the Tsar. On the other hand the more conservative group, led by Alexander Wielopolski, urged loyal co-operation with the Tsar in the hope that this would be rewarded by substantial reforms. The society did not commit itself either to Wielopolski or to the radicals.

POLISH IN 1772 : AUSTRIAN 1815-1914
  "   "   "   : PRUSSIAN 1815-1914
BOUNDARY OF POLAND IN 1772
  "   "   RUSSIA " 1815
  "   "   CONGRESS KINGDOM

0   100   200   300 Miles

St. Petersburg

Reval

LIVONIA

Riga

KURLAND

Memel

LITHUANIA   R. Dvina   Smolensk

Tilsit
Königsberg   Kovno
Danzig   EAST   Vilna

POMERANIA   PRUSSIA

Stettin   R. Niemen   Minsk   Mogilev

GERMAN   Białystok

Berlin

EMPIRE   Poznan (Posen)   R. Vistula

R. Oder   R. Warta   CONGRESS   Warsaw   R. Bug   R. Pripet   R. Dnieper

R. Elbe Dresden   Lodz   KINGDOM   Kiev

Prague   Breslau   SILESIA   Lublin   Chernigov

Cracow   VOLHYNIA   Kiev

WESTERN   R. San
GALICIA   Lwow
          (Lemberg)

AUSTRIA   EASTERN
                 GALICIA

R. Danube   Czernowitz   PODOLIA   R. Bug

Vienna

Budapest   R. Dniester   BESSARABIA

HUNGARY   Kishinyov   Odessa

R U S S I A N   E M P I R E

3. POLAND

On 25th March 1861 however the Tsar accepted Wielopolski's proposals for reform in Poland. He set up a Council of State which would examine complaints or petitions submitted to it by Polish citizens. A Commission of Public Instruction and Religion was appointed to reform the schools and to establish a Polish system of higher education. Provincial and local assemblies were also to be created as organs of self-government. By a decree of 27th March, Wielopolski was made the head of the Commission and was given the task of organising the Council. He was also to supervise land reform and the emancipation of the Jews in Poland, and received wide powers over the administration of Justice and over the Polish representatives of the Ministry of the Interior. He was to advise the Governor-General on army affairs in Poland. During the following months real progress was made in reintroducing the Polish language into the schools and the administration. Little however was done for the peasants, who received proportionately much less land than was granted to the Russian peasants under the emancipation decrees. The Polish middle class disliked Wielopolski's liberal attitude to the Jews, their economic rivals. Radicalism was not checked. During the summer several nationalist demonstrations took place in Polish cities. The biggest, which occurred in Warsaw on 15th October, the anniversary of the death of the eighteenth-century Polish patriot, Kościuszko, caused Wielopolski to resign his offices.

Since 1830 the Polish exiles in Western Europe had had a great influence inside Poland. They were divided in two groups. The aristocratic and conservative group, led by Prince Czartoryski, hoped to restore Polish independence through their influence on the diplomacy of the Great Powers. Their complete failure at the Paris peace conference of 1856, which ended the Crimean War but never considered the Polish question, brought discredit on them. Their rivals, the radical group whose main spokesman was General Mierosławski, believed that Poland would only be freed by armed revolt of her people. Inside Poland, the radical programme was supported by many middle-class Poles. Its chief champions were found among students and graduates of the Russian universities of St. Petersburg, Dorpat and Kiev and of the Warsaw Academy of Medicine.

In June 1862 Wielopolski accepted office in a second attempt at collaboration with the Russian authorities. In August the liberal-minded Grand Duke Constantine, brother of Alexander II, became Viceroy in Warsaw. This conciliatory gesture did not appease the

Polish nationalists. After a few weeks an attempt was made on the Viceroy's life. Wielopolski, determined to convince the government of his good faith and of the possibility of Polish-Russian co-operation, had the would-be assassins publicly hanged. This enraged Polish public opinion. The radicals decided the time was come for action. They set up a Central National Committee, and called themselves the government of Poland. Even the moderate Agricultural Society began to protest against Wielopolski's regime. He dissolved the Society, and its leaders declared they would never be satisfied with less than a national Polish government, to rule not only the Congress Kingdom but also Lithuania and the Ukrainian borderlands. There clearly remained no basis for co-operation between the Russian government and the real leaders of the Poles. The Tsar would not give Poland independence, the Poles would not agree to half-measures. Wielopolski's statesmanship had failed, and only force could decide.

Insurrection broke out in January 1863.[1] Its occasion was a sudden levy of recruits to the army from the Polish towns, intended to remove able-bodied men from the chief centres of radical opinion. Many of those called up fled to the forests. On 16th January the revolutionary committee called the Polish nation to armed resistance. The revolt lasted for most of the year. It was weakened by disputes among the military commanders, and by the indifference of the peasants in a large part of the country. This was a result of the reluctance of the aristocracy in the preceding years to take practical steps towards land reform. The revolutionary committee "decreed" complete emancipation from serfdom on 22nd January, and sent its propagandists into the villages. But they seem to have met with little response. The reaction of the non-Polish population varied. In Lithuania they supported the revolt, and were brutally punished by the Russian general Muraviev, who conquered the Baltic regions in June. In the Ukrainian provinces however little sympathy was shown for the Polish cause. The revolt ended in the autumn in Warsaw. Its last commander, Traugutt, was captured by the Russians, and was hanged in August 1864.

The Polish revolt was the object of a series of ineffective diplomatic representations to Russia by the Great Powers. The only friend of Russia among the Powers was Prussia. Clearly recognising a common interest with Russia in holding down the Poles, the

---

[1] For a brief summary of the background to the Revolt, its politics and its military operations, see *The Cambridge History of Poland* (Cambridge, 1941), Vol. II, chapter 16 (by Dr. A. P. Coleman).

new Prussian Premier, Count Otto von Bismarck, concluded a convention with the Russian government on 7th February. This provided for repressive action by Prussia should the revolt spread to the Polish provinces of Prussia, and allowed Russian officials to look for Polish revolutionaries on Prussian territory. In France and Britain, public opinion was sympathetic to the Poles. The French and British governments, with lukewarm support from Austria, took up the Polish question with the Russian government on the ground that Polish autonomy had been granted as a result of the 1814 treaties, of which the three Powers were signatories. A personal request by Napoleon III to the Tsar in February, to restore Polish self-government, was refused. On 2nd March the British Foreign Secretary, Earl Russell, made a formal request to the Russian Foreign Minister, Prince Gorchakov, to restore the situation of 1815 and to grant an amnesty. The utmost Russian concession was a promise, made on 1st April, of an amnesty to all who should lay down arms by 1st May. Three separate but similar notes addressed by the French, British and Austrian governments to St. Petersburg on 10th–12th April asked for the creation of a self-governing Polish territory to include the Congress Kingdom, Lithuania and Ruthenia. Gorchakov's reply pointed to the amnesty, insisted that the self-government of 1815 was a free act of the Tsar withdrawn after the revolt of 1830, and maintained that the present revolt was not a movement of the Polish people but an intrigue by revolutionaries from abroad, which had found some support among the gentry, priests and artisans, but was ignored by the peasant masses. A further note was delivered by the three Powers on 11th June. It put forward six points[1] for future settlement, and asked for suspension of hostilities and a conference of the Powers that had signed the Vienna Treaty. Gorchakov replied that no concessions could be considered until the revolt was suppressed. Further British and French notes in August merely put the blame for the bloodshed on the Russian government. Gorchakov's last reply, in September, repeated that there would be no negotiations until the revolt was over, and declared that the Tsar would assume full responsibility for Poland's destiny. There the matter ended.[2]

The events of 1863 cast little credit on British or French diplomacy. Neither Power was at any time prepared to go to war,

[1] These were a general amnesty, a National Assembly, an autonomous Polish administration, freedom for the Catholic Church, use of the Polish language in public affairs and in the schools, and a regular and legal system of army recruitment.
[2] For a brief summary of the diplomatic aspects of the Polish Revolt, see R. W. Seton-Watson, *Britain in Europe* (Cambridge, 1935), pp. 432–8.

and only the threat of force could have held Russia back. With Prussian support, and fearing no armed action from the West, Russia went ahead. Her victory was thus not only military but diplomatic. It did much to restore her international prestige, shaken by the Crimean War. The fact that Russia had become still more hateful to foreign liberal opinion did not disturb her rulers. The Polish crisis also had effects in Central Europe. Prussia's attitude won her the gratitude of Russia, which was useful in her wars of 1866 and 1870. Austria further antagonised Russia, already embittered by her attitude in the Crimean War, which had seemed rank ingratitude for Russian support against the Hungarian revolution in 1849. Austrian policy in 1863 was particularly inept. Not only did she antagonise Russia, though she, as a beneficiary of the partitions of Poland, had an interest in common with her: she also rejected the advances of Napoleon III for a Franco-Austrian alliance. Thus the crisis strengthened Prussia and Russia, humiliated France and Britain, and weakened Austria.[1]

Russian policy in Poland after the revolt was designed both to repress the revolutionaries and to split the national ranks. The new administration, under Prince Cherkasski and N. A. Milyutin, introduced the Russian emancipation of the peasantry, but gave it a particularly liberal interpretation. The peasants received a larger share of the landlords' land, and paid much lower redemption dues, than in Russia. A reform of local government granted much greater powers to the rural commune (*gmina*). Its aim was to win peasant sympathy against the nationalist landlords.

If Russian social policy was progressive, educational policy was extremely illiberal. The fight against the Polish religion and language was now extended from the borderlands to the centre of Poland, whose official designation was now changed from "Kingdom of Poland" to "Vistula provinces". In 1869 the Polish University of Warsaw was suppressed, and a purely Russian university was set up in its place. Russification of the school system reached its climax in the eighties under Governor-General Gurko and Curator of Education Apuhtin. State-supported education was confined to Russian schools, private Polish schools were not permitted, and obstacles were placed in the way of religious education by the Catholic Church. The Russian legal system involved the use of the Russian language in courts. Russian was also

---

[1] For a brief summary of Austrian foreign policy at this time, which is an important part of the diplomatic background to the Revolt, see A. J. P. Taylor, *The Habsburg Monarchy* (1948 edition), chapter 9.

introduced on the railways and in State enterprises in Poland, and
Polish banks and factories were made to conduct their correspondence in Russian.

In the following years Polish opinion to some extent turned away
from romantic nationalism. "Realism" became the slogan. The
best must be made of a bad situation, and the most promising field
was economic. From the seventies a modern Polish industry grew
up, which was soon in a position to benefit from the vast market of
the Russian Empire. The textile industry centred in Łódź at first
produced only for local consumption. But by the seventies its
goods were being sold in the Ukraine, and in the eighties in New
Russia, the Caucasus and the Volga region. In the nineties Polish
cloth was going to Siberia and Central Asia, and was being exported
to Turkey, Persia and China. Polish industrialists took a growing
interest in Asiatic markets, and began to organise exhibitions of
Asiatic countries in Polish towns. The successes of Polish industrialists caused alarm to some Russian business circles, especially to
the Moscow textile producers, who tried to enlist government
support, demanding internal tariffs and higher taxation of Poland.
The Moscow industrialists were also annoyed because Polish factories, being organised in a more modern fashion and employing a
working population of higher education and skill than in central
Russia, were able to pay higher wages. But the influence of Moscow
textile manufacturers on Russian government policy was not overwhelming. There were other business interests in Russia which
gained from Poland's progress, for instance, the railways and their
suppliers, and raw-material producers. In general, the real rivalry
was not between Russian and Polish industry, but between different
Russian and Polish business interests within the Russian Empire.
Moreover the Russian government to some extent backed Polish
industry in the hope of obtaining in the Polish bourgeoisie an ally
against the "rebellious" nationalist-minded Polish nobility. The
decade 1895–1905, during which Russian foreign policy turned
from the Balkans to seek expansion in the Far East, was of special
benefit to Polish industry. At the same time superior education
and technical skill secured many individual Poles employment as
engineers, managers of landed estates, and administrators in State
service and in industry, in European and Asiatic Russia, far away
from Poland.[1]

[1] For the early years of Poland's industrial development, see Rosa Luxemburg,
Die industrielle Entwicklung Polens (Leipzig, 1898). The rivalry between Moscow
and Łódź is described in Part II, chapter 3.

During the last decades of the century considerable social changes took place in Poland. Agriculture, as in most of Europe, experienced a severe depression, whose main cause was the competition of overseas grain. Many estates went bankrupt, and land was sold. It passed partly into the hands of the banks, and partly of the peasants. According to a Russian socialist estimate in 1905, about 15 per cent of the agricultural land was acquired by peasants up to the end of the century.[1] This development was of course welcome to the Russian authorities, whose policy backed the peasants against the nobility. The economic strengthening of the peasantry made it more important for Polish political movements to appeal to the peasants, and so to broaden the social content of their programmes. At the same time the children of impoverished landowners were compelled to seek employment in the towns. As the State bureaucracy in Poland was increasingly reserved for Russians, Poles were obliged to enter the free professions or business. In both they found the Jews strongly entrenched. Here then were a number of new motives for a revival of nationalism, which took on a middle-class rather than an aristocratic character, though the new Polish middle class was largely of aristocratic origin. Finally, these years saw the rise of an industrial working class, whose numbers, including dependent members of families, by the end of the century ran into several hundred thousands.

During the second half of the century, Ukrainian nationalism developed, both in the Polish borderlands and further east. Its first political manifestation was the secret society of SS. Cyril and Methodius, founded in 1847. Its leaders were the poet Shevchenko, the historian Kostomarov and the writer Kulish. Its ideas were derived from the French Revolution. It hoped for the overthrow of the dynasty and the formation of a democratic federal republic of all Slav nations, one of whose members would be the Ukraine. The society was betrayed to the police, and its leaders arrested and banished, During the sixties and seventies the Russian authorities in Kiev showed greater tolerance to Ukrainian nationalist intellectuals. Books were published in Russian on Ukrainian subjects by the "South-western section of the Russian Geographical Society" in Kiev. In 1876 this section was denounced to the government by Yusefovich, the Curator of Kiev educational region, as a centre of separatism and it was, dissolved. There then followed an ukaz of 30th May 1876 directed against the use of the Ukrainian language. It forbade the import of works in

---

[1] *O.D.*, Vol. I, p. 358.

"Little Russian dialect" published abroad (i.e. in Austria), without special permission of the censorship. Inside the Empire no works in Ukrainian might be published except historical documents or pure literature, and this only after previous examination of the manuscript by the censorship. All theatrical productions, lectures and the publication of musical scores in the "Little Russian dialect" were banned. From this time the Russian authorities regarded with hostility all manifestations of Ukrainian cultural separateness.

The Uniate Church, which included many Ukrainians in the south-western provinces, had for some time been subjected to persecution, and was finally suppressed in 1874. Zemstvo institutions were not introduced in the provinces of Kiev, Podolia and Volhynia, which remained subject to the Governor-General of Kiev.[1]

Expansion in Asia

The defeat in the Crimean War put an end to Russian designs in the Balkans for twenty years.[2] In the sixties and early seventies Russia's main effort, military and diplomatic, was directed to Asia. Here considerable success was achieved in two distinct regions, in the east towards the Pacific coast and in the south towards Persia and Afghanistan.

Russia's border with China had been fixed by the Treaty of Nerchinsk, of 1689. This permitted Russia to establish some scattered settlements in the north-east corner of the continent, but left the basin of the Amur river to China. The boundary between the two empires was to follow the line of the Stanovoy mountains to Ohotsk, on the sea of that name. Communications with the Russian posts in this remote region were maintained by sea, not across Siberia. In 1707 Russia declared the Kamchatka peninsula a part of her territory, and Petropavlovsk was built as a Russian naval base on its coast. Alaska, on the American side of the Bering Sea, was also Russian. For the next 150 years there was no change in the northern Pacific, and the Great Powers showed no interest.

In 1847 Nicholas I appointed as Governor-General of East Siberia Count Nicholas Muravyov.[3] The new governor encouraged

[1] Ukrainian affairs in this period are briefly described in Hrushevski, *op. cit.*, pp. 180-94, and in *Velika Istoria Ukrainy*, pp. 703 ff.

[2] The only exception to this statement, the successful attempt to abolish the restrictions on naval armaments in the Black Sea imposed by the Treaty of Paris of 1856, is discussed below, pp. 94,·96.

[3] The official biography is Barsukov, *Grof N. N. Muravyov-Amurskii* (Moscow, 1891).

exploration of the Pacific coast. Russian parties reached the mouth of the Amur and established themselves on the island of Sahalin and in the Kurile archipelago. In 1854 Muravyov himself led an armed expedition down the Amur river to its mouth. He had now decided that it was essential to annex the lower course of the river in order to maintain communications with the Russian settlements to the north of the river mouth. The outbreak of the Crimean War brought further justification of his policy. An Anglo-French naval force attacked Petropavlovsk, and patrolled the Sea of Ohotsk. Russian naval weakness made land communications more important than ever.

In 1856 war broke out between China and the Crimean allies. The Chinese, much more alarmed by British and French designs on Canton and Tonking than by Russian encroachments in the far north, and weakened by the Taiping rebellion in the Yangtse valley, were in no position to withstand Russian pressure. The Russian government came forward as a mediator between the Western Powers and China, and required a handsome reward for its good offices. By the treaty of Aigun of May 1858, the Chinese government agreed that the Amur should form the frontier between the two empires as far as its junction with the Ussuri, and from that point should pass eastwards to the coast. The area to the north of this line should be jointly administered by Russia and China. In the following year Peking attempted to revoke this concession and also to refuse the terms which had been agreed with the Western Powers. The British and French attacked again and occupied Peking. The Russian government sent an envoy, Count Paul Ignatiev, who arrived in the capital at the time when the Western troops were about to enter. He found the Chinese government in chastened mood, and was able to obtain better terms for Russia than those of Aigun. By the Russo-Chinese Treaty of Peking, signed in November 1860, the frontier was to follow the Amur to the junction of the Ussuri, then follow the Ussuri to its source and then cut across the thin strip which separated it from the sea. Thus Russia acquired both sides of the lower course of the Amur and a large band of territory stretching down the coast to the south. It was at the bottom of this strip that was founded in 1861 the city of Vladivostok, which has been since then Russia's main Pacific base. At the same time the treaty recognised Russian sovereignty in the area of Lake Balkash and Lake Issik Kul, in Central Asia on the border of Chinese Turkestan.

In 1861 a Russian naval force landed on the island of Tsushima, in the straits between Japan and Korea. The Japanese government appealed to the British, who sent a ship to investigate. The incident was peacefully solved by the withdrawal of both parties. During the following decade the status of Sahalin provided friction between Russia and Japan. Agreement was not reached until 1875, when Japan recognised Russian sovereignty over the whole island while Russia ceded the Kurile archipelago to Japan. The only other important event in the Pacific area during this period was the sale of Alaska by the Russian government to the United States in 1867, for the sum of $7,200,000. This transaction aroused little interest at the time in either country or elsewhere. When it is considered, in the light of later developments, what would have been the effect of a consolidation of Russian power on the American continent, the sale appears almost a major historic event.

As the Russians had expanded during the seventeenth and eighteenth centuries into Siberia they had come into contact with various tribes of Finnish or Turkish type. By the beginning of the nineteenth century Russian rule was well established across central Siberia, its main bases being Orenburg on the Ural river and Omsk and Semipalatinsk on the river Irtysh. To the south lived more or less organised nomadic tribes, the most important of which were the Kazah. The Kazah—who were erroneously called Kirghiz by the Russian authorities—were divided at this time into three groups known as the Little Horde, Middle Horde and Great Horde. The Little Horde lived between the north-east corner of the Caspian Sea, the Ural river and the Aral Sea; the Middle Horde between the upper Ural and the upper Irtysh; and the Great Horde between Lake Balkash and the river Syr Darya (Jaxartes). By the middle of the century the Hordes had been subjected to Russia. Between 1847 and 1853 Perovski, governor of Orenburg, built a line of forts from the north-east corner of the Aral Sea along the Syr Darya for about 300 miles. In the same years a similar line was built southwards from Semipalatinsk. A Russian fortress was built at Vernoe (Alma Ata), under the Tien Shan mountains, in 1854. In the central part of the frontier a Russian fortress had been founded at Akmolinsk in 1830.

By these conquests Russia was brought into contact with the peoples of Central Asia, not mere nomads like the tribes of the steppes but a settled civilisation with an ancient history based on the great river valleys. The most important of the various nationalities of this region were the Uzbeks, a Turkish people, inseparably mixed with the Sarts, who were of Iranian origin, but had

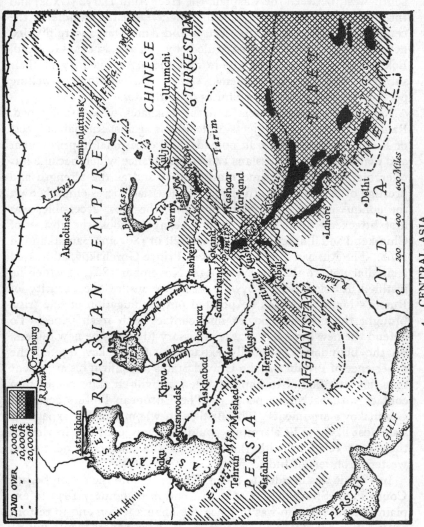

LAND OVER   3,000 ft.
    "   " 10,000 ft.
    "   " 20,000 ft.

4. CENTRAL ASIA

adopted the language of the Uzbeks. In the south-east corner lived the Tadjiks, Iranian in both race and language. To their north, along the frontier with China, were the Black Kirghiz. In the south-west, between the Caspian, the river Amu Darya (Oxus) and the Persian border, were the Turcomans.[1] In the middle of the century the valleys of the Syr Darya and Amu Darya were divided between three principalities, ruled by Uzbek khans—Kokand, Bokhara and Khiva. The rulers and the great majority of their subjects were Sunni Moslems. Only the mountain-dwelling portion of the Tadjiks were Shiites or Ismailites.

Relations between Russia and the khanates were usually bad. Raids and robbery by subjects of the khans against Russian subjects or Russian-protected Kazah nomads, and occasional imprisonment and maltreatment of Russians caused annoyance which became less tolerable as Siberia became more settled and as the strength and prestige of Russia grew. In the sixties Russian forces embarked on the conquest of the khanates. Kokand, the most accessible, was first attacked. In 1864 General Chernyaev took the towns of Chimkend and Turkestan. Tashkend fell in 1865 and Samarkand in 1868. The Russian Foreign Minister, Prince Gorchakov, addressed a circular note to the Powers on 21st November 1864, in which he justified Russian policy by the need to ensure the security of Russia's boundaries. As he pointed out, subjugation of one tribe brought the civilising power into contact with fresh tribes. To defend the new boundary it was necessary to crush the new raiders. So the boundary continually expanded. Gorchakov quoted the experience of Britain and the United States to confirm his argument that this was bound to happen when a civilised state comes into contact with barbarous peoples. The European Powers accepted Gorchakov's arguments. The British, to whom Russian expansion was most likely to be alarming, could hardly reject them in view of their own relations with the tribes of the northern and north-western frontiers of India.

In 1872 it was decided to attack Khiva. Before the action began, Count Peter Shuvalov was sent to London in January 1873 to explain that its sole aim was to teach the khan a lesson and to restore order. The khanate would not be annexed, and there would not be a prolonged occupation. The expedition started in March, and on 10th June the city of Khiva surrendered to General Kaufmann. A

---

[1] The various nationalities are described by W. Jochelson, *Peoples of Asiatic Russia* (American Museum of Natural History, 1928). A brief Soviet summary is I. Zarubin, *Spisok narodnostei turkestanskovo kraya* (Leningrad, 1925).

treaty was signed between Russia and Khiva on 24th August 1873, whose terms could hardly be reconciled with Shuvalov's assurances. All territory north of the Amu Darya and the river delta itself, were ceded to Russia, an indemnity of 2,200,000 roubles was paid, and Russian merchants were to be exempt from duties. The khan declared himself the humble servant of the Tsar, and undertook to maintain no direct relations with other rulers. On 28th September 1873 a similar but milder treaty was signed with Bokhara. Its khan also accepted the status of Russian protectorate and granted privileges to Russian merchants, but did not have to pay an indemnity or yield territory. The khanate of Kokand was formally incorporated in the Russian Empire in 1876.[1]

Russian expansion in Central Asia was completed by the conquest of the Turcomans on the east shore of the Caspian Sea. In 1869 the fortress of Krasnovodsk was built on the east coast. During the seventies minor fighting took place. It was not until 1881 that a serious attempt at conquest was made. In that year General Skobelev captured the Turcoman stronghold of Dengil Tepe and massacred the civil population. The main Turcoman city of Ashkhabad was annexed. In 1884 Russia annexed the Merv oasis.

Though security of the frontier had been the original aim of Russian expansion, the conquest brought both economic and diplomatic advantages. The region possessed considerable mineral wealth, which attracted the interest of Russian industrialists. More immediately important were its uses as a source of raw cotton. From the mid-eighties American cotton was planted there. By the end of the century Central Asia provided a large part of the raw material for the textile industry of Moscow, though much less for the textiles of northern and western Russia. Both economic and strategic aims were furthered by the building of railways. In 1879 the Transcaspian railway was begun. It reached Merv in 1886 and Samarkand in 1888. In 1898 a line was completed from Merv to Kushk on the Afghan frontier. Another line was built from Orenburg south-east into Turkestan. It reached Tashkend in 1906. The Turkestan railway was not however linked up with the Siberian railway until after the Revolution.[2]

The diplomatic value of the Central Asiatic conquests lay in the ability to put pressure on Britain at times when concessions were required elsewhere. In fact the physical obstacles to a Russian invasion of India were overwhelming. This did not however

[1] The texts of the treaties are in Krausse, *Russia in Asia* (London, 1899).
[2] For a summary of Russian railway building in Asia, see Sumner, *Tsardom and Russian Imperialism in the Middle East and Far East* (British Academy, 1942).

prevent public opinion in both Britain and Russia from taking it seriously. Fear for the Indian frontier was for long a major factor in British foreign policy, and limited Britain's freedom of action in other parts of the world. The three periods of tension in Central Asia between Britain and Russia—or Russia's Asiatic *protégés*— (1855–7, 1878, 1885)—coincided with war or tension between Britain and Russia in Europe. On the second and third occasions this was probably of less advantage to Russia than to Germany. But the threat from Central Asia was valued highly at times by Russian generals and diplomats.

It is also important to understand that the remoteness of Central Asia made control by St. Petersburg difficult. Irresponsible action by men on the spot sometimes made Russian policy appear more sinister than it really was. In the Russian capital the Ministries of Foreign Affairs, Interior, Finance and War quarrelled with each other for authority over the distant provinces. The War Ministry was perhaps the least unsuccessful. The Central Asiatic territory annexed by Russia was organised as the Governor-Generalship of Turkestan, which also handled relations with the protected khanates of Khiva and Bokhara. General Kaufmann, who was Governor-General from 1867 to 1883, had in practice something of the status of a viceroy, and often treated the St. Petersburg ministries with scant respect. In 1874 however his authority was somewhat reduced by the transfer of Transcaspia from his command to that of the Governor-General of the Caucasus. In 1899 it was once more transferred to Turkestan.

Russo-British tension was concerned with the status of Afghanistan and Persia. After the peace of Turcomanchai of 1828, which ended the long Russo-Persian struggle for the Caucasus, Russian influence in Persia became strong. The Persians had long wished to seize Herat, in western Afghanistan, a position which the British authorities in India considered to possess great strategic value. In 1838 the Persian Shah, encouraged by Russia, attacked Herat but did not capture it. In 1851 the newly acceded ruler of Herat, Said Mohammed, made overtures to the Persians. Though the Shah signed in 1853 a convention with Britain, in which he promised not to take Herat, the temptation proved in the end too great for him. In 1855 he occupied the city, was expelled and reconquered it. This involved him in war with Britain. The defeat of Russia in the Crimean War put an end to his hopes, and in 1857 he signed a treaty with Britain in Paris by which he abandoned his claim.

The next round in the Anglo-Russian struggle came in Afghanistan. Its ruler, Shere Ali, was alarmed by the Russian conquest of Kokand. In 1870 he asked for British protection but received only vague assurances. After the Russian conquest of Khiva he repeated his request. The British government was annoyed by the disparity between the assurances of Shuvalov and the terms of the Russian treaties with Khiva and Bokhara, but it was still unwilling to commit itself to the Afghan Amir. Shere Ali came to Simla in 1874 but still received no firm promise of support. He decided to come to terms with Russia. When the next viceroy, Lord Lytton, made overtures to him it was too late. In 1878 Shere Ali received an official Russian embassy in Kabul, under General Stolyetov. Lytton demanded that a British embassy be accepted, but the Afghans turned it back at the border. This insult led to the Second Anglo-Afghan War of 1878–80, at the end of which British influence was re-established in Afghanistan. Shere Ali had fled, and his heir had been killed. The new Amir, Abdurrahman, convinced the British government that he would preserve his independence against Russia and would cause no trouble to India.

The most dangerous Anglo-Russian crisis concerning Central Asia came in the spring of 1885.[1] The Russian conquest of Merv, and occupation of Astrabad, at the south-east corner of the Caspian, had greatly alarmed government and public opinion. On 30th March 1885 Russian troops defeated an Afghan force at Penjdeh, on the Afghan border. The incident caused the more alarm as the Russian government had failed to send a representative to a joint frontier commission to which it had agreed in the previous summer. The British government not unnaturally attributed to Russia gross deceitfulness when at least a large part of the true explanation lay in the lack of co-ordination between St. Petersburg and Turkestan. War with Russia seemed imminent, and the alarm was increased when it was known that Bismarck, with the support of the other Powers, was insisting that the Straits should be kept closed, thus making it impossible for Britain to strike Russia in her most vulnerable spot. Neither Power however wished war. In May agreement was reached on conditions for arbitration of the frontier dispute. Then it was decided not to invite arbitration but to discuss the frontier delimitation directly. The replacement of the Gladstone Ministry by that of Salisbury somewhat prolonged the discussions, but the agreement was signed on 15th September 1885.[2]

[1] For this crisis, see Meyendorff, *Correspondance diplomatique du baron de Staal* (Paris, 1929), Vol. I, pp. 155–262. Staal was Russian Ambassador in London.
[2] W. L. Langer, *European Alliances and Alignments* (New York, 1931), pp. 310–15.

Panslavism and the Balkans

Russian interest in the Balkan Peninsula and the Straits of the Black Sea was very old and was well known to the governments of Europe. To the Russian Tsars, rulers of the only great state whose religion was Orthodoxy, the spiritual centre of Orthodoxy, Constantinople, always held a special attraction. In the fifteenth century when Tsar Ivan III of Moscow had married a Byzantine princess, Russian ecclesiastical spokesmen had maintained that after the fall of Constantinople to the Turks Moscow had become the "Third Rome". In the nineteenth century romantic ideologues sometimes revived the claim. The Tsars and the Orthodox Church also took an interest in the fate of Orthodox Christians living under Ottoman rule. These included the Slav Serbs and Bulgarians, and the non-Slav Roumanians and Greeks. Since the treaty of Küçük Kainarci in 1774 the Tsar had claimed a right to protect all these Christians. The Turkish government and the Great Powers however maintained that the right of protection was confined to the people of Serbia and of the Danubian (Roumanian) principalities. The religious claim had been one of the factors in Russian policy during the Greek War of Independence and in Russian intervention in the Roumanian principalities during the first half of the nineteenth century. A third reason for Russian interest in the Balkans was strategic. Turkish control of the Straits meant that the Sultan was able as he wished to open or shut to other Powers Russia's back door, to grant or to deny to Russia access to the Mediterranean and world trade routes. This was becoming an important matter by the middle of the nineteenth century, when the industrialisation of Russia was gathering speed and was based on imports of raw materials in exchange for exports of grain, and when the building of railways in the southern provinces gave the landowners of the black-earth region the chance to enrich themselves as never before.[1]

To these three reasons for Russian interest in the Balkans was added a fourth in the growth of Panslav ideas, which gave Russia the task of protecting not only those of Orthodox religion, but those of Slav speech or race.

Panslavism may be described as the application of the Slavophile ideology in the field of foreign affairs. But as there were shades of Slavophily, from radical to reactionary, so there were shades of Panslavism. In varying degrees such very different men as Herzen, Bakunin, Shevchenko, Dostoevski and Katkov were

[1] See below, pp. 115-6, 120, 121-2.

affected by Panslavism. The two main questions which divided Panslavs were whether the notion of Slavdom should extend to all who spoke a Slav tongue or only to Slavs who were Orthodox by religion, and whether the Russians should have a dominant position in the Slav world or all Slav nations should be treated as equal brothers.

An interesting parallel can be made between Panslavism and Pangermanism. The three divisions of Greater Germanism, Lesser Germanism and Pangerman Imperialism, have rough counterparts which may be called Greater Slavdom, Lesser Slavdom and Russo-Panslav Imperialism.

The Greater German idea[1] was essentially democratic. It appealed to all Germans, whatever their religion, history or state loyalty. It appealed to them in the name of the German people, not of any dynasty. The Greater Slav idea, as proclaimed for example by Shevchenko or Bakunin, appealed to all Slavs, regardless of religion or history or state, in the name of the Slav peoples and against all dynasties. The Lesser German idea emphasised the role of the Hohenzollern dynasty, the Prussian state and the Protestant religion. It was never associated with a democratic programme, and became increasingly hostile to democracy. The Lesser Slav idea emphasised the role of the Romanov dynasty, the Russian state and the Orthodox religion. Though not absolutely opposed to reform, its exponents were on the whole strong conservatives, and became more so with the passage of time. The Pangerman Imperialists added the territorial aims of the Greater Germans to the Lesser German programme, while abandoning the original ideological basis of the Greater German idea. The Russo-Panslav Imperialists extended Lesser Slav ambitions to the whole Slav world, while rejecting the wish of the smaller Slav peoples to preserve their own traditions and outlook. The Russian Tsar would liberate the Slavs, but would impose on them Russian political supremacy, Orthodoxy and autocracy.

Russo-Panslav Imperialism is perhaps most clearly expressed in the famous book of Danilevski, *Russia and Europe*, published in 1871. It explained history as a succession of "cultural-historical types", each dominant for particular periods. The period of the Slav cultural-historical type was at hand, and would replace the

[1] For further material on Great German, Little German and Pangerman ideas, see A. J. P. Taylor, *The Course of German History* (London, 1945); Friedjung, *The Struggle for Supremacy in Germany* (abridged English translation, London, 1935); Molisch, *Geschichte der deutsch-nationalen Bewegung in Österreich* (Jena, 1926); Werner, *Der alldeutsche Verband* (Berlin, 1935).

earlier Latin and German types. Danilevski declared that, apart from God and the Orthodox Church, the highest ideal for all Slavs must be Slavdom—higher than freedom, science, education or knowledge, which cannot be attained without the existence of an independent Slav world. This argument has a curious similarity with that used during the Dreyfus affair, twenty years later, by Charles Maurras, the father of French fascism, that France is more important than justice, because there can be no justice without France. Another Panslav imperialist was Fadeyev, who served with distinction in the army in Asia for twenty years and took to politics in his forties. He is chiefly memorable for the phrase that Russia must either advance to the Adriatic or retire behind the Dnieper. For her the alternative was "Slavdom or Asia". Both Danilevski and Fadeyev denounced as enemies of the Slavs not only the Turks but also the German Powers.

It is interesting to note that the frontiers in Central Europe which Danilevski set forth as the aim of the Panslavs were not very different from those which were in fact established by the peace settlement of 1919. The dominance of Russia over Central Europe, which Danilevski considered essential to their realisation, did not however come about until 1945, and then in the name of ideas of which he would hardly have approved.

The first important Panslav organisation was the Moscow Slavonic Benevolent Committee, founded in 1858. It had close connections with the Orthodox Church and with the Asiatic Department of the Foreign Ministry.[1] Its aims were to spread among Russians interest in other Slav nations, and to help young Slavs to study in Russia. It was mainly interested in Bulgarians. Its chief spokesman was Ivan Aksakov. Moscow remained the centre of Panslavism in Russia, and had a following not only in the university and the Press of the city, but also among the increasingly powerful business class of the central Russian textile region.

The Panslavs were much impressed by the Polish revolt of 1863. Russian public opinion condemned the Poles almost unanimously. Only the voices of Herzen and Bakunin in exile were raised in their defence. A prominent Panslav, Yuri Samarin, called Poland "a poisoned dagger which the West thrust in Slavdom's heart". The Moscow editor Katkov (who should perhaps be called a Russian nationalist rather than a Panslav, but was long regarded abroad as

[1] This department dealt with the whole Ottoman Empire, including Turkey in Europe. The organisation of the ministry is described in the official publication, *Ocherk istorii ministerstva inostrannih del* (SPB., 1902). The best English account is in Sumner, *Russia and the Balkans 1870–80* (Oxford, 1937), pp. 18–33.

the mouthpiece of Russian Panslavism) denied that there was a Polish nation. The Polish Slav peasants, he argued, had been corrupted by an aristocracy and a priesthood which had succumbed to Western influences.[1] After 1863 the Panslavs as a whole moved to the right, forgot their liberal criticisms of the imperial regime, and identified the Panslav cause increasingly with the causes of Russia, Orthodoxy and autocracy. The Polish revolt struck a blow at the Greater Slav idea from which for long it did not recover. The Lesser Slav idea now dominated. Liberation of the Orthodox Slavs was a less ambitious aim, but one of which the Russian government was less suspicious. From the official point of view it had two good points; it coincided with the old ambitions of the Russian state towards Constantinople, and it involved conflict only with Turkey, not with the German Powers, whom official Russian policy wished to conciliate.

The only non-Orthodox Slavs who continued to be well viewed by Russian Panslavs were the Czechs. At the Slav Ethnographic Exhibition held in 1867 in Moscow, however, Czech speakers made themselves unpopular by arguing that the first step towards Russo-Polish reconciliation must come from the Russian side. Russian suggestions that Czechs should adopt the Cyrillic alphabet roused no enthusiasm, and the suggestion made in the following years, that they should abandon the Church of Rome "which had burned Hus" for Orthodoxy, was a failure.[2] Though the St. Petersburg Slav Committee, founded in 1868, kept some contacts with Czechs, the Moscow group, and the new branches in Kiev (1869) and Odessa (1870), were now interested almost solely in the Orthodox Slavs of the Balkans who, it was hoped, were longing for Russia to liberate them from the Moslem yoke.

．　　．　　．　　．　　．

The crisis came in the Balkans in 1875. It was not immediately caused by the problem of the Straits. Yet the future of the Straits was throughout an important factor in the policy of the Powers, and

---

[1] Fischel, *Der Panslawismus bis zum Weltkriege* (Berlin, 1919), pp. 371–2.

[2] There is a curious parallel between the movement among some Czech intellectuals to leave Rome for Orthodoxy in order to please the Russian Tsar, and the movement among German intellectuals of the same Bohemian borderlands to leave Rome for Protestantism in order to please the Prussian King and his Chancellor Bismarck. But the Czech movement, which was supported by some members of the Young Czech Party (see Fischel, *op. cit.*, pp. 423 ff.) had insignificant support, whereas the German "Los von Rom" movement, led by the anti-semitic fanatic Georg von Schönerer in the eighties and nineties, had considerable support (see Molisch, *op. cit.*), and also provided the intellectual training of the Austrian house-painter Adolf Hitler.

especially of Russia and Britain. It is therefore convenient at this stage to examine the problem, which recurs from time to time during our whole period.[1]

It was generally assumed that the Straits would always be open to merchant shipping in time of peace. The controversy concerned the passage of warships, either in time of peace or when a Black Sea Power was at war but Turkey was not. When Turkey herself was at war, it was assumed that the Turkish government would make its own decisions.

The ideal situation from the Russian point of view was that Russian warships should be allowed to pass through the Straits into the Mediterranean, but that warships of non-Black Sea Powers should not be allowed to pass through the Straits into the Black Sea. This was secured by the Treaty of Unkiar Iskelesi of 1833. Extorted from the Sultan at a time when Russian help was sorely needed against his rebellious vassal, the Pasha of Egypt Mohammed Ali, the treaty provided for a military alliance between the two Powers in which the Turkish contribution was to be the closure of the Dardanelles against the warships of any Power "under any pretext whatever". Thus Russia could count on her ally's approval for her warships to pass out into the Aegean should she ever wish to send them, while if she were ever at war she would be protected from any attack against her Black Sea coast.

This state of affairs was ended by the London Convention of 13th July 1841, signed by Russia, Austria, France, Britain and Prussia. This provided that as long as Turkey was not at war, she would allow no warship of any belligerent foreign Power into the Straits. Thus Russia was still protected from an attack on her Black Sea coast unless her attacker was allied to Turkey. She lost however the possibility of sending her own warships out into the Aegean, and she lost the domination over Turkey's foreign policy which she had secured at Unkiar Iskelesi. Nevertheless on the whole her situation was still favourable.

After the Crimean War, by the terms of the Treaty of Paris of 1856, both Russia and Turkey were forbidden to have battle fleets in the Black Sea. Though officially aimed at neutralisation and pacification of the Black Sea, this situation clearly operated to the disadvantage of Russia, as well as wounding her prestige. The sacrifice of a navy was much greater for Russia, a great state, than for Turkey, whose naval strength was small. Moreover Turkey was

---

[1] The authoritative work on this subject is Goriainov, *Le Bosphore et les Dardanelles* (Paris, 1910). A useful general survey is Anchieri, *Constantinopoli e gli stretti* (Milano, 1948).

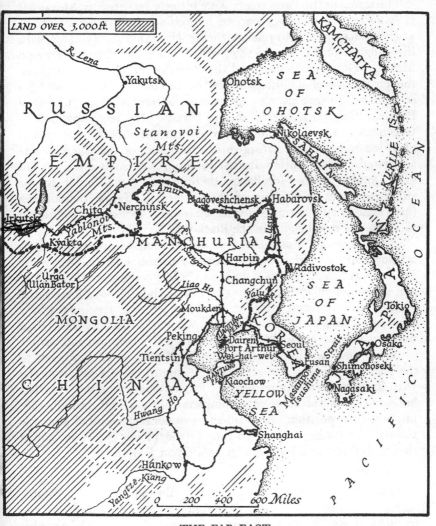

LAND OVER 3,000 ft.

R. Lena

Yakutsk

RUSSIAN

SEA
OF
OHOTSK

Ohotsk

KAMCHATKA

Stanovoi
Mts.

EMPIRE

Nikolaevsk

SAHALIN

R. Amur

Blagoveshchensk   Habarovsk

Chita   Nerchinsk

Irkutsk   Yablonoi
Mts.

MANCHURIA

Harbin

Kyakta

Vladivostok

Urga
(Ullan Bator)

Liao Ho

Changchun
Yalu R.

SEA
OF
JAPAN

JAPAN

Tokio

MONGOLIA

Moukden

KOREA

Peking

Dairen
Port Arthur
Wei-hai-wei

Seoul

Osaka

Tientsin

Fusan

Shimonoseki

CHINA

Kiaochow

Masampo
Tsushima Strait

Nagasaki

YELLOW
SEA

Hwang Ho

Shanghai

PACIFIC

Hankow

Yangtze Kiang

0   200   400   600 Miles

OCEAN

5. THE FAR EAST

able to keep naval forces in the Aegean and the Marmora, while Russia had no navy nearer than the Baltic. Thus in the event of war Russia would be in a dangerous position.

The terms of the Paris treaty were bitterly resented by Alexander II, who later fiercely reproached himself for having signed them, and was determined to change them. His opportunity came with the collapse of France in 1870. In August the Russian Foreign Minister Gorchakov consulted the Prussian Premier Bismarck on the possibility of an international conference to revise the 1856 settlement. Bismarck was against a conference, but supported Russia's aims with regard to the Straits. He recommended to Gorchakov that he should simply inform the Powers that Russia regarded the clauses relating to neutralisation of the Black Sea as abrogated. He promised Prussian support for such a move. On 31st October 1870 Gorchakov therefore sent a circular to his ambassadors at the courts of the signatory Powers, denouncing these clauses and stating Russia's willingness to see the restoration to Turkey of equal rights in the Black Sea.

Of the Powers, France was in no position to oppose Russia's actions, Britain and to a less extent Austria were hostile, while Prussia was friendly. It was agreed to hold a conference in London, and it opened on 17th January 1871. The right of both Russia and Turkey to have naval forces in the Black Sea was recognised by a separate Russo-Turkish convention of 16th March. The 1856 treaty was also modified by a new treaty whose second article provided that the Sultan might open the Straits in time of peace to the fleets of friendly and allied fleets, should the execution of the 1856 Paris peace treaty require it. Russia could thus not feel that her security in the south was complete, but she had undoubtedly improved her position. She had also won an impressive diplomatic victory. Following on that of 1863 in the Polish Question, it had thoroughly restored her prestige as a Great Power.

. . . . .

The Balkan crisis of 1875 came in Bosnia and Hercegovina. These two provinces formed the north-western corner of the territory of the Ottoman Empire in Europe. They formed a wedge between the coastal strip of Dalmatia—once the possession of the Venetian Republic and now a province of Austria—and the central European river valleys of Sava and Danube—the southern borders of the kingdom of Hungary. The presence of this wedge driven between the lands of the Habsburgs was a nuisance, and in the event of a naval threat from the new and hostile kingdom of Italy might be a danger. Thus in military circles in Vienna there had long been a wish to round off the empire's dominions by acquiring Bosnia and Hercegovina. The people of the two provinces were South Slavs, all of whom spoke the same Serbo-Croatian language, but were divided by their religions—Orthodoxy, Islam and Catholicism—into three communities so different as to constitute separate nationalities. The Catholics, the least numerous of the three, considered themselves part of the Croatian nation, and looked to their brothers under Habsburg rule. The Orthodox, the most numerous, considered themselves part of the Serbian nation, and looked to their brothers in the principalities of Serbia and Montenegro. The Moslems, despite occasional disagreements with the authorities appointed by the distant Sultan, were on the whole loyal subjects of the Ottoman Empire. Of the three communities, they were the most privileged. In particular, a large part of the small quantity of good land which these rugged provinces possessed was in the hands of Moslem beys. The peasants, whatever their religion, were poor and were heavily taxed. During the century however a middle class of rich cattle dealers and merchants had grown up among the Bosnian Serbs. These men had built trade connections with Austria and Serbia, had visited those countries and had become aware of a form of society more advanced than their own. Their children read books, and some studied abroad. It was from this incipient educated class that nationalism developed in Bosnia and Hercegovina.

In Hercegovina there were revolts against Turkish rule, helped by Montenegro, in 1852, 1857 and 1861. In Bosnia there was a peasant rising in 1858. In 1866 an organisation was created called the "United Serbian Youth" (*Omladina*). Its ideas were liberal and nationalist, and had first been expressed in a newspaper published on Hungarian territory, in the town of Novi Sad. It profited from the liberal attitude of the Hungarian authorities of the sixties. The Serbian merchants of south Hungary also contributed generously to the *Omladina*. In Serbia Prince Michael (1860–8), who favoured a forward policy of the Christian Balkan states against Turkey, encouraged the *Omladina*. It began to organise conspiratorial groups in Bosnia. Some of its leaders were arrested by the Turks in 1869, tried for treason, and exiled to Asia Minor. But the work went on.[1]

---

[1] Sumner, *Russia and the Balkans*, chapter 3, surveys the background in Bosnia, Hercegovina, Montenegro and Bulgaria. A special study of Bosnia is Ćubrilović, *Bosanski ustanak 1875–8* (Belgrade, 1930). The best work on Serbia at this time is Slobodan Jovanović, *Vlada Milana Obrenovica* (Belgrade, 1934), 3 vols.

In April 1875 Emperor Francis Joseph visited Dalmatia, and Prince Nicholas of Montenegro came down from his mountains to talk to him. The emperor gave no encouragement to rebellion, but his presence probably raised false hopes in Hercegovina, where petty acts of tyranny by Moslems against Christians had appreciably increased during the preceding year. In June 1875 a revolt broke out in the small town of Nevesinje, and spread through the province. Nicholas of Montenegro hesitated, but it was too late to hold the insurgents back. In August a revolt broke out in Bosnia. Its leaders had connections with Montenegro rather than Serbia. Among the Bosnian rebels was a certain Peter Mrkonjić, a pseudonym which was soon found to conceal Peter Karadjordjević, the pretender to the Serbian throne from the dynasty that was the rival to the Obrenović, which reigned in Belgrade.

Serbian opinion was strongly sympathetic to the rebels. The ruling Prince Milan was for neutrality, but was forced by public opinion to replace the government of the conservatives by one of liberals, who were for war. Milan however managed to keep the peace until the winter set in.[1] Meanwhile the Great Powers were working to prevent war. In December 1875 a note circulated by Count Andrássy, Foreign Minister of Austria-Hungary, proposing reforms for the rebellious provinces, was accepted by the Powers and by the Sultan but was rejected by the rebels. During the winter the rebels held their ground, and military operations on a larger scale were not possible. In May 1876 the Foreign Ministers of Austria, Russia and Germany put forward the Berlin Memorandum, considerably more favourable to the rebels. Britain refused to associate herself with it. In Turkey, Moslem hostility to the Ottoman Christians and to their European protectors increased. In Serbia nationalism became fiercer and more widespread. Milan still tried to keep peace, though at the same time making overtures to Greece and Montenegro for common action in case of war. Advice to Milan from the Great Powers appeared contradictory. The Austrian consul strongly urged maintenance of peace. Official Russian advice was to the same effect, but the Russian consul Kartsov made little attempt to conceal his Panslav sympathies, and gave Milan the impression that the Russian government was really in favour of war. Panslav agitation in Russia was obvious and loud, and Russian Panslav volunteers streamed into Serbia to help the Serbs fight the infidel. On 30th June 1876 Serbia declared war on Turkey, and a few days later Montenegro did the same.[2]

[1] Jovanović, op. cit., Vol. I, pp. 421 ff.   [2] Ibid., pp. 507 ff., Vol. II, pp. 1–35.

Meanwhile revolt had also broken out in Bulgaria. Bulgarian national revival dated from the second half of the eighteenth century. The struggle against the Greek hierarchy of the Orthodox Church, which ended with the recognition in 1870 by the Sultan of a Bulgarian autonomous church under its own Exarch, had greatly increased national feeling among all sections of the Bulgarian people. From the fifties a political movement had begun, whose aim was national independence. Its leader was George Rakovski (1821–67), who spent twenty-five years plotting, agitating and leading guerrilla bands in Bulgaria and in the independent Balkan countries, seeking foreign help and also telling Bulgarians to organise themselves for freedom. From 1866 Roumania became the centre of Bulgarian revolutionary activity. There two committees were set up, of which the second or "young" was the more important. Its leaders were Karavelov, Botev and Levski. The first two had studied in Russia, and there learned socialist ideas. They were pro-Russian in the sense that they loved the Russian people, and believed in a brotherly relationship between Bulgarians and Russians. But at the same time they were bitter opponents of the autocracy for which Russia stood. They were determined that the new free Bulgaria was to be an independent and democratic state. This combination of love for Russia with hatred of Russian forms of government has appeared many times in the last seventy years in the relations between Russia and the Balkan states. It has seldom been understood by the rulers of Russia, whatever their political outlook. Levski was the most successful of the three men as a conspirator. From 1871 to 1873 he organised revolutionary groups in various parts of Bulgaria. In December 1873 he was betrayed to the Turks by a priest and hanged. His successor as chief organiser was Stambolov, who later became the chief opponent of Russian policy in liberated Bulgaria. The rising in Bosnia and Hercegovina convinced the revolutionaries in Bucarest that the moment was ripe for a rising. In August 1875 leaders of guerrilla bands went to Bucarest to consult the committee, and plans were laid for the spring. In April 1876 the revolt broke out. For some weeks part of the Sredna Gora mountains, in central Bulgaria, were held by the insurgents. The poet Botev, who had been the effective leader of the committee since Levski's death, crossed the Danube with 200 men on 25th May. Within a month his band had been dispersed and he was dead. During the summer the Turks stamped out resistance and carried out savage reprisals. The Bulgarians had not liberated their country, but they had created a heroic legend and had fired the imagination of Europe, especially of Russia.[1]

From the beginning of 1876 Panslav agitation in Russia had been growing. In May General Chernyaev, the conqueror of Kokand, had arrived in Belgrade and taken command of a Serbian army. The Bulgarian rising, and the atrocities committed by the Turks in its suppression, followed by the Serbian declaration of war, greatly increased the excitement in Russia. The Moscow Slav Committee issued an appeal in hysterical language. On 13th July the Metropolitan of Moscow held a special service for the Serbian and Montenegrin cause. Ladies of high society in St. Petersburg collected money for help to the Serbs. Volunteers left to fight with the Serbian army. The government at first permitted regular officers of the Russian army to enlist as volunteers, and did not stop the public collection of money, though this had never previously been allowed to voluntary bodies.[2] The war however soon brought disappointments. The Serbs were decisively defeated by the Turks, though the Montenegrins, protected by their mountain deserts, held out. The Serbs blamed the incompetence of the Russian volunteers, mostly officers, each expecting positions of command, not knowing the terrain or the military organisation of Serbia. The Russians blamed the Serbs as inferior soldiers and ungrateful Slavs. Whatever the truth in these accusations, there is no doubt that friction between Serbs and Russians on the spot was serious, and that Serbia obtained a reputation for military incapacity which was not corrected for more than thirty years. Serbia had gone to war in the belief that if she was to gain Bosnia she must prove her right on the field of battle. She had failed in the test, and from now onwards her wishes were ignored by the European statesmen throughout the ensuing international crisis.

Disillusioned by Serbia, the Russian Panslavs turned to Bulgaria, which, as Ivan Aksakov wrote in December 1876, was "much more important for us and for the future of Slavdom than Serbia". It is true that the Bulgarian rising had been crushed even more quickly than the Serbian army had been beaten. But at least the Bulgarians had not shown themselves ungrateful to Russia, if only because they had had no chance. Bulgaria was of course far more attractive to

[1] For Bulgaria before the revolt, and for the revolutionary activities which prepared it, see Hajek, *Bulgarien unter der Türkenherrschaft* (Berlin, 1925), pp. 140-293. The most authoritative Bulgarian work on the leaders of Bulgaria is Simeon Radev, *Stroitelite na savremenna Blgariya* (Sofia, 1911). A work by a Bulgarian Communist is Todor Pavlov, *Botev, Levski i Markovich* (Sofia, 1946).

[2] Sumner, *op. cit.*, pp. 159, 189, 194-5.

the Russian government than Serbia: it was much nearer the Straits, and it was not near enough to Austria to arouse alarm in Vienna. The sentimental enthusiasm of the Panslavs for martyred Bulgaria, the defenceless and innocent little brother, was thus not a grave embarrassment to the St. Petersburg Foreign Office. At the same time Panslav influence in the highest quarters was having its effect. During September and October 1876 the Tsar was in his summer palace of Livadia in the Crimea, surrounded by the chief figures of court, government and diplomacy. The brilliant Panslav Ignatiev, Russian ambassador in Constantinople, was there. The Foreign Minister Gorchakov was also there, but the dominant atmosphere was one of Panslavism. The heir to the throne, who favoured the Panslavs, arrived in October. The very geographical situation of Livadia favoured the Panslavs, "with all the news from the West arriving late and all the news from the Balkans arriving early".[1] Even Gorchakov, infected by the surrounding feelings and led on by the hope of a dramatic success that would flatter his ambition, was moving closer to the Panslavs.

The immediate tasks before the diplomats of the Great Powers were to hold back the Turks from completely crushing Serbia, and to obtain a change in the status of Bulgaria which would satisfy Russia. For Russia the Powers whose attitude was most immediately important were Austria, Germany and Britain. Of the diplomatic negotiations conducted by Russia with Austria, Britain and Germany between the beginning of the Serbo-Turkish war in July 1876 and her own declaration of war on Turkey in April 1877, which have been described and analysed in great detail in several authoritative works, only the barest outline is here needed.[2]

Russia's relations with the two Empires had improved since September 1872, when William I, Alexander II and Francis Joseph met in Berlin. The meeting was followed by the signature of a German-Russian military convention in St. Petersburg in May 1873, and of a more general Austro-Russian convention (with no military commitments) in Schönbrunn in June 1873. The *Dreikaiserbund* thus created was an indication of the desire of the

[1] Sumner, *op. cit.*, p. 206.
[2] The authoritative work on Russian policy during this crisis is Sumner, *op. cit.*, on British, R. W. Seton-Watson, *Disraeli, Gladstone and the Eastern Question* (London, 1935). A work based partly on Serbian official sources is M. Stojanović, *The Great Powers and the Balkans* (Cambridge, 1939). Rupp, *A Wavering Friendship, Russia and Austria* (Harvard University Press, 1941), deals with Russo-Austrian relations. An excellent summary of the crisis as a whole is Langer, *op. cit.*, chapters 3–5. A Soviet view is *Istoria Diplomatii* (ed. V. P. Potyomkin), Vol. II, pp. 22–50.

three monarchs to stand together in defence of the monarchical principle and in resistance to all Polish claims, rather than a firm foundation of their foreign policies. Its practical importance was bound to be tested by Austro-Russian relations in the Balkans.[1]

On 8th July 1876, the Austrian and Russian Foreign Ministers, Count Andrássy and Prince Gorchakov, met at Reichstadt. They agreed that in the event of Turkish defeat Russia should take southern Bessarabia in order to give her access to the mouth of the Danube, and that Bosnia-Hercegovina should be divided between Austria, Serbia and Montenegro. But the Austrian and Russian texts differ as to the respective shares of this territory which should go to the three states.[2] The two statesmen also agreed that the Sandjak of Novi Bazar, lying to the south-west of Serbia and the south-east of Hercegovina, should be divided between Serbia and Montenegro. The explanation of the difference in the texts may be simply that the two Foreign Ministers were ignorant of geography. It was however to be a cause of bad feeling later. For the time being, the defeat of the Serbs made this agreement inoperative.

During the summer the Serbo-Turkish situation kept up tension between the Great Powers and between Russia and Turkey. On the whole Britain supported armistice conditions relatively favourable to Turkey, while Russia insisted on better terms for the defeated Serbs. On 31st October the Sultan accepted a Russian ultimatum to give Serbia an armistice of six weeks. Panslav agitation in Russia had now reached its climax, and the Tsar himself was affected. On 11th November Alexander made a speech to the nobility and civil authorities of Moscow, in which he declared that if guarantees of Russia's "just demands" were not obtained from Turkey, he would "act independently". The speech referred to the sufferings of Christians in the Balkans and to "the cause of Slavdom". It ended with the words "May God help us to fulfil our sacred mission". The speech was the more effective, not only because it was quite exceptional for the emperor to make a public speech on such a subject but also because two days earlier Disraeli had made a speech at the Guildhall, in which he had said that though England seeks peace and will not go to war "except for a righteous cause",

---

[1] For further details on the 1872–3 contacts, see Langer, op. cit., pp. 21–6.
[2] The Austrian version provided that Serbia should have "an extension of territory towards the Drina in Bosnia", and Montenegro "an adjacent part of Hercegovina", "the rest of Bosnia and Hercegovina" to be annexed to Austria. The Russian version gave all Hercegovina to Montenegro and "some parts" of Bosnia to Serbia, while Austria was to annex "Turkish Croatia", and "some parts of Bosnia contiguous to her frontiers". Texts are in Sumner, op. cit., pp. 584–7.

her resources are inexhaustible and once she does enter a conflict she "will not terminate until right is done".

On 23rd December, a conference of the ambassadors of the six Powers met at Constantinople to work out the conditions of a settlement in the Ottoman territories. They agreed on the following. Serbia was to receive slight frontier rectifications, and Montenegro to annex a part of Hercegovina and north Albania. The greater part of Bosnia-Hercegovina, Macedonia and Bulgaria were to form three widely autonomous provinces, each with a governor-general appointed by the Sultan for five years with the Powers' approval, and a provincial assembly. The governors of the second and third provinces—which were called the "Bulgarian twin vilayets"—must both be Christians. Conditions were laid down on the composition of the police forces and on the expenditure of taxation, and a European commission was to supervise the execution of the scheme. It was a real achievement that the Powers should have agreed on such a plan, and its provisions seem in retrospect reasonable. But it failed owing to Turkish opposition. On 20th December Sultan Abdul Hamid had granted a constitution, and his vizier, the liberal general Midhat Pasha, declared that as the new regime guaranteed all liberties, no special reforms were necessary. The Powers somewhat reduced their demands, but they were still unacceptable. On 18th January 1877 Midhat summoned the assembly, and it formally rejected them, the Greek and Armenian Christians on this occasion voting with the Moslems.

The next step was a military convention between Austria and Russia, signed in Budapest on 15th January 1877. In the event of a complete breakdown, it was agreed that Russia might invade Bulgaria and Austria take Bosnia. It was also agreed that in the event of the dissolution of the Ottoman Empire, no large compact state, Slav or other, would be established, but a number of small states might be set up as mentioned at Reichstadt.

Discussions on military collaboration were also conducted between Russia and Roumania. Agreement in principle had been reached in December 1876, but signature was delayed until the eve of war, 16th April 1877. The convention provided for passage of Russian troops through Roumania in exchange for a payment in gold, and also engaged the Tsar to "maintain and defend the existing integrity of Roumania". This last provision was in direct conflict with Russia's intention, already stated to the Austrians and agreed to by them, of annexing southern Bessarabia.

On 28th February 1877 peace was signed between Turkey and

Serbia. But the future of the Christian provinces of the Ottoman Empire had not been decided, and Russian demands were not satisfied. Further discussions between the Powers led to the conclusion of an agreement, prepared in London by Lord Derby and the Russian ambassador, Count Peter Shuvalov, signed on 31st March by all the Powers, and known as the London Protocol. It invited the Turkish government to demobilise and to put reforms into effect in the Christian provinces. It took note of the recent more conciliatory attitude of the Turkish government (Midhat Pasha had fallen on 5th February) but declared that the representatives of the Powers would carefully watch the execution of the promises of reform. If hopes of reform were once more disappointed they would consider this "incompatible with their interests and those of Europe". In this case they would consult on measures best fitted to assure the well-being of the Christian populations. An additional statement by Shuvalov declared that if Turkey showed herself willing to put her forces on a footing of peace and to undertake reforms, she might send a special envoy to St. Petersburg to discuss the disarmament of both Powers. On 9th April the Turkish government rejected the Protocol, protested against the proposed foreign tutelage, and appealed to the Treaty of Paris of 1856 which had guaranteed Ottoman independence and territorial integrity. On 24th April Russia declared war.

After fairly quick progress to the Shipka Pass on the main Balkan range, the Russian invasion was held up by the resistance of the Turkish fortress of Pleven, which lay north of the mountains. This setback made Russia more eager for the support of the small Balkan states. Montenegro had never concluded peace, and continued to engage Turkish troops in her mountain fortress above the Adriatic. In August Roumania was persuaded to join the war, and made an effective contribution to the capture of Pleven. In December Serbia again declared war on Turkey. Greece remained neutral. Pleven surrendered on 10th December, the Russian armies crossed the mountains, and advanced rapidly south-east. By the middle of January 1878 they had reached the shores of the Sea of Marmora. For some days it was uncertain whether they would make a direct attack on Constantinople. On 31st January armistice was signed at Adrianople. Russian troops then occupied all but the peninsula of Gallipoli and the immediate vicinity of Constantinople.

February and March marked the height of Anglo-Russian tension. Refusal to see the Straits in Russian hands had long been a dogma of British foreign policy, and Disraeli felt as strongly on this as Palmerston. Since 12th February the British fleet had been in the Marmora. Absence of naval support, and a growing doubt whether his troops could storm the defences of the city, which the Turks had been frantically improving, caused the Russian commander to decide against attack.

War in the Straits had been averted, but Russian demands on defeated Turkey caused a deeper conflict between the Powers. On 3rd March a peace treaty was signed at San Stefano on the Marmora coast. Montenegro and Serbia were to become independent states and to gain small amounts of territory. Roumania was to become independent, but was to give southern Bessarabia to Russia in return for compensation in the province immediately south of the Danube delta, Dobrudja. Russia was to annex territory on the Caucasus frontier. Bosnia and Hercegovina were to remain in the Ottoman Empire, but to be granted reforms. A large Bulgarian state was to be created, including all Macedonia except Salonica and part of Thrace.

This treaty was insufferable to Britain, as it brought a state which was expected to be a vassal of Russia down to the Aegean, and to Austria because it created the "large compact Slav state" which the Budapest convention had precluded and failed to grant Austria's claim for Bosnia and Hercegovina. A further point, which may not have seemed so important then but must in the light of later events be so judged, is that the San Stefano Bulgaria, stretching in the west almost to the Adriatic, would have cut off Austria's access to the Aegean down the Vardar valley to Salonica.

On 6th March Andrássy issued invitations to the Powers for an international conference, to be held in Berlin. The following months were filled with further negotiations. Shuvalov, who had worked untiringly throughout the crisis for Anglo-Russian peace, concluded an agreement with Britain on 30th May by which Russia agreed to reduce the territory of Bulgaria in the west and the south in return for British agreement to Russian territorial gains in the Caucasus. On 23rd May an Anglo-Turkish convention provided that if Russia acquired territory in the Caucasus, Turkey would cede Cyprus to Britain to administer under nominal Turkish sovereignty. In return Britain would guarantee Turkey's Asiatic provinces. On 6th June an Anglo-Austrian agreement dealt with the frontiers of Bulgaria and provided British support for Austria's claim to Bosnia and Hercegovina. Austro-Russian negotiations during these months did not lead to a definite agreement.

On 13th June 1878 the Berlin Congress opened. Russia had her way in the Caucasus and in Bessarabia, at the expense in the latter case of a small ally, Roumania, which had given her valiant military aid. Bulgaria was shorn of Macedonia, and the remnant was divided into a northern and southern half, bounded by the main Balkan range. The northern half became the Principality of Bulgaria, the southern the autonomous province of Eastern Roumelia. Bulgaria was to be subject to the nominal suzerainty of the Sultan but in effect independent. Russian troops were to leave after nine months. Eastern Roumelia was to be under Turkish military control. Macedonia was to remain simply a Turkish province, with no special autonomy or European supervision. Serbia gained Nish and Vranje on her south-east border. Greece gained no territory. Montenegro was promised some gains, and in fact acquired in 1880 the town of Ulcinj. In the northern part of the peninsula Austria had everything her way. She acquired the right to occupy both Bosnia and Hercegovina and the Sandjak of Novi Bazar. The first was carried out against the hostility, and even armed opposition, of the population, which desired union with Serbia, announced by the insurgents already in 1875. The second separated Serbia from Montenegro, and kept open a line of communication between Austrian territory and Salonica without passing through the territory of either.

From the point of view of Balkan peace, the defect of the Berlin settlement was that it changed too little. To leave Thessaly, Albania, Macedonia and Thrace in Turkish hands was to lay up trouble for the future. Yet, granted the attitudes of Austria and Britain, no better solution was possible than to leave things as they were. Austria's gains represented a triumph of the military party in Vienna, which laid the greatest emphasis on providing a safe hinterland to the exposed Dalmatian strip, over the more cautious Hungarian politicians, who opposed any increase in the Slav population of the Empire. Andrássy was himself a Hungarian aristocrat, but abandoned the Hungarian point of view. It may be doubted whether his change of attitude proved ultimately wise either for Hungary or for the empire as a whole. In the short term however it established Austrian domination over the northern half of the peninsula, and forced Serbia into the position of Austria's vassal. It may also be doubted whether the seizure of southern Bessarabia by Russia was worth the hostility which it naturally caused in Roumania.

Two more general effects of the Berlin settlement deserve

mention. The first is that Britain gained by it the reputation of an enemy of the small Slav peoples. This was of course especially true in Bulgaria, where San Stefano became the slogan of the nationalists for at least seventy years, and where the adoration of Gladstone, the man who put the "Bulgarian atrocities" before the conscience of Europe, was outweighed by the execration of Disraeli. The legend of Britain the selfish imperialist Power, willing to perpetrate the most barbarous oppression of young nations as long as it is advantageous to her, a legend that has been used at various times by various enemy Great Powers, dates as far as South-Eastern Europe is concerned from 1878.

The second effect is the rage caused in Russia against Germany. The Panslavs had of course always regarded Austria, the ruler over many Slav peoples, as a potential enemy. But Germany, which had previously shown such friendship for Russia, which had always pursued a common policy towards the faithless Poles, was felt to have betrayed the trust in which she had been held. Berlin had been chosen as the place of the congress, and Bismarck had made much of his role as "honest broker". But the congress had resulted in concessions by Russia. Bismarck may have tried his best to hold the balance between Russia, Austria and Britain. But in St. Petersburg, and still more in Moscow, he appeared as the arch-enemy of Russia. The personal disappointment of the vain elderly Gorchakov combined with the ideological frenzy of the Panslavs to produce a bitter anti-German atmosphere in the Russian educated class. With the accession of Alexander III this was modified, not because the new Tsar was pro-German—on the contrary, he was more sympathetic to Panslavism than his father had been—but because he had no use for public opinion in foreign policy, and preferred to hand it back to the professional diplomats, who were less influenced by popular passions. In the new reign better relations with the German Powers were for a time restored, But the anger created by Berlin remained beneath the surface, and found expression when a new major crisis occurred in the Balkans.

PART TWO
REACTION, 1881–1904

Chapter IV

ECONOMIC DEVELOPMENT

THE period between the emancipation of the serfs and the Revolution of 1905 was marked by stagnation in agriculture, progress in industry, and the creation of an industrial working class. These problems, which form the economic and social background to Russian political life in these four decades, will be the subject of this chapter.

The Agrarian Problem

The immediate problems of agriculture after the emancipation were the financial burdens on the peasants, the land shortage, and the various attempts to secure a living by labour outside the family holding. Underlying these was the basic question of rural over-population.

The burden of redemption debts in the years after emancipation was extremely heavy, and in fact was not fully supported. Already in 1875 the sum of arrears in payments from the peasants to the State had reached 22 per cent of the average annual assessment for the preceding five years, and in 1880 it was 27 per cent. The Government more than once in the following years reduced the total redemption debt charge. Nevertheless by 1900 arrears had grown to 119 per cent of the average annual assessment for the years 1896–1900.[1] Another heavy burden was indirect taxation. This was in Russia, as in most countries of backward economy, the principal form of government revenue. It was placed on articles consumed by the whole population, and therefore relatively hit the poorest class the heaviest.[2]

Methods of cultivation remained primitive, and output per acre very low. The usual system was a three-field rotation of crops—winter grain, spring grain and fallow. In some areas in the north the same crop was produced for years in succession and the land

[1] Robinson, *op. cit.*, pp. 95–6.   [2] See also below, pp. 120–3.

was then left fallow for ten years or more. Every year the population rapidly increased while the means of subsistence remained almost stationary. In 1891–2 a disastrous famine occurred. At the turn of the century investigations by an official commission showed a huge excess of labour power in the villages over the number required for the cultivation of the peasant allotments.[1] By 1900 rural over-population was already the basic economic malady of Russia.

Relief could be sought from this situation in three ways—by obtaining more land through purchase or rent; by employment outside the family holding; and by emigration to distant parts, within the empire or abroad. In fact all three ways were used.

In 1883 was founded the Peasants' Land Bank, to assist the buying of landlords' land by peasants. Between the emancipation and 1877 some 6·5 million *desyatin* of land had already been bought by peasants. By 1905, with the help of the bank, this amount had risen to over 23 million, or nearly one-third of the area left in the nobles' hands at the time of the emancipation. Not all land sold by landlords went to peasants. Townsmen had acquired 11·7 million by 1877 and a further 4·5 million by 1905. Alarm was felt by the nobility, and also by the government, which continued to regard a strong landed gentry as an essential support to the regime. In 1885 the government therefore set up a Nobles' Land Bank, which made loans to landowners at rates more favourable than those granted by the Peasants' Bank to the peasants. By 1904 more than one-third of the land still belonging to landlords was mortgaged to the Nobles' Bank. Its loans totalled 707 million roubles. Arrears of interest payments to it by landlords were nearly 15 million, and were rising yearly.[2]

In 1905 some 4,300,000 *desyatin* were held by mixed societies, some of whose members were peasants.[3] This makes it difficult to determine exactly the amount of land held by peasants at this time. An authoritative estimate however is that, of approximately 21 million desyatin sold by the nobility between 1877 and 1905, about 7 million went to big peasants, and 7 million to mixed societies and to townsmen. This would mean that not much less than one-third of the land sold passed to small peasants.[4]

In 1905 municipalities owned 2 million *desyatin*, and the Ortho-

---

[1] Robinson, *op. cit.*, p. 98. As Robinson comments, these estimates are only approximate, and so of dubious value. They do however give some indication of the dimensions of the problem.

[2] Robinson, *op. cit.*, pp. 131–4.

[3] They included also townsmen or members of the rural middle class (shop-keepers, officials, etc.).

[4] Robinson, *op. cit.*, p. 134.

dox Church about the same amount. The imperial family's estates were nearly 8 million, of which less than a quarter was arable. State lands amounted to the enormous figure of 138 million, but only 4 million of this was arable, pasture or meadow. The rest was mainly forests.

Still more important than purchase, as a means of increasing the peasants' livelihood, was renting of land. In the eighties it was calculated that more than one-third of the peasants were renting some land, and the amount rented averaged one-sixth of the area of their allotments. It is worth distinguishing three types of rent relationship. Firstly, some of the poorest peasants leased their small allotments to wealthier peasants, and worked entirely for an employer for wages. Secondly, some of the richest peasants rented large quantities of land from landlords, and adding these to their own already large holdings created more or less efficient farms. The third category, far more numerous than either of these, consisted of smallholders who rented, from nobles or from State or Crown estates, further small areas to support their families. With the steady increase of population, competition for land drove rents higher and higher. The tenants were forced to get the last possible ounce out of the land. With their primitive tools and methods this sometimes meant what has been called an "economy of devastation", and seriously harmed the land for the future. Even so it became difficult to avoid a net loss on the transaction.

In many cases land was rented collectively by village communes from the nobles' estates. The communes then distributed the rented land among households according to the number of persons in each family. In the last decades of the century the collective type of renting increased proportionately to the individual type.

Throughout this period the repartitional type of commune was more widespread than the hereditary type. The powers of the repartitional commune were appreciably reduced by a decree of 1893, which empowered the Land Commandants[1] to intervene in the redistribution of land between households.

Various forms of paid labour were available. One was in agriculture. The census of 1897 showed 1,800,000 persons as permanently occupied in this manner. If family dependents are included the number affected would be at least doubled. In seasons of intense activity, for instance the harvest, the number was greatly increased. The real wages of agricultural labour can be roughly estimated by relating money wages to the price of rye, the basis of the bread most

[1] See below, p. 136.

widely consumed in Russia. This shows a decline in the eighties, a rise in the nineties, and a further fall in the first years of the new century. A second form of paid labour available to peasants was handicraft production. Especially in the central provinces, the peasants worked in their houses and sold the product (for instance cloth, sacking, cutlery, leather or woodwork) to a merchant entrepreneur. In some areas *artels*[1] marketed their members' wares. Finally there was employment in the factories, especially in the textile region round Moscow, in the metallurgical area of the south, and in St. Petersburg.

There was a considerable migration within European Russia. From the central provinces, north of the black-earth line, peasants moved to the industrial cities, especially to the two capitals. From the northern part of the black-earth region they moved to the sparsely populated agricultural areas towards the Black Sea coast and to the Don and Lower Volga steppes. Migration to Siberia was at first discouraged by the government. At the end of the eighties this policy changed, largely for reasons connected with the new expansionist policy in the Far East. In the last years of the century the yearly average of emigrants to Siberia exceeded 100,000. This figure appears less impressive when it is recalled that the yearly increase of population in European Russia was more than ten times as high.

During the decades following the emancipation a process of differentiation of the peasantry into a richer and a poorer class went on in the villages of Russia. But its extent is a matter of controversy. Marxist writers have stressed it, while those of conservative, liberal or populist sympathies have minimised it. Available statistics do not finally prove either view. An indirect indication is provided by figures for renting of land, dated 1905. These show that less than 5 per cent of those peasants who rented non-allotment land held an area larger than that rented by 50 per cent of all individual holdings of this kind. But as a great deal of the renting of land was done through various forms of peasant associations, this evidence is not conclusive. Another indication is given by figures of the same date on ownership by peasants of horses. Thirty-nine per cent of holdings had two horses or more each, 29 per cent had one horse, and 32 per cent had none. Statistics from the military survey of horses for 1888–91, quoted by Lenin,[2] show that 11 per

---

[1] See below p. 117.
[2] Lenin, *Razvitie kapitalizma v Rossii* (SPB, 1899); *Sochinenia*, 3rd edition, ed. L. B. Kamenev, 1931, Vol. III p. 103.

cent had four or more horses, and owned 37 per cent of the total number of horses. Further data compiled by Lenin from the statistics of a number of provincial administrations certainly show a contrast in wealth within the peasantry. On the one hand the *kulaks*, or prosperous farmers, own substantial holdings, and rent a further considerable area. They have many horses and cattle, employ hired labour, possess minor industrial plants (such as mills or distilleries), spend a large part of their income on improving their farms, and consume wheat bread and meat. At the other extreme are the poorest smallholders. They are poorly equipped with draft animals and tools. Several members of the family work for a wage. The greater part of the family cash budget is devoted to buying food, with very little left over for clothing or for improvements. Rye bread is almost the only item in their diet. These two extremes undoubtedly existed, and were undoubtedly increasing during the period. But between them was the mass of medium holders. To what extent the medium class was being eliminated by the process of concentration at the two extremes has always been a controversial question. Reliable data are not sufficient to decide it. Certainly as late as the time of the 1917 revolution the medium peasants were the most numerous category.

From time to time the government took measures to relieve peasant distress. In 1886 the poll tax was abolished. Though yielding very little revenue, it had been strongly resented by the peasants. In 1894 the interest rate on loans from the Peasants' Bank was reduced. In 1896 redemption payments were postponed, and the land tax paid by peasants to the State was reduced by half for the following ten years. At the same time the Peasants' and Nobles' Banks were brought under one administration, and the interest rates made the same for both. On the other hand the order of 1900 that zemstvo revenue from taxation must not increase by more than 3 per cent per year[1] was a doubtful blessing to the peasant ratepayers, since it made it difficult for the zemstvos to finance various enterprises which were of real benefit to the peasants.

Various government bodies at the turn of the century investigated the state of agriculture. In 1897 was set up a "Special Conference on the Needs of Agriculture", under the presidency of the Chairman of the Committee of Ministers. In 1900 was formed an "editing commission" attached to the central administration of the Ministry of the Interior, to examine the situation of the peasantry. In 1901 another commission was attached to the central adminis-

[1] See below, p. 138.

tration of the Ministry of Finance, to study the economic decay
of the central provinces. At the beginning of 1902 the Finance
Minister Witte was put in charge of a "Special Conference on
the Needs of Agriculture", which was to create committees in
the provinces under the chairmanship of the governors, and in
districts under the chairmanship of the marshals of the nobility.
The zemstvos requested that the conference's programme be
submitted to them for their opinion, but this was refused.

In March–April 1902 serious peasant riots broke out in the
provinces of Harkov and Poltava. The deliberations of the government bodies continued, but led to small results. By the manifesto
of 26th February/11th March 1903 the collective responsibility of
communes for tax payments was abolished. At the same time the
powers of provincial governors were generally increased, and district police forces were strengthened, on the basis of roughly one
policeman for 2,500 inhabitants. Throughout this period the conflict between the Ministries of the Interior and Finance, which
affected most major fields of Russian policy, was reflected in the
agricultural field in the rivalry between the "editing commission"
of the former and the "special conference" of the latter. By the
summer of 1903 the Ministry of the Interior had the upper hand.
Its policy was to entrust reforms entirely to the bureaucracy, to
weaken the zemstvos and in general to exclude all non-official
opinion from the discussion of reform.

The Growth of Industry

The last decades of the 19th century were a period of rapid
industrial growth. This growth forms the essential background to
the country's political development. In the following brief survey
we shall first give some facts on the development of the main
branches (textiles, railways, metallurgy and oil). We shall then
consider the rise of a business class, the support given to it by the
government, and the various links between industrialists and
officials. We shall then briefly describe government trade and
taxation policy, and its effects on the population as a whole. The
problems of industrial labour, and its relations with both employers
and government, form the subject of a separate section.

The emancipation of the serfs affected different branches of
industry in different ways. Those enterprises which had been
worked by serf labour were severely damaged, since the liberated
serfs at once took the opportunity of leaving the hated mines and
factories. The most important victim was the government-owned

metal industry of the Urals: in the Bogoslovsk district of Perm province, for instance, some 3,000 out of 10,000 workers left. Cast-iron production in the Urals fell between 1860 and 1862 from 14,500,000 *pud* to 10,400,000;[1] by 1867 it had only recovered to 12,400,000. Another important branch of industry which suffered a serious decline in its labour force were the formerly serf-employing cloth factories in the central and eastern Russian provinces of Simbirsk, Voronezh, Kazan, Oryol and Smolensk.[2]

Industries which already before 1861 had relied on free wage labour profited from the emancipation. The influx of labour from the villages to industrial centres was made easier by the removal of the personal restrictions of serfdom. The Moscow textile industry made great progress. After experiencing some difficulty with raw cotton supplies during the American civil war, it went rapidly ahead. Another important textile centre grew up in and around Łódż, in the west of Russian Poland. Some indication of the progress of the Russian textile industry (including both these areas) is given by figures for Russian imports of raw cotton. These were (in millions of *pud*, 62·2 *pud* = 1 ton):

1863	.. ..	1·1
1877	.. ..	5·2
1881	.. ..	9·7
1894	.. ..	15·4

The early seventies were a great period of railway building in Russia. During the eighties construction was slower, but in the nineties it was again rapid. In the first period most was done by private companies. The government encouraged private enterprise, but exercised a general technical supervision through the Ministry of Communications. At the end of the eighties, 76 per cent of the railway track of Russia (21,000 *versts*)[3] was owned by 42 private companies and 24 per cent by the State. Confusion was caused by the variety of freight tariffs, which were repeatedly lowered to attract custom from one line to another. In 1889 the government decreed that no tariff might be applied by a private line until it was approved by the Ministry of Finance. From this time the Ministry of Finance tightened its grip on the financial side of the railways, while the Ministry of Communications continued as before to exercise technical control. During the nineties the government bought most of the lines belonging to small companies, and

[1] One *pud* is equal to 36 lb. One ton equals c. 62·2 *pud*.
[2] Tugan-Baranovski, *op. cit.*, pp. 371–6.
[3] One *verst* is equal to 0·66 mile, slightly more than one kilometre.

encouraged a few major private lines to buy up other small companies. In 1894 the old-established Chief Society of Russian Railways, which controlled the St. Petersburg–Moscow, St. Petersburg–Warsaw and Moscow–Nizhni Novgorod lines, passed into State ownership. In 1902 the total length of line in Russia was 53,000 *versts*, of which 35,000 (67 per cent) was State property. Of the remaining 18,000 versts, 15,000 belonged to six companies.[1] Railway mileage had thus nearly doubled between 1889 and 1902. In 1897 the total receipts of all railways in Russia were 437 million roubles, of which 74 per cent came from goods traffic. Total goods transport in the same year was 111 million tons, of which slightly less than a quarter consisted of the four main items of cereals, coal, timber and petrol. The revenue from the State railways was controlled by the Department of Railway Affairs in the Ministry of Finance.[2]

The railway boom gave a strong incentive to the rise of a metallurgical industry. A great new industrial area grew up in the south, based on the coal-mines of the Donetz basin and the iron ore of Krivoi Rog: it soon far outstripped the old metallurgy of the Urals. In 1869 a Welshman named Hughes obtained a concession for a company, to be called the New Russia Company, for the production of coal, iron and rails. The concession included the exploitation of large mineral fields. From a tiny village arose a city, named after him, Yuzovka, which at the end of the century had 30,000 inhabitants. Production of pig-iron in Russia grew as follows (in millions of *pud*, 62·2 *pud* = 1 ton): 1862 15, 1886 32, 1896 98. In the decade 1886–96, whereas the population increase for Russia as a whole was 15 per cent, for the southern and south-west provinces it was 30 per cent and 35 per cent. The towns grew especially fast. Ekaterinoslav grew from 47,000 to 120,000, Rostov-on-Don from nearly 80,000 to nearly 150,000.[3] Similar progress took place in the oil-bearing region of the Caucasus, whose capital Baku increased from 46,000 to 108,000. Production figures of crude oil were 5 million pud in 1875, 116 million in 1885, and 348 million in 1895.

At the same time Russian economists noted a growing concen-

---

[1] These were the Vladikavkaz Railway; the Moscow-Kazan Railway Co.; the Ryazan-Ural Railway Co.; the Kiev-Voronezh Railway Co.; the Moscow-Rybinsk Railway Co.; and the South-Eastern Railway Co.

[2] For an account of the administration and finances of the Russian railways, see *Rossia v kontse XIX veka*, ed. V. I. Kovalevski (S.P.B., 1900), pp. 692–740.

[3] This greater increase is accounted for not solely by the new industry, but also by immigration of labourers to the grain-bearing provinces of "New-Russia", formerly sparsely inhabited.

tration of industry in the hands of big enterprises. The Marxist Tugan-Baranovski collected and analysed statistics for the cotton industry, dividing it into categories according to the number of workmen employed. His figures showed that in 1866 43 per cent of the workers in this industry were employed in factories employing more than 100 persons, in 1879 51 per cent, and in 1894 72 per cent. He found a similar tendency in other branches of the textile industry, and in paper, chemicals and metal-working. In the coal industry, the largest mines between 1882 and 1894 multiplied their output sevenfold, while the remainder were almost stationary. The only exceptions to this process of concentration were in the food-preparing industries, especially sugar factories and vodka distilleries, in which small units continued to be important.[1]

From the eighties onwards there was a decline in the craft industries which—especially in the central provinces—had been an important means of livelihood for peasants under serfdom. The decline was especially marked in textiles, sacking, nails (Tver province), nets (Kazan province), and locks (Nizhni Novgorod province). In some areas the decline was caused by direct competition from big factories, which might be located hundreds of miles away, as in the case of the nail trade, or in the same region, as with the textile crafts in the provinces around Moscow. In other cases it was caused by amalgamation of craft enterprises into larger units, which eventually transformed themselves into factories. An example of this is the cutlery trade in Nizhni Novgorod province. An example of a craft which still flourished at the end of the century was the brush trade in Moscow province, but here too capitalistic methods were penetrating. The craftsmen sold their wares to big merchants from Moscow, whose relationship to them more and more approximated to that of an employer of hired labour. Both the central government and the zemstvos tried to assist craft industry. A special Rural Economy section was set up in the Ministry of Finance. Exhibitions of their products were organised. Some products were even sold abroad, for instance lace work. Some protection was ensured by a type of artisans' co-operative known as an *artel*. Members contributed only their labour, and each member had an equal vote. The *artels* pooled members' resources for the purchase of equipment, and were able to arrange better marketing conditions than individual producers could obtain. At the end of the century it was estimated that 7 million to 8 million persons were partly or fully employed in crafts, and earned a yearly

[1] Tugan-Baranovski, *op. cit.*, pp. 427–37.

total of about 500 million roubles. Average yearly earnings per head were thus 70 roubles, but in some trades they were as low as 15 and in others as high as 200.[1]

A class of industrialist came into being during the last decades of the century, partly derived from the traditional merchant class and partly connected with the foreign capital that was beginning to pour into Russia. In 1874 was held the first congress of southern mine-owners, in Taganrog. From the fifth (1880) onwards, these were held yearly in Harkov. Between congresses affairs were managed by a Council selected by the congress. Voting power at congresses depended on the figures of output of the firms represented. At first it included only mine-owners, but from the nineties onwards metallurgical factories were also represented. Government officials attended the congresses, whose chairman was appointed by the Ministry of Finance. The main subjects of discussion were requests for various forms of State subsidies, and conflicts with the land-owning class, for instance with regard to representation at zemstvo assemblies. In 1887 was founded the Permanent Consultative Office of Iron Industrialists, which represented factories from all over Russia, but was dominated by the big southern enterprises. The Congress of Petrol Industrialists was founded in 1884. It was dominated by the three biggest firms, Nobel, Rothschild and Mantashev, which together held 27 per cent of the votes. All-Russian congresses of industrialists were not of great importance at this time. One was held in 1870 and two in 1882. They included not only industrialists but also government officials, engineers and professors interested in industrial matters. They therefore did no more than discuss subjects of general interest. They were not effective organisations for the defence of industrialists' interests. The same is true of the All-Russian congress of trade and industry held in Nizhni Novgorod in 1896.[2]

Throughout this period the government strongly supported the rising Russian industry. Its first interest was in the railways, which it encouraged for strategic reasons. From this developed support to coal-mining, pig-iron production and the manufacture of rails. State contracts played an enormous part in Russian production. It is estimated that in 1899 nearly two-thirds of Russian metallurgical production was taken by the State. Close links developed between officials and industrialists. Officials sat on many bodies supervising

[1] The decline of craft industries is discussed from a Marxist point of view in Tugan-Baranovski, *op. cit.*, Part II, chapter 4. See also Kovalevski, *op. cit.*, pp. 511–17 and 601–8, for semi-official views of crafts and artels.
[2] *O.D.*, Vol I, pp. 332–47 (A. Yermanski, *Krupnaya burzhuazia do 1905 goda*).

industrial activities. This of course gave them the opportunity to intervene in business, but it also enabled industrialists to win them over to their point of view. One of the most important of these bodies was a committee for the allocation of government orders for rails, which had immense opportunities of patronage. Much effort was expended in contests between firms for government orders.[1]

Another most important form of support given by the government to industrialists was the imposition of import duties. Russia's commercial policy was traditionally protectionist. The tariffs of 1857 and 1868 had however been low, in accordance with the prevailing European belief in free trade. But in 1887 the duty per *pud* of pig-iron was raised from 5 to 25 kopeks, and in 1891 to 30. Heavy duties were put on consumption goods, lighter but still severe duties on imported raw materials. There were three motives for protection—support to Russian industry, increase of the State revenue, and creation of a favourable balance of trade in order to make possible the introduction of the gold standard.

The interests of different industries varied. The main demand for protection came from the Moscow textile group. With easy access to the great Volga waterway and the Caspian, Moscow could supply itself with the liquid fuel of the Caucasus and the raw cotton which was being increasingly developed in Russian Central Asia. Thus assured of raw materials from domestic sources, it could afford to indulge in economic patriotism. The textile mills of Łódź and St. Petersburg, whose easiest access to raw materials was by sea or rail from abroad, were less enthusiastic. It is no coincidence that the traditional rivalry in ideas between Slavophile Moscow and Westernising St. Petersburg should now take on a new, economic form.[2]

The fiscal and currency motives for protection became especially important during Witte's tenure of the Ministry of Finance (1894–1903). Witte was able to create a large favourable balance. By 1903 the value of Russian exports was 1,000 million roubles and of imports 682 million. During the last two decades of the century, receipts from tariffs enormously increased. In the years 1877–80 their average yearly yield was 84 million roubles, in 1901–3 the average was 227 million. Tariff receipts as a percentage of the total value of imports were, on a yearly average, in 1877–80 15·8 per cent and in 1901–3 38 per cent. The structure of Russia's foreign trade

[1] *O.D.*, Vol. I, pp. 170–4 (M. Bogolyepov, *Gosudarstvennoe hozyaistvo i finansovaya politika pravitelstva*).
[2] There is an interesting discussion of Russian protectionism in Schulze-Gävernitz, *Volkswirtschaftliche Studien aus Russland* (Leipzig, 1899), pp. 269–82.

also changed considerably in this period. In 1865–7 foodstuffs formed 39 per cent of Russia's exports, in 1903 62 per cent, the largest item in this being grain from the southern provinces. In the same period the share of raw and half-finished goods declined from 50 per cent to 32 per cent. In imports, raw and half-finished goods increased in the same years from 44 per cent to 53 per cent, and manufactures declined from 37 per cent to 27 per cent.[1]

The effect of Witte's policy was to create a large gold reserve, and to make possible the adoption of the gold standard in 1897. This greatly increased foreign confidence in the Russian economy, and thus made it possible to attract foreign capital on a large scale, which was also one of Witte's main aims. In 1900 according to official sources there were 269 foreign companies in Russia, of which all but 16 had been founded since 1888. One hundred and sixty-two were Belgian, 54 French, 30 German and 19 British. The French companies had the largest total capital. The French and Belgians were mainly interested in mining and metallurgy, the Germans in chemicals and electrical engineering, the British in oil.[2]

Of the government's revenue from taxation, the largest share was borne by the peasants and the town workers. The land tax on estates of the nobility was in practice assessed by themselves, and even so was reduced by half in 1896. Inheritance tax was imposed, after intense opposition, in 1882. It was always very light, and was reduced in 1895. The business tax, introduced in 1898, was based on very low assessments of the income of industrial and commercial enterprises. Zemstvo land taxation was approximately twice as high on peasant-owned land as on estates of the nobility. Canton taxes were paid only by the peasants, but the services performed by canton authorities were used by all inhabitants of the canton. Thus the peasants paid for the rest. Indirect taxation continued to be heavy. The salt tax was abolished in 1880. The spirits tax was converted in 1894 into the State spirits monopoly. Witte later declared that his intention in introducing this measure was not merely to get revenue for the State but also, for moral reasons, to reduce the curse of drunkenness in the villages. He blames his successors for concerning themselves only with the financial side. Be that as it may, huge sums certainly rolled into the Treasury from the government wine-shops. Another very important tax was the

[1] O.D., Vol. I, pp. 130–8 (Mukoseyev, *Vnyeshnyaya torgovlya*).
[2] Kovalevski *op. cit.*, pp. 615–21. I have not been able to find figures for the proportions of the total foreign investments belonging to citizens of the different countries for this period. These figures for the period immediately before 1914 are given below, pp. 285–6.

sugar duty, which was used to subsidise sugar exports. Money was thus taken by the government from the poor consumer and handed to the big exporting sugar producers of the south-west provinces.

A picture of the economic policy of the Russian government can be seen from the following figures, which show the main items of revenue and expenditure in the years 1878, 1886, 1895 and 1897.[1]

GOVERNMENT REVENUE (millions of roubles)

Taxation of the Peasantry	1878	1886	1895	1897
Poll tax, land tax and forest tax	122	86 [2]	49	39
Redemption payments by landlords' peasants		41	42	35
Redemption payments by State peasants	4	5	56 [3]	48
Other direct taxation				
Business tax	15	28	43	46
Tax on share capital		10	14	15
Indirect taxation				
Alcohol[4]	215	237	298	332
Tobacco	12	20	34	35
Sugar	5	15	47	55
Mineral oil			20	23
Matches			7	7
Customs revenue	98	113	168	195
Stamp duties	18	18	30	32
State properties				
Agricultural land	7	11	14	16
Forests	11	13	28	38
Railways	6	13	194	278
Post	14	16	25	26
Telegraph and telephone	7	9	14	18

[1] Schulze-Gävernitz, *op. cit.*, pp. 540 ff.
[2] Poll tax was abolished in 1886.
[3] These payments came regularly into force from 1887 onwards.
[4] Including State spirits monopoly receipts after 1894.

GOVERNMENT EXPENDITURE (millions of roubles)[1]

	1878	1886	1895	1897
Service of State debt	140	246	277	258
War Ministry	189	213	285	294
Naval Ministry	26	44	57	85
Ministry of Communications	12	26	163	227
Ministry of Finance (including the cost of operating the spirits monopoly after 1894)	91	116	140	204
Ministry of Interior	58	72	86	80
Ministry of Education	17	21	23	26

The aim of the Russian government was to increase the military might and prestige of the Russian State. The enormous development of the railways was an integral part of this process. Industrial development was welcomed as modernising the country. Foreign capital was welcomed as a means of developing economic resources. If foreign capital was to be attracted, interest on loans must be punctually and fully paid. These payments were, after defence, the most important item in government expenditure. The burden of these vast expenses was placed on the poorest classes of the population, and especially on the peasants. The total sum paid in 1897 in direct taxes by the peasantry (122 million roubles) is only twice that paid by the business class (61 million roubles), although the peasants were probably at least twenty times more numerous. But the peasants' cash incomes were so very small that this burden was in fact very heavy. Indirect taxation, amounting to 452 million roubles, of course hit the poor in town and village. Of the import duties, those levied on luxury goods were paid by the wealthy, but those affecting raw materials were passed on to all consumers of Russian industrial products, and those on manufactured goods of wide consumption hit the peasants and workers. The income of the State railways came from the big landlords and industrialists whose goods were transported, but here too part of the cost was passed on to the urban consumers of these goods.

The burden on the peasantry was not only financial in the narrow sense. The repayment of foreign loans, and the maintenance of the currency, depended on a favourable balance of trade, and this was secured above all by great grain exports. The grain available for export was the property of the big landowners, and to a much lesser extent of the richer peasants (*kulaks*). It was produced by the

[1] Schulze-Gävernitz, *op. cit.*, p. 549.

labour of the landless peasants and dwarf holders, who received low wages, in cash or in kind or in both. If the land had belonged not to the big landlords but to these peasant labourers, they would have eaten more, and less would have been available for export.

Thus the prestige of the autocracy, the military power of the empire, and the modernisation of the economy were paid for directly by grain exports and foreign loans and investments, and indirectly by over-taxation and undernourishment of the peasants and workers.

Labour Policy

During the second half of the century an industrial working class was being formed, distinct from the peasantry from which it sprang. The number of workers in industry was a subject of controversy among Russian economists. In the interests of their respective theories, Marxists and Populists overestimated and under-estimated the number, including or excluding various categories of labour as "industrial workers". According to the calculations of the Marxist Tugan-Baranovski the number of industrial workers in 1896 was about 2,200,000. But he believed that this was too low a figure owing to gaps in the official statistics, and estimated that by 1900 the number must be at least 3,000,000.[1] Of these approxi-mately 550,000 were employed in the textile group, 500,000 in metallurgy and 400,000 were railwaymen. The connection between the workers and villages was beginning to wear thin. According to the researches of Dementyev in the central Russian provinces in 1884–5, an average of only 14 per cent of factory workers regularly left the factories for the villages every harvest season. In the big machine-run factories the percentage was smaller. About half the workers whom he interrogated were children of parents who had at least partly worked in factories. Most owned no land in the villages, but were still recorded as members of village communes and so officially regarded as peasants.[2] Already in the seventies Plehanov noted a difference between the experienced workers and those recently arrived from the countryside, who were called "grey" and despised by the former.[3] The Ministry of Finance inspector for the Moscow region in the period 1883–93 found that 82 per cent of the factory workers were permanently employed and only 18 per cent went to the villages in summer.

[1] Tugan-Baranovski, *op. cit.*, p. 425.
[2] Ibid., pp. 520–1, quotes a work which I have not been able to find, Dementyev, *Fabrika, chto naseleniu dayot i chto u nyevo beryot* (Moscow, 1897).
[3] Plehanov, *Russkii rabochii v revolyutsionnom dvizhenii*, pp. 12–14.

These figures however come only from central Russia. Similar information was not at this time available about other industrial centres. It seems probable that the formation of a working class distinct from the peasantry had gone equally far in St. Petersburg and in the industrial region of Poland, but that the process was less advanced in the new metallurgical and mining areas of south Russia or in the Urals.

Wages rose after 1861, but at first the prices of foodstuffs rose more rapidly. For instance, in Ivanovo-Voznesensk at the beginning of the eighties wages were between 15 and 50 per cent higher than in the fifties, but rye cost 100 per cent more, butter 83 per cent more and meat 220 per cent more. But from the mid-eighties there was an improvement. In Vladimir and Moscow provinces from 1883 to 1896 money wages increased by 10 per cent to 15 per cent, while grain prices fell.[1]

The first important strikes took place in St. Petersburg cotton mills in 1878 as a protest against lowering of wages by the management. The strikers sent a petition to the heir to the throne. There were further stoppages in the following autumn, and in January 1879 simultaneous strikes were organised in several mills by previous agreement. The workers' demands included wage increases, shorter hours, abolition of fines and dismissal of certain unpopular foremen. The demands were printed in the "Land and Liberty" press. The short-lived Northern Workers' Union of Halturin played a part in these events.[2] The next important strike was at the Morozov textile factory at Orehovo-Zuevo, near Moscow, in 1885. It led to legislation in the following year obliging employers to pay wages at regular intervals and in cash, and reducing the use of fines for breaches of factory discipline. In 1896 there were serious strikes again in St. Petersburg cotton mills. Some 35,000 workers came out, and the strike lasted for nearly a month When the promises made by the employers were not fulfilled, the strike was repeated in January 1897. The Marxist organisation, "League of Combat", took an active part in the organisation of these strikes.[3] In the late nineties the strike movement spread to other provinces, involving the metal industry of the south, dockers in Riga, miners and textile workers in Poland, and railwaymen in various parts of the empire.

[1] Tugan-Baranovski, op. cit., pp. 515–19.
[2] For an account of the Union's activities, see Plehanov, op. cit., pp. 65 ff.
[3] See below, p. 148. The League's activity is described in a pamphlet by "Peterburzhets" (Tahtarev), Ocherki peterburgskovo rabochevo dvizhenia 90-h godov (London, 1902). Also in Y. Martov and F. Dan, Geschichte der russischen Sozialdemokratie (Berlin, 1926), pp. 31 ff.

During the eighties and nineties labour legislation was introduced, despite considerable opposition from employers. This was mainly the work of Bunge, for some years professor at Kiev university and from 1881 to 1886 Minister of Finance. The first law was passed in 1882. It forbade labour of children under 12; limited to eight hours labour by those between 12 and 15 years; obliged employers to allow child employees to attend school; and introduced a government inspectorate, under the orders of the Finance Ministry. Its value was diminished by a provision that during a transition period of two years exceptions to these rules could be allowed by special permission of the Ministry.

The law was willingly accepted by the industrialists of St. Petersburg, who even suggested further provisions to the advantage of women and adult male workers. It was bitterly opposed by the Moscow industrialists, in the name of "freedom of labour". The reason lay in the different conditions of the labour market in the two regions. In St. Petersburg the supply of labour lagged behind the demand, and wages were relatively high. The industrialists found that it paid them to introduce machines, modernise their factories and raise the productivity of labour by giving their workers better living conditions. In Moscow, the centre of an over-populated region, the supply of labour was more than sufficient and profits were most conveniently made by exploiting a cheap and inefficient labour supply for long hours. The Polish centre, around Łódź, in this matter resembled St. Petersburg rather than Moscow.[1]

In 1884 and 1885 Bunge passed further laws regulating school attendance for child employees and forbidding night work in cotton, linen and wool factories for women and adolescents. The passing of these laws was helped by the fact that industry was now experiencing a depression, factories were not working at full capacity, and so had less need to exploit labour to the full. It was also helped by the desire of the Ministry of the Interior, which had been alarmed by the Morozov strike of 1885, to pacify the workers in the interest of "public order". A law of 1886 regulated employment contracts and the method of paying workers. It also imposed penalties for striking—two to four months' prison for strikers and four to eight months for ringleaders. Breach of contract by a worker was punished with a month's prison, but by an employer with only 300 roubles fine.

In 1886 Bunge, who by now was thoroughly unpopular with the

[1] Tugan-Baranovski, *op. cit.*, pp. 460–3. See also Luxemburg, *op. cit.*

industrialists, was replaced at the Finance Ministry by Vyshne-gradski, who showed more sympathy for them. A law of 1890 allowed in certain cases the employment of women and adolescents on night work. The most important of the whole series of labour laws was passed in July 1897, when Witte was Minister, after the big St. Petersburg textile strikes. It imposed a maximum $11\frac{1}{2}$ hours' working day for all workers, male or female, of all ages, and a maximum of 10 hours for all who were engaged in any night work.

Despite these concessions to labour, the general trend of government policy was hostile to the workers and supported employers. For instance, the police collaborated with industrialists in measures for "protection of order in the factories". Cossack detachments were sometimes sent at request. In 1880 employers were permitted by law to maintain at their own expense special police on their premises. At the end of the century the Minister of Interior Sipyagin stated that sometimes employers gave funds to the police for the maintenance of agents in their factories, and sometimes paid secret agents of their own whose reports were put at the disposal of the police.[1]

The government also assisted industrialists in recruiting labour from the villages. In 1897 an "Office for the Hire of Workers" was set up in Harkov, which received information on the labour supply from commanders of gendarmerie at railway stations and from Land Commandants[2]—in the latter case with the express authorisation of the Ministry of the Interior. But still the industrialists were not content, on the grounds that conditions were not so favourable to them as to big landowners, whose recruitment of hired labour was more thoroughly organised.

There was however an important difference in the attitude to the workers of the Ministry of Finance and the Interior. The Finance Ministry considered its task to be the "just reconciliation of the interests of both sides, capital and labour". Its inspectors in the factories were to pursue this aim. In practice, the close connections of the Ministry of Finance with the industrialists ensured that it took the side of the employers. On the other hand, the Ministry of the Interior was concerned with the preservation of public order, without any special sympathy for any single class. Its servants often felt their task to include the removal of potential causes of disorder. For instance, the town commandant of Odessa, Count Shuvalov, wrote in 1899 that revolutionary activity among the workers could

---

[1] *O.D.*, Vol. I, pp. 422–82 (F. Danilov, *Obshchaya politika pravitelstva*); I. H. Ozerov, *Politika po rabochemu voprosu* (Moscow, 1906), chapter 6.
[2] See below p. 136.

not be removed merely by deporting agitators, but only by shortening hours of work and developing adult education. Count Svyatopolk-Mirski, as Chief of Gendarmes in 1901, wrote that conditions of labour, and especially the lack of provision for old age or incapacity due to illness, favoured revolutionary agitators. "In the last three to four years, from the good-natured Russian lad has been formed a peculiar type of semi-illiterate intellectual, who considers it his duty to deny religion and the family, to ignore the law, to disobey it and to make jokes about it."[1]

Though ruthless in suppression of strikes or other "mutinous" activities, the Ministry of the Interior wished to satisfy the workers' demands provided they were kept out of politics. The Ministry wished police to be stationed inside factories and to get to know factory conditions. The employers, and the Ministry of Finance, preferred that the police should hold themselves available outside the factories, and come in only when asked by the employers to restore order. A decree of February 1899, which strengthened police in factories, was a victory for the Ministry of the Interior. Another conflict concerned the position of factory inspectors, whom the Ministry of the Interior wished to have placed under its command, instead of the Ministry of Finance. This time a compromise was made. The Ministry of Finance retained authority over the inspectors, but they were also to be responsible locally to provincial governors. Inspectors and police were instructed to collaborate and to supply each other with information. In practice, the position of inspectors was unenviable. If they were too friendly to the workers, and took up their grievances with higher authority, they were denounced by the employers as "agitators". If they tried to collaborate with the employers, they found themselves being used as spies and censors, and lost any hope of winning the workers' confidence and so fulfilling the Ministry's directives on "conciliation".[2]

Trade unions were illegal. Their formation was prevented under article 318 of the penal law of 1874, which imposed varying sentences of prison or exile on those organising a society which stimulated hatred between employers and workers. Early attempts at the organisation of illegal unions were a "Workers' Alliance" at Ivanovo-Voznesensk in 1895 and a "central fund" in Nikolaev in 1897. The latter devoted half its funds to strike pay, one-third to relief and one-sixth to the establishment of a members' library. The most successful organisation was the "Society for Mutual Aid to Persons employed in Artisan Labour", founded in Harkov in 1898,

---

[1] Ozerov, *op. cit.*, p. 131.   [2] Ibid., chapters 6 and 7.

which gave their first training to the later labour leaders of southern Russia.[1]

An important step in the development of Russian workers' organisations came from an unexpected source. The Head of the Moscow branch of the Defence Section (Ohrana) of the Department of Police, Zubatov, had the idea of canalising working-class discontent by setting up a workers' organisation under police leadership. In 1901 some professors of Moscow University were persuaded to assist in drafting the statute of a workers' society, which was approved by the city Police Chief and referred to the Minister of the Interior. In February 1902 was formally founded, with official permission, the "Society of Mutual Help of Workers in Mechanical Production".[2] The society, under police direction, organised workers' demonstrations in favour of the Tsar, communal singing of patriotic songs, and the reception of workers' representatives by the Minister of the Interior Pleve. At the advice of Pleve two new labour laws ware passed in June 1903. One introduced elections by the workers of factory "elders" to represent their interests before the employers. The other obliged employers to provide medical assistance to workers injured during their work, to pay them half their normal wage during illness, and to contribute a sum to their funeral expenses.

But for all its ingenuity, the Ministry of the Interior's policy was not successful. The Moscow association got out of hand and organised strikes. In practice it provided the agitators of the Social Democratic Party with opportunities to increase their influence over the workers. A similar organisation created in the south by an agent of the Ministry of the Interior, Shaevich, under the name of "Independent Workers' Committee" was used by the Socialists and led to a general strike in Odessa in the summer of 1903. The Zubatov policy did not long deceive the workers, and it antagonised the employers. It was not possible to divert the workers' discontent without carrying out reforms more radical than the ruling class of the Imperial regime could accept. Zubatov resigned his post in 1903.[3] This was not however a final victory for the Ministry of

---

[1] *O.D.*, Vol. I, p. 192 (in article by D. Koltsov, *Rabochie v 1890–1904 gody*). V. Grinevich, *Professionalnoe dvizhenie rabochih v Rossii* (SPB., 1908), chapter 2, gives details of attempts to create unions in the nineties.

[2] Ozerov, *op. cit.*, chapter 8.

[3] There is some information on Zubatov in M. Laporte, *Histoire de l'Okhrana 1880–1917* (Paris, 1935), and P. Zavarzin, *Zhandarmy i revolyutsionery* (Paris, 1930). The latter author also gives some details about the working of the secret political police in *Rabota tainoy politsii* (Paris, 1924). The Socialist-Revolutionary leader Chernov describes an interview with Zubatov when under arrest in his *Zapiski sotsialista-revolyutsionera* (Berlin, 1922), chapter 7. According to the diary of the

Finance. Witte himself was surpassed by Pleve in the favour of the Tsar, and had to give up his Ministry in August 1903. The feud between the two State departments continued. It represented he deep rivalry between traditional bureaucratic Russia and the rising forces of capitalism and the bourgeoisie.

After more than a decade of growing prosperity, which even the famine of 1891–2 had not for long reversed, Russian industry in 1899 entered a period of depression. The first signs appeared in August 1899. The State Bank's discount rate rose sharply, and the prices of company shares began to fall. A reassuring statement by the Ministry of Finance did not restore confidence. Two large concerns, Von Derviz and Mamontov, both of which owned railway companies and various factories, went bankrupt. In the following year industrial prices began to fall, and this continued for two years. For example, pig-iron fell from 70–80 kopeks per *pud* in mid-1900 to 45–48 kopeks at the end of the year; Donetz coal from 9–10 kopeks per *pud* in early 1900 to 6–7 kopeks at the end of 1902; crude oil from 17–18 kopeks in 1900 to 4–6 kopeks in early 1902. Fall of prices was followed in 1902 by fall of production. Total output of pig-iron in Russia in 1901 was 172·8 million *pud*, in 1902 156·5 million, in 1903 149·1 million. Iron ore output in Krivoi Rog fell from 156·2 million *pud* in 1900 to 111·8 in 1902, but recovered to 149·5 million by 1903. An important feature of the slump is that it had a much bigger effect on the metallurgical and petrol industries than on light industry. The internal market for cotton goods saved the Moscow textile industry from very serious loss. In the southern metallurgical industry the slump eliminated a number of weaker firms, and furthered the concentration of capital in large enterprises. By the end of 1903 business had almost recovered from the slump. But further improvement was retarded by the outbreak of war with Japan.[1]

The depression years 1899–1903 had important effects on the working-class movement. Slumps are usually unfavourable to economic strikes. Unemployment rose, and employers were able to use the labour reserve to refuse wage claims. But if economic hardship placed the workers at a disadvantage in regard to their

---

War Minister, General Kuropatkin (*Krasny Arkhiv V*, pp. 81–2, entry of 31st October/13th November 1903), Zubatov fell from favour because he made some derogatory remarks about Pleve, which were repeated to Pleve by Prince Meshcherski.

[1] Lyashchenko, *Istoria narodnovo hozyaistva S.S.S.R.* (Moscow, 1948), Vol. II, pp. 230–42; Migulin, *Reforma denezhnovo obrashchenia v Rossii i promyshlenny krizis 1893–1902* (Harkov, 1902), chapter 4, pp. 236–324.

employers, it also increased their discontent and so made easier the work of the revolutionary agitators. Whereas the prosperous late nineties had been marked by economic strikes, the first years of the century were filled with short political strikes and street demonstrations, in many cases accompanied by violence. The revolutionary leaders paid great attention to demonstrations, believing that they gave the workers valuable training in discipline and increased their hatred of the rulers. On the whole it seems that the stupidity and brutality of police and Cossacks justified the revolutionaries' hopes.

On 4th/17th November 1902 there was a strike in Rostov-on-Don. The workers made sweeping demands including a nine-hour day and increases of wages. On the 6th there were mass demonstrations and political speeches. On the 8th a general strike was declared in the whole city. For the first few days, the majority of the population showed sympathy for the workers, but then became lukewarm. On the 15th troops occupied the city in force. By the 25th the workers were back at their jobs. The police authorities insisted that the employers should not grant any of the workers' demands. Economically the strike was thus a failure, but as "political education" it was important. In July 1903 there was a big strike in Baku, affecting most enterprises in the city. Troops were brought in, there were riots and fires were started.[1] Strikes broke out at the same time in Tiflis and Batum, and "sympathetic" strikes were declared in Odessa, Kiev, Nikolaev and Ekaterinoslav. A feature of these strikes was that crowds of workers moved from factory to factory appealing to each to stop work. There were also big open-air political meetings, and clashes with police or troops. It was clear that the workers' movement was passing out of the stage of mere instinctive discontent. Political ideas, and illegal political organisations, were gaining a following.[2]

---

[1] Recent Soviet historians all assert that the workers' movement in the Caucasus at this time was led and organised by Comrade Stalin. In fact however Djugashvili played a small part at this time. The socialist movement in the Caucasus, which was a strong one, was led by men who subsequently became Mensheviks. The Stalinist case is largely based on the statement of Beriya, *On the history of the Bolshevik organisations in Transcaucasia*. This lecture, delivered in 1935, is available in an English translation (Moscow, 1949). The case against the Stalinists is in Wolfe, *Three who made a Revolution* (New York, 1949). See also Trotski, *Stalinskaya shkola falsifikatsii* (Berlin, 1932). I. Deutscher, *Stalin, a Political Biography* (Oxford, 1949), is more cautious in his judgment.

[2] *O.D.*, Vol. I, pp. 213–24.

Chapter V

POLITICAL DEVELOPMENT

Central and Local Government

THE new Tsar, Alexander III, was a convinced autocrat and extreme conservative. He had regarded his father's reforms with displeasure, and was keen to return to the safe path of his grandfather. He opposed any concessions to liberalism, and was resolved to maintain the supremacy of the Russians and of Orthodoxy over all other nationalities and religions of the empire. His sympathy with Panslavism caused him to dislike the German element, and to wish to reduce its influence in the bureaucracy and in cultural affairs. But conservative principles applied to foreign policy required good relations with the two German emperors. He did his best to ensure this by prudent diplomacy. Foreign policy was best left, he believed, to the Tsar and his diplomats, and should not be affected by public opinion. Though Panslav public opinion was less distasteful to him than any other, he considered that it should be kept within safe limits. In fact it was not his Panslav sympathy so much as his wounded personal feelings which led him into the only serious diplomatic crisis of his reign.[1] Though disliked by all liberals, Alexander III was respected for his sincerity, strength of character and devotion to duty. His tall and massive figure was the last impressive symbol of Russian autocracy.

His most important adviser was K. P. Pobedonostsev, a former professor of constitutional law and since 1880 Procurator of the Holy Synod.[2] A bitter opponent of Western liberal influences, he coined the famous phrase that parliamentarism is "the great lie of our time". Autocracy and bureaucracy should be the sole basis of government. Not only elected legislatures but even consultative representative bodies met with his whole-hearted disapproval. He distrusted even the local self-government created by Alexander II.

[1] See below, pp. 173–5.
[3] Some of the correspondence of Pobedonostsev has been published under the title, *K. P. Pobedonostsev i yevo korrespodenty* (Moscow, 1926). There is also a French edition. *Mémoires politiques, correspondance officielle et documents inédits relatifs à l'histoire de règne d' Alexandre III* (Paris 1927).

His advice to Alexander III consistently favoured conservatism, Orthodox clericalism and narrow Russian nationalism. He found in his imperial pupil a ready listener.

Alexander III was faced on his accession with a difficult choice. He had to take a decision on Loris-Melikov's proposed reforms. His own inclinations were against them, but he knew that his late father had approved them, and hesitated to begin his reign with an act of filial impiety. On 8th/21st March he summoned a conference of ministers and high officials to discuss the proposals. Milyutin and Loris-Melikov defended the proposals on the ground that they in no way amounted to a "constitution". Pobedonostsev fiercely denounced them on the ground that they were a first step towards further changes in the structure of the State, which would in the end lead inevitably to a constitution. The Tsar was visibly impressed by these arguments but did not yet make up his mind. A further conference was held on 21st April/4th May. On this occasion, Loris-Melikov, while not abandoning his first proposals, went further and suggested that there should be a "united government", that is, that the duties of individual ministers should be co-ordinated in what would amount to a cabinet (the word was not spoken, owing to its West European associations) instead of being separately responsible to the emperor. This suggestion decided the Tsar against Loris-Melikov. He entrusted Pobedonostsev with the preparation of a suitable manifesto to his subjects. This was published on 29th April/12th May, and announced the Tsar's firm resolve to maintain unchanged the ancient principles of autocracy. Loris-Melikov was not informed beforehand of the content of the manifesto. He rightly interpreted this as a loss of the monarch's confidence. He, Milyutin and the Minister of Finance Abaza immediately offered their resignations, which were readily accepted.

The extreme conservatives, shocked by the assassination of Alexander II, and feeling that this had proved the incompetence of the State machine, felt that they must take independent action to safeguard public order. Some of them created an organisation called the "Sacred Company" (*Svyashchonnaya druzhina*). It was to be secret and conspiratorial, and was intended to ensure the protection of the imperial family, to infiltrate the ranks of the revolutionaries and to organise counter-revolutionary propaganda. The first task was entrusted to a "Voluntary Defence" section, which had committees in the two capitals and was ready to watch the streets during visits of members of the imperial family. The second task could hardly be successful, if only because the revolutionary organisation had been broken up after the assassination. The third task was handled with some ingenuity. The Company had influence over two papers published by Russian exiles. In one it attacked the "People's Will" from the point of view of the moderate revolutionaries. In the other it put out revolutionary ideas in wildly fantastic language with the aim of making them ridiculous. It is doubtful whether in fact the Company had any importance. It is interesting mainly as an indication of the ideas held at the time by some extreme conservatives on the means of combating revolution. The existence of the Company was intended to be a secret, but became known to the public through the indiscretions of officials. Its name thus became a symbol of reaction in the eyes of Russian liberals and democrats, and as such was long remembered. Its total membership appears to have been only 700, though 14,000 persons were believed to have belonged to the Voluntary Defence. It dissolved itself in November 1882, by which time the activities of the official police and administration were sufficient to satisfy all conservatives.[1]

Loris-Melikov's successor as Minister of the Interior was Count Ignatiev, the eminent Panslav and former ambassador in Constantinople. Ignatiev took his ideas on internal politics from the Slavophiles. Like them, he felt that the bureaucracy needed reform. He appointed a commission to examine the working of the administration, under the senator Kahanov. The commission made some proposals for reform of the police, and also considered the replacement of the existing cantonal authority, which treated the peasants as a separate class under special law and custom, by a new authority which would cover all classes in each canton. Ignatiev also carried out several reforms to the advantage of the peasantry. All this reforming zeal displeased Pobedonostsev, who had originally approved of the Tsar's choice of Ignatiev in the belief that he was a "safe" reactionary. In the spring of 1882 Ignatiev went still further, and proposed to the Tsar the creation of a consultative assembly, to be based on the *zemskii sobor* of the sixteenth and seventeenth centuries.[2] This had long been the aim of the Slavophiles, who believed that such assemblies would re-establish an ideal contact between people and Tsar, which they believed had existed in the past. They hoped that the assemblies would short-cut the bureaucracy, which they regarded as a pernicious growth of the eighteenth and nineteenth centuries and a

[1] For details on this organisation, see *Krasny Arhiv*, XXI, pp. 200–17.
[2] See above, p. 23.

result of German influence encouraged by Peter the Great and his successors. Ignatiev's project was prepared by a Moscow Slavophile intellectual named Golohvastov. It provided for an assembly representing all classes of Russian society and numbering some 3,000 persons. It was wildly impracticable, and would not in fact have been more than a sort of parade before the Tsar of his devoted subjects. But it was enough for Pobedonostsev, who had now lost all confidence in Ignatiev, and was able to convince the emperor that this was a sinister preliminary manœuvre for the creation of a constitution. Ignatiev was dismissed, and in his place was appointed Count Dmitri Tolstoy, the former Minister of Education, friend of Pobedonostsev and convinced conservative.[1]

One of Tolstoy's first measures was to strengthen the police. One of the Assistant Ministers of the Interior was placed in direct control of the gendarmerie and of the Department of Police. By a decree of July 1882 this official was given authority, in matters of State security, over all ranks of both gendarmerie and general police. City police chiefs, provincial governors and city commandants were subordinated in these matters to him. In 1883 the Judicial Department of the Ministry of the Interior was merged with the Department of Police. Special courts continued to exist for various offences, and even judges of regular courts were increasingly subordinated to the Minister of Justice. A decree of 1885 empowered the Minister to demand "explanations" from all ranks of the judicial hierarchy and to give "warnings" and "indications" to them.[2] Administrative arrest and exile continued to be used, though the suggestion was made by officials of the Ministry that it should be abolished, as it was not a sufficient deterrent. Reform of the prisons was discussed but little change was made. In the years 1879–89 a number of new prisons were built, and in the latter year their administration was handed from the Ministry of Interior to the Ministry of Justice. Conditions in penal settlements, in the Far East and Sahalin, were made more severe.[3]

In August 1882 censorship was tightened again. Newspapers which had been three times "warned" by the censor were thenceforth obliged to submit their texts to the censor one day before publication. This regulation was not relaxed until 1901, when it was decreed that the duration of one "warning" could not exceed one

[1] There is a good summary of these events in Kizevetter, *Na rubezhe dvuh stoletiy* (Prague, 1929), pp. 112–24.
[2] *O.D.*, Vol. I, p. 437.
[3] *Ministerstvo Vnutrennih Dyel, istoricheskii ocherk* (SPB, 1902), Vol. III, p. 215.

year, or of two "warnings" two years, after which the paper could start again with a clear record. In 1882 was also created a Special Conference, consisting of the Ministers of Interior, Justice and Education and the Procurator of the Holy Synod, with power to suspend or suppress any periodical considered "specially harmful", and to forbid an editor or a publisher from ever carrying on his profession in future. In 1884 were issued special regulations on public libraries and reading-rooms. Particular attention was paid to those to which access was free and to those used by the poorer classes. By an instruction of 1888 of the Ministry of Education, these were allowed to contain only such books as had been approved by the Scientific Committee of the Ministry. Later the instruction was extended to include all publications that had been passed for secondary schools or by the church hierarchy. In 1890 the opening of libraries or reading-rooms with small subscriptions or with none was made dependent on permission by the provincial governors' offices. The government also tried to spread "sound" ideas among the peasants by a periodical, *The Village Courier*, and a series of small books known as *God Help*. The mentality of the censors is indicated by some recurrent official phrases. For instance a frequent ground for the banning of some work from a library was that it "does not correspond to the level of intellectual development and understanding of the simple people". On the other hand, the authorities were encouraged to spread "information which has as its aim the development and maintenance among the people of religious and moral convictions."[1]

In 1884 the government introduced a new statute for the universities, to replace the liberal statute of 1863. This reduced the autonomy of the university, weakened the council of professors, and put an end to the election of university officers by the members of the university. The Rector was to be appointed in future by the Minister of Education, and the Deans of faculties by the Curators. The new statute strengthened the powers of the inspectors over the students.

Tolstoy also took steps to confirm the privileged position of the nobility. In April 1885, the centenary of Catherine II's privileges,[2] an imperial manifesto was issued in which it was stated to be essential that "Russian nobles should keep their leading position in the conduct of war, affairs of local administration and courts, and in the diffusion by their own example of the rules of faith and loyalty and sound principles of national education". The first concrete

---

[1] *Ministerstvo Vnutrennih Dyel, loc. cit.*, pp. 217–20.   [2] See above, pp. 12, 16,

expression of these intentions was the foundation in the same year
of the Nobles' Bank.[1] In 1889 came the abolition of elected justices
of peace, and their replacement by nominated "Land Commandants" from the ranks of the nobility, with both administrative and
judicial powers over the peasants. This law was prepared at the
orders of Tolstoy by a former marshal of the district nobility in
Simbirsk province named Pazuhin, who had made a reputation by a
pamphlet in defence of the traditional class system as the foundation
of the Russian State.[2] A further step in the same direction were the
zemstvo regulations of 1890, introduced by I. N. Durnovo, who
succeeded Tolstoy on the latter's death in 1889. These reduced the
proportion of peasant representation in the district zemstvo
assemblies, and made it less representative. They provided that
the peasant electors[3] should not directly elect their representatives
but choose a list of candidates from which the governor would select
those who were to sit in the assembly.

In November 1894 Alexander III died and was succeeded by his
son Nicholas. The new Tsar had his father's reactionary outlook
without his father's strength of character. He had personal charm
and natural intelligence. He liked to make a good impression and
was easily influenced. This led him often to change his mind, to
raise hopes and disappoint them, and to give those who worked
with him an impression of deceitfulness which may or may not
have been justified. Yet most of those whom he treated badly seem
to have succumbed to his charm, and few could bear a grudge
against him.[4] His prejudices were those of a Russian conservative
landowner—nationalism, anti-semitism, contempt for the "rabble"
combined with paternal affection for the peasants, at least as far
as he understood them. His virtues were those of the same class.
He was a devoted husband and father, loved the country and wild
life, and was a good landlord. Of constitutional, social and economic problems he understood little. Even in foreign affairs, of
which he knew much more, his attitude was essentially personal.
He was greatly influenced by his wife, Princess Alexandra of Hesse-
Darmstadt, who, having embraced the Orthodox religion, became
a fanatical supporter of Russian autocracy and constantly urged
Nicholas to perform his duty to God by upholding it unchanged.
Neither he nor his wife was a good judge of character. They
chose as their advisers inferior bureaucrats or mere adventurers,

[1] See above, p. 110.   [2] Kizevetter, *op. cit.*, pp. 143–5.   [3] See above, pp. 49–50.
[4] The exception was Witte, who writes maliciously of Nicholas in his memoirs.
On the other hand, Kokovtsov and Rodzianko both show affection despite the
injustice they suffered. See also below, pp. 252, 268, 271.

and when they were served by men of real qualities failed to appreciate their value.

Under the next three Ministers of Interior there was little change in government policy. The first two, Durnovo (1889–95) and Goremykin (1895–9) were colourless bureaucrats, the third, Sipyagin (1899–1902) a reactionary landowner. The main feature of this period was the struggle between the Ministries of Interior and Finance, to which we have already had cause to refer in connection with agricultural and industrial development.[1] The series of conferences and committees on the needs of agriculture set up in the years 1901–3 threw into relief the conflict between the central authorities and the zemstvos. In this conflict the position of the Minister of Finance Witte was ambiguous. In a long memorandum addressed to Goremykin in 1899, and published in Struve's exile paper *Osvobozhdenie*,[2] Witte had argued that autocracy and zemstvo institutions are incompatible, that one or the other must go.[3] He stated that he preferred autocay to a constitution of the Western type, which was the inevitable result of the process that had begun when zemstvos were introduced. But if autocracy was to be maintained, the administration must be radically improved, and for this the co-operation of Russian society with the authorities was essential. He believed that the government could and should make use of what he called "the Russian man's capacity to think of himself not otherwise than as a member of a social union". This was the language of the Slavophiles, of Ignatiev's "Zemskii Sobor" of 1882. It is not clear what were Witte's aims, apart from his desire to discredit the Ministry of Interior as responsible for the bureaucracy whose faults he decried. Witte was no romantic looking back to the days of Ivan the Terrible. Much of his memorandum can be interpreted as a plea in favour of development on Western lines, though he was at pains to deny such a wish. In general, Witte and his Ministry stood for the modernisation of Russia, above all economic, but to some extent inevitably political. They supported the rising Russian capitalism against the traditional bureaucracy and the political ideas associated therewith. Though Witte no doubt disliked zemstvo institutions and the zemstvo leaders, he was less hostile to them than were the old bureaucrats, and he was willing to use them for his own ends against his rivals.

Some reforms were carried out at the beginning of the century.

---

[1] See above, pp. 114, 126–7.   [2] See below, p. 146.
[3] Witte, *Samoderzhavie i zemstvo* (Stuttgart, 1901).

The manifesto of 26th February/11th March 1903 promised religious toleration and economic and administrative measures to the advantage of the agricultural population, both peasants and landlords. The abolition of collective responsibility for taxes and the new factory labour legislation have already been mentioned.[1] The St. Petersburg municipal franchise was extended to include a section of the professional class which did not own houses. At the same time the police force in the countryside was increased, in order to guard against a repetition of the disorders which had taken place in 1902. Special village police guards were created, and their expenses were to be covered by taxation of the peasants.

In August 1903 Witte was removed from the Ministry of Finance. The new Minister of the Interior, V. K. von Pleve, believed above all in repression. He also believed that a "small victorious war" would have a salutary effect on Russian opinion, and would divert the people's thoughts from revolution. But before the war with Japan had ended, not in victory but in defeat, Pleve had lost his life and the Russian State had been shaken to its foundations.[2]

Despite restrictions and hostility, the zemstvos had considerable achievements to their credit during this period. In the first decades after 1864 they had, as we have seen, been greatly impeded by the obligation to carry out at their own expense various duties on behalf of the central administration. These obligations were however reduced in 1895 and in 1901. By 1903 they took up only 8 per cent of zemstvo expenditure. The main sources of revenue were the taxes on land and on immovable non-agricultural property. In 1903 the first yielded 47 million roubles to the zemstvos, the second 16 million roubles. A regulation of 1900, by which zemstvo revenues were not to increase by more than 3 per cent in one year, did less damage to the zemstvos than might have been expected, and was not in fact strictly observed. There were great variations between different areas. In 1901 fifty district zemstvos derived more than 70 per cent of their revenue from land tax, while forty-seven derived less than 30 per cent. For provincial zemstvos, the share of land tax in revenues averaged 20–40 per cent (in three cases out of thirty-four it was more than 50 per cent and in two cases less than 10 per cent). In 1903 the main items of expenditure were as follows:

---

[1] See above, pp. 114, 128.   See below, pp. 220 ff.

DISTRICT ZEMSTVOS (average for all districts affected)

administration	..	5–10 per cent
roads	..	1– 3 „
education	..	20 „
medical	..	25–30 „
economic measures	..	3 „

PROVINCIAL ZEMSTVOS (average for all provinces affected)

administration	..	10–15 per cent
roads	..	5 „
education	..	5–15 „
medical	..	25–30 „

Elementary education was the concern of the district zemstvos, secondary of the provincial. Little progress was made in either field before 1890, but then the pace quickened. In 1903 it was estimated that the establishment of universal primary education, then one of the main demands of Russian liberal opinion, could be achieved by doubling existing facilities.· Medical services were still of poor quality, and depended too much on semi-skilled medical orderlies in the absence of qualified doctors in many areas. From the turn of the century however standards greatly improved. The increased organisation of the medical profession itself contributed notably to this result.[1]

The Political Revival

The regime of Dmitrii Tolstoy and Pobedonostsev silenced political opinion in Russia, but did not prevent educated Russians from thinking about politics. Contact with political ideas was still possible by travelling or studying abroad, and the writings of Russian political exiles penetrated in small numbers into Russia.

The only free political discussions among Russians in the eighties thus took place abroad, especially in Switzerland. Here were groups of Populists and also the first important Russian Marxist group. The latter was called the "Liberation of Labour". Its leaders were Plehanov, Akselrod and Vera Zasulich. All three had been active in "Land and Liberty", and had followed the "Black Partition" fraction after the split of 1879. In exile they became converted to Marxism, and Plehanov became not only the greatest

[1] The work of the zemstvos in the first forty years of their existence is carefully described and analysed in B. Veselovski, *Istoria zemstva za sorok let* (SPB, 1909), 2 vols. The first volume contains information on revenue and expenditure, public health and education, the second on economic activities.

of Russian Marxist theorists but a great figure in the whole international Marxist movement. The group was formed in 1883, and in the following year published two pamphlets by Plehanov which have an important place in Russian political history.

The first was entitled *Our Differences*, and put the Marxist case against Populist theories. Its main argument was that in Russia as in other countries socialism cannot be based on the peasantry and the bourgeoisie, but only on the industrial working class. The liberation of the workers can come only from their own conscious efforts. The growth of the working class is an inevitable result of the growth of capitalism, which is going ahead in Russia. The village commune is an anachronism, a survival of the pre-capitalist order. It will yield place not to a special Russian form of agrarian socialism but to capitalism. Only when capitalism has replaced the old economic system of Russia will advance towards socialism be possible.

In the second pamphlet, *Socialism and the Political Struggle*, Plehanov argued that the preparation of the socialist revolution cannot be separated from action in the political field. Russian socialists must not only educate and organise the workers, but must also fight against the Tsar's autocracy. With these views, Plehanov was denying his earlier beliefs as a member of "Black Partition".

These ideas were discussed in intellectual circles inside Russia in the eighties. In the nineties they even began to be discussed in camouflaged form in the legal press. The censors would of course at once suppress any discussion of political action. The fight against the autocracy could not be mentioned. But arguments about economic doctrine did not appear dangerous to the censors. And so the controversy on the role of the village commune, the main point of dispute between Populists and Marxists, could be conducted in public, both in newspaper articles and at gatherings of university students and teachers.

Far the most important of the Populist writers was N. K. Mihailovski. A man of independent thought and integrity, Mihailovski does not easily fit into any precise political category. He was a moralist and a philosopher as well as a politician. He first attracted attention by an article "What is Progress?" published in 1869 in the liberal periodical *Otechestvennie zapiski* (Notes of the Fatherland). He was always a champion of individual freedom, and of the development of the individual personality. He opposed excessive specialisation and division of labour. He considered that the life of a peasant was more balanced than that of a worker. He wished to see Russia spared the agonies of capitalism, but did not close his eyes to the facts of capitalist development. He wrote some of the articles of the "People's Will" underground press in 1879–80. He stressed the necessity of political action both then and later. During the eighties and nineties he made it his task to express in the legal press, in disguised and "Aesopian" form, the main ideas of the revolutionary movement. He was a fierce defender of social utilitarianism in literature, and attacked Tolstoy for his doctrine of non-resistance. Though difficult to define, Mihailovski's influence was immense, up to his death in 1904 and even after. To a whole generation of Russians he was not merely a political and moral theorist, but a great preacher and master, indeed a prophet.[1]

Two other important Populist writers were V. P. Voronstov and N. Danielson, who wrote under the pseudonyms "VV" and "N.—on". Vorontsov wrote in the periodical *Russkoe Bogatstvo* ("Russia's Wealth"). He defended the Populist cause chiefly on the general ideological plane, Danielson on the economic. The Marxists did not have a paper of the standing of *Russkoe Bogatstvo*, but controlled for brief periods several provincial papers which acquired an ephemeral fame in intellectual circles before the censors discovered that Marxism was a subversive doctrine. The two most important were *Samarskii Vestnik* in Samara (1896–7) and *Novoe Slovo* in St. Petersburg (1897–9). The chief spokesmen of Marxist economic doctrines in Russia at this time were P. B. Struve and Tugan-Baranovski. Two younger men who also made a contribution to Marxist economic studies in Russia in the nineties were A. Potresov and V. I. Ulyanov, known to history as Lenin.[2]

The philosophical arguments seem, after sixty years, to have lost the qualities which then roused passions on both sides. But the economic arguments are essential to an understanding of Russia's development. Danielson the Populist admitted that capitalism had made some progress in Russia, but maintained that it had impoverished, not enriched the economy, and could not develop much

---

[1] On Mihailovski, apart from his own works, see Ovsyanniko-Kulikovski, *Istoria russkoy intelligentsii* (SPB, 1912), Vol. VIII; Y. Gardenin (V. M. Chernov), *K pamyati N. K. Mihailovskovo*, (1904).

[2] Among the more important books in this controversy may be mentioned: V. P. Vorontsov ("VV"), *Nashi napravlenia* (SPB., 1893); N. Danielson ("N.—on"), *Ocherki nashevo poreformennovo hozyaistva* (SPB, 1893); P. B. Struve, *Kriticheskie zametki k voprosu ob ekonomicheskom razvitii Rossii* (SPB, 1894); V. I. Lenin ("V. Ilyin"), *Razvitie kapitalizma v Rossii* (SPB, 1899); Tugan-Baranovski, *Istoria russkoy fabriki* (SPB, 1898). All these were passed by the censor. Lenin's polemic against the Populists, *What are the Friends of the People?* was produced and circulated secretly.

further. Capitalist industry had damaged local industry. Peasants
in central Russia no longer made their own clothes, but bought them
from the towns, to which they were obliged to sell, at low prices, an
increased proportion of their crops. The Russian people were
worse fed and worse clad, and had been deprived of subsidiary
employment from which they had previously won considerable
earnings. The advance of capitalism had been achieved at the
expense of the economy as a whole. The internal market, which
capitalism should serve, was not expanding. "The limits of the
development of capitalism are set by the growing poverty, which is
itself caused by its development, by the growing number of
workers who have no employment and cannot obtain employment."
Obviously, Danielson argued, there could be no return to the past.
The only way forward was "to develop the productive forces of the
population in such a form that they can be used not by an insignificant minority but by the whole people". The peasant commune
was to be the instrument of this change. The technique of modern
agriculture and industry must be adapted to the commune. The
commune would thus become "a suitable instrument to organise
big industry and to transform big industry from a capitalistic form
to a social form".[1]

Struve maintained that Danielson's arguments were disproved
by the facts. It was of course true that the Russian people were
worse fed and clad, and that unemployment was growing. These
evils had been clearly and horribly exposed by the famine of
1891–2. But they were due, not to capitalism, but to the effects of
the period of serfdom. It was not true that capitalism was not
developing an internal market: the facts of railway building and
metallurgical construction showed the contrary. Struve denounced
as "national vanity" the idea that Russia could take a short cut, and
could "by the constructions of our own critical thought", escape
"the long difficult cultural work and the efforts of generations, the
fierce struggle of social classes, economic forces and interests".
His concluding sentence was, "No, let us confess our lack of
culture, and go and take a lesson from capitalism".[2]

[1] Danielson, *op. cit.*, pp. 343–4.
[2] Struve, *op. cit.*, p. 288. Marx himself preserved an open mind on Russia's prospect of avoiding capitalism. He admired Chernyshevski, and learnt Russian in order
to study the economic and social problems of Russia. In the preface to the Russian
edition (1882) of the Communist Manifesto, Marx and Engels wrote, " If a Russian
revolution serves as a signal for a workers' revolution in the West, so that both com-
plement each other, then the contemporary Russian form of land tenure may be the
starting-point of communistic development". In a letter addressed to " *Otechestvennie Zapiski*" in 1883, and provoked by an article of N. K. Mihailovski, Marx

It is important to note the apparent similarity between the views of the Marxists and the supporters of capitalism, and of the Populists and the supporters of bureaucratic paternalism. The similarity was of course superficial. Both Marxists and Populists were revolutionaries. Both intended to destroy the autocratic state. But since the censorship made it impossible to mention political aims, the economic arguments of the two opposing groups appeared to be a defence either of capitalism or of the old order in the villages. The Marxists wished to speed up the development of capitalism in Russia, in order that the conditions which they considered essential for the preparation of socialist revolution should quickly be achieved. The capitalists wished to speed up capitalism because that was their real interest. The Populists wished to preserve the village commune and the artisan artel from the onslaught of capitalism in order that they might be transformed into organs of socialist government. They therefore urged the authorities to protect commune and artel in the columns of *Russkoe Bogatstvo*. The paternalist bureaucrats wished to preserve these institutions because they regarded them as the very antithesis of instruments of revolution. They believed them to be strongholds of the old Russian national spirit, bulwarks against the tide of Western, individualist, disintegrating influence. The hostility between Russian capitalism and Russian paternalism was of great benefit to both types of Russian revolutionary. These two trends within the ruling class and the government machine were represented respectively by the Ministry of Finance and the Ministry of the Interior. Ministry of Interior and Populists both wished to save the commune, Ministry of Finance and Marxists to abolish it. Ministry of Interior and Marxists agreed in their analysis of the commune, which made the former defend it and the latter attack it. Ministry of Finance and Populists agreed that capitalism was an obstacle to revolution, which caused the former to encourage it and the latter to denounce it. The Ministry of Interior distrusted the supporters of capitalism as liberals, almost revolutionaries, while the Populists condemned them as reactionaries. The Ministry of Finance attacked the Ministry of Interior as an obstacle to the growth of a sound and truly conservative Russia, the Marxists attacked it as a bulwark of the old order they were sworn to destroy.

---

wrote that if the Russian revolution were delayed, Russia would "miss the rarest and most suitable opportunity, ever offered to a country, to avoid the phase of capitalistic development". If the opportunity were missed, then Russia would "fall under the sway of the ineluctable laws" of capitalism. This letter is quoted as an appendix to Gardenin (Chernov), *op. cit.*

Not only the two branches of socialism, but also liberalism, made progress during the nineties. The centre of the more moderate form of liberalism were the zemstvos. A generation of experience in local administration had given zemstvo men confidence in their ability to govern. They felt that the powers of elected bodies should be extended. They began to discuss broad national issues, especially the introduction of universal elementary education and the abolition of corporal punishment of peasants. They also felt, like their predecessors in the sixties, that there should be some central elected assembly, which the bolder spirits wished to be legislative while the more conservative would have been content that it should be consultative. The accession of Nicholas II raised hopes. The Tver zemstvo, in its address to the new sovereign, expressed the hope that "the voice of the people's need will always be heard from the height of the throne". In reply to these innocuous words, the Tsar referred to "senseless dreams of the participation of zemstvo representatives in the affairs of internal administration", and declared his firm resolve to maintain the principle of autocracy.

The presence at the coronation of Nicholas II in 1896 of the presidents of all zemstvo administrations caused one of their number, D. N. Shipov, of Moscow, to suggest that yearly congresses of presidents be held. The first congress was held the same year in Nizhni Novgorod. It discussed matters of general interest to zemstvos, including the critical state of agriculture, the food supply, and elementary education for all. The second congress was to be held in 1897 in St. Petersburg, but was banned by order of the Minister of Interior Goremykin.

The more radical branch of Russian liberalism was associated with the professional classes, and especially with the considerable number of experts employed by the zemstvos. These became known by a name first uttered by the Governor of Samara province at the opening of his provincial assembly in 1899—"the third element".[1] From the mid-nineties, professional congresses began to be frequent. In 1896, for example, there were congresses of agricultural experts, doctors, and teachers in technical establishments. All of these demanded the introduction of universal elementary education and abolition of corporal punishment.

During the nineties university students began to be an important political force. In Moscow university a body called the Union Council (*soyuzny soviet*) was formed, which was supposed to

[1] Kizevetter, *op. cit.*, p. 226.

defend the direct interests of the students in relations with the authorities. It was composed of representatives of the various clubs of students from the same part of the country (*zemlyachestva*). In practice the Council did not confine itself to matters affecting the immediate interests of its members. It was influenced by political ideas, and had some contact with revolutionary groups.[1] Its example was followed in other Russian universities. These student organisations arranged meetings of protest against actions of the Ministry of Education authorities, and called "strikes" of students. To refuse to attend examinations or lectures was a form of protest which for obvious reasons was not unattractive to students. In 1895 a demonstration of students was held in Moscow to demand the repeal of the university statute of 1884 and a return to that of 1863, the abolition of inspectors, and the admission of women students to the universities. In the following year occurred the famous Hodynka disaster at the Tsar's coronation. A great crowd watched the ceremonies on a field which was crossed by rows of ditches, cut for previous military manœuvres. The police lost their heads and stampeded the crowd into the ditches. Several hundred people were crushed to death. The funeral of the victims was used as an opportunity for a student demonstration. On this occasion the student Council openly stated that its aim was "the preparation of political fighters". In November 1896 the leaders of the Council were arrested and several hundred students were expelled from the university, some sent to terms of exile. The next two years were quieter, but in 1899 there was a strike in all universities of the empire in protest against the flogging of some students by the police in St. Petersburg. The government's reply was a decree that students expelled from the university for disorders should be conscripted into the army. Those guilty of "especially harmful participation" in riots should serve for three years. In 1900 a big meeting of protest was held in Kiev. It was surrounded by police and cossacks, who arrested 500 students, of whom 200 were conscripted and the rest expelled. Further riots took place the same year in Harkov, St. Petersburg and Moscow. Student demonstrations were joined in some cases by factory workers. In this political climate it is not surprising that the extreme parties won support among students. The most successful were the Socialist Revolutionaries, whose method of assassination was more attractive to many students, as a heroic act of individual revolutionary sacrifice, than the more humdrum work of agitation among workers

[1] Kizevetter, *op. cit.*, pp. 244–6.

6

in which the Social Democrats specialised. But Marxism also had a substantial following among students. It was a student of Socialist Revolutionary sympathies who on 1st/14th February 1901 asassinated the Minister of Education, Bogolepov.

In the first three years of the new century the political temperature continued to rise. Business slump, political strikes, student disorders and liberal meetings all helped to keep it high. Professional congresses—for example, the agricultural advisers' congress in Moscow in February 1901 and the local industries' congress in Poltava in the following autumn—gave more attention than ever to political questions. It was in this year that Struve, who had now abandoned his earlier Marxism for radical liberalism, proposed to the leaders of the constitutionalists in the zemstvos and in the free professions the foundation of a liberal newspaper abroad. The idea was well received, and in 1902 Struve went to Germany and began publication, in Stuttgart, of the journal which was called *Osvobozhdenie* (Liberation).

In April 1902 the Minister of the Interior, Sipyagin, was assassinated by a Socialist-Revolutionary. His successor was the former Head of the Police, and recent Secretary of State for Finland, V. K. von Pleve. Despite occasional fair words to zemstvo representatives, Pleve in practice opposed all attempts by the zemstvos to take a larger share in public affairs. Official rebukes were administered to prominent zemstvo men who had dared to discuss broad political issues. The manifesto of 26th February/11th March 1903 and the trifling concessions of Pleve to the zemstvos of March 1904 could not satisfy even the most moderate liberal opinion.

In the summer of 1903 a meeting of zemstvo leaders with Struve and his colleagues in Stuttgart resulted in the formation of the "League of Liberation". The League's programme was discussed at a zemstvo congress in Harkov in September 1903. It won the support of the professional organisations, the "third element" and the more radical zemstvo assemblies. Organisations of the League were set up in the main political centres. Thus at the outbreak of the war with Japan, Russian liberalism was a force to be reckoned with.

The Social Democratic Movement

The first organised Marxist groups inside Russia were formed during the eighties in several cities. The earliest seems to have been founded in 1883 among technological students in St. Petersburg.

Its leader was a Bulgarian named Dimiter Blagoyev, who later became the founder of the Bulgarian Socialist, and later still the Communist Party. It had some contact with the workers of the Putilov factory. A second group was the "Society of Petersburg Manual Workers" created by a Pole named Tochinski in 1886 and divided into a workers' and an intellectuals' section. A third group in Kazan in 1888 was led by Fedoseev and had some influence in central Russia. One of its members was the young Ulyanov (Lenin). A fourth in 1889 in St. Petersburg was the "Social Democratic Society" created by Brusnev and composed of technological students. It closely followed German Social Democracy, circulated duplicated proclamations, and organised in 1891 a May Day demonstration of one hundred workers. These organisations were little more than secret study and discussion groups. Their organisers were students. In so far as factory workers were drawn into their activities, it was for education in socialist ideas rather than for action. The only visible concrete achievement was the publication for a short time by the Blagoyev group of an illegal paper *Rabochii*, whose readers were only a few dozen people. Nevertheless these early groups had their importance in training leaders for later action.

Another centre of Marxist ideas was Vilna, the chief city of the Lithuanian borderlands, whose population was largely Jewish.[1] The Vilna Marxists felt that secret study groups were not advancing the cause. Contact with the masses was essential, and required new methods. Marxists must find out what issues most interested the workers, and agitate along these lines. They would gain their confidence by making themselves spokesmen for their grievances. Having gained their confidence, they could begin to organise them into a political force. The most important task of revolutionaries must thus be "agitation", defined as the presentation of one idea to many people, rather than "propaganda", the presentation of many ideas to a few leaders. In the immediate future, day-to-day matters affecting the workers' life were more important than "politics". Some of these ideas were expressed in a famous pamphlet, *On Agitation*, written by Arkadii Kremer, with the assistance of Julius Martov. Though it provoked opposition from the champions of the secret study groups, who accused its authors of neglecting the education of workers in political issues, it served to concentrate the attention of Russian Marxists on the need for contact with workers.

[1] The beginnings of the Marxist movement in Vilna are described in the memoirs of Martov, *Zapiski Sotsial-Demokrata* (Berlin, 1922).

In 1895 a more efficient Marxist organisation was built in St. Petersburg. Formed from two secret groups, which bore the nicknames "The Old" and "The Young", it took the name "League of Combat for the Liberation of the Working Class". Among its leaders were Lenin and Martov, both of whom had now come to St. Petersburg. Branches of the League were also formed in Moscow and Ekaterinoslav. In 1896 a group was created in Kiev with the name "Workers' Cause". It published an illegal paper, *Vperyod* ("Forward"). The St. Petersburg league strongly opposed the non-political tendency. It took part in the workers' day-to-day struggles, stressed economic issues, and played a part in organising and supporting the textile strikes of 1896 and 1897. But it also emphasised the need for a political struggle against the autocracy. In December 1895 the police caught most of the League's leaders, including Lenin. The manuscript of the first number of its illegal newspaper, *Rabochee Delo* ("Workers' Cause") was found on the person of one of those arrested, and so was never printed. In January 1896 Martov and some other leaders were caught. Those arrested were sent to banishment for some years in Siberia, but a remnant of the League continued its activity.

The controversy about the necessity of a political struggle was not decided, and still divided the working-class organisations. In 1897 a group was created in St. Petersburg which opposed the use of political slogans and resented the influence of non-worker intellectuals in the incipient working-class movement. This point of view was expressed in the illegal paper *Rabochaya Mysl* ("Workers' Thought"). Its chief exponent was Tahtarev.[1] This group co-operated with the League in St. Petersburg but neither wholly trusted the other. In 1898 an agreement was made by which *Rabochaya Mysl* became the official mouthpiece of the two groups but the struggle for control of its policy continued. It was decided to hold a congress of existing Marxist groups and to form a Russian Social Democratic Workers' Party. This took place at Minsk in February 1898. Representatives were present from the League's branches, from the Kiev Committee and from the Jewish Socialist Party (the "Bund").[2] The programme of the new party was drawn up by Struve, who was then still a theoretical Marxist but had hitherto stood aside from the political struggle. The manifesto stressed the leading role of the industrial workers in the struggle for political freedom in Russia. A memorable passage stated: "The further to the east one goes in Europe, the weaker in politics,

---

[1] See Peterburzhets, *op. cit.*   [2] See below, p. 160.

the more cowardly and the meaner becomes the bourgeoisie, the greater are the cultural and political tasks that fall to the lot of the proletariat." The party statute allowed a relatively loose organisation. The Bund was allowed to enter it while remaining "autonomous only in questions touching specially the Jewish proletariat". Local committees of the party were to execute the instructions of its Central Committee in the form which they might consider most suited to local conditions. In exceptional cases they had the right to refuse to execute the Central Committee's demands, and would then inform it of their reasons for refusal.

Almost immediately after the congress, the new party's central committee was caught by the police and arrested. There had been no time to set up a new organisation. The tenth article of the Statute had said that the "League of Russian Social Democrats Abroad" was a part of the party and its foreign representative. This body was located in Switzerland, and now took over the functions of party leadership. It was in exile that the important internal controversies of Russian Social Democracy took place in the next few years.[1]

The League Abroad had been set up in 1895. It included within its ranks both Plehanov's "Liberation of Labour" group and the supporters of the St. Petersburg *Rabochaya Mysl* which was now printed outside Russia. The League's official paper was *Rabochii* ("The Worker"). But within the League the controversy on the political struggle raged, and the non-political tendency, which became known as "Economism", prevailed. The name of the paper was changed to *Rabochee Delo*, and it took a non-political attitude, though less markedly so than *Rabochaya Mysl*. Plehanov was strongly opposed to this tendency. He published in 1899 the pamphlet *Once more Socialism and the Political Struggle*, reiterating in up-to-date form his arguments of 1884. In 1899 the "Economists" abroad published a pamphlet, written by Kuskova, which became known under the name *The Credo*, and which defended the tactics of "Economism". It argued that Social Democrats should concern themselves with the organisation of the workers' economic and social struggle only. The political struggle against the Tsar should

[1] For the history of Russian Marxism up to 1914 the best single work is Martov and Dan, *Geschichte der russischen Sozialdemokratie* (Berlin, 1926). The works of Lenin are of course indispensable. The version of the party's history in favour at the present moment in the U.S.S.R. is the *Short History of the All-Union Communist Party (Bolshevik)*, published in 1937 in Moscow under the personal supervision of Stalin and since translated into many languages. This should be used with caution. Other works will be quoted in later footnotes.

be left to the middle-class liberals: to the proletariat it was of minor interest. The argument was in essence the same as Plehanov himself had used 20 years earlier against People's Will. *Credo* was answered abroad by Plehanov's *Vademecum* and Akselrod's *Letters to the Comrades*, and in Russia provoked the protests of the three leaders of the League of Combat banished in Siberia—Lenin, Potresov and Dan. In their banishment they enjoyed considerable freedom of speech, and found means of sending their written views abroad. Yet a third group at this time were the so-called "Legal Marxists", the most eminent of whom was Tugan-Baranovski. Their policy was similar to that of the "revisionist" section of Bernstein within the German Social Democratic Party. They put forward Marxist economic views, but in their political attitude became hardly distinguishable from liberals.

It was increasingly felt that the schism in the party must be brought to an end, and the best means seemed to be another congress. Lenin and his group of exiles were allowed to return to European Russia in 1900, and began to plan for the new congress. Arrests in the southern cities in this year delayed the arrangements, and Lenin and Potresov decided to go abroad. Their supporters who remained in Russia were instructed to spread their view of the importance of the political struggle, and to capture for this view as many as possible of the underground Marxist committees in Russian cities.

The "political" group of exiles set up in Munich a paper called *Iskra* ("The Spark"), which was smuggled back into Russia and was read by considerable numbers. Its editors were Lenin, Martov, Plehanov, Akselrod and Potresov. In 1902 appeared Lenin's pamphlet, *What is to be Done?* Its title was taken from Chernyshevski's novel. In it Lenin argued for a strongly centralised and disciplined party, to consist of "professional revolutionaries". These would at first come mainly from the intelligentsia, but recruits from the working class must be found and trained as soon as possible. The party must form the revolutionary vanguard, leading the workers' masses forward. Special attention must be paid to Marxist theory, which alone could effectively unify and discipline the revolutionaries. Lenin particularly denounced mere "trade unionism", and what he called an "elemental" policy. This meant any tendency to leave the initiative to the masses themselves, to follow passively behind the movement of the workers for economic betterment.[1] The revolutionaries must educate the workers. They

---

[1] Another name also used for this sin by Lenin and his Soviet successors is "Hvostizm" (Tail-ism), or following behind the tail of the workers.

must explain to them the political obstacles to the attainment of their economic aims, and show them that they could only improve their lot by fighting the political power of the ruling class. To ignore political issues just because the workers were not naturally interested in them was mere defeatism. The party must understand the workers' interests better than the workers themselves, and lead them into battle for them.

In July 1903 the second congress of the party met, first in Brussels and then in London. Its most important discussions concerned the nature and organisation of the party. Lenin argued for a centralised disciplined party of professional revolutionaries, even if in practice it would have to be small in numbers. Quality was more important than quantity. The test was to be the first article of the proposed party Statute, which laid down the conditions for membership of the party. Lenin wished to admit only those who would take an active part in one of the party's organisations. The opposite point of view was that anyone who accepted the party's political programme should be allowed to enter, even if this meant that many party members would not be active. This point of view was argued by Martov, although he had been Lenin's colleague on *Iskra*, which had stood for a centralised disciplined party. At the congress Martov's view prevailed over Lenin's. [2]

Shortly after the debate on the Statute, however, the representatives of the Jewish Bund left the congress and seceded from the party, as they had not obtained their demand for federal status within the party as the exclusive representatives of the Jewish workers. Their defection gave the followers of Lenin a majority in the congress. The next discussion was on the composition of the editorial board of *Iskra*, which was to be the official organ of the party, and was to be published as before in exile. The division of votes on this issue gave Lenin's group the victory. It is from this vote that were taken the names which became attached thenceforth to the two sects into which the party was divided—"majoritarians" (Bolsheviks) and "minoritarians" (Mensheviks).

Some months later the positions were reversed. Plehanov, who had at first sided with Lenin, was impressed by the amount of support shown to the Menshevik case at a conference of the League Abroad, held in Geneva, and suggested that the old editors of *Iskra*— Martov and Potresov, now Mensheviks—should be co-opted on to

---

[2] The text of the Congress proceedings is to be found in *Vtoroy ocherednoy s'yezd R.S.D.R.P.* (London, 1903). See also Lenin's pamphlet, *One Step Forward, Two Steps Back*, first published in Russian in Geneva in 1904.

the editorial board. Lenin refused, and when Plehanov insisted he
resigned. In the summer of 1904 *Iskra* thus passed under Menshevik control, while Lenin founded a "Union of Committees of
the Majority", with its own "Bureau" and its own paper *Vperyod*
("Forward"). Henceforth there were in fact two separate Russian
Marxist parties.

The whole episode seems trivial when the bare succession of facts
is related. To many members of the party at the time it appeared
an unedifying wrangle between hair-splitting doctrinaires, or a bad-
tempered clash of personalities. Yet it was not a trivial issue. It
was in some sense a repetition, in a new movement, of the quarrel
which had split "Land and Liberty" after the congress of Lipetsk
in 1879. It was an important issue, which any revolutionary
organisation working in an autocratic state must face. From this
dispute on party organisation, and the clash between Lenin and
Martov, developed, as we shall see later, vital differences of policy.
Much more was to happen before the Russian Marxist movement
was irreparably split, and before Russian Bolshevism broke with
European socialism. But the first origins of the breach are to be
found in the debates of the 1903 congress. It gave to history two
important words, Bolshevik and Menshevik.

The revolutionary events of 1905—discussed in a later chapter—
found the factions still separate but both asserting their desire for
reunion. In the summer of 1905 the third congress of R.S.D.R.P.
was to be held, but in fact two separate "conferences" took
place, a Bolshevik conference—which has claimed ever since the
title of "Third Congress"—in London, and a Menshevik conference—which did not claim to be a congress—in Geneva, both in
May.

In July Lenin published an important pamphlet entitled *Two
Tactics of Social-Democracy*. In it the depth of the differences
between Mensheviks and Bolsheviks began to appear more clearly.
Its main argument was that though the future Russian revolution
(which the stormy events in Russia suggested was not far off)
would be a "bourgeois revolution", taking Russia approximately
through the stages passed in France after 1789, and therefore not a
"socialist revolution", yet it must be led not by the bourgeoisie
but by the working class, in alliance with the peasantry. The
bourgeoisie was weak and cowardly. It would betray the revolution
and seek a compromise with the ruling class. But if the transformation of Russia from a still semi-feudal to a bourgeois state
could be achieved not by "reformist" but by revolutionary means,

and if the leadership in action could be maintained by the working class, then the bourgeois revolution would be of greater benefit to the workers than to the bourgeoisie. In such a policy the natural allies of the workers were the peasants. Lenin of course shared the common Marxist view that the peasantry was a politically backward class with a "petty bourgeois" outlook. He was also well aware of the divisions between rich and poor peasants. But in the struggle against Tsardom and for the partition of the great landed estates the vast majority of the peasants could be won for the revolution. Only after the bourgeois revolution had been completed would development of the class struggle in the villages become important.[1] Lenin denounced those who argued that support by the workers to peasant violence would "frighten away" the bourgeoisie into the reactionary camp, and that in order to prevent this the party should back the zemstvo liberal campaign, and merely push the liberals on from behind against the Tsar. Lenin insisted on the need to give battle-training to the workers and the peasants, to give them arms and prepare them mentally and physically for armed action, for a national uprising.

When the Tsar's regime was overthrown, Lenin argued, there would be a "provisional government" which would be a "revolutionary-democratic. dictatorship of the proletariat and the peasantry". The social and political regime which this dictatorship would install would be bourgeois-democratic, not socialist. But its task would be to maintain in being a revolutionary state of affairs, in order for Russia to "carry the revolutionary conflagration in to Europe". If the party, at the head of the working class, could not only win the mass of the peasantry for an armed bourgeois revolution, but could also maintain the support of the proletarian elements in the peasantry after the end of the bourgeois revolution; and if the more advanced proletariat of some major industrial country of Europe could embark on a socialist revolution, then it might be possible for Russia to pass on much sooner from the bourgeois to the socialist revolution. But Lenin did not—and indeed could not—commit himself as to the length of the period of transition between the two stages of revolution in Russia.

The Mensheviks made the same distinction between the bourgeois and socialist revolutions as did Lenin. They also admitted that the spread of revolution to Western countries would greatly assist and accelerate development in Russia. But they were

[1] For further discussion of Bolshevik, Menshevik and Socialist-Revolutionary views on the peasant problem, see below, pp. 278–280.

extremely sceptical about the revolutionary potentialities of the peasantry, and they were much less contemptuous than Lenin towards the radical elements of the urban middle class. They therefore not only regarded as inevitable, but accepted more or less contentedly the prospect of a long period of bourgeois democracy in Russia.

A third position was taken by a brilliant young Marxist, L. D. Bronstein, better known as Trotski, who soon became prominent as a leader of the St. Petersburg Soviet.[1] Trotski believed that the Russian proletariat might lead the revolution in its bourgeois stage, and so find itself in power, but he did not believe that if this had once happened the proletariat could limit itself to pursuing a bourgeois policy. Once the proletariat had power, it would have to move on to the socialist revolution. But this could not be successful in Russia unless there were a socialist revolution also in industrial Europe. Trotski's answer to the problem was not the artificial self-limitation of the proletariat to a bourgeois policy, but the "permanent revolution". In this last point Trotski's views were not far from those of Lenin. He differed from Lenin however in being sceptical—though less so than the Mensheviks—about the role of the peasantry. In questions of party organisation also he was much closer to the Mensheviks than to the Bolsheviks.[2]

Party organisation, relations with the peasantry, and the prospects of the bourgeois and socialist revolutions—these were the great questions for Russian Marxist socialism after 1903. In later chapters they will be mentioned again in connection with the events of 1905–6 and with the political issues of the last years before 1914. During those years the differences between Bolsheviks and Mensheviks spread in breadth and depth until they became quite distinct and mutually hostile movements.

The Socialist Revolutionaries

The revival of political opinion affected also the Populists. At the beginning of the nineties some of those exiled at the end of the reign of Alexander II returned from Siberia. They included the veteran Natanson, founder of "Land and Liberty", and Breshko-Breshkovskaya, who became known as the "grandmother of the

---

[1] See below, pp. 223, 224.
[2] Trotski's views were influenced by his experiences in the St. Perersburg soviet. They were expressed most clearly in his work, *The Year 1905*, published in Vienna in 1909 in German, and in Moscow in 1922 in Russian in slightly different form. There is also an Italian edition, Milano, 1948, the only copy to which I have had access.

revolution". In 1894 the first attempt was made to create a new Populist central organisation. Natanson formed a group which took the name *Narodnoe Pravo* ("The People's Right"). It had branches in some towns of central Russia and the Volga valley. It published a "Manifesto" in February 1894, in which it declared its aim to unite all oppositional elements in the country in a struggle for political liberty. Its programme included representative institutions, universal suffrage, civil and personal liberties, and the right of self-determination for the nationalities of the empire. The organisation was short-lived. Its secret printing-press was discovered by the police in Smolensk, and its most active members were arrested and exiled "administratively" to northern provinces.

During the nineties however other secret Populist groups were formed.[1] In 1896 a "Union of Socialist-Revolutionaries" was founded in Saratov by Argunov. It published occasional leaflets and pamphlets, and in the following year transferred its centre to Moscow. Here its leaders collaborated with the editor of the legal journal *Russkoe Bogatstvo*, Peshehonov. The group became known as the "Northern Union". From 1901 it published in Finland a journal called *Revolutionary Russia*. In 1897 another Populist group was created in Minsk. Among the founders were Breshko-Breshkovskaya and a young chemist named Gershuni. The group, which called itself "Workers' Party of National Liberation of Russia", was broken up by arrests in 1900. A third centre of Populist activity at the turn of the century was Tambov province, where the brothers Chernov were actually able to organise some peasant supporters in secret discussion circles.[2] Victor Chernov had been involved in the *Narodnoe Pravo* of 1894. He left Russia for Switzerland in 1899, but something remained of his work. From exile Chernov sent back to Russia pamphlets for agitation among the peasants. His group called itself the "Socialist Agrarian League". The indefatigable Breshko-Breshkovskaya travelled in the Volga provinces on its behalf. Fourthly, in 1900 a meeting of Populists from the southern provinces was secretly held

[1] An interesting work on the Socialist-Revolutionary movement, by a former high police officer, is General Spiridovich, *Histoire du terrorisme russe, 1886–1917* (Paris, 1930). Among memoirs by members of the party are Breshko-Breshkovskaya, *Reminiscences* (Boston, 1917); Gershuni, *Iz nedavnevo proshlovo* (Paris, 1908); and Burtsev, *Borba za svobodnuyu Rossiyu* (Berlin, 1923). Chernov's volume of memoirs ends before the foundation of the party. A Menshevik view of the movement is in *O.D.*, Vol. I, pp. 372–5 and 414–21

[2] This work is described in Chernov, *Zapiski sotsialista-revolyutsionera* (Berlin, 1922), chapters 8 and 9.

in Harkov. It decided to form a "Socialist Revolutionary Party" and issued a manifesto, which was printed in Voronezh. The party was in touch with other Populist groups, who expressed sympathy with it but wished to preserve their independence. The Harkov group became known as the "southern party."

In 1902 representatives of the groups inside Russia met with Populist exiles in Switzerland to discuss the creation of a united party. The leading figures were the exiles V. Chernov and M. Gotz (a veteran from the seventies), and the emissaries from Russia, Gershuni and Azeff.[1] They agreed to form a single Socialist Revolutionary Party. *Revolutionary Russia* became the party's official newspaper. It was published abroad and smuggled in. The party gained support in Russia in the next three years, especially among students and among teachers in provincial towns and villages. The agrarian revolts of 1902 were used for further agitation among the peasants. Pamphlets specially designed for peasant readers were published both abroad and in secret printing presses in Russia.

An important part of the party's machinery was the "combat organisation", which arranged assassinations. Among its eminent victims in the next years were Minister of Interior Sipyagin (April 1902), Minister of Interior Pleve (July 1904), and Grand Duke Sergei (February 1905). Its first chief was the chemist Gershuni. After his arrest in May 1903 it was managed by Azeff. The "combat organisation's" relation to the rest of the party was theoretically defined at the 1902 conference. It was to carry out the directives of the central committee with regard to the choice of persons to be "executed", and with regard to a general increase or reduction of terrorist activity. Its operations were however secret, and were not revealed to the party as a whole. It was linked with the party machine through the person of its chief, who was always a member of the Central Committee.

The first congress of the party was not held until the end of 1905. The events of that year, especially the peasant revolts and the formation of the Peasant Union,[2] had shown that the party was potentially extremely strong. Its greatest successes were won in those areas where the peasant commune had the strongest hold on peasant loyalty, and where rents were paid to landlords in produce, that is in the central agricultural provinces and in the Volga valley. In regions where private holdings were well developed, and where rents were paid only in money, the Social Democrats were able to

[1] On Azeff's role in the movement, see below, pp. 300–1.   [2] See below, pp. 229–30.

compete with the Socialist Revolutionaries for peasant support. These conditions were found especially in the non-Russian parts of European Russia and in the Caucasus—the Ukraine, Lithuania, the Baltic provinces and Georgia.

The congress assembled in Finland at the beginning of January 1906. Its programme stated that the party "considers itself a detachment of the international socialist army, and pursues its activity in the forms which correspond to the concrete conditions of the Russian present reality". In fact the party was recognised, though somewhat hesitantly, by the Second International as a member party up to 1914. Apart from demands for civil liberties, labour legislation and taxation according to wealth, such as would be expected from any radical party, the Socialist Revolutionary programme, prepared by Victor Chernov, contained two specific features. One was its emphasis on a federal structure of the Russian State, with complete self-determination for non-Russians. In fact, of all Russian parties, the Socialist-Revolutionaries had the best relations with the radical movements of the nationalities— especially with the Finnish Activists, the Georgian Socialist-Federalists, the Armenian Dashnyaks, the Latvian Social Democratic League and the Polish socialists (P.P.S.).[1] The second specific feature of the programme was its agrarian policy. The party did not believe that capitalism could develop well in Russia. The factors favouring revolutionary socialism in Russia were, it believed, the existence of a socialist intelligentsia and the strength of a communal outlook and form of organisation among the peasants. The party accepted as its principle the common belief of the peasants that "the land belongs to no one, and labour alone confers the right to use it". The party therefore demanded the socialisation of the land, its "conversion from the personal property of individual persons or groups into the general possession of the whole nation". Land was no longer to be bought or sold. All the arable land which would be taken from landowners was to pass under the control of elected local authorities. These would grant suitable amounts to individual peasants on a basis of "labour ownership". Great forests and fisheries were to be administered by higher administrative authorities, while the subsoil was to be State property. Landowners would not receive compensation, but would be maintained from public funds during a transitional period while adapting themselves to conditions and obtaining new employment.

[1] See below, pp. 163, 165, 186, 237.

The organisation of the party was a subject of controversy. The old issues which had divided "Land and Liberty" in the seventies and the Social Democrats at the turn of the century reappeared. A section represented by the *Russkoe Bogatstvo* group of Peshehonov, wished to make the party entirely overt and legal. It was defeated, and subsequently formed a separate party called the Popular Socialist Party. The extreme exponents of terrorism were also defeated, in so far as "agrarian terror" or crop-sabotage was condemned. But "partisan actions" or raids on the property of landlords or public authorities by armed bands, were approved, on the grounds that they drew the masses into the revolutionary struggle. "Flying groups" of combatants were also to be formed to perform "more complicated terrorist acts". Sabotage of com-_nunications and assassination of official personnel were also permitted. The structure of the party was a compromise between centralists and federalists. A party member must obey orders and belong to one of the party's active organisations. Party offices were to be as far as possible elective, but co-optation was permitted when conspiratorial conditions were essential. The Central Committee was to have five elected members, but could co-opt up to a total of ten. The Central Committee must summon a congress once a year. There was also to be a Council of the party, composed of the five elected members of the Central Committee and a representative from each provincial committee and from the committees of St. Petersburg and Moscow. The Council's decisions could be overruled only by decisions of the party congress. The five Central Committee members elected by the first congress were Natanson, Chernov, Argunov, Azeff and Rakitnikov.

The Nationalities

The years 1882–1905, in which the dominant ideology was that of Pobedonostsev, were marked by a policy of discrimination and russification against the nationalities. The Polish and Ukrainian questions, and the conquest of Central Asia, which affected Russia's relations with other Powers, have been treated elsewhere. Here we shall consider the Jews, Balts, Armenians and Finns.

The Jews were obvious victims of the reaction after the assassination of Alexander II.[1] In April and May 1881 *pogroms*— attacks on Jewish shops and houses, beatings of Jews—took place

[1] The policy of the Russian authorities towards the Jews under Alexander III and Nicholas II is described, from a strongly Jewish point of view, in Dubnow, *History of the Jews in Russia and Poland*, Vols. II and III (Philadelphia, 1916–20).

in Elizavetgrad, Kíev and Odessa. The extreme reactionaries incited the people against the Jews. In August 1881 commissions were set up in provinces to investigate "the injurious influence of the economic activity" of the Jews, and to "protect the Christian population" from it. On 3rd May 1882 were published the "Temporary Rules", which imposed further restrictions on Jews and remained in force for thirty years. Jews were forbidden to live outside towns or large villages. Any transactions still in course for the acquisition of rural property by Jews were cancelled. The rules were not supposed to affect Jews already settled, but in practice many were expelled on the initiative of village communes, on the grounds that they were "vicious members" of the commune. The Pale restrictions remained in force. Jews who had done military service outside the Pale were compelled to return to the Pale when their service was over. The Ministry of War limited the proportion of Jews serving as military doctors or medical orderlies to 5 per cent of army medical personnel, and ordered that no further Jews be accepted for such duties in units stationed in the western military districts. These measures were justified by the insulting assertion that Jews showed "deficient conscientiousness in discharging their duties and an unfavourable influence on the sanitary service in the army". In 1887 a *numerus clausus* for Jews at universities and secondary schools was introduced. Jewish pupils were not to exceed 10 per cent of all pupils in the Pale, 5 per cent in the provinces outside it, or 3 per cent in St. Petersburg or Moscow. The result was that all Jews who could scrape together the funds went and studied abroad, mostly in Germany or Switzerland. Admission of Jews to the Bar required, by a law of 1889, the permission of the Minister of Justice, which was in practice not given. Jewish doctors did not get jobs under central or local authorities. Zemstvos advertising for medical officers would often add the phrase "Jews need not apply". The zemstvo regulations of 1890 deprived Jews of a vote for zemstvo assemblies, though they continued to pay zemstvo rates. In 1891 Jewish merchants and artisans were expelled from Moscow in large numbers and sudden harsh conditions. A further blow at the Jews was the introduction of the spirits monopoly in 1894. Jews were thenceforth refused licences to sell spirits, which deprived many village Jews of a living. A government commission under the former Minister of Justice Pahlen, set up in 1883, studied the position of the Jews for five years. In 1888 it reported on the miserable conditions in which Jews lived, pointed out that they were not "foreigners" but 5,000,000 Russian subjects, attributed their aloofness to the discriminatory laws, and recommended a "graduated system of emancipatory and equalising laws". The Tsar, no doubt influenced by Tolstoy and Pobedonostsev, ignored it.

These developments inevitably weakened the assimilationist trend within Russian Jewry, and strengthened both the revolutionary and the nationalist trends.[1]

Jews were found among supporters of both the Populist and the Marxist branches of socialism. In a Russian socialist republic it was to be assumed that Jews would enjoy the same rights as other citizens. The main specifically Jewish socialist group was the "Bund", founded in 1897, which was, as we have seen, one of the constituent groups of the Russian Social Democratic Party. But, though opposed in principle to nationalism, even the Bund demanded "national-cultural autonomy" for Jews. In 1902 the fourth conference of the Bund decided that it regarded the Jews in Russia as a nation. It therefore demanded, at the 1903 congress of R.S.D.R.P., more far-reaching autonomy within the party than it had been granted by the first programme of 1898. It now demanded that it should be recognised as the sole representative of Jewish Social Democrats within the Russian Empire, wherever they might dwell. The refusal of this demand by the congress led to the secession of the Bund from R.S.D.R.P. It was readmitted in 1906, but its relations with the Russian movement were never placed on a satisfactory basis. The Bund's claims were to cause dissensions within the socialist ranks right up to the final breach between Mensheviks and Bolsheviks in 1912.

The nationalist trend within Russian Jewry was first clearly expressed in a pamphlet entitled *Auto-emancipation*, by Pinsker. This urged the establishment of a Jewish territory, in Palestine or in America, to be obtained by the common endeavour of Jewry in all lands. Published in Berlin in 1882, the pamphlet had little effect in Western Europe, but considerable in Russia. An important centre of Jewish nationalism in Russia was the circle led by Ahad Ha'am (Ginzberg) in Odessa. His plan was to found a centre in Palestine, of a small number of intellectually first-class and strongly patriotic Jews, who would exercise an influence over all Jewry, and so ultimately create a powerful Jewish national feeling, and an effec-

---

[1] The first chapters of the autobiography of Dr. Chaim Weizmann, *Trial and Error* (London, 1949), contain some material on the condition of the Jews in the Pale in these years, and on the beginnings of Zionism.

tive demand for a Jewish state, for which however the time was not yet ripe.

Zionism became known internationally with the publication in 1896 of Herzl's *Der Judenstaat*. During the eighties and nineties some 20,000 Jews had individually entered Palestine, and fifteen agricultural colonies had been set up. In 1897 the first Zionist congress was held in Basel. It revealed a conflict between the orthodox (religious and conservative) and the progressive (liberal or socialist) tendencies which continued throughout Zionist history. In 1901 was formed within the Zionist movement a socialist party called "Poale Zion", whose relation to the Bund may be very loosely compared with the relation of the Polish P.P.S. to Polish Social Democracy.[1]

The Jewish problem in Russia became still more acute in the first years of the new century. The scene of the most violent anti-semitic agitation was Bessarabia, and its chief instigator a certain Krushevan, who edited a paper called *Bessarabets*. In April 1903 a violent pogrom took place in Kishinyov. For two whole days Jews were maltreated, their houses sacked, and innocent persons killed. When at last the army appeared, the rioters immediately stopped. In August 1903 a similar pogrom took place in Homel, in White Russia. The authorities were, to say the least, slow in taking action against the hooligans, but when the Jews began to organise a Self-defence Force of their own this was officially regarded as sub-versive. The sensational visit of Herzl to Russia in July 1903, and his conversation with Pleve, did not improve the lot of the Jews.

In the Baltic provinces, russification was principally directed against the Germans. The Estonians and Latvians derived some advantage from the introduction in 1882 of Russian municipal institutions, which reduced the powers of the German element. In 1886 all schools in the Baltic provinces were placed under the Russian Ministry of Education. Russian was introduced as the language of instruction in all but the lowest classes of primary schools. This change hit the Germans most severely. Soon their secondary schools, including the ancient Domschule in Reval, had to close down. In 1893 the German university of Dorpat was closed, and shortly afterwards reopened as a Russian university now named Yuryev. By 1900 the number of its students, which had been over 1,000 in 1890, had fallen to 268.

The russification of schools was relatively less damaging to the

---

[1] See below, pp. 186–7. The Bund of course became considerably more "nation-alistic" than was Polish Social Democracy.

Esthonians and Latvians, to whom it merely meant that one obstacle
to further education was replaced by another. Russification in
church policy was however equally harmful to Germans, Esthonians
and Latvians. From 1885 onwards construction of new Lutheran
churches required permission from the Holy Synod, while the
building of Orthodox churches was subsidised from funds placed
at the disposal of the Russian governors. The Orthodox Church
conducted a vigorous campaign of conversion. Up to 1905 everything remained outwardly calm in the Baltic provinces. But both
Esthonian and Latvian nationalism were growing, and were now
directed not only against the German "Baltic Barons" but also
against Russia. The causes of agrarian discontent remained as
before. Meanwhile in Riga, Reval and other towns a working class
was springing up. Especially among the Latvians, socialism was
making progress.[1]

The Armenians had made good use of the relative tolerance of
Alexander II's reign, and of the favourable Russian attitude to the
Christians of lands bordering Turkey which resulted from the
Russo-Turkish war, to found schools, newspapers and theatres in
their language on Russian soil. In the following reign these gains
were attacked. Revolutionary ideas, with a Populist tinge, gained
ground. In 1890 was founded the Armenian Revolutionary
Federation (Dashnyaks), which operated on both Russian and
Ottoman territory. The organisation's aim was by crimes, assassination and consequent reprisals and massacre in Ottoman territory,
to create an international scandal, and so provoke the intervention
of the Great Powers on behalf of the Armenian cause.[2] These
tactics, and the increasingly revolutionary attitude of the Armenian
educated class inside Russia, had the opposite effect as far as Russia
was concerned. Whereas in the seventies she had looked with
favour on the Armenians as victims of the Turks and allies in her
conflict with Turkey, she now showed sympathy for Turkey as a
monarchical state threatened, like herself, by revolutionary agitation. The Russian authorities in the Caucasus began to repress the
Armenians. In 1897 Armenian schools, of which there were then
more than 500, were closed. On 12th/25th June 1903 an imperial
decree transferred the Armenian "national fund", held by the Head

---

[1] A brief account of the Russification policy in the Baltic provinces, from the
point of view of a German Russophile, is Hoetzsch, *op. cit.*, pp. 487 ff., An interesting piece of polemical literature is the pamphlet by the Lutheran pastor Hermann
Dalton, *Offenes Sendschreiben an den Oberprokurator des heiligen Synods K.P.
Pobedonostsev* (1889).

[2] On the international aspects of this problem, see below, p. 195.

of the Armenian National Church, the Catholics in Echmiadzin, to the Russian administration. This action produced bitter and active opposition from the whole Armenian community, led by the Dashnyak organisation. Armenians boycotted Russian courts and schools, and refused payment to their Church now that it was controlled by the Russian authorities. The Dashnyak central committee set up illegal schools and courts, which were attended and obeyed by the population. In the last months of 1903 there were clashes between Armenian civilians and Russian forces, and Russian officials were assassinated. Thus Russian action had united the Armenian people behind the Dashnyaks.[1] The only other political party of importance among the Armenians was the Armenian Social Democracy, which had a socialist programme but insisted on remaining separate from other Russian socialist parties and on maintaining contact with Armenian socialist groups in other countries. This attitude made its federation with R.S.D.R.P impossible. There were however Armenians who belonged to R.S.D.R.P. and thus accepted the discipline of a single socialist party for the whole empire.[2]

In Georgia peasant discontent with oppressive agrarian conditions had favoured Marxist socialism. At the turn of the century social democracy was the strongest political force in the Georgian provinces. It was represented by R.S.D.R.P. There was also a specifically Georgian party, the Socialist-Federalists. This party, founded in the nineties, demanded autonomy for the Georgian lands within a federal Russian state, and a share in schools, budget expenditure and political representation proportionate to their numbers for Georgian minorities in other provinces. The socialism of the Socialist-Federalists was Populist rather than Marxist.[3]

The most eminent Moslem figure in this period was Ismail Bey Gasprinski, a Crimean Tatar from Bahçesaray, who in 1883 founded in that city a newspaper entitled *Tercüman* (The Interpreter). The only paper published in Turco-Tatar during some decades, it had great influence among Russian Moslems. It specialised in giving cultural news from the different Moslem territories of Russia, in interesting their people, separated by thousands of miles, in each other's affairs. He also sought to create a common language for all Turkish peoples in Russia, based on Ottoman Turkish. In this he was less successful. The Volga Tatars rightly felt themselves cultural equals, if not superiors, of the Ottoman Turks, and pre-

---

[1] *O.D.*, Vol. I, pp. 369–71, Pasdermadjian, *op. cit.*
[2] Ibid., III, pp. 313–16.   [3] Ibid., pp. 316–18.

ferred their own dialect. Far more important was the school
reform. The model school founded by Gasprinski at Bahçesaray
in 1884 was widely copied. By 1905 there were 5,000 such primary
schools among Russia's Moslems. Their pupils were equipped
with an education as modern at least as that of their Russian con-
temporaries. Great progress was also made in the emancipation
of women, a cause to which Gasprinski gave his enthusiastic
support. The new Tatar intelligentsia included a growing number
of women. The modernising movement among the Tatars had
to face the opposition of both the Russian authorities and the
traditional elements among the ulema. It had patrons among the
prosperous Tatar merchants. In all this Kazan was the centre,
but Crimea and Azerbaijan were strongly affected. Central Asia
was much more backward.[1]

The pressure of Russian nationalism in the bureaucracy and in
the highest class of society during the nineties was bound in time to
affect the autonomy of Finland. During the reign of Alexander III
the Grand Duchy was respected. The only infringements of its
rights were a project in 1890 to place Finnish posts under the
imperial postal system, and the rejection in 1891 of the criminal code
prepared by the Finnish Diet. In 1891 however a commission was
appointed under the former Finance Minister Bunge to define
matters which should be regarded as of common imperial interest,
and so of concern to both the Russian and the Finnish governments.
There was also a marked tendency to fill the offices of State-
Secretary for Finnish affairs in St. Petersburg, and of Governor-
General in Helsingfors, with Russians, and even to suggest that
preference should be given in official jobs in Finland to persons
who knew the Russian language as well as their own. These early
moves towards russification were received with indignation by the
Diet and public opinion of the Grand Duchy. The death of
Alexander III in 1894 however postponed the crisis. For the first
years of Nicholas II there was calm.

The change came in 1898, and was marked by the appointment
of General Bobrikov to the governorship-general.[2] The immediate
aim of Russian policy was to obtain a larger military contribution
from Finland. Hitherto Finland had had only an army of 5,600
men with a reserve of 20,000. Military service was compulsory, but
amounted only to a total period of ninety days spread over three

---

[1] Mende *op. cit.*, pp. 44–71.
[2] See Schybergson, *op. cit.*; Wuorinen, *op. cit.*; and von Törne, *op. cit.* Brief
accounts may be found in Hoetzsch, *op. cit.*, pp. 495–502, and Hampden Jackson,
Finland, chapter 4.

years. The Finnish army might not be sent outside the borders of the Grand-Duchy save for a small regular force known as the Guard. The new law drafted Finnish recruits to Russian units, placed Russian officers in command of Finnish units, and provided for five years' service, which was to be reduced only for persons speaking Russian.

It might indeed fairly be claimed that the Finns, who benefited from the security of the great Russian Empire, should make greater sacrifices for its defence than in the past. But the 1898 law was going very far. It provoked universal and fierce opposition. A mass petition, signed by 500,000 persons from a population of 3,000,000, was taken to the Tsar, who refused to accept it. Nicholas also refused to receive deputations from the Finnish Senate and Diet. In February 1899 a manifesto of the Tsar was proclaimed by the governor-general, in which it was stated that imperial laws had precedence in Finland over Finnish laws. The Finnish Diet was thus reduced to the status of a provincial assembly. In August 1899 the former police chief of the empire, Pleve, was appointed State-Secretary for Finland.[1] In 1901 the Russian conscription system was finally introduced into Finland by imperial decree.

The Finnish reply was passive resistance. The pastors refused to proclaim the law in the villages, the judges and lawyers to apply it, the conscripts to execute it. In 1902 Russian subjects were made eligible for State service in Finland. The personnel and the powers of the police were greatly increased. Bobrikov took over the greater part of the high administration, the posts and the railways. The Russian language was introduced into administration and schools. In April 1903 the constitution was suspended, and Bobrikov assumed dictatorial powers. In the Senate, a section of the Old Finns, hoping that Russian control would finally eliminate Swedish influence in Finland, co-operated with Bobrikov. But Finnish opinion was overwhelmingly against the new policy. Passive resistance continued, and violence was also used. In June 1904 Bobrikov was assassinated by a young Finn named Schaumann.

During the last two decades of the century the Finnish economy underwent important changes. The peasantry became differentiated more than ever between rich and poor. In 1901 there were 110,000 families who owned land, 170,000 families of tenants—of whom the majority were poor—and 207,000 families of landless agricultural labourers. The same years saw a growth of industry, based on

[1] Pleve left this office in 1902 to become Minister of Interior of the Empire. See above p. 138.

timber and water-power. In 1885 industry employed 38,000 workers and had an output to the value of 117 million Finnish marks. In 1906 the number of workers was 113,500 and the value was 439·5 million marks. The growth of Finnish industry, and the cheapness of its raw materials, alarmed Russian industrialists. The Russo-Finnish tariff was revised in 1885 and 1897, each time in favour of protection to Russian industry. Its effect was to direct Finnish exports to other countries, and still further to reduce the Finns' community of interests with Russia.[1]

The growth of a factory working class, and the impoverishment of a large part of the peasantry, favoured the rise of socialism in Finland. In 1896 a congress of workers' delegates was held in Tampere (Tammerfors). Three years later a Workers' Party was founded at a congress in Turku (Abo). In 1903 the party took the name Social Democratic Party.[2] During the nineties there also emerged a progressive liberal party, the Young Finns, who broke away from the conservative Old Finnish Party. The Swedish political leaders at first hoped to influence the Russian court, and to obtain foreign diplomatic intervention, through their aristocratic contacts,[3] but when this yielded no results they joined with the Young Finns and with the more patriotic section of the Old Finns to form a single movement for the defence of the constitution. They published a newspaper abroad, and had contacts with the Russian liberals grouped round Struve's *Osvobozhdenie*. In opposition to them were a group called the "Party of Active Resistance", which resembled the Socialist Revolutionary Party in Russia and advocated the use of assassination. The Diet elections of 1904 gave a large majority to the constitutionalist block, and three Social Democrats were also elected.

[1] For the development of Finnish industry and the growth of a Finnish working class, see *O.D.*, Vol. IV, Part 2, pp. 247–262 (from article by Alexandra Kollontay).

[2] J. Paasivirta, *Arbetarrörelsen i Finland* (Stockholm, 1948), pp. 11–18.

[3] The most influential champion of the Finnish cause was the Empress Dowager, Marie Fyodorovna (formerly Princess Dagmar of Denmark). But Nicholas II would not be persuaded by his mother to change his policy. See *Letters of Tsar Nicholas and Empress Marie* (London, 1937), pp. 162–4 (letter of the Empress dated 1st October, 1902) and 165–8 (letter of the Tsar dated 20th October 1902).

Chapter VI

FOREIGN RELATIONS

The Three Empires and the Balkans

THE basis of Bismarck's Balkan policy, as revealed at the Berlin congress, was to draw a line from north to south through the peninsula, leaving an Austrian sphere to the west and a Russian sphere to the east. The border chosen between Serbia and Bulgaria was a reasonable one, and has caused little trouble since. By all the diplomatic rules, the division of interest should have worked. But diplomatic rules alone could not cope with the Balkans. The division did not work, for two reasons. The first was that Macedonia and Thrace, with their large non-Turkish, mainly Slav and mainly Christian populations, were left under Turkish rule, and provided an object for the appetite of the three small Balkan states. It is difficult to blame Bismarck, or any other statesman, for this. As we have seen, the San Stefano frontier was unacceptable to two of the Great Powers, and no other frontier would have been likely to satisfy the Macedonians. The second reason for the failure of the policy is more complicated, and concerns the internal politics of Serbia and Bulgaria.

The Great Powers were agreed that Serbia should be Austria's vassal, and Bulgaria Russia's, and the rulers of the two countries were content to play this role. But neither they nor their protectors took account of the Serbian and Bulgarian peoples. Austria backed the dictatorial and reactionary regime of Prince Milan, and so turned the majority of the Serbs, who were already embittered at the loss of Bosnia and alarmed at the treatment of the Serbs of Hungary, into enemies of Austria. Russia intervened in the affairs of Bulgaria, not so much backing the Prince or the democrats as alternately encouraging and frustrating both, and so turned the great majority of Bulgarians against her. Thus each Power became unpopular in the country which the Powers had allotted to her as her vassal, and by contrast enjoyed popularity in the country recognised as the vassal of her rival. Serbian democrats looked to Russia because they hated Austria, Bulgarian liberals to Austria

167

because they feared Russia. Friendship for Austria or Russia became an issue of internal party politics in Serbia and Bulgaria. Austro-Russian relations inevitably suffered.

The political parties of Serbia and Bulgaria were very similar, as indeed was to be expected in two countries of so similar social structure. Neither had a land-owning aristocracy. In both a ruling class arose after liberation. It consisted of bureaucrats, army officers and a westernised intelligentsia, all of which arose from the peasantry, especially from the families of village merchants and Orthodox priests which formed the top layer of rural society.

In Serbia by 1880 there were two parties based on these social elements, the Liberals and the Progressives. The main differences between them were that the Liberals were pro-Russian and the Progressives pro-Austrian, and that the Progressives had some organised support in the small towns and villages while the Liberals had not much influence outside the educated class in Belgrade. In the following years the Liberals declined, and a new force arose in the Radical Party, which possessed an efficient organisation among the peasants. The founders of the Radicals were Populist socialists, disciples of Chernyshevski. The life of their most eminent ideologue, Svetozar Marković, in some ways resembles that of the hero of Turgenev's *On the Eve*.[1] But in the eighties the Radical Party's policy became more moderate. It abandoned its revolutionary socialism, and became a party of parliamentary democracy, defending the interests of the peasants and receiving the great majority of peasant support. Its rivals the Progressives stood for the supremacy of the educated class and the modernisation of the Serbian economy by contact with Western capitalism. The Progressives introduced foreign capital, modern banks, railways, and a professional army and civil service, modelled on European experience. The financial burden of their policy lay on the peasant taxpayers.

In Bulgaria the Conservatives represented the same forces, and stood for the same policies, as the Progressives in Serbia. But while the Serbian Progressives were Austrophile, the Bulgarian Conservatives were Russophile. Their rivals, the Liberals, were a less homogeneous party. Some of their leaders were Populist

---

[1] His most important work, *Srbija na istoku*, published in Novi Sad (Ujvidék or Neusatz), in southern Hungary in 1872, urged a democratic federation of the Balkan peoples. Two essays on Marković are, Slobodan Jovanović, *Političke i pravne rasprave* (Belgrade, 1932), Vol. I, pp. 59–299; and Masleša, *Svetozar Marković* (Belgrade, 1945). The first is by Serbia's greatest historian, the second a posthumous work by a brilliant young Serbian Communist.

socialists, others were moderate democrats. Events made the Liberals Austrophile, and also placed them in power for a decade, during which they became more conservative and more dictatorial. The result was that other parties sprang up on their left. In 1891 a Bulgarian Social Democrat Party was formed, twelve years before an effective Marxist group appeared in Serbia. Its leader was Blagoyev, who had organised the first Marxist group in Russia in 1885.[1] In general it may be said that though Bulgarian political life began later than Serbian, it developed more quickly in a radical direction.

Bulgaria was ruled from 1877 by a Russian Commissioner, with a Chancery divided into six departments and five provincial administrations. A temporary Organic Statute was introduced, based on the existing constitutions of Serbia and Roumania. In February 1879 a Constituent Assembly met at Trnovo, and under the influence of its democratic majority produced at the end of April a constitution of a parliamentary democratic type. The Assembly chose as Prince of Bulgaria Alexander of Battenberg, who was fortunate in being popular with the governments of all the Great Powers.[2]

Russian policy in Bulgaria was not united. The Ministry of Foreign Affairs wished to fulfil the terms of the Berlin treaty, to co-operate with the Powers, and to trust the Prince and support his constitutional prerogatives. The Ministry of War, influenced by the Panslavs, distrusted the Prince because of his German origin and British connections, wished to establish a dominant position for Russia at the expense of the other Powers, and for this reason supported the Bulgarian Liberals as the most powerful force in Bulgarian public opinion. From July 1879 to April 1880 the Conservatives were in power while the parliamentary majority was Liberal. From April 1880 to May 1881 the Prince, who had been advised by Alexander II to give the Liberals a chance, had Liberal ministries. In May 1881 with the approval of Alexander III, and in accordance with the reaction in Russia which ·followed the assassination of Alexander II, the Prince dissolved the parliament and amended the constitution. He now relied mainly on advice from the Conservatives. In 1882 however the Conservatives became alarmed by Russian plans for the economic penetration of

[1] See above, pp. 146–7. Blagoyev's own work, *Prinos km istoriyata na sotsializma v Blgariya* (Sofia, 1906), is of considerable interest for Bulgarian development in these years.

[2] The outstanding work on these years is C. E. Black, *The Establishment of Constitutional Government in Bulgaria* (Princeton University Press, 1943).

the country, especially in railway construction. Two Russian generals who were members of the government made themselves unpopular by intervention in civil administration and in Church affairs. The Prince himself grew restive of Russian influence, and the generals sent hostile reports about him to St. Petersburg. The Liberals were now courted by the Prince, the Conservatives and the Russians. In the end they came to terms with the Prince and the Conservatives, and on 17th September 1883 the Prince, with the approval of the Austrian and British representatives, restored the Constitution of 1879 and formed a coalition government. The Russian generals resigned, and Alexander III became convinced that the Prince was an enemy of Russia.

In Serbia the disappointments of Berlin and the inclination of Prince Milan made close co-operation with Austria inevitable. But Austria was determined to strike a hard bargain. The first task was the conclusion of a trade treaty and a railway convention. The Liberal leader, Jovan Ristić, objected to the Austrian terms, which included most-favoured-nation status for Austria in Serbia but not for Serbia in Austria. The result was an Austrian boycott of Serbian livestock which brought hardship to Serbian peasants and caused the fall of Ristić in 1880. The Progressives now came to power, and accepted the Austrian terms in April 1881.[1]

In June 1881 a political treaty was also signed with Austria. This contained a promise by Serbia not to tolerate on her territory any political, religious or other activities directed against Austria, and (article 4) not to conclude an agreement with any other Power without previously consulting Austria. Austria promised to support Milan's desire to take the title of King and to support Serbian territorial aims to the south, except in the Sandjak of Novi Bazar, if circumstances should later favour this. The Premier Pirocanac threatened to resign unless article 4 was changed. Milan then visited Vienna and obtained a modifying clause, but at the same time gave the Austrian government a letter in which he stated that he personally considered the original article binding.[2]

In February 1882 Milan took the title of King. Shortly afterwards a crisis was caused by the Radicals, who left the parliament when their demand for an enquiry into a railway scandal had been refused. The government kept itself in power by exceptional measures. In September 1883 the Radicals had a clear majority in elections, but the King formed a cabinet of bureaucrats. In October

---

[1] Jovanović, *Vlada Milana Obrenovića*, Vol. II, pp. 267–305.
[2] Ibid., *op. cit.*, Vol. II, pp. 333–52.

there was a peasant rising, supported and led by the Radicals. Its suppression was followed by some executions and many prison sentences. For the next two years the King and the Progressives ruled by police methods.[1]

Thus within six years of the Berlin Congress the Balkan situation had once more become inherently unstable. Before we consider the Balkan crisis of 1885–7 however a few words are needed on the relations of the Great Powers in these years.

The first major diplomatic event in Europe after the Congress of Berlin was the German-Austrian alliance, signed in October 1879. Bismarck seems to have had two motives in making this treaty. One was fear of the anti-German agitation in Russia which had followed the Berlin settlement, and consequent desire to guard against any Russo-French combination against Germany. The second was the wish to prevent Austria from coming to terms with France, and perhaps Britain, and thus reviving the "Crimean combination". Bismarck took seriously at this time the problem of political Catholicism, with which he was engaged in a struggle in Prussia. A Franco-Austrian alignment would not only have exercised an attraction on the Catholic subjects of the Reich, but would have placed Germany at the mercy of Russia, whose friendship in these circumstances she would have had to buy dear. It seems clear that it was these diplomatic calculations, rather than any Greater German ideology, which induced Bismarck to commit the Reich to the defence of the Habsburg Empire. But after Bismarck had left the scene, and the supremacy of the Prussian landowners, generals and diplomats in the Reich was increasingly challenged by the rise of a German nationalist public opinion, strong in the business and professional classes, the ideological element in the German-Austrian alliance became dominant, with results ultimately disastrous to both Germany and Europe.

In 1882 the German-Austrian alliance was extended by the adhesion of Italy, and in 1883 both Austria and Germany made alliances with Roumania. There is a certain similarity between the situations of Italy and Roumania. Both feared Austria and had territorial claims on her (Italy in Trentino and Trieste, Roumania in Transylvania and Bucovina), but both also feared one other Power even more—Italy France and Roumania Russia. Both came to terms with Austria as the lesser evil, and largely because their relations with Austria were guaranteed by Germany, a Power for which both Italians and Roumanians had respect, and with which

[1] Jovanović, *op. cit.*, Vol. III, pp. 1–170.

neither had a quarrel. Roumania's relations with Russia were affected adversely by Russia's annexation of southern Bessarabia in 1878 despite the military aid granted to Russia during the war with Turkey; by suspicion of Russian intentions in Bulgaria, which could be used as the lower arm of a pincer directed from St. Petersburg; and by the interest of Roumanian public opinion in the fate of the Roumanian population in the whole province of Bessarabia. At the same time concern for the Roumanians under Hungarian rule in Transylvania grew as the "magyarisation" policy of Budapest became more aggressive.[1]

Bismarck never abandoned his desire for friendship with Russia. At the same time, despite the hostility of Russian public opinion to Germany, the Russian government was anxious to restore good relations with Germany. During 1880 exploratory conversations took place between Bismarck and the Russian ambassador, Saburov, the initiative being from the Russian side. These discussions eventually bore fruit in the revival of the Three Emperors' League by the signature of a treaty in June 1881.[2] The three Powers recognised the principle of the closure of the Straits. If Turkey should make an exception to this principle to the advantage of a belligerent Power, the three governments would warn her that she had put herself in a state of war with the Power thus injured— which of course meant Russia—and was thus deprived of the security assured her by the Berlin treaty. This was a great gain to Russia, which was thus protected against attack in the Black Sea. At the same time the treaty recognised the right of Austria to convert her present occupation of Bosnia and Hercegovina into formal annexation when she should think fit, and agreed that the three Powers would not oppose the reunion of Bulgaria and Eastern Roumelia at a later stage. The treaty was renewed in 1884 when the three emperors met at Skierniewice in Poland. On this occasion it appears that the Russian Foreign Minister Giers[3] assured the Austrians that they would not support the Karadjordjević dynasty against the Obrenović, and that they recognised that Serbia must depend mainly on Austria. In Bulgaria Russia would take no action against Prince Alexander. In August 1885 Giers met

[1] R. W. Seton-Watson, *History of the Roumanians* (Cambridge, 1934), pp. 360–6 (for the treaty) and 397–409 (for magyarisation in Transylvania).

[2] Useful sources for these discussions are Simpson, *The Saburov Papers* (Cambridge, 1929), and Skazkin, *Konyets avstro-russko-germanskovo Soyuza* (Moscow, 1928).

[3] Giers had previously served as Russian Minister in Berne (1869) and Stockholm, and had been Assistant Minister of Foreign Affairs from 1875 to 1882, when he succeeded Gorchakov.

Alexander of Bulgaria at Franzensbad. Giers stated that Russia wished the *status quo* in the Balkans to be maintained, and did not at present desire the union of Bulgaria and Eastern Roumelia. Alexander stated that he did not expect trouble in this direction, and Giers appears to have regarded this as an undertaking by the Prince not to intervene in Roumelia.

Only a month later, on 18th September 1885, the Bulgarian nationalists in Eastern Roumelia seized the capital, Plovdiv, and proclaimed the unity of the province with Bulgaria. Prince Alexander, forced to incur the wrath of either his subjects or the Tsar, decided that the second was the less formidable, and accepted the union. Alexander III, who since September 1883 had regarded the Prince as an enemy, was determined that he should not win popularity by his action. On 25th September the Tsar therefore ordered all Russian officers serving in the Bulgarian army to return to Russia. This was an invitation to attack against Bulgaria. The blow came however not from the Turks but from Serbia.

King Milan was well aware of the unpopularity of his regime, and was alarmed at the proposed increase in territory of Bulgaria. He therefore demanded compensation. Austria urged patience, and promised that she would do her best with the other Powers to obtain something for Serbia. But Russia was not willing to see Austria's vassal strengthened, Bismarck did not wish to oppose Russia, and Britain did not wish to weaken Turkey. So the prospect of satisfaction for Serbia by diplomatic means seemed poor. At the same time Milan had reason to believe that both the Hungarian government and the Austrian General Staff favoured Serbian action against Bulgaria, and that he could therefore disregard the official warning of the Vienna Foreign Office.[1] On 13th November he attacked. The Bulgarians, however, despite their scarcity of officers, defeated the Serbian forces at Slivnitsa, west of Sofia, and in turn invaded Serbia. They were stopped only by the arrival of the Austrian Minister in Belgrade, Count Khevenhüller, who informed Prince Alexander that if he advanced further Austrian troops would enter Serbia, in which case it was probable that Russian troops would occupy Bulgaria, which would cost him his throne.

In April 1886 the problem of the union of Bulgaria and Eastern Roumelia was settled between the Powers and Turkey by recognition of the Prince of Bulgaria as Governor-General of Eastern Roumelia. Prince Alexander's name however was not mentioned,

---

[1] For Milan's attitude during the crisis, see Jovanović, *op. cit.*, Vol. III, pp. 219–60.

as a result of Russian pressure. It was now clear to the Bulgarians that the Tsar was implacably opposed to their Prince. The Russo-phile elements were hostile to him, and a group of officers organised a conspiracy against him. On 20th August he was kidnapped and deported to Russian territory. In Bulgaria however the Liberal leader Stambolov seized power and asked Alexander, who had now reached Austrian territory, to return. On arrival in Bulgaria, the Prince was met by the Russian consul in Rustchuk, who told him that an emissary of the Tsar was on his way to take over the government of the country. An appeal to the Tsar's mercy brought the reply from Alexander III that he "could not approve" the Prince's return. The Prince decided that he could not face the wrath of Russia, and abdicated.

Russia's intervention in Bulgarian affairs aroused a storm of protests in Britain and in Hungary. Kálnoky, the Austrian Foreign Minister, declared that Austria would take a "determined attitude" if Russia should send troops or a commissioner to assume control of Bulgaria. Lord Salisbury denounced the action of "officers debauched with foreign gold". Queen Victoria wrote to the Premier of "Russian fiends". Most important of all, the Bulgarians themselves refused to surrender. The Russian military attaché in Vienna, General Kaulbars, was sent to Bulgaria in September. He found Stambolov firmly in charge. Elections were held, and despite Kaulbars' threats and intrigues Stambolov won a victory. The Grand National Assembly was then summoned to Trnovo to elect a new Prince. On 17th November Kaulbars left Bulgaria and Russia broke diplomatic relations.[1]

During the winter an international crisis developed. Its main feature was that Austro-Russian tension was accompanied by anti-German agitation in France. With the rise of General Boulanger *revanche* propaganda had become a serious force in France—the only time that this was so between 1871 and 1914. Bismarck feared common Franco-Russian action. At the same time he was having difficulties with the Opposition in the Reichstag, and found it convenient to rally German patriotism against the foreigner. He made a sensational speech on the French danger on 11th January 1887, dissolved the Reichstag, and conducted a fiercely nationalist election campaign. In February the Triple Alliance was renewed, and Bismarck was able loosely to associate Britain with it by an exchange of notes between Britain, Austria and Italy, known as the Mediterranean Agreement, in which the three Powers expressed

---

[1] For later developments in Bulgaria, see below, pp. 193-4.

their community of interests. This Agreement was strengthened at the end of the year, after the strongly Germanophile and Francophobe Crispi had become Premier in Italy. On 12th December 1887 an exchange of notes between Britain, Italy and Austria provided that the three Powers would support Turkey in resistance to any "illegal enterprises" by a third Power in relation to Bulgaria or Asia Minor, and would combine to occupy points on Turkish territory should the Turkish government become the accomplice of such enterprises.[1]

Meanwhile the situation had improved by the peaceful solution of the Schnaebele incident between France and Germany in April 1887 and the formation of a new French cabinet without Boulanger in May. In Russia Giers, who favoured the traditional co-operation with the German Powers, recovered influence, while that of Katkov and the Panslavs waned.[2] Giers may have shared the belief of the Panslavs that the Bulgarian nation was devoted to Russia and that the anti-Russian turn of Bulgarian policy was due only to a handful of Austrian or British agents: he was probably no more capable than Katkov of understanding that Russian arrogance had alienated the Bulgarian people.[3] But Giers was a more realistic statesman than the Panslavs, and understood that anti-German fulminations would do Russia no good. He preferred a return to the Three Emperors' Alliance. This was too much for the Tsar, who in April 1887 definitely refused to renew the agreement as far as Austria was concerned. Friendship with Germany, however, the Tsar was eager to preserve. Count Paul Shuvalov, Russian ambassador in Berlin, was instructed to discuss an agreement with Bismarck.

The result of the discussions was the famous Russo-German Reinsurance Treaty of 18th June 1887. Its first article provided for benevolent neutrality in the event of either party being involved in war, with the reservation that this should not apply to a war against either Austria or France if this resulted from an attack on either of those Powers by one of the two signatories. The second article recognised the preponderant influence of Russia in Bulgaria and Eastern Roumelia. The third article reaffirmed the principle of the closure of the Straits. An "additional and very secret protocol" promised that Germany would help restore a regular government in Bulgaria, would not consent to the return of Battenberg, and

---

[1] For a thorough survey of the diplomatic events of 1886–7 see Langer, *op. cit.*, chapters 10 and 11. For Bismarck's financial measure against Russia, see below pp. 177–8.

[2] Baron Nolde, *L'alliance franco-russe* (Paris, 1936), pp. 447 ff.

[3] Molotov made almost exactly the same mistake about the Serbs in 1948.

would give her benevolent neutrality and diplomatic support should Russia find it necessary to "defend the entrance to the Black Sea".

This treaty was Bismarck's last attempt at co-operation with Russia. It has been the object of minute discussion by diplomatic historians.[1] It may be doubted whether it could ever have stood the test of a Franco-German or Austro-Russian war, whether aggressive or not. But as long as peace was kept, as an indication of Germany's disinterestedness in the Balkans and desire ultimately to get back to co-operation between the three empires, it is of great significance.

The Franco-Russian Alliance

When Count Paul Shuvalov arrived in Berlin on 17th March 1890 to renew the Reinsurance Treaty of 1887, he learned that Bismarck had just resigned from the Imperial Chancellorship. The news so impressed him that he decided to ask for further instructions from St. Petersburg before proceeding with negotiations. But on 21st March William II received him with extreme cordiality and insisted on his friendship for Russia and his determination to renew the treaty.

On 23rd March a conference was held between the new Chancellor, General von Caprivi, the new Foreign Secretary, Baron Marschall von Bieberstein, and several senior diplomatic officials, of whom the most important was Baron von Holstein. Holstein was against renewal, and was in general against a policy of too close relations with Russia. His main arguments were, that the treaty was incompatible with the Austro-German and Triple alliances; that it was too complicated for anyone of smaller stature than Bismarck to handle; and that in any case there was no danger of a Russo-French combination if it were not renewed. Holstein also persuaded the able and experienced General von Schweinitz, German ambassador in St. Petersburg, who was at the time on a visit to Berlin, to support his views. Caprivi accepted Holstein's recommendations, and William II, who two days earlier had been so eager to renew, changed his mind. He now instructed Schweinitz to tell Giers that though Germany's friendship for Russia remained as strong as ever, the change of personalities in the highest positions made it desirable to pursue a modest policy and to enter into no far-reaching commitments.

[1] See Langer, *op. cit.*, chapter 11, which also has excellent bibliographical references. A modern critical treatment by a German liberal scholar is Eyck, *Bismarck* (Zürich, 1944), Vol. III, pp. 477–90.

The refusal to renew was a bitter blow for Giers, who had considered the treaty a personal triumph in his own battle against the Panslav and nationalist elements in Russia led by Katkov. On 15th May 1890 he made a last attempt to save something from the wreck. He was willing that the secret protocol, with its specific references to Bulgaria and the Straits, should be dropped, and did not even ask for a formal treaty at all. He was content that the two emperors should simply exchange letters to the effect that good relations between the two countries are firmly based and do not depend on personalities. Schweinitz strongly advised that this proposal should be accepted. But Holstein and Marschall opposed even this moderate request. Caprivi interpreted it as a manœuvre to split the Triple Alliance and to engage Germany in an anti-British policy. William II agreed with his Chancellor, and Schweinitz was instructed to repeat the assurances of friendship but to refuse the proposal. The treaty therefore lapsed on 18th June 1890, and an atmosphere of distrust was created on both sides. It was from this time that Russia began to turn towards France.[1]

In France, traditional sympathy for the Poles, dislike of the Russian autocracy, and fear of antagonising Germany had hitherto combined to commend a reserved attitude to Russia. It was only the extreme nationalists and champions of revenge for Alsace, who were not numerous and whose influence has been greatly exaggerated, that already in the eighties urged a Franco-Russian alliance. The most obvious persons are Déroulède, leader of the *Ligue des Patriotes*, who visited Russia in 1886, and Mme Juliette Adam, the friend of Gambetta. The greatest French expert on Russian affairs, Leroy-Beaulieu, was sceptical. But from about 1887 a change took place. The Russian ambassador in Paris, Baron Mohrenheim, made many friends, and his embassy became an important social centre.[2] Slight contacts grew up between the French and Russian armies. Russian officers were allowed to study French rifle and munitions manufacture. The influence of Boulanger at the War Ministry to some extent survived his fall. General Boisdeffre, the Assistant Chief of General Staff, had known Russia, and strongly favoured military collaboration with her.

Financial links also became important. One of Bismarck's few serious blunders in foreign policy was his action on 10th Novem-

---

[1] The best work on the origin and negotiation of the Franco-Russian alliance is Nolde, *op. cit.* Two other useful works are Langer, *The Franco-Russian Alliance* (Harvard, 1929), and Michon, *L'alliance Franco-Russe* (Paris, 1927).
[2] Nolde, *op. cit.*, pp. 488–92.

ber 1887 in forbidding the Reichsbank to accept Russian securities
as collateral for loans. This seems to have been a reprisal for a
Russian decree of May 1887 which had forbidden foreigners to
hold land in border areas, and which had in practice fallen most
heavily on German subjects in Russian Poland. Bismarck does not
appear to have realised the significance of his action for German-
Russian relations. This *Lombardverbot* was maintained until 1894.
During these years Russian securities were bought in France.
In 1889 the Finance Minister Vyshnegradski floated a 4 per
cent conversion loan, which was taken up in France. A second
conversion loan, in 1890, was still more successful in France.
During the nineties was built up the dominant position of France
among foreign holders of Russian bonds, which had such important
political results.

In Russia an alliance with France was not seriously considered
in the early eighties, though the rage of the Panslavs after 1878 and
the fiery speech made in Paris in 1882 on German-Slav antagonism
by General Skobelev, the conqueror of Central Asia, attracted some
attention in the European capitals. The nearest approach had been
a campaign by Katkov during the 1886–7 crisis in favour of "freedom of action". Katkov had argued that Russia's diplomatic
reverses were due to her excessive desire for the goodwill of Germany, and that she would do well in future to choose her friends
with an open mind.

Franco-Russian negotiations began in 1891. The visit of the
Empress Frederick, mother of William II of Germany, to Paris in
February alarmed Giers, who advised the Tsar to confer the Order
of St. Andrew on the President of the Republic, Sadi Carnot, as a
demonstration. Giers wrote to Mohrenheim on 3rd March,
stressing the importance of maintaining the existing *entente
cordiale*[1] between France and Russia. Mohrenheim read too
much into the letter, asked at once for an appointment with the
French Foreign Minister, Ribot, and read it aloud to him. In
June 1891 the renewal of the Triple Alliance, combined with
Italian statements about the importance of Anglo-Italian friendship, persuaded Giers that Britain was associating herself with the
Central Powers. An unofficial visit by Clémenceau, most Anglo-
phile of French politicians, to London, during which he had a
discouraging conversation with Joseph Chamberlain, diminished
his opposition to alliance with Russia. If Britain was not prepared
to make concessions to France, what alternative was there to Russia?

[1] Nolde, *op. cit.*, pp. 605–6.

Though Clémenceau was not in the government, his attitude was a political factor of some importance.[1]

On 16th July Giers suggested to the French ambassador that the relations of Britain with the Triple Alliance were such as to make desirable a step further in the Franco-Russian entente. Ribot replied to this overture with a draft agreement on consultation between the two Powers and common mobilisation in the event of international danger. On 23rd July a French naval squadron visited Kronstadt, and was visited by the Tsar, who stood bareheaded at attention when the *Marseillaise* was played. It was this incident which revealed to Europe that Franco-Russian relations were being seriously changed. The agreement was signed on 27th August 1891. The two Powers would consult each other on any matters which put the general peace in doubt. If peace was threatened, and one of the two Powers was in danger of aggression, both governments would agree on the "measures which this eventuality would require the two governments to adopt immediately and simultaneously". The details arising out of the second point would be studied by "special delegates".[2]

Eighteen months more passed before a military convention was signed. During the winter of 1891–2 Russia was weakened by the famine, and French politics were dominated by the Panama scandals. But German-Russian relations deteriorated owing to the conciliatory policy of Caprivi towards the Poles,[3] and owing to trade difficulties. In 1891 the Russian tariff was greatly increased, and preferential agreements were made between the Powers of the Triple Alliance. Paul Shuvalov visited Berlin in March 1892, but was unable to settle outstanding commercial disputes. In the Balkans a Russophile turn in Serbian foreign policy,[4] and the hospitality extended in Serbia to refugees from Bulgaria who were enemies of the pro-Austrian Stambolov, aggravated Austro-Russian relations. These factors reduced the hesitancy of Giers, who seems hitherto to have hoped to use the agreement with France as a means to force Germany into concessions rather than make it the basis of Russian foreign policy.

In August 1892 General Boisdeffre came to St. Petersburg, and on the 17th reached agreement with the Russian Assistant Chief of General Staff, General Obruchev, on the military convention. The draft terms were as follows. If France were attacked by Germany, or by Italy with German help, all available Russian forces would be

---

[1] Nolde, *op. cit.*, pp. 609–12.   [2] Ibid. p. 636.   [3] See below, p. 188.
[4] See below, p. 192.

used against Germany. If Russia were attacked by Germany, or by Austria with German help, all available French forces would be used against Germany. If the Triple Alliance, or one of its members, should mobilise, both France and Russia would mobilise. The French force to be used in support of Russia would be 1,300,000 men. The Russian force to be used in support of France would be 700,000 to 800,000 men.[1] These terms contain a contradiction. France was obliged to mobilise even if only Austria mobilised, but was obliged to go to war only if Germany joined Austria in attacking Russia. The same applied to Russia's obligations towards France with regard to Italy. The convention in fact was not really clear, but represented a compromise between the original French and Russian proposals, of which the first had aimed at bringing in Russia against Germany, the second at engaging France against Austria.[2]

After the Boisdeffre-Obruchev agreement had been initialled there was a further delay before ratification. The consequences of the Panama affair continued to preoccupy French political leaders. In April 1893 Giers made another overture to Germany, through the German ambassador in St. Petersburg, Werder. He insisted on Russia's desire for German friendship, and the very general nature of the 1891 entente—whose existence was known to Europe only by the Kronstadt visit and the gesture of the Tsar. But the German Foreign Office, dominated by Holstein, did not take the hint.[3] In May and June 1893 the election campaign for the new Reichstag was largely fought on the issue of increased military estimates, and the military law was in fact passed in July with the votes of the Polish members. In December the new French ministry, under Casimir-Périer, began to pay more attention to foreign policy than its recent predecessors. Already in July a sensational article had appeared in *Figaro* entitled "Alliance or Flirtation". It contained the phrase, "Just as a Franco-Russian alliance is desirable, so also is a perpetual flirtation without conclusion imprudent". The French need for the alliance was increased by tension with Britain in Siam in the summer. In October a Russian naval squadron visited Toulon. British warships visited Taranto, a rather ineffective counter-demonstration. By December it was clear to Giers that relations with the German Powers were definitely worse than

---

[1] The reason why the French contribution was larger is that France would have only one major enemy to fight (Italy's strength was discounted), whereas Russia would have to face both Germany and Austria.

[2] This is discussed by Langer, *op. cit.*, pp. 260–3.

[3] Nolde, *op. cit.*, pp. 678–82.

they had been in Bismarck's day and showed no sign of returning to their former state. Russia needed the alliance as much as France. On 30th December 1893 Giers therefore wrote to the French ambassador that the Boisdeffre-Obruchev agreement could be considered valid, and on 4th January 1894 received official confirmation from the French side.[1]

The Franco-Russian Alliance remained a basic factor in European diplomacy until the First World War. Its terms remained secret, but the fact of its existence became apparent during the nineties. Public signs of Franco-Russian friendship included official visits of Nicholas II and the Empress to Paris in October 1896 and of President Félix Faure to St. Petersburg in August 1897. A second visit of the Tsar took place in September 1901. The alliance was steadily reinforced by French loans, which began to play a major part in the Russian economy.[2]

The terms of the alliance were modified in August 1899, when the French Foreign Minister Delcassé visited St. Petersburg. Official notes were exchanged between him and Muraviev, the Russian Foreign Minister, which introduced two new points. Firstly, the duration of the military convention was no longer made dependent on that of the Triple Alliance, but was extended until denounced by either Power. Secondly, the aims of the alliance were stated to be not merely (as in August 1891), the maintenance of peace but also the preservation of the Balance of Power in Europe.[3] The reason for the changes was the fear that the Habsburg Empire, weakened by the German-Czech crisis,[4] might disintegrate, and its German provinces be united with the Reich.

Rational discussion of the Franco-Russian alliance has long been made impossible by the passions aroused by the circumstances in which it broke up. In 1918 both Frenchmen and Russians of both right and left were convinced that they had had the worst of a disreputable bargain. French conservatives pointed out that millions of francs of French savings had been lost when the Bolsheviks repudiated the loans, and that France had been bled of her best sons on the Western Front while her eastern ally betrayed her word. Frenchmen of the left had always denounced the alliance with the Tsar, the most reactionary despot in the world, and now declared that it had done France nothing but harm. Russians of the right declared that the alliance had tied Russia to the cause of Western decadent liberalism, which had undermined her foundations and

[1] Nolde, op. cit., pp. 687-9.   [2] See below, pp. 316-7.
[3] See Michon, op. cit., pp. 84-8.   [4] See below, p. 196.

prepared the ground for revolution. Russia should have kept the well-proved friendship with conservative monarchical Germany and refused to be drawn into war on behalf of French *revanche*. Russians of the left argued that the alliance had made the Russian people a plaything of Western imperialist capitalists, that French rentiers had stolen the product of the Russian workers' toil and sweat and made profits from the blood of millions of Russian peasant soldiers. Influenced by these polemics, by the frantic attempts of disappointed men to find a scapegoat for their failures, even objective British and American historians have concluded that the alliance was a mistake, and involved both countries in disaster.

The simplest comment on this controversy is to compare the events of August–September 1914 with those of May–June 1940. The merit of the French army and of the small British expeditionary force in 1914 are in no way diminished by the undoubted fact that a large part of the German army was then tied down on the Russian front. If Germany had been able to throw her whole army against France in 1914, as she was able in 1940, she would have had as complete a victory. The Russian army saved France in 1914, but it is also true that the French army saved Russia. If the whole German and Austrian strength had been thrown against Russia in 1914, she could not have held out. For three years the balance held. When at last Russia broke, Britain had reached her full military strength and the United States had joined the allies. It remains an extraordinary fact that Russia's war effort up to 1917 has been underestimated by military historians and almost completely forgotten by politicians. Among those who forgot in 1939 were Chamberlain and Stalin, both of whom paid a heavy price.[1]

The Franco-Russian alliance can only be considered a mistake on one of two assumptions, or a combination of both. The assumptions are, first, that France had no grounds for fearing Germany, and could and should have stayed out of all complications in Eastern Europe that might embroil Russia and Austria: or, second,

---

[1] It is extraordinary that a scholar of the standing of Langer could write in 1929: "No one appears to have discovered what concrete advantages the alliance brought to France" (*op. cit.*, p. 399), and: "The alliance was from start to finish a Russian instrument which operated to Russia's advantage almost exclusively" (*op. cit.*, pp. 416–17). Yet it would be unfair to blame the eminent American historian when the French people themselves seem unable even in 1950 to understand that it was Russia's action which saved them in 1914 and doomed them in 1940. As long as Russia is regarded as a bogey or a paladin—Slavonic aggressor against Germany the bulwark of Europe, or liberator from Teutonic aggression endowed with all the attributes of Bayard—clear thinking about her policy and about France's security will remain impossible.

that Russia could have satisfied her aims in the Balkans by ag
ment with Germany, and could and should have refused to beco...
entangled in the rivalry of the Western Powers with Germany.
If neither of these assumptions is justified by the facts of Great
Power foreign policy between 1890 and 1914, then it must surely
be admitted that the alliance proved its value. It saved France,
and if it did not save Russia at least it postponed Russia's collapse.
It may of course be argued that rapid defeat of Russia by the
German Powers, followed by a status of satellite to Berlin, would
have saved Russia from revolution and benefited her in the long
run. But the Russian statesmen who negotiated the alliance in
1891–4 could not reasonably be expected to show such subtly
imaginative conservative defeatism.

Fear of British intentions had, as we have seen, played a part in
the making of the alliance. During the nineties both Powers were
in more serious conflict with Britain than with the Central Powers
—France in Africa and South-east Asia, Russia in China. The two
General Staffs held discussions on 2nd July 1900 and 21st February 1901 to discuss common action in the event of war with
Britain alone or with Britain supported by the Triple Alliance.
The discussions envisaged a French landing in Britain; a Russian
invasion of India; French naval action in the Mediterranean with
support from the Russian Black Sea fleet; and Russian naval action
in the Pacific with support from a French Indian Ocean fleet based
on Diego Suarez in Madagascar. The Russian General Staff however made clear that, until the completion of the Orenburg–
Tashkent line made possible the transportation of 300,000 troops
to the Indian frontier area Russia could do no more than make a
minor demonstration along the Afghan border. The French
General Pendezec declared that the French government attached
the greatest importance to the construction of the line, which
should be "poussée avec la plus grande rapidité".[1]

It would be a mistake to take these plans very seriously. For
geographical reasons, a conflict in Asia between British and Russian
armies was improbable. Even after the Orenburg-Tashkent line
was completed it would have been difficult for Russia to undertake
major operations in that area. If on the other hand war had broken
out between Britain and France in Africa, which was much less
unlikely, there would have been little that Russia could have done to
help France. The most valuable help would have been an attack
towards the Middle East. But this, whether with or against the

[1] *Documents diplomatiques français*, 2nd Series, Vol. I, p. 146; Vol. III, pp. 601 ff.

consent of Turkey, could hardly have failed to provoke the intervention of Austria, and so of Germany, which would not have been
to the advantage of France. Whatever the feelings and intentions
of the two governments and General Staffs, the fact remains that
the Franco-Russian alliance was an unsuitable instrument against
Britain, but a valuable weapon against the German Powers.

Poland, the Ukraine and the Three Empires

Though the Polish question did not, in the years between the
conclusion of the Franco-Russian Alliance and the war with Japan,
cause a major diplomatic crisis, it was always present in the calculations of Russian, German and Austrian statesmen. Opposition
to Polish nationalism remained of course a basic common interest of
all three states. But the alternative policy, of granting favours to
Poles in order to embarrass the neighbour empire, was adopted to
some extent throughout the period by Austria, and for a few years
even by Germany. The period was marked by a revival of political
nationalism among the Poles themselves in all three regions.
Though Balkan questions continued until 1914 to be the main
source of friction between Russia and Austria, yet the Polish and
Ukrainian problems also played their part in building up hostility
on both sides. This factor can only be explained by a brief survey
of political developments in Poland and the Ukraine and of the
attitude of the three partitionary governments.

The revival of militant nationalism in Russian Poland dates from
the middle of the eighties. It was in part a reaction against the
special severity of the Gurko-Apuhtin regime, and was also
encouraged by the tension between Russia and Austria-Hungary
in the Bulgarian crisis of 1885. In 1886 was founded in Warsaw a
weekly paper called *Głos* ("The Voice"), edited by Popławski.
Within the limits imposed by the Russian censorship, it expressed
radical views, preaching sometimes a mild socialism. It insisted
especially on the duty of placing the interests of the Polish nation
above those of any single class, and denounced social privileges
among Poles. The paper was finally suppressed in 1894.

The first signs of socialist organisation in Poland appeared
already at the end of the seventies. A conspiratorial group called
Proletariat was created by Ludwik Waryński. It was strongly
internationalist, put social revolution above Polish independence,
and was influenced by the Russian *Narodnaya volya*, with whose
remnants it made an agreement for co-operation in 1884. In 1885
four leaders of this group were hanged, and Waryński was imprisoned

in the Schlüsselburg, where he died soon afterwards.[1] Another early socialist leader was Bolesław Limanowski, who founded a group called *Lud polski* ("The Polish People") in Austrian Poland. He later published a paper in Paris, and smuggled copies across the Russian frontier. Limanowski urged the workers not to ignore the struggle for political liberties and for Polish national independence. In 1887 a Polish student at Harkov university, named Jozef Piłsudski, was arrested for socialist activities and sent to Siberia.[2]

The two most important parties in the partition period of Polish history, the National Democrats and the Polish Socialists, came into being in the nineties.

The first organisation of the former was the *Liga narodowa* (National League), founded in Switzerland by Miłkowski, one of the leaders of 1863. Its declared aim was to gather together all national forces for a struggle to restore Poland's independence within the frontiers of 1772. The Polish nation must achieve this by its own strength. It must win for itself such prestige that the European Powers would be compelled to reckon with it. In 1891 a "Union of Polish Youth" was founded, also in Switzerland, by Balicki. In 1895 there appeared in Lwów (Lemberg), in Austrian Poland, a periodical called *Przegląd Wszechpolski* ("All-Polish Review"). One of its three directors was Balicki, who had made himself a reputation by a pamphlet published in 1892 entitled *National Egoism in Relation to Ethics*, in which he defended extreme nationalism. The second was Popławski, the former director of *Głos* in Warsaw, who retained a populist socialist outlook and now also founded in 1896 in Lwów a monthly called *Polak* intended for peasant readers. The third was Roman Dmowski, also an exile from Russian Poland, who became for thirty years the leader of Polish nationalism. Dmowski maintained that the old liberal outlook was outmoded. He expressed admiration for Prussian methods and urged Poles to imitate them. He was bitterly anti-Semitic and anti-Ukrainian. In contrast to the socialist doctrine of the class struggle, he urged that "the nation is a living social organism".

---

[1] Waryński's action is described in Feliks Perl ("Res"), *Dzieje ruchu socjalistycznego w zaborze rosyjskim* (Warsaw, 1910), pp. 128–196. See also the interesting article by M. K. Dziewanowski, *The beginnings of Socialism in Poland*, in The Slavonic Review, June 1951. This article is partly based on publications in Poland since 1944.

[2] For the development of political ideas in Poland up to 1905, see J. Feldman, *Geschichte der politischen Ideen in Polen seit dessen Teilungen, 1795–1914* (Munich, 1917), pp. 310–355. Chapter 17 (by Professor W. J. Rose) of the *Cambridge History of Poland*, Vol. II (Cambridge, 1941), is a useful brief summary.

His ideas were expressed in book form in 1903 under the title *Myśli nowoczesnego Polaka* ("Thoughts of a Modern Pole"). This book influenced a generation of Polish nationalists.

The Polish Socialist Party (P.P.S.) was founded in 1892 in Paris.[1] There were from the beginning two trends within its ranks. One was for Polish national independence: the Polish socialist movements in the three empires were to be linked with each other, and P.P.S. was to be the socialist party of all Poland. The other was internationalist Social Democracy, which recognised between the Polish socialists of the three empires no more solidarity than between all workers of all lands. The Galician socialists, led by Ignacy Daszyński, began as internationalists, but by the nineties had come round to the "patriotic" point of view. Under Austrian laws they were able to operate legally. In 1904 the Social Democratic Party of Galicia and Silesia made at its congress a declaration of the closest collaboration with P.P.S. For Prussian Poland a Polish socialist paper was founded in 1890 in Berlin, and in 1893 was set up a Polish branch of the German Social Democrat Party, which also enjoyed freedom of organisation under the law. It strongly sympathised with P.P.S. In Russian Poland P.P.S. was of course illegal, but it was here that it had its greatest strength. From 1894 onwards it published an illegal paper *Robotnik*. Its first editor was Piłsudski, who stood for the most nationalistic policy.

P.P.S. was strongly opposed to all forms of Panslavism. With regard to the eastern provinces,[2] it declared, at its Sixth Congress, held in 1902, that the future of Lithuania should be decided, after liberation from the Tsarist yoke, by the multinational population of the Lithuanian lands, but that till then there should be maximum unity of Polish and Lithuanian workers. It was not anti-semitic, but reserved judgment as to whether the Jews were entitled to consider themselves a separate nation. It combated the "Bund", which since 1902 argued that they were,[3] and deplored the alleged tendency of Polish Jews to help Russian Jews to combat the Polish independence movement. It was sceptical of the value of the Russian revolutionary movement, and had only scanty contact with it.

This nationalist trend, represented especially by Piłsudski, was combated by Polish internationalist socialists led by Roza Luxem-

---

[1] Perl, *op. cit.*, pp. 383–401.
[2] Of former Poland, that is the "western" and "south-western" provinces of the Russian Empire, ruled by the Governors-General of Vilna and Kiev. See above, p. 32.
[3] See above, p. 160.

burg. This group, which had in exile its own paper, *Sprawa Robotnicza* ("The Workers' Cause"), stood for the closest co-operation between the Polish, Lithuanian and Russian proletariats. It regarded Polish independence as an illusion. Roza Luxemburg maintained that the maintenance of the partitions, with frontiers as they were, was to the advantage of the Polish workers. Their economic interests were bound to the industrial development of the three great states. The future of the Polish workers lay, she believed, not in an independent Polish state, but in three socialist republics of Russia, Austria and Germany. Luxemburg and Karski founded in 1900 the Social Democracy of the Kingdoms of Poland and Lithuania (S.D.K.P.L.). Still another group was the "P.P.S. Proletariat", founded by Kułczycki, which agreed with S.D.K.P.L. on most issues but specified that the Russian socialist republic of the future should have an "autonomous-federative" structure, while S.D.K.P.L. was for centralism.[1]

The policy of the two German Powers to the Poles differed, because their interests in the Polish question were different. Firstly, Prussia was a Protestant country, in which the Poles were a Catholic minority. The religious issue therefore strengthened German-Polish antagonism. Secondly, it was the aim of Prussian policy definitely to secure for the German population the possession of the land along the eastern march. This territory had to be germanised, and the Poles to go under. Thirdly, the German Empire had no direct conflict of interests with Russia. It had indeed become a Prussian tradition to seek Russian friendship. In the case of Austria all three conditions were reversed. First, Catholicism was the religion of the Habsburg emperors and of the great majority of their subjects, as well as of the Poles. It was therefore a link rather than a barrier. Secondly, Vienna never intended to colonise Galicia with Germans, who were a small minority of the population of the whole empire and enjoyed a relatively high standard of living in Austria and Bohemia. Thirdly, Austria had good reasons to be opposed to Russian policy in the Balkans, and as the South Slav movement grew within her borders her rulers increasingly feared Russian intervention in her own affairs. Therefore Polish nationalism could not be ignored as a weapon to use in self-defence against Russia. In both the German and Austrian empires, in contrast to Russia, most of the personal civil liberties normal in Western countries existed. In so far as they possessed these liberties, the Polish subjects of Germany and Austria were more for-

[1] Feldman, *op. cit.*, pp. 334–42.

tunate than those of Russia. But though methods of policy in both German states were relatively civilised, the aims were quite different. Prussian policy aimed at the destruction of Polish national feeling, Austrian did not.[1]

The main points of conflict between Germans and Poles in Prussia were the Church, the schools and the land.[2] Bismarck's *Kulturkampf* against the Catholic Church in the seventies was especially severe in the Polish areas. Archbishop Ledochowski of Poznań, appointed in 1865, had been anything but provocative. He had even antagonised Polish opinion by discouraging the clergy from opposing the German authorities in any way on the national issue. But when Bismarck began his anti-Catholic policy, Ledochowski had to resist. He was imprisoned in Ostrow in 1874, released after two years and went to Rome. His see was vacant for twelve years. Side by side with the religious struggle went measures against the Polish language, which in 1874 was excluded from schools "except where no other language can be understood". In 1876 Polish was excluded from the transactions of public offices, and in 1877 of the law courts. An *Ausnahmsgesetz* prevented the application to the Polish-inhabited Poznań province of the local government system established for the rest of Prussia in 1872. Colonisation of the land by Germans was promoted by a law of 1886, which set aside public funds to assist the process. Resistance was organised by the local Polish "agricultural societies". An increasing part was played by the co-operatives in which Polish priests were active. The number of co-operative branches in Prussian Poland increased between 1878 and 1910 from 73 to 265. The Polish population increased more rapidly than the German. Whereas in 1867 it formed 62 per cent of the total population in Poznań province, by 1910 it was 71 per cent. During the whole period the Polish population in the towns also grew. By the turn of the century Poles were engaged, side by side with Germans and Jews, in both commerce and industry.

After the dismissal of Bismarck, Prussian policy under his successor Caprivi was milder. Caprivi received the leader of the Polish Club of the Reichstag, and a delegation of the Polish nobility called on Emperor William II. The immediate effect of this change in policy to the Poles was a deterioration of German-Russian relations,

---

[1] Brief summaries may be found in *Cambridge History of Poland*, chapter 18 (on Prussian Poland, by Professor W. J. Rose) and 19 (on Galicia by Professor S., Estreicher).

[2] See Feldman, *Bismarck et la question polonaise*, *Revue historique*, Vol. CLXXIII (Paris, 1934). A German account is Bernhard, *Die Polenfrage* (Leipzig, 1910).

already exacerbated by the failure of commercial negotiations. It was a short honeymoon. At about the same time as the German-Russian tariff war was concluded by a trade treaty (1894) German policy reverted to its anti-Polish traditions. In 1899 was founded the *Deutsche Ostmarkenverein*, the first syllables of the names of whose three leaders, Hannemann, Kennemann and Tiedemann, provided the word "Hakatist", which has passed into the Polish language as a description of extreme anti-Polish German nationalism. It was at the turn of the century that the word *Ausrottungspolitik* ("policy of extermination") began to be used of German policy in the borderlands. It is however only fair to add that it was used in the economic and cultural senses only. The battle for ownership of land and for teaching in the schools was fought within the framework of the laws, even if these were reactionary laws. It was only in the age of Adolf Hitler that the word *Ausrottung* received literal physical significance.

In Austria, the Galician Poles had enjoyed since 1867 a large measure of self-government. A Diet for Galicia met in Lwów. It was elected on a restricted franchise by a system of colleges. Local government was based on district, town and commune councils. Within the competence of the Diet were matters relating to local agriculture, forestry, public health and education. A law of 1883 gave it very wide powers over the schools. The head of the executive power, and representative of the Emperor, was the Viceroy. This office was always given to a Pole. He had executive departments under him, of which the Schools Board was perhaps the most important. Apart from this, Galicia was represented in the Imperial Parliament, or Reichsrat in Vienna. For the first six years the Diet elected the Reichsrat delegates, but from 1873 they were elected directly by the public, also on a restricted franchise. In Vienna was also a Minister for Galicia, who acted as a link between the imperial ministries and the Viceroy's government. The practical result was that Galicia enjoyed almost complete autonomy, the Galician administration was staffed by Poles, and the schools—together with the two universities of Lwów and Cracow and the Lwów engineering college—were controlled by Poles.

Of the political parties, the two most important, the National Democrats and the Socialists, pursued essentially the same aims as in Russian Poland. There was also a Conservative Party, representing the landowners and influential until the introduction of universal franchise in 1907. There was a marked difference in attitude between the Cracow conservatives and the so-called Podolian group, representing the landowners of the eastern part of Galicia. The former co-operated loyally with the Vienna government. The latter, alarmed at the growth of Ukrainian nationalism and discontented with the tolerance shown by Vienna towards the Ukrainians, were inclined to sympathise with Russia. A fourth party of growing importance was the People's Party, which drew its strength from the peasantry. It was formed in 1903 from the union of various small groups, and became powerful after universal suffrage was introduced.

Galicia was the only land in Europe where free political and literary activity was possible for Ukrainians. In Lwów was founded in 1868 the society *Prosvita* ("Enlightenment"), which opened reading-rooms and organised lectures in Ukrainian in the small towns and villages. In 1873 was founded the Shevchenko Society, which became in time a sort of Ukrainian Academy. The leading Ukrainian intellectual in the seventies was Drahomaniv, who had been Professor at Kiev university and in 1875 founded in Geneva a paper called *Hromada*. He later came to Lwów. Among his pupils was the poet Ivan Franko. Drahomaniv was close in his general political ideas to the Russian Populists. He opposed the separation of Ukraine from Russia, but wished all Russia to be reorganised as a federal Slav state. The first political party among the Ukrainians of Galicia were the so-called Old Ruthenes, who co-operated with the Austrian and Galician authorities. In the early eighties grew up in opposition to them the Populists (Narodovtsi) or Young Ruthenes. In 1889 the left wing of this party, consisting of pupils of Drahomaniv, broke off to form the Radical Party. In 1890 the Narodovtsi in their turn came to an agreement with the government, while the Radicals remained in opposition. In 1894 a Chair of Ukrainian History was founded at Lwów university, and was taken by Hrushevski, an exile from the Russian Ukraine, who became the greatest Ukrainian historian, and had a great influence on the next generation on both sides of the frontier. Hrushevski was more conservative than Drahomaniv, and considerably more nationalistic. He was bitterly anti-Russian. He was largely responsible for the formation in 1899, from the Narodovtsi and the Radicals of the National Democratic Party, thenceforth the most important Ukrainian political party in Galicia. On the extreme left there was founded in 1899 a Ukrainian Social Democratic Party for Galicia.[1]

---

[1] *Narys Istorii Ukrainy* (Kiev, 1942), p. 130; *Velika Istoriya Ukrainy*, pp. 740–2.

During these years political activity in the Russian Ukraine had to be underground. The left elements of the Ukrainian national movement founded in 1901 the Revolutionary Ukrainian Party (R.U.P.). It was both socially radical and strongly nationalist. Its first illegal pamphlet, giving its programme, was entitled *Samostii-na Ukraina* ("Independent Ukraine"), and had the slogan "One single indivisible free independent Ukraine from the Carpathians to the Caucasus". During the following years it split several times. First the extreme nationalists seceded to form the Ukrainian People's Party, whose ideas can be described as a Ukrainian variant of Polish National Democracy. Then the extreme left broke off to form the Ukrainian section (*spilka*) of the Russian Social Democratic Party. Then in 1905 the remnant split into the Ukrainian Social Democratic Party (corresponding to P.P.S. in Poland) and the Radical Democrat Party (corresponding to the liberals of the League of Liberation in Russia). The last was the strongest of all these groups, and also drew to itself the left wing of the People's Party.[1]

The relations of Poles and Ukrainians to each other and to the three imperial governments can be briefly summarised as follows. The Russian government was systematically hostile to both Polish and Ukrainian nationalism, but attempted to use any discontented social elements within either nation against the nationalists. The Prussian government was systematically hostile to every class of the Polish nation, but the economic and political structure of the German Empire allowed Poles greater opportunities of expression and development than they enjoyed in Russia—opportunities which they used against the Germans. The Austrian regime allowed much more freedom to both Poles and Ukrainians, playing them off against each other and keeping both as weapons to use against Russia. The triangular relationship between Russians, Poles and Ukrainians is complicated. On the whole each of the three hated the other two. Yet among both Poles and Ukrainians there were Russophile minorites, and Polish-Ukrainian friendship also found some support on both sides of the frontier. While both Poles and Ukrainians looked to Vienna, Ukrainians also looked to Berlin, against which they had no grounds for hatred. Poles however could expect from Berlin nothing but enmity.[2]

[1] *O.D.*, Vol. III, pp. 197 ff.
[2] On the triangular relationship, see also below, pp. 321–2.

The Balkans in the Nineties

Russian foreign policy in the nineties was concentrated on Asia. In the Balkans Russia wished to maintain the *status quo*, to prevent any territorial changes in the Ottoman Empire, and to keep such influence as she possessed in the Balkan states. During these years Austria was weakened by internal conflicts. As these principally concerned her German and Czech subjects, whose interests were not directly connected with the Balkan peninsula, she could not hope to solve them by gaining territory or influence in the Balkans. She therefore pursued a more moderate Balkan policy than in the seventies and eighties. Germany did her best to encourage Russian action in Asia and to hold back Austria from any action in Europe which would annoy Russia. Britain, on the other hand, feared Russian action in Asia, and had much less objection to Russian intervention in the Balkans. In place of the older British policy of protection of Turkey, Salisbury suggested common action with Russia in Turkish affairs. British overtures however met only with suspicion in St. Petersburg. Austria valued co-operation with Britain, but was too weak to make her German ally agree. The result was stalemate and comparative quiet in the Balkans. Nevertheless the forces which were making for Austro-Russian conflict— the unsolved Macedonian problem and the connection between internal Balkan politics and Great Power interests—continued to develop.

In Serbia, Milan's position was seriously weakened by the defeat of 1885. In the following year he felt obliged to grant an amnesty to the Radical leaders imprisoned after the rebellion of 1883. Then estrangement from his wife and a love affair with the wife of one of his own subjects took up most of his attention. In 1888 he granted a new, and much more democratic, constitution, obtained the consent of the Orthodox Church to a divorce, and abdicated.[1] His son Alexander was an irresolute young man, influenced alternately by his mother, who was Russophile, and his father, who remained Austrophile. The Austro-Serbian treaty expired in 1895 and was not renewed. For the first years of the new reign the Regency, dominated by the veteran statesman Ristić, inclined towards Russia. In 1894 Milan returned to Belgrade and re-established his influence over his son. Policy veered towards Austria. In 1896 however a tariff dispute with Austria, caused by pressure from Hungarian landowners for protection against

[1] Jovanović, *Vlada Milana Obrenovića*; Vol. III, pp. 443–95.

imports of Serbian pigs, brought a swing back to Russia. At the end of 1897 Alexander introduced a personal dictatorship, with Vladan Djordjević as Prime Minister. Milan's influence was again strong in these years, and Serbia's relations with Austria were once more good. In 1900 however Alexander decided, despite the bitter opposition of his father and of Djordjević, to marry his mistress Draga Mashin, whose friends were strongly pro-Russian. This year was the turning-point in Serbia's foreign policy, from which it did not again swerve. In 1901 Alexander introduced a new constitution, revoked it in March 1903, and was assassinated, with his wife, in extremely horrible circumstances, by officer conspirators, in May. The murder was followed by the restoration of the Karadjordjević dynasty. This was at first expected to cause a recovery of Austrian influence, but for reasons which will be considered later it did not have that effect.[1]

In Bulgaria the Grand National Assembly had decided in 1887 to elect as its ruler Ferdinand of Coburg, who had connections with Austria and actually held a commission in the Hungarian army. Ferdinand accepted despite the discouragement or hostility of the Powers, and came to Bulgaria in July 1887. For the first seven years of his reign the country was effectively ruled by Stambolov. It was diplomatically isolated, and stood in constant fear of Russia. In 1890 an attempt was made on Ferdinand's life by a Russophile officer, and in 1891 Stambolov narrowly escaped assassination. In 1892 tension was reduced when Stambolov visited Constantinople and the Sultan recognised Ferdinand. Next year the Prince married Princess Marie-Louise of Parma. Stambolov ensured passage of a constitutional amendment to enable the heir to be brought up as a Catholic, which was the demand of the bride's family. This action infuriated the Tsar, but was followed by better relations with Austria. Having got what he wanted from Stambolov, Ferdinand now broke with him. A quarrel about an appointment led the Premier to offer his resignation in May 1894, and to his surprise it was accepted. Out of office, Stambolov bitterly attacked the Prince. But his long period of power, during which he had sometimes used cruel methods of repression, had won Stambolov many enemies. In July 1895 during Ferdinand's absence abroad, Stambolov was brutally murdered in a Sofia street while the police were conveniently out of sight.

The death of Stambolov prepared the way for better relations

---

[1] For Serbian politics in this period, the best work is Slobodan Jovanović, *Vlada Aleksandra Obrenovića* (Belgrade, 1935), 3 vols.

with Russia, where the change of Tsar had also made possible a more conciliatory spirit. The price was the reconversion to Orthodoxy of the heir to the throne, Prince Boris. This meant a breach between Ferdinand and his wife. Unlike Milan and Alexander of Serbia, who sacrificed politics for matrimonial satisfaction, Ferdinand was willing to put politics first. On 15th February 1896 the reconversion took place, and Nicholas II recognised Ferdinand as ruler of Bulgaria. The Russophile period coincided with the Ministry of Stoilov, who had succeeded Stambolov in 1894 and remained in power until 1899. From 1899 to 1901 the Austrophiles were again in power, but were succeeded by two years of Russophile governments.[1] In 1902 the Russian Foreign Minister Lamsdorff paid a visit to both Sofia and Belgrade. In the same year a Russo-Bulgarian military convention was signed. The two Powers were to assist each other in the event of an attack on either by Roumania.[2] Thus by 1903 Russia's diplomatic position in the Balkans had substantially improved. Both Serbia and Bulgaria were more inclined towards Russia than Austria.

During the nineties the discontent of the Macedonians with Turkish rule was growing. Small-scale guerrilla activity became a permanent feature of the province. The bands fought not only the Turks but each other. Bulgarian, Serbian and Greek bishops claimed authority over Macedonian Orthodox parishes; Bulgarian, Greek and Serbian schools competed for the instruction of Macedonian children; and Bulgarian, Greek and Serbian "komitadjis"[3] fought each other and the Turkish troops in the hills and forests.

The majority of the Macedonian Christians were Slavs, and were more closely akin to the Bulgarians than to the Serbs. There were two main points of view among them, the one favouring incorporation in Bulgaria, the other an independent Macedonian state. The first was led from Sofia, and its leadership was organised in the so-called Supreme Committee, founded in 1896. The second was led by the Internal Macedonian Revolutionary Organisation (V.M.R.O.), founded in 1895 by Damian Gruev and Gotsi Delchev. It declared as its aim the liberation of all Macedonia and equal

---

[1] For Bulgarian politics in these years the following are of some use: Blagoyev, *op. cit.*; Y. Sakazov, *Blgarite v svoyata istoriya* (Sofia, 1922); Kosta Todorov, *Politička istorija savremene Bugarske* (Belgrade, 1938); Madol, *King Ferdinand of Bulgaria* (London, 1933).

[2] On this convention, see article by E. C. Helmreich and C. E. Black in *Journal of Modern History*, Vol. IX (Chicago, 1937), pp. 471–82.

[3] The literal meaning of this Turkish word is "committee-man". In practice it meant a member of an insurgent band.

rights for all its nationalities—Slavs, Greeks, Albanians, Vlachs[1] and Turks. In practice it was a Slav organisation, and tended to be pro-Bulgarian. But before 1914 it was always much more independent of Sofia than was the Supreme Committee.[2]

The first international crisis which affected Russia and the Ottoman Empire in this period was caused by the activities of the Armenian revolutionaries, the Dashnyaks. In the autumn of 1894, the winter of 1895-6 and the summer of 1896, risings and outrages by Armenians in Constantinople or other Turkish cities were followed by massacres of Armenian civilians by Turkish troops or mobs.[3] The outcry in Europe was greatest in Britain. Public opinion urged action to force the Sultan to reform, and Salisbury thought the opportunity favourable for a far-reaching settlement of the problems of the Near East. But the Russian government had little sympathy for Armenian revolutionaries whom its own officials were repressing in the Caucasus; France was interested in the survival of the Ottoman Empire in which she had substantial investments; and Germany was anxious to avoid any question that might lead to Russo-Austrian tension. In St. Petersburg there was alarm at the prospect of any European control over the Ottoman Empire which would reduce Russia's influence. Nelidov, the Russian ambassador in Constantinople, proposed to his Government in November 1896 that if any British naval action were taken against Turkey, Russia must occupy the Bosphorus with her troops. Despite opposition from Witte, the Tsar approved a detailed plan submitted by Nelidov.[4] It did not however materialise, as France strongly discouraged action by Russia, and William II assured the Russian Foreign Minister that British action was most improbable. In February 1897 an agreed scheme of reforms for the Ottoman Empire was prepared by the ambassadors of the Powers in Constantinople. But before it could be presented to the Turkish government, a new crisis arose in Crete.

During the nineties relations between the Christian Cretans and

---

[1] The Vlachs speak a language similar to Roumanian. They were at this time scattered through Macedonia, and also formed a compact group in the Pindus mountains of Greece. The best account of the Balkan nationalities at the turn of the century is the brilliant work of Sir Charles Eliot (" Odysseus "), *Turkey in Europe* (London, 1900). Another extremely useful work is H. Brailsford, *Macedonia* (London, 1906).

[2] For the intricacies of Macedonian Slav organisations see, besides Brailsford, *op. cit.*, Swire, *Bulgarian Conspiracy* (London, 1939).

[3] For an account of these incidents and the diplomacy to which they gave rise, see W. L. Langer, *The Diplomacy of Imperialism* (New York, 1935), Vol. I, chapters 5–7.

[4] *Krasny Arkhiv*, I, pp. 152–163; *Mémoires du Comte Witte* (Paris, 1921), pp. 164–6. The episode is discussed in Langer, *op. cit*, Vol. I, pp. 205–9.

the Turkish authorities, which had been uneasy since the Berlin Congress and earlier, grew rapidly worse. In 1895 guerrilla bands were operating in the mountains. Nationalist agitation was encouraged from Greece. Two organisations were especially active in Greece itself—the Cretan Committee, which was an overt organisation, and the *Ethnike Hetairia*, a secret society founded in 1894, which was especially concerned with Greek interests in Macedonia. In the summer of 1896 the revolt in Crete spread, and supplies were shipped from the Greek mainland. The Greek government took no steps to stop the traffic. In February 1897 the Cretan rebels declared the union of the island with Greece, and appealed to Athens for help. Prince George, second son of the King, arrived off the coast with four torpedo-boats, but left again the following day. A force of 1,500 men was however landed under command of a Greek colonel. In the next two months the Powers unsuccessfully discussed organising a common blockade of the Cretan coasts. Britain showed sympathy for Greece and Russia for the rights of the Turks. Germany supported Russia. Meanwhile in Thessaly troops were concentrated on both sides of the frontier. On 17th April 1897 the Greeks attacked, and Turkey declared war. The Turks defeated the Greeks and advanced southwards during May. The German and Russian governments, which at first had supported Turkey, now intervened in favour of the Greeks. A personal appeal from Nicholas II to the Sultan resulted in an armistice. The subsequent peace denied Turkey any important gains. The Powers could not at first agree on the future settlement of Crete. Eventually however Prince George of Greece was appointed governor in November 1898 on the advice of Britain, France, Russia and Italy. Germany dissociated herself.[1] This treatment by the Powers of Turkey undoubtedly encouraged all the Balkan States to pursue forward policies. If the Greeks, though routed by the Turks, were able to get what they wanted through the help of the Powers, the Serbs, Bulgarians and Montenegrins could also hope for gains at fairly small risk.

The disagreement between Britain and Germany, and the cold response of Russia to British overtures, which were a constant feature of the years 1895-7, were embarrassing to Austria. Torn by dissensions in Bohemia, the Austrian government could not refuse German pressure to reach an agreement with Russia. In May 1897, during the visit of Francis Joseph and his Foreign Minister, Count Gołuchowski, to St. Petersburg, an agreement

---

[1] Langer, *op. cit.*, Vol. I, p. 377.

was signed. Both Powers disclaimed territorial annexations in the
Balkans, and agreed to oppose acquisition of Balkan territory by
any other Power. They both also accepted the principle of clcsure
of the Straits. Should disintegration of the Ottoman Empire in
Europe be unavoidable, Austria would have the right to change her
status of occupying Power in Bosnia-Hercegovina and Novi
Bazar into one of full sovereignty. An Albanian state would be
created along the Adriatic coast between Scutari and Yanina. The
rest of the Ottoman territory would be divided between the existing
Balkan states in such a way as to secure an equal balance between
them, and prevent a "marked preponderance of any particular
Balkan principality to the detriment of the others".[1]

Agreements between the Powers could not prevent an increase of
disorders, reprisals and further disorders in Macedonia. These
reached their culmination in August 1903, when V.M.R.O.
ordered a general insurrection on St. Elijah's day (Ilinden). After
a few successes, it was suppressed by Turkish troops. Despite some
support from Macedonian organisations in Bulgaria to the rebels,
and much agitation on their behalf, the Bulgarian government
stood aside. Once more European public opinion demanded
reforms and foreign supervision. In October the Austrian and
Russian emperors met at Mürzsteg and agreed on a programme.
There was to be an inspector-general, appointed by the Turkish
government, to organise reforms. He was to have two civil advisers,
one Austrian, one Russian. Under him was to be a gendarmerie
staffed by the Powers, each of which was to have its territorial
zone.[2] This scheme received the agreement of all the Powers
except Germany, which would not accept a gendarmerie zone.

Mürzsteg was the last Austro-Russian agreement in Balkan
matters. On the eve of the war with Japan, the Balkans seemed
quiet, and Russian influence seemed solidly based. But the defeat
of Russia, and the entry of new factors into Russian political life,
brought far-reaching changes.

The Far East

The territorial gains of 1860 had established Russia as a Pacific
Power, but they could not be regarded as a satisfactory settlement

[1] Full text in Pribram, *Secret Treaties of Austria–Hungary, 1870–1914* (Harvard,
1920), Vol. I, pp. 184–90.
[2] The Russian sector was Salonica city and the western part of Salonica province
(*vilayet*); the Italian sector Bitolj (Monastir); the Austrian sector Skoplje (Üsküb);
the French sector Seres; the British sector Drama. The Commander of the gendarmerie was to be the Italian general De Giorgis. See Brailsford, *op. cit.*, pp.
305 ff.

for two reasons. The Amur-Ussuri frontier left Manchuria as a great salient thrust into Russian territory between the maritime province and Siberia, and the newly acquired coast had no ice-free port. To shorten the frontier, and so reduce the number of troops needed to guard it, was a constant aim of the Russian military command, which always considered that its main tasks lay in Europe. The search for a warm water preoccupied the Russian Admiralty. It could be satisfied only by a port in the Yellow Sea or in Korea. The Yellow Sea would be unsatisfactory unless the port were linked with Russia by land communications through Manchuria, and the latter were effectively dominated by Russia. Korea, lying nearer to Russia's existing frontiers, seemed more satisfactory. But as it was separated only by a narrow channel from Japan, it was the most important point on the Asiatic mainland to that Power. Any Russian attempt to seize part of Korea's southern coast must involve Russia in conflict with Japan.

Korea was nominally a vassal of the Chinese Empire, but in the third quarter of the nineteenth century was in practice independent. As an independent state it made commercial treaties with Japan and with the European Powers between 1876 and 1886. In 1883 a German named Möllendorff took over the administration of the Korean customs, under nominal Chinese authority. He then proposed that Russian officers be sent as instructors to the Korean army.[1] The Russian government asked, as a price for sending the instructors, for a base on the Korean coast at Port Lazarev. The British government then sent a naval force to occupy an island at the entrance to the Straits of Korea. The two governments then agreed to withdraw both forces.

In 1884 a group of young Korean reformers seized power at the capital Seoul. The reformers enjoyed the sympathy of the Japanese. The Chinese government, as suzerain of Korea, sent troops to restore order. The Japanese did the same. Conflict was averted by a Chinese-Japanese convention of April 1885. Both Powers were to withdraw their forces, but in the event of further disorders in Korea they might jointly intervene after previous consultation. Thus Chinese suzerainty was replaced by a sort of negative protectorate by the two Powers.

In July 1894 another rebellion broke out against the Korean government, which appealed to China for aid. In accordance with the 1885 convention, the Japanese also announced their intention to intervene. The Chinese force numbered some 3,000 men, the

[1] B. Romanov, *Rossiya v Manchzhurii* (Leningrad, 1928), p. 8.

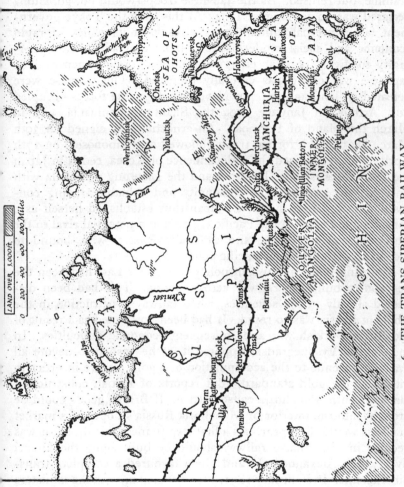

6. THE TRANS-SIBERIAN RAILWAY

Japanese nearly 10,000. The rebellion was soon crushed, but the Japanese refused to evacuate until the Korean government had accepted a far-reaching programme of reforms under Japanese supervision. The Chinese were invited to participate in the programme, but refused, As the Japanese troops would not go, China declared war on 1st August 1894. At this time the Tokyo government faced internal difficulties as a result of its policy of rapid economic and social modernisation, and was glad of the opportunity to divert popular energies against a foreign enemy. The Japanese war effort was carefully prepared. The Chinese were defeated on land and sea. In November Japanese forces occupied Port Arthur, in January 1895 the Shantung peninsula, and in March the island of Formosa. An armistice was signed on 30th March 1895, and a formal treaty followed at Shimonoseki on 17th April. This recognised the independence of Korea, ceded to Japan the Pescadores islands, Formosa and the Liaotung peninsula with Port Arthur, and gave an indemnity and valuable trading concessions to Japanese subjects. Japan thus established herself as a considerable Power in the Pacific region and a potential rival to the European states. These, and especially Russia, were bound to reconsider seriously their Pacific policy.

A turning-point in Russian policy in the Far East had been the decision to build the railway across Siberia. This had been discussed already in the seventies, when railway construction in the whole of Russia was so rapid. It had been postponed as a result of the Russo-Turkish war and subsequent economic difficulties. In the eighties Vyshnegradski opposed it, as he wished to devote all available revenue to the accumulation of a gold reserve in order to introduce the gold standard. But reports of British construction plans in south Manchuria caused alarm. If British goods could be brought into the interior of Manchuria Russia's hopes of a market in China would disappear. As a first step to meet this threat, it was decided in 1890 that a railway should be built along the Ussuri river. Both Alexander III and Giers favoured a complete trans-Siberian line. In February 1891, after discussions with the ministers concerned, the Tsar definitely decided in favour of the project, which was to begin simultaneously from Chelyabinsk and from Vladivostok.[1]

When Vyshnegradski, who had first opposed and then delayed the plan, was replaced as Minister of Finance by Witte, who had previously been Minister of Communications, work really

[1] Romanov, *op. cit.*, chapter 1.

went ahead. Witte was able to persuade the Tsar of the urgency of the plan. He argued that it would greatly assist the exportation of Siberian wheat to West and East. The Chinese tea trade, threatened by Indian tea carried in British ships, would revive to the advantage of Russia, which could both satisfy home demand and profit from transit trade to Europe. Internal migration and transportation of food, the need for both of which had been horrifyingly demonstrated by the famine of 1891–2, would be made much easier. Witte believed that there were good prospects for Russian exports of both textiles and metal goods to China by land. The railway would resist British penetration of northern China and Korea and would develop Russia's trade with the United States. The railway in fact would do for Russia some of the things that the Canadian Pacific Railway was doing for Canada.

Witte was helped by the activities of a Buryat Mongol doctor named Badmaev, who had access to the Tsar. A memorandum of February 1893, addressed by Badmaev to Witte with the request to bring it to the Tsar's attention, urged that a railway be built not only to Vladivostok but also through Mongolia to Lanchow on the upper Hwang-Ho. Badmaev had fantastic projects for a revolt of the Tibetans, Chinese and Mongols of north China against the Manchu dynasty, and for an appeal by their feudal lords and merchants to the "white emperor" to take them under his protection. He himself with a few thousand Buryat traders and gun-runners would prepare the ground. Witte used this curious document to support his pleas for an active policy in the Far East. In his own recommendation to the Tsar occurred the sentence, "Russia from the shores of the Pacific and the summits of the Himalayas will dominate not only Asiatic but also European affairs".[1] The Tsar was sufficiently impressed to give his assent to a request by Badmaev for a loan of 2,000,000 roubles from the Treasury for the trading concern which he proposed to create in Mongolia with these ambitious aims. Despite misgivings, Witte had to hand out the money. In fact nothing came of Badmaev's plans. He is interesting as the first of a series of adventurers who influenced Russian policy in the Far East. While he made money the real work of railway building went ahead.[2]

Thus when the Sino-Japanese war came, Russia was already committed to expansion in the Far East. The crisis compelled the

[1] Romanov, *op. cit.*, p. 63.
[2] Documents relating to Badmaev, including some of his letters and memoranda, are contained in a Soviet publication, *Za kulisami tsarizma* (Leningrad, 1925).

Russian government to decide its attitude to the parties at war and
to the other Great Powers. Giers wished an agreement for common
action with Britain. This was opposed by the other ministers, who
feared that it would give Britain too much influence over China.
Opinions were divided between support of Japan and support of
China. At a conference of ministers held on 6th April 1895, the
new Foreign Minister, Prince Lobanov-Rostovski[1], assumed that
the object of Russia's policy was the old naval aim of an ice-free
port in Korea. This he believed could be obtained by agreement
with Japan. Russia could recognise Japanese annexation of Liaotung peninsula in return for compensation on the Korean coast.
Witte, on the other hand, was less concerned with an ice-free port
at once than with Russian control of the Chinese market, and
political domination of all north China, in the more distant future.
In his view it would be better to support China against Japan,
which was a potential future rival to Russia. The price of Russian
support to China would be extensive economic concessions in
Manchuria. Witte argued that Chinese integrity must at present
be defended in order to prevent a premature partition between the
Powers. A few years later, when the trans-Siberian railway was
completed, Russia would be in a position to take the lion's share in
any partition, of territory or of economic advantages. Meanwhile it
was to her interest to preserve the *status quo*.[2]

Witte's arguments were strengthened by the known attitude of
Germany, which was willing to join Russia in forcing Japan to give
up her gains from the war. It was during this crisis that the policy
took shape which William II pursued with regard to Russia for the
next ten years. In order to keep Russian attention away from the
Balkans, and so minimise the Austro-Russian friction which was so
embarrassing to Germany, he encouraged Russian expansion in
Eastern Asia. In this policy there was also an ideological element, of
fear and hatred of the "yellow races", which seems to have been
sincere. On 26th April 1895 William wrote to Nicholas that "the
great task of the future for Russia is to cultivate the Asian continent and defend Europe from the inroads of the Great Yellow
race". On 10th July he wrote that he himself would "let nobody
interfere with you and attack you from behind in Europe during the
time you were fulfilling the great mission which Heaven has shaped

---

[1] Before his appointment as Minister of Foreign Affairs, Prince Lobanov-
Rostovski had been Russian Ambassador in Constantinople (1878-9), London
(1879-82), Vienna (1882-94), and Berlin (1894-5).
[2] Romanov, *op. cit.*, pp. 67-81.

7. THE BALKANS 1875–8

for you". On 25th October he personally assured Lobanov that he considered it his duty to keep Russia's back free in Europe.[1]

After first inclining to the point of view of Lobanov and the Admiralty, the Tsar decided in favour of Witte. On 8th April 1895 the Russian government proposed to the governments of Germany, France and Britain that the four Powers should together require the Japanese to abandon the Liaotung peninsula. The Germans agreed to the Russian proposals, both because it was their policy to encourage Russian interference in that region and because they themselves wished to prepare for territorial gains in China. France decided to support her newly won ally, even though the region was one to which the provisions of the 1891 agreement did not apply. Britain however refused to associate herself with the other Powers. Already in July 1894 the Japanese government had consulted the British, and had been told that Britain's main concern was that the Shanghai area should not be involved in hostilities. This reply had in fact encouraged the Japanese to go ahead in Korea.[2] At the outbreak of war British official sympathy was rather on the Chinese side, but public opinion moved to the side of Japan. Moreover the British government was not averse to a strengthening of Japan which might bar the door to Manchuria to Russia.

Thus it was only the Russian, French and German governments which on 23rd April 1895 presented notes in Tokyo, asking for the abandonment of Liaotung. The notes were similarly phrased, but the German minister in delivering his note used insulting language and threatened Japan with force. The Japanese accepted the demand of the Powers and gave up the peninsula. But the behaviour of the German minister was remembered against his country.[3]

The result of this diplomatic action confirmed Witte's hopes. On 6th July 1895 the Russian government guaranteed a loan of 400 million francs to the Chinese government, provided by French and Russian banks, to enable China to pay her indemnity to Japan. In December 1895 was formed the Russo-Chinese Bank. Most of its capital was provided by French banks. Its chairman was Prince Uhtomski, a prominent advocate of a forward policy in the Far East, and among its directors were high officials of the Russian Ministry of Finance. In May 1896 the leading Chinese statesman Li-Hung-Chang came to Moscow to the coronation ceremonies of Nicholas II. He had several conversations with Witte, and on 22nd

[1] *Briefe Wilhelms II an den Zaren, 1894–1914* (Berlin, 1920), pp. 291, 293, 299.
[2] *The Secret Memoirs of Count Hayashi*, ed. A. M. Pooley (London, 1915), p. 72.
[3] Hayashi, *op. cit.*, pp. 77–9.

May signed a treaty of alliance between Russia and China. Russia undertook to defend China against attack, and in order that it might be possible for her to fulfil this obligation a railway was to be built across Manchuria from west to east, thus shortening the link with Vladivostok by cutting off the Amur salient. The new enterprise was to be called the Chinese Eastern Railway. It was to be financed by the Russo-Chinese Bank. A substantial zone of land on both sides of the line was to be placed at the disposal of the company. Russian personnel might be employed on the line, and Russian armed police, under the command of the Russian Ministry of Finance, might keep order within the railway zone. The concession was to be for eighty years, at the end of which it would pass into the ownership of the Chinese government without compensation. The Chinese government might however buy the railway after thirty-six years. In practice, for the following twenty years there was on Manchurian soil a strip of Russian territory which was ruled by the Finance Ministry. The town of Harbin was in effect a Russian colonial city.[1]

After the victory over China, Japan intended to make Korea a Japanese protectorate. Her policy was however opposed by Russia. The Admiralty's interest in Korea, especially in the port of Mosampo, was still strong. In May 1896 an ambassador from the king of Korea visited Nicholas II and requested that his country be taken under the protection of Russia. The Tsar accepted the request on the spot, but was later persuaded by Lobanov that this was not possible.[2] In June 1896 was signed an agreement, known as the Lobanov-Yamagata convention. It created a Russo-Japanese condominium, similar to the Sino-Japanese arrangement of 1885. The two Powers agreed to combine against any other Power that might seek to interfere in Korea. In the event of disorders they would intervene together after consultation. During 1897 Russian officers were sent to Seoul to train the Korean army, and a Russian was appointed to direct the Korean customs. In November 1897 a Russo-Korean Bank was set up, financed mainly by French capital. At the end of the year the Japanese obtained a concession for a railway from Seoul to the southern coast at Fusan.

The next stage in the rivalry of the Powers in the Far East began with action by Germany. In November 1897 two German Catholic missionaries were murdered in Shantung province. On 3rd Decem-

---

[1] The organisation of the Chinese Eastern Railway is described in *Ministerstvo Finansov, istoricheskii ocherk* (SPB, 1902), Vol. II, pp. 589–602.
[2] Baron Rosen, *Forty Years of Diplomacy* (London, 1922), Vol. I, pp. 125–6.

ber German forces occupied the town of Kiao-Chow. This was a surprise to the Russian government, which decided that it must have compensation. The Foreign Minister, Count Muraviev, proposed the seizure of Port Arthur. Witte opposed this as it would be a provocation of Japan, which Russia had obliged to give up this territory only two years earlier. Admiral Tyrtov, of the naval general staff, was also opposed, on the ground that Port Arthur, though an ice-free port, would be useless to Russia as it was separated from Vladivostok by the Korean peninsula and straits. The Tsar however supported Muraviev. On 14th December 1897 the Russian government informed Germany of its intention to send a naval force to Port Arthur, and received enthusiastic German support. On 27th March 1898 China granted Russia a lease for twenty-five years of the peninsula of Liaotung with the ports of Port Arthur and Dairen, and a concession for a South Manchurian Railway, from Harbin to Dairen, on the same terms as the Chinese Eastern Railway. Thus Harbin became a great railway junction and a centre of Russian strategic and economic strength in the Far East, while Manchuria was well on its way to becoming a Russian colony. This new concession was only obtained by offering a large bribe to Li-Hung-Chang. Witte was opposed to the transaction. He believed that northern China would fall under Russian control if only Russia would pursue her peaceful penetration, without antagonising other Powers and so putting them prematurely on their guard.[1]

The Japanese government was in fact infuriated by the Russian action, but tried to console itself with the hope that, having now obtained an ice-free port, Russia would abandon her designs on Korea. The Japanese Foreign Minister, Baron Nissi, proposed to the Russian ambassador, Baron Rosen, a delimitation of spheres of influence. Japan was willing to recognise all Manchuria, with its coast, as outside its zone of influence, if Russia would do the same with regard to Korea. Rosen forwarded the proposal to St. Petersburg with a strong recommendation, but received the reply that, while Russia would welcome a Japanese statement of disinterestedness in Manchuria, she could not give up her own interests in Korea. Thus Russia lost an opportunity of conciliating Japan. All that was achieved was an agreement of April 1898, known as the Rosen-Nissi convention, by which both Powers pledged themselves to respect Korean sovereignty and not to interfere in her internal affairs. Russia would not interfere with commercial relations

[1] Witte, op. cit., p. 208.

between Japan and Korea. Neither Power would send further advisers to Korea without consulting the other beforehand. Shortly afterwards the existing Russian military and financial advisers were withdrawn from Korea.[1]

The other European Powers gained concessions from China as a result of the crisis initiated by the German action. Germany herself received a ninety-nine years' concession of Kiao-Chow and three railway concessions in Shantung province (6th March 1898). Britain obtained the port of Wei-hai-wei, near the tip of the Shantung peninsula, by an agreement signed on 1st July. On 27th May France, which during the preceding year had received two railway concessions in southern China, obtained a ninety-nine years' lease of the southern port of Kwang-chow-wan.

In the same year the United States formally annexed Hawaii and acquired the Philippines from Spain, thus becoming in her turn a Pacific Great Power. The United States strongly championed the principle of "open door" in China. Equal opportunities for trade and investment should be available to citizens of all countries. This principle was still applicable to trade, but was hardly applicable to investments. During 1898 and 1899 the main Powers established zones in which each had special rights of railway building. The French were supreme in the south, towards the frontier of their own colony of Indo-China, and hoped to draw some of the trade of the Yangtse valley southwards. The British were dominant in the Yangtse valley itself. The Germans had the privileged position in Shantung province. North of the Great Wall was the Russian zone. An Anglo-German agreement of September 1898 allocated the Hwang-ho valley to the Germans and the province of Shansi as well as the Yangtse valley to Britain. An Anglo-Russian agreement of April 1899 left all territory north of the Wall to Russian enterprise, thus allowing the Russians to proceed with a project for a railway in Jehol province, in return for a Russian promise to seek no concessions in the Yangtse basin.[2]

In September 1899 the United States Secretary of State, John Hay, addressed to the Powers a note requesting acceptance of the "open door" principle in trade. In particular, the Powers were asked to promise not to interfere with the existing free ports, established by treaties with China in the past, and not to introduce

[1] Rosen, *op. cit.*, Vol. I, pp. 156–61.
[2] For a brief and clear summary of the division of spheres of influence and territorial concessions during these years, see G. F. Hudson, *The Far East in World Politics* (Oxford, 1939); Renouvin, *L'extrême Orient* (Paris, 1946). Both provide excellent surveys of Far Eastern affairs throughout the period up to 1914.

discriminatory tariffs on their railways. Britain, France and
Germany agreed, but the Russian reply was evasive. It accepted the
principle for the leased territories but gave no assurances concerning its railway rates in Manchuria.[1]

The Boxer rebellion of 1900 gave Russia a further opportunity
to strengthen her position in China. In August 1900 a joint force of
the Powers occupied Peking. But the Russian government decided
at the same time to occupy the chief cities of Manchuria and to
increase the Russian forces in the railway zone. Thus Russia, the
only European Power to possess a land frontier with China, was in
a position to force her terms on China. Britain in particular feared
that Russia would press the Chinese government, situated in
Peking perilously near to Port Arthur, to make difficulties for the
other Powers which had concessions further south.[2]

Against Russian policy Britain sought German support. On 16th
October 1900 was signed the so-called "Yangtse agreement"
between the two Powers. Both governments declared their wish
that the maritime and river ports of China should be open to the
trade of all nations. Both declared that they themselves had no
territorial aims, were opposed to territorial gains in the region by
any third Power, but if such gains were made would require compensation for themselves. The agreement did not however specify
what action they would take against an extension of the territory
of another Power—Russia was of course understood—and it was
not clearly stated whether the region referred to included all Manchuria. Subsequently it became clear that Germany was not
prepared to take any action to prevent Russia from dominating
Manchuria. Bülow, the German Chancellor, declared in the
Reichstag on 15th March 1901 that Germany had "no interests of
importance" in Manchuria, and that "the fate of that province was
a matter of absolute indifference to Germany".[3] This German
reluctance was in fact one of the principal reasons for the failure
of the general Anglo-German negotiations for an alliance or close
co-operation which took place in 1901.[4]

---

[1] See Tyler Dennett, *John Hay* (New York, 1933). For a general survey of
American policy, see S. Bemis, *Diplomatic History of the United States* (London,
1937), chapter 27. Another very useful work is Zabriskie, *American–Russian
Rivalry in the Far East* (Philadelphia, 1946).

[2] British investments in China, mostly in the Yangtse valley, were large and growing. In 1902 they amounted to about $260 million, in 1914 $600 million. At these
two dates Russian investments in China amounted to $240 million and $270
million, German to $170 million and $270 million. See chart in Bemis, *op. cit.*,
p. 499.

[3] Langer, *Diplomacy of Imperialism*, Vol. II, p. 722.

[4] For a summary of these negotiations, see Langer, *op. cit.*, Vol. II, chapter 22,
and F. Meinecke, *Geschichte des deutsch-englischen Bündnisproblems* (Munich, 1927).

As Germany had little to offer, Britain looked for another friend. Inevitably her choice fell on Japan. The first overtures came from the Japanese side, in April 1901. During the summer and autumn discussions continued. The Japanese government, led by Count Katsura, were in favour of an alliance with Britain, but two influential "elder statesmen"[1] Marquess Ito and Prince Inouye, preferred to reach agreement with Russia. On 25th November Ito arrived in St. Petersburg via Paris and Berlin, to the great embarrassment of Baron Hayashi, the Japanese ambassador in London, who was charged with the conduct of the negotiations. After discussions between Ito, Witte and Lamsdorff, draft proposals were exchanged. There seemed some possibility of the conclusion of an agreement by which Japan should be dominant in Korea and Russia in Manchuria. The obstacles were however serious. In Russia the naval, and to a lesser extent the military, influences were against concessions to Japan in Korea. The British government was understandably suspicious of Russo-Japanese negotiations. Lansdowne told Ito, when he came on to London in January 1902, that it "would obviously be improper that Japan should enter into a bargain with us affecting our common interests in the Far East and should then enter into another bargain of a conflicting character with a third Power". The Tokyo government, faced with a choice between a definite alliance with Britain or a limited agreement with Russia which might be repudiated by the Russian extremists, preferred the former. In fact it seems possible that the government only agreed to Ito's mission in order to be rid of him when the decision was taken. The Japanese emperor made up his mind to conclude the treaty with Britain after holding a council of elder statesmen on 7th December 1901. Definite instructions were sent to Hayashi on 10th December.[2] The British government had originally hoped to include Germany in the alliance, and in April and May Eckardstein, of the German Embassy in London, had shown interest in the idea. But by the end of the year hopes of

[1] The "elder statesmen" were a small number of persons who had rendered distinguished service to the state, and were consulted by the Emperor on matters of national policy. During the first years of the Meiji restoration they formed a Senate, but after this body was abolished a few continued to enjoy great authority, outside the framework of the constitution, at least until the end of the century. For the background to modern Japan, see Sir George Sansom, *The Western World and Japan* (London, 1950); and G. C. Allen, *A Short Economic History of Japan* (London, 1946).

[2] Hayashi, *op. cit.*, pp. 135-62. See discussion by Langer, *op. cit.*, Vol. II, pp. 758-71. Among the sources used by Langer are some of Ito's documents, available only in Japanese, which confirm Hayashi's account. Russian documents relating to Ito's visit are in *Krasny Arkhiv*, LXIII, pp. 7-54.

Anglo-German co-operation had faded. Speeches by Chamberlain in Birmingham and by Bülow in the German Reichstag showed a bitterness on both sides which closed the issue.[1]

The Anglo-Japanese alliance was signed on 30th January 1902. If either Power were involved in war with a third Power in defence of its interests in the Far East, the other would remain neutral, but if any further Power should join in hostilities against it, the ally would come to its assistance. Neither Power would enter into arrangements with a third Power to the prejudice of its ally's Far Eastern interests without consulting its ally. The Far Eastern interests to which these obligations referred were defined in the first article of the treaty as follows. Those of Britain "relate principally to China, while Japan, in addition to the interests which she possesses in China, is interested in a peculiar degree politically as well as commercially and industrially in Korea". Either Power might safeguard these interests "if threatened either by the aggressive action of any other Power or by disturbances arising in China or Korea". The original attempt of the British to extend the area covered by the treaty to include India was abandoned. The gain to both parties was considerable. Britain had emerged from an isolation which, at the time of the Boer War and of Russian expansion in Manchuria, had begun to be alarming. Japan was able to face Russia with the knowledge that she would be protected from any further attack.[2]

In St. Petersburg opinions were divided. Witte still favoured peaceful penetration of Manchuria, in the belief that this would bring China under Russian domination in the end. He therefore wished the Russian forces which had occupied cities outside the railway zone during the Boxer rebellion to be withdrawn to Russian territory. Lamsdorff shared Witte's view of the Far East, and wished to avoid any entanglements which would limit Russia's freedom of action in Europe. In particular, he wished to pursue a more active policy in the Balkans. The War Minister, General Kuropatkin, also wished an active policy in Europe. He regretted Far Eastern commitments as distracting Russia from her historic tasks in the region of the Straits and in defence of the Slavs. But his plan differed from that of Witte and Lamsdorff. He wished to annex northern Manchuria in order to shorten Russia's eastern frontier and so reduce her military commitments. He considered

[1] See Langer, *op. cit.*, Vol. II, pp. 774–5.
[2] The British documents relating to the Anglo-Japanese alliance are in *B.D.*, Vol. II, pp. 89–122.

this an urgent task as he feared the long-term effects of the rapid colonisation of Manchuria by immigrants from the over-populated provinces of China. He believed that agreement could be reached with Japan if north Manchuria became a Russian sphere, south Korea a Japanese sphere, and south Manchuria and northern Korea were neutral zones.[1] The Admiralty continued to maintain an interest in Korea.[2]

The Tsar himself vacillated between these points of view, generally expressing his agreement with each adviser in turn. But from 1901 onwards he fell under the influence of an adventurer, a former cavalry officer named Bezobrazov, who was introduced to him by the Grand Duke Alexander Mihailovich. Bezobrazov persuaded the emperor to send him on an official mission to the Far East in November 1902 to study the natural resources of the area. Witte was instructed by the Tsar to place secretly at Bezobrazov's disposal in the Russo-Chinese Bank a sum of 2,000,000 roubles.[3] Bezobrazov took special interest in the timber resources of the Yalu river valley, the frontier region between Manchuria and Korea. In 1903 he formed a company for the exploitation of these forests. He hoped not only to make money from the enterprise but to use it for the political penetration of Korea. He wished regular Russian troops to be assigned to the company as guards in civilian clothes, but Kuropatkin was able to prevent this. Instead the company enlisted various Chinese toughs and attracted unfavourable attention from both the Chinese and the Japanese authorities. Economically it was a failure, but politically it made its contribution to the Russo-Japanese tension of 1903.

Bezobrazov was denounced by the Tsar's ministers, but kept his influence. He was even given information on secret defence plans on the Polish frontier, and used his influence to press for the transfer of troops from Europe to the East. In this he was of course helping German policy. That William II was aware of Bezobrazov's activity is suggested by a remark of Lamsdorff to Kuropatkin in December 1903. "They are pushing the emperor towards war even from the German side. William keeps on asking whether

---

[1] See Kuropatkin's diary for 5th/18th January 1903, 28th January/10th February 1903, and 27th October/9th November 1903, in *Krasny Arkhiv*, II, pp. 21–2, 28, 85, 87–9.

[2] For an expression in 1900 of a naval view on the value of a Korean port, see memorandum by Admiral Tyrtov, acting Minister of the Navy, in *Krasny Arkhiv*, XVIII, pp. 19–20.

[3] Witte, *op. cit.*, p. 103. There is much valuable material on Besobrazov's activities in Romanov, *op. cit.*, and in the papers of Witte, *Prolog russko-yaponskoy voiny*, ed. B. B. Glinski (SPB, 1916).

Bezobrazov is still well, for he is their reliable ally."[1] Kuropatkin himself spoke bitterly to Witte in February 1903 of the Tsar's views on foreign policy and Bezobrazov's influence. The emperor, he said, wants Manchuria, hopes to unite Korea with Russia, and dreams of seizing Tibet, Persia and the Straits. He believes he understands better than his ministers "problems of the glory and advantage of Russia. For this reason any Bezobrazov, who sings in unison with him, appears to the emperor to understand his thoughts better than we, his ministers."[2]

The Anglo-Japanese alliance was followed on 20th March 1902 by a Franco-Russian declaration. Both Powers expressed their desire to maintain the independence of China and Korea, and noted that this was also the declared intention of Britain and Japan. They added that if aggressive action by third Powers threatened their own interests, the two allied governments would consider means to safeguard them.[3] This was not very much, and the Franco-Russian alliance remained confined to Europe.

Lamsdorff proposed to the German government a similar common declaration, but Bülow refused on the grounds that this would force the United States into closer co-operation with Britain and Japan and damage German commercial interests in China. This reserved official attitude was however to some extent compensated by William II's personal encouragement of the Tsar. William did his best to frighten Nicholas with a picture of "twenty to thirty million Chinese trained and helped by half a dozen Japanese divisions and led by fine undaunted Christian-hating Japanese officers".[4] As the crisis approached its climax, he urged the Tsar not to yield Korea to Japanese control. Between Vladivostok and Port Arthur, he argued, "is a tongue of land which may—in an adversary's hand—become a new sort of Dardanelles. These 'Dardanelles' (Korea) must not threaten your communications. . . . It is evident to every unbiased mind that Korea must and will be Russian."[5] Though this did not represent the official view of the German Foreign Office, it can hardly be doubted that it influenced the Tsar.

On 8th April 1902 a Russo-Chinese agreement provided for the evacuation of Manchuria by three stages, to be completed in eighteen months. The first stage was completed in time, but not the second.

[1] Kuropatkin, diary for 11th/24th December 1903, *Krasny Arkhiv*, II, p. 94.
[2] Kuropatkin, diary for 16th February/1st March 1903, *Krasny Arkhiv*, II, pp. 31–2.
[3] Renouvin, *op. cit.*, pp. 214–15.   [4] *Wilhelm II*, p. 328.   [5] Ibid., pp. 334–5.

On 28th July 1903 the Japanese government proposed to the Russian that both Powers should examine together all points in the Far East where their interests met.[1] The Japanese view was stated in six points, of which the essence was that Japan should have a dominant interest in Korea and Russia in the Manchurian railway system. The Korean railways should be linked with those of southern Manchuria. Each Power should guarantee trading rights to the other in the zone which it controlled. Japan should have the exclusive right to advise the Korean government on reforms. All previous Russo-Japanese agreements about Korea should be superseded.

For two months there was no Russian reply. Meanwhile on 13th August the Tsar appointed Admiral Alexeev, who on the whole supported an extreme policy, and was on friendly terms with Bezobrazov, as Regent for the Far East, with his headquarters in Port Arthur. All powers normally handled by St. Petersburg ministries were transferred to the Admiral. On 29th August Witte was dismissed from the Ministry of Finance. This marked the victory over Witte of his main rival Pleve, who had rallied to the side of the extremists. Pleve believed that Russia needed "a little victorious war to stop the revolutionary tide".[2] On 12th September a special Far Eastern Committee was created. Bezobrazov, who had been given the rank of Imperial Secretary, was made its secretary.

It was not until 3rd October that the Russian government replied to the Japanese note. It summarised Russia's aims in eight points. The independence and integrity of Korea were to be recognised by both Powers, but nothing was to be said of China. Thus Russia demanded a free hand for herself in Manchuria but would not grant the same to Japan in Korea. The attitude was the same as at the time of the Nissi overture of 1898.[3] Russia was to recognise Japan's economic interests in Korea, but no part of Korea was to be used for strategic purposes, and there were to be no military installations on the Korean coast. All Korean territory north of 39 degrees latitude was to be a neutral zone. Japan was to recognise that

[1] The negotiations are conveniently summarised in Franke, *Die Grossmächte in Ostasien* (Brunswick, 1923). The activities of the Bezobrazov clique and the financial adventurers are recounted in detail in Romanov, *op. cit.*, chapter 6. The same author's *Diplomaticheskii ocherk russko-yaponskoy voiny* (Moscow, 1947), is useful, but is marred by the preoccupation—dictated by the current "party line"—to explain everything by the sinister plans of the British and American (*sic*) imperialists.

[2] According to Witte, Pleve made this remark to Kuropatkin in his presence. Witte, *op. cit.*, p. 222.

[3] See above, p. 206.

Manchuria and its coast-line were outside the Japanese sphere of interest. The Japanese reply of 30th October rejected the neutral zone and the phrase about "strategic purposes", and insisted that Japan must have rights in Korea equal to those of Russia in Manchuria. In subsequent exchanges during December 1903 and January 1904 the two points of view did not substantially change. A last attempt at mediation was made by the French government on 6th January 1904. Delcassé suggested that Japan should give up certain claims she still maintained in regard to Japanese colonists' rights in Manchuria, in return for which he would ask the Russians to reduce the extent of the proposed neutral zone in north Korea. Neither side responded to the French effort.[1]

Japan now made thorough military preparations. The Russians however were far from ready. As late as 15th January Kuropatkin urged at a conference of ministers that war be postponed for sixteen months until the section of the trans-Siberian line round Lake Baikal be completed. In any case a four months' delay was essential in order to allow reinforcements to reach the theatre of war.[2] But though not prepared for war, the Russian government would not yield. The Tsar may have wished for peace, but he was unable to impose his will on his advisers, or even to stop their intrigues and disputes with each other. Alexeev from Port Arthur was advising a rupture, and Nicholas could not reach a definite decision. On 5th February the Japanese government declared the negotiations ended and broke off diplomatic relations with Russia. On the night of 8th–9th February Japanese forces made a surprise attack on Russian warships in Port Arthur.

The war was a series of Russian disasters. The Japanese fleet soon established its mastery of the seas between Port Arthur and Vladivostok. In May the Russian land forces were defeated on the Yalu, in August they were forced back towards Mukden. In the autumn, strengthened by reinforcements, the Russian army in Manchuria, under Kuropatkin's personal command, opened an offensive to relieve Port Arthur. It was defeated at the battle of Cha-ho in October, and in January 1905 Port Arthur capitulated. At the end of February the Japanese, anticipating an offensive by the Russian army, still a formidable force, attacked the Russian positions south of Mukden. An eight days' battle, with more than 100,000 men engaged on each side, ended with the Russian evacuation, in good order, of Mukden. The last hope of the Russian command was to regain mastery of the seas by sending

---

[1] Renouvin, *op. cit.*, p. 220.   [2] Kuropatkin, diary, *Krasny Arkhiv*, II, p. 105.

the Baltic fleet to the Far East. The Black Sea fleet was of course compelled by the existing Straits convention[1] to remain in the Black Sea. All the European Powers were obliged to enforce this, and Britain, as the greatest naval Power and the ally of Japan, had special cause and special ability to ensure it. The Baltic fleet, under Admiral Rozhdestvenski, reached the coast of China in May. On 27th May 1905 it was engaged off the island of Tsushima by the Japanese navy under Admiral Togo, and decisively defeated.

The passage of the Baltic fleet had led to an incident which nearly had grave consequences. On 21st October 1904 the Russian admiral alarmed by rumours (subsequently shown to be false) of the presence of Japanese vessels in the North Sea, and by excited signals from a straggling ship of his fleet whose skipper was drunk, opened fire on two of his own cruisers and some British fishing-boats on the Dogger Bank. Two boats were sunk and several persons killed or wounded. The British government demanded compensation, an inquiry, and punishment of the officers responsible. The Russian government, relying on the report of the admiral (who, as later transpired, deliberately suppressed facts known to him), promised compensation but resisted the other British demands.[2]

Anglo-Russian relations were already tense on account of the behaviour of Russian vessels of the so-called "volunteer fleet", which had been allowed to leave the Black Sea as merchant vessels, had been re-equipped in Baltic ports as warships, and had then held up British ships in the Red Sea in search of contraband of war—a concept which was more widely interpreted by the Russians than was normal in international usage. Russian nationalist opinion at this time regarded Britain as Russia's main enemy. The Japanese were felt to be mere pawns of the British. There was even loose talk, not in high military circles—where the practical difficulties were known—but in Press and conversation, of an attack on India to wipe out the shame of the defeats in the Far East, and to crush the true villain.[3] The Tsar himself appears, as so often, inconsistent. In conversation with the British ambassador he was courteous and even friendly. In his correspondence with William II he spoke sharply of British impudence. In his own diary on

---

[1] See above, p. 94.

[2] For an account of what really happened in the Russian fleet, see Baron Taube, *Der grossen Katastrophe entgegen* (Leipzig, 1937), chapter I. British documents on the crisis are in *B.D.*, Vol. IV, pp. 5–41; French in *Documents diplomatiques français*, 2nd Series, Vol. IV, pp. 464–571.

[3] See dispatch by Sir Charles Hardinge, British Ambassador in St. Petersburg, of 7th November 1904, in *B.D.*, Vol. IV, pp. 33–5.

16th/29th October he referred to the British as "our mangy enemies".[1]

Both the British and Russian Foreign Offices were however keen to avoid war, and their wish was shared by the French government, which made great efforts to conciliate its old ally and its new friend. Eventually both parties agreed to submit the dispute to an international commission of inquiry, in accordance with the Hague Convention. The commission, which had a French president and American and Austrian members in addition to representatives of the parties concerned, met at the end of the year and made its report in February 1905. On 9th March the Russian government paid compensation to the extent of £65,000. The incident was thus settled without public humiliation to Russia. Relations between Russia and Britain, which had reached their worst point since 1878, were able once more to improve.[2]

After the Battle of Tsushima both Russia and Japan wished to end the war. Russia still had vast reserves of troops, but the unpopularity of the war and the growing revolutionary movement discouraged the government from resorting to them. Japan had suffered a severe economic strain, which could not be maintained indefinitely. The Russians had been cleared from the area which interested the Japanese, and the conquest of northern Manchuria or the Russian Maritime Province would have required a great effort. The other Powers were also keen that peace should be restored. Britain and France, whose relations had so markedly improved since the signature of the entente of April 1904, were embarrassed by the continuance of war between their respective allies. William II of Germany fancied himself in the role of peacemaker. Finally the United States, which under the leadership of President Theodore Roosevelt was taking a greater part in international politics than ever before, was concerned to maintain the Pacific balance of power, which had earlier been threatened by Russia and now seemed likely to be upset by the successes of Japan.

On 31st May 1905 the Japanese government informed Roosevelt that it hoped he would "directly and of his own motive and initiative invite the two belligerents to come together for the purpose of direct negotiations". On 3rd June William II telegraphed to the President, offering to support him in representations to the

---

[1] *Dnevnik Imperatora Nikolaya II* (Berlin, 1923), p. 177.

[2] *B.D.*, Vol. IV, p. 38. For a brilliant summary of the results of the crisis, which was however proved wrong by subsequent events, see despatch by M. Bompard, French Ambassador in St. Petersburg, in *Documents diplomatiques français*, 2nd Series, Vol. V, pp. 562–4.

Tsar, and at the same time wrote to Nicholas strongly urging him to make peace and to use the good offices of Roosevelt. On 6th June the Tsar received the American ambassador and gave his consent, on the understanding that this be kept secret until the Japanese answer was seen. Knowing that he could count on a favourable reply from both parties, Roosevelt made a public and official offer of mediation on 8th June. After several weeks of argument about the details of the meeting, it was decided to hold the conference in the United States, and it opened on 10th August at Portsmouth, New Hampshire.[1]

The chief Russian delegate was Witte, assisted by Rosen, former ambassador in Tokyo and now ambassador in Washington. The Japanese representatives were the Foreign Minister, Komura, and the minister in Washington, Takahira. During the weeks of negotiation Witte showed great skill. He was especially clever in his treatment of the American Press, which soon adopted an attitude much more friendly to Russia. Witte made no attempt to preserve Russian influence in Korea or southern Manchuria, but he refused any limitation of Russia's right to keep naval forces in Far Eastern waters; rejected the claim for an indemnity on the ground that Russia had suffered reverses but not been beaten; and insisted that Sahalin, which was a part of the Russian Empire, must remain Russian. In the end a compromise was reached about Sahalin; the island was divided between the two Powers by a west-east line. The question of an indemnity nearly caused a breakdown, but the Japanese at last gave up their claim. The treaty was signed on 5th September 1905. The lease of the Liaotung peninsula, with Dairen and Port Arthur, and the concession for the South Manchurian Railway south of Changchun,[2] were transferred from Russia to Japan. Russian influence in northern Manchuria remained as before. The conditions of the Chinese Eastern Railway concession remained as under the Russo-Chinese treaty of 1896. Japanese rights in Korea were recognised, and it was in fact understood that that country would be a Japanese protectorate. Thus the first stage of Russia's expansion into China had ended in a defeat which was also the first considerable victory of an Asiatic people over white men since the Middle Ages. But Russia still possessed not only the basic resources but also the essential strategic positions from which once more to take up the challenge.

---

[1] On Roosevelt's part in the peacemaking, see Tyler Dennett, *Roosevelt and the Russo-Japanese War*, 1925.

[2] The section from Changchun north to Harbin, the junction of the two railways, remained in Russian hands. See map, facing p. 198.

PART THREE
THE LAST CHANCE, 1905–1914

<hr>

Chapter VII

THE DAYS OF LIBERTY

The Revolutionary Movement

RUSSIAN industry had barely begun to recover from the slump of 1899–1903 when the war with Japan brought fresh disruption. Mobilisation of peasant sons dislocated agriculture and food supplies. Scarcities of raw materials caused unemployment in some branches of industry. To these economic hardships were added general and growing discontent with the conduct of the war, and alarm at the series of defeats. Though public opinion at first supported the war, the attitude of the authorities quickly damped patriotic enthusiasm. In February 1904 the zemstvo leaders proposed to create an organisation for help to the wounded. Pleve did not welcome this initiative: his main concern was, not to make use of it on behalf of the men at the front, but to hedge it round with restrictions to ensure that it would not embarrass the official authorities. When the first conference of its leaders rejected his proposals, he removed some of the most active from their positions. Special indignation was caused by his refusal to confirm the election of D. N. Shipov, one of the most conservative of the zemstvo leaders but a figure most popular and respected throughout the country, as chairman of the zemstvo administration of Moscow province.[1]

On 15th/28th July 1904 Pleve was assassinated by a Socialist-Revolutionary named Sazonov. His successor as Minister of the Interior was Prince Svyatopolk-Mirski, a man of slightly liberal tendencies. The new minister aroused some expectations by a statement, on 16th/29th September, that he would be guided by the principle of "confidence in the public". His good intentions were put to the test when a congress of zemstvo representatives was announced for the beginning of November in St. Petersburg. The

<hr>

[1] For the reaction of liberals to the Shipov incident, see Kizevetter, *op. cit.*, pp. 356–8.

minister at first wished to authorise the congress, then officially
forbade it, then allowed it to meet as a "private gathering" in a
private house. The congress demanded representative institutions.
The majority wished a legislative assembly, but a minority led by
Shipov asked only for a consultative assembly, such as had long
been the aim of the Slavophiles. After the congress the individual
zemstvos carried on a campaign for the congress's demands, which
were summarised in "eleven theses". These became the immediate programme of both the zemstvo movement and the "League
of Liberation." In the two capitals and in some of the large
provincial cities, professional organisations held banquets at which
outspoken liberal speeches were made. On 1st/14th December an
imperial *ukaz* was published. This promised various administrative reforms and measures to the advantage of the peasants, but
said nothing of representative institutions. Liberal opinion was in
no way satisfied, and the movement gained impetus.

The first important expression of working-class unrest was
a one-day general strike in Baku on 30th November/13th
December. Some days later a strike began in the Putilov works
in St. Petersburg. Its cause was the dismissal by the management of some workers who belonged to the "Assembly of Russian
Workers", a trade union founded in December 1903 by a priest
called Gapon, and sanctioned by the authorities in February 1904.
It had been intended, like the earlier "Zubatov unions"[1] to be anti-
revolutionary and anti-Social Democrat, but in fact became
penetrated by Social Democrat agitators. The strike began on
3rd/16th January 1905. During the following week several public
meetings were held in St. Petersburg by the district sections of the
Assembly. By 7th/20th January work had stopped in most factories
of the capital. On Sunday, 9th/22nd January, Gapon led a deputation, followed by a crowd of workers, to present a petition to the
Tsar at the Winter Palace. The troops opened fire, and several
hundreds were killed or injured. This was the "bloody Sunday"
massacre which is usually considered to have opened the "1905
revolution".

The immediate results were a general strike in St. Petersburg
and sympathetic strikes in other big cities—Moscow, Saratov,
Ekaterinoslav, Riga, Łódż, Warsaw, Vilna. Svyatopolk-Mirski
felt unable to cope with the situation. He was replaced on 22nd
January/4th February by Bulygin, a professional bureaucrat. A
few days earlier General Trepov, son of Zasulich's intended victim

[1] See above, p. 128.

of 1878,[1] was appointed Governor-General of St. Petersburg with dictatorial powers. Early in February peasant revolts began in the province of Kursk, and spread to the neighbouring provinces of Oriol and Chernigov. On 4th/17th February the Tsar's uncle, Grand Duke Sergei, was murdered. The assassin was once more a Socialist-Revolutionary. The murder deeply impressed Nicholas, and was the immediate cause of his Rescript to Bulygin of 18th February/3rd March. This announced the emperor's intention of creating a consultative assembly. It was to be composed of "the most worthy people, endowed with the confidence of the people, elected by the population to take part in the preliminary consideration of projects of law". This pompous statement, which might have been well received in the 1860's, now fell far short of the wishes of even the moderate opposition.

While a Special Conference of experts, with Bulygin as chairman, prepared a draft for the decree on the consultative assembly, disorders spread through the country. The strike movement spread to cities and to trades which hitherto had been little or not at all affected. An example of the first is the strike in the textile town Ivanovo-Voznesensk, which lasted from 12th/25th May to 1st/14th July, and led to political meetings and demonstrations; of the second the Moscow bakery workers' strike in April.[2] During these months the workers' movement won growing sympathy in the middle class. Co-operation of workers and intellectuals increased as the city professional class and the zemstvo "third element" began to organise themselves more closely. It reached its peak with the creation in May of the "Union of Unions". The peasants too were affected by the general trend. In March agrarian riots broke out in the central and north-west provinces. In June a Peasant Union was founded.[3] Nor did the armed forces escape revolutionary influence. The morale of the sailors in the Black Sea fleet, prevented by the closure of the Straits from taking part in the operations in the Far East, yet subjected to the severer discipline and restrictions of war, fell rapidly. Many listened readily to the agitators of the revolutionary parties. In June the crew of the battleship *Potyomkin* mutinied in the harbour of Odessa, where a general strike was in progress at the time. They resisted attack from loyal ships, and finally sailed to the Roumanian port of Constantsa and surrendered.

During spring and summer the Constitutionalists were active. At a congress of zemstvo representatives held in Moscow at the

---

[1] See above, p. 68.   [2] *O.D.*, Vol. II, Part 1, pp. 205, 217–19.
[3] For the Union of Unions and the Peasant Union, see below, pp. 228–230.

end of April, the Shipov group definitely separated from the majority, which committed itself to the demand for a legislative assembly. On 6th/19th June the Tsar gave an audience to a zemstvo delegation at Peterhof. Its leader, Prince Sergei Trubetskoy, urged the Tsar to ensure that the whole Russian people, without distinctions of class, should be represented in the future assembly. Nicholas replied that his determination to call an assembly was unshaken, but referred vaguely to "essential Russian principles". On 21st June/4th July he received a deputation of extreme conservatives led by Count Bobrinski, who recalled the words of the Tsar's ancestors "who called themselves the first among the nobility of Russia". Bobrinski's speech, which was a direct attack on Trubetskoy's plea for representation without class distinctions, received a friendly answer from Nicholas, who declared that those states alone are strong which "preserve as sacred the traditions of the past".

During June a committee of representatives of city councils was formed, and at the end of the month a congress was held in Moscow with representatives of eighty-six cities. It supported the demands of the zemstvos for civil liberties and a legislative assembly elected by universal suffrage. On 6th/19th July a joint congress of zemstvo and city representatives met in Moscow, in defiance of the Governor-General and police chief. Though they had forbidden it, the authorities decided not to prevent it from meeting but merely sent police to attend its sessions. The congress adopted as its aim a draft constitution prepared by Kokoshkin, a prominent member of the League of Liberation.

On 6th/19th August Bulygin's proposals were issued in an imperial decree. The electorate was divided into the three traditional classes—nobility, burghers and peasants. Election was indirect, in two stages for the first two classes and in three stages for the peasants. The town franchise was limited by a property qualification which in effect excluded a large part of the intelligentsia and the whole of the working class. The assembly's powers amounted to no more than the right to submit measures to the Council of State for consideration as laws.

This half-hearted and grudging proposal could not satisfy the liberals, still less the radicals. Agitation for a Constituent Assembly increased. The concession to the universities on 26th August/8th September of the right to manage their own affairs and to hold meetings without police interference provided the revolutionaries with safe meeting-places. Throughout the summer peasant riots grew in number and intensity. They spread from the northern black-earth region to other parts of the empire. There were outbreaks west of St. Petersburg, in the south-west Ukraine, Caucasus, Poland and the Baltic provinces. In September mass revolts occurred in the Volga region. The peasants cut down landlords' forests, took over farm buildings, in some cases burnt down manor houses and escorted the landlords out of the village. During these months there were many minor mutinies among troops returning from the Manchurian front along the Siberian railway.

At the end of September a congress of railwaymen was held in Moscow, and on 8th/21st October a railway strike was declared. In the next week it spread to St. Petersburg, central and south Russia, Poland, the Caucasus, the Urals and the Asiatic lines. By the end of October the Russian railway system was almost at a standstill. In St. Petersburg there was for a few days a general strike of all workers. On 13th/26th October was formed the first St. Petersburg Soviet (council) of workers' deputies. The Soviet, which was at first a council of strike committees, soon became a political body, and put forward demands to the City Duma and to the police authorities on behalf of all the city's workers. In mid-November it consisted of 562 elected deputies, of whom 351 were from the metallurgical industry, 57 from textiles and 32 from printing and paper. It had an Executive Committee of 31, of whom 22 were workers' deputies and 9 were party representatives (three each from Mensheviks, Bolsheviks and Socialist Revolutionaries). The chairman was a radical lawyer named Nosar (Hrustalev). Of the other leaders the most important was Bronstein (Trotski). The Soviet was also supported by the bodies representing the professional classes. Another Soviet was formed shortly afterwards in Moscow.

The formation of the Soviet, the railway strike, and the mass peasant disturbances together forced the Tsar to issue the manifesto of the 17th/30th October, which gave Russia the embryo of a Constitution.[1] The manifesto provided for the election of a legislative Duma, on an indirect but wide franchise. It also announced the reorganisation of the government as a Council of Ministers, with a President whose position corresponded to that of a West European Prime Minister. A week later Witte was appointed by the Tsar to this post.

The October manifesto marks the flood tide of the 1905 revolution. It split the ranks of the opposition movement. The most

[1] See below, pp. 245-7, 251.

radical elements among the professional class and the zemstvo men were still far from satisfied, since the Manifesto gave substantially less than the Constituent Assembly which they demanded. But the moderates in both groups felt that this was real progress, and their opposition thus greatly weakened. By this time also the forces of the Right had begun to organise themselves. It was in October 1905 that the "black hundreds" became prominent. This name was given to gangs of toughs led by uncompromising supporters of the autocracy, which distinguished themselves by attacks on Jews, and on Russian intellectuals, including teachers, students and even school-children. Their leaders were often landowners, and many priests played a part in their agitation. The police authorities tolerated and sometimes even assisted them. Their mass support came from the lower middle class and unskilled workers of the towns.

Meanwhile the workers were becoming isolated. The Soviets concerned themselves with exclusively working-class demands. They ordered a campaign for the eight-hour working day. This was much less likely to unite the professional class behind the workers than the earlier more general slogan of a Constituent Assembly. Some of the bourgeoisie opposed this demand, others were indifferent, but few were likely to show enthusiasm for it. In November the Soviet of St. Petersburg ordered a general strike for the eight-hour day. When it was clear that there was little sympathy for this outside the working class, and that the workers alone were not strong enough, it was called off. This failure encouraged the employers, who now began a campaign of lock-outs which caused great hardship to the workers. At the beginning of December the St. Petersburg police decided to risk the arrest of the leaders of the Soviet. Nosar-Hrustalev was arrested on 27th November/10th December. On 3rd/16th December the Soviet was dissolved by troops. There was no resistance in the capital, but the St. Petersburg committee of the Social Democratic Party appealed to the workers of other cities for a new general strike. The appeal was effectively obeyed only in Rostov-on-Don and in Moscow. In Rostov there were minor armed clashes between strikers and police in the week from 8th/21st to 16th/29th December. In Moscow a general strike led to street fighting, barricades, and a regular armed rising. Troops had to be called in large numbers. The fighting lasted from 8th/21st December to 20th December/2nd January 1906. There were over a thousand dead.

The Moscow rising was a failure, and it was clear that the revolution was over. The army's loyalty was by now ensured. The peasant riots died down as winter came on. The workers had been defeated. The concession of a legislative Duma had satisfied a large part of the bourgeoisie. The bureaucratic apparatus and the police hierarchy remained untouched. The government now had demogogic allies in the form of the Extreme Right movement with its "black hundred" auxiliaries. The year ended with the passing of the electoral law for the First Duma. The country prepared in comparative order for the elections.

Social Classes in 1905

The revolutionary year brought important changes in the organisation and the political attitude of the principal social classes.

The most active class were the industrial workers. It was their strikes and demonstrations which made the opposition movement an effective and dangerous force. The origin of the first strikes had been genuinely economic, especially in the textile industry. It was the metal workers who took the lead in political strikes. But the spread of economic strikes to large areas, and the brutal reaction of the authorities, gave political agitators their opportunity. The workers of several great industrial centres where hitherto there had been little sign of political unrest, or even interest in political questions—for instance the textile workers of Ivanovo-Voznesensk and the miners of the Urals—were thus brought into the political movement.

During the "days of liberty" trade union organisation made great progress. During the summer of 1905 members of the Society of Mechanical Workers of Harkov[1] discussed with some Moscow and St. Petersburg workers the formation of a general trade union body. In November was founded a Central Bureau of St. Petersburg Unions in which the printers took a leading part. During the autumn foundations were also laid in Moscow, Nizhni Novgorod, Odessa, Saratov, Kazan and some of the central towns. In the Urals, where the workers were still backward, the movement grew from nothing with great rapidity. At the end of the year there was, at least on paper, a single Ural workers' organisation under Social Democratic leadership.

It was planned to hold a first All-Russian Congress of trade unions in Moscow in December, but as a result of the rising this had to be postponed. A congress did however meet in February 1906 in Moscow. At this time there were 44 unions in St. Peters-

[1] See above pp. 127–8.

burg with a membership of 35,000; 40 to 50 in Moscow with 25,000–30,000; and 18 in Nizhni Novgorod with 8,500. The congress rejected the suggestion that the unions should abandon all conspiratorial organisation and come out into the open—that they should "legalise" the movement. It was however in favour of making every possible use of any forms of organisation permitted by the Government. A law on associations of March 1906 in practice made things somewhat easier for unions.[1] The congress prepared a Statute, and set up an "Organising Commission". After the dissolution of the First Duma,[2] persecution by police and employers revived, lock-outs increased, and great hardship was caused by unemployment. In March 1906 in St. Petersburg and Moscow a League of the Unemployed had been created at the initiative of the socialist parties. It sent deputations to the City Dumas, but obtained no more than minor relief and promises of public works.

At the beginning of 1907, according to figures published in *Professionalny vestnik*, the official and legal organ of the unions, the trade in which the largest number of workers were organised was printing. The printers' union included 43 per cent of all printing workers. The next two strongest unions were metal workers (8·6 per cent of workers in the industry, and a total membership in Russia of 54,000), leather trades (7·1 per cent) and food industry (7·2 per cent). The cities with the largest number of workers belonging to a union were St. Petersburg (52,000), Moscow (48,000), Łódź (26,000), Warsaw (17,000), Baku (12,000) and Odessa (10,000). In the whole Russian Empire there were 652 unions, with 245,000 members. Poland and the Caucasus together accounted for about a quarter of the membership.[3]

During 1905 and 1906 a sharp rise in food prices increased the workers' interest in consumers' co-operatives. The workers attempted both to get control of existing societies—such as the Moscow Union of Consumers' Societies, founded in 1897, which had 179 branches, and also to found new societies of their own. The most important of these were *Trudovoy soyuz*, *Truzhenik* and *Prikazchik* in St. Petersburg, *Rabochii* in Baku, and *Trud* in Harkov. All these were run by the workers, and were based on Rochdale principles.[4]

The most striking embodiment of the workers' increased political

---

[1] See below, p. 291.   [2] See below p. 256.
[3] Figures in Grinevich, *op. cit.*, pp. 277–8, 284–5.
   O.D., Vol. II, Part 1, p. 335. A detailed study of co-operatives is S. N. Prokopovich, *Ko-operativnoe dvizhenie v Rossii, yevo teoriya i praktika* (Moscow, 1913).

conscience were the Soviets which arose in St. Petersburg and Moscow. It is important here to stress that these were not just elected bodies representing workers' interests, but actually attempted to become organs of government, challenging both municipal and central authorities. For a time they possessed great prestige among all classes of the population, hostile as well as friendly. Citizens brought their private troubles and disputes to the St. Petersburg Soviet instead of going to the legal authorities. There was much talk of two rival governments in the capital. The question on all lips was, Will Witte arrest Hrustalev, or Hrustalev Witte? The ease with which in the end the Soviets were overthrown showed that their power had been overrated. They were not strong enough to replace the State machine, yet their appearance was a fact of historical significance.

The industrialists had hitherto kept out of politics. They had been satisfied with State support in the form of tariffs and government contracts. Their only grievance had been what they considered the unduly privileged position of agriculture, and they had believed the way to counteract this was to convince the government of their greater value to it. They had therefore left politics to the Tsar's ministers, in return for solid advantages. But the storm of 1905 inevitably affected them. Individual industrialists felt sincere sympathy for the more "moderate" oppositional demands. Most were not opposed to political reforms, provided these did not involve radical social changes. During the early months several liberal-flavoured memoranda were put forward by various provincial committees of business and industry.[1]

But when the government suggested mild reforms to the advantage of the workers, the employers strongly objected. At the end of January 1905 a commission was appointed, under Senator Shidlovski, to discuss with representatives of employers and workers. The workers' delegates were elected in nine separate sections of St. Petersburg, and on 16th/29th February were allowed to meet together to formulate their demands. These were refused by Shidlovski on 18th February/3rd March. The workers' delegates then abandoned the commission, whose work came to an end. Another commission with similar terms of reference was appointed about the same time under the Finance Minister Kokovtsov. This time it was the industrialists who resisted the government. All Kokovtsov's main proposals for concessions to the workers were rejected. The commission dragged on through the spring, until in May the

[1] *O.D.*, Vol. II, Part 2, pp. 30-41.

industrialists broke off further discussions on the ground that after the defeat of Tsushima the general preoccupation with "patriotic considerations" made it impossible to continue such petty materialistic work.[1]

As the tide of revolution ebbed, the industrialists grew bolder. Their political liberalism was ever more outweighed by their economic conservatism. Now for the first time a strong employers' organisation appeared. Unions of employers developed throughout the country, some uniting businesses in the same branch of industry in various regions, and others businesses in various branches in the same region. The main purpose at this stage was common resistance to workers' demands. Agreements were made not to raise wages except after approval by the union, to circulate to members "black lists" of striking workers, to take common action in lock-outs, and to give financial help to members whose workers were on strike.

Later these unions were also used to increase pressure on the Government with regard to taxation, tariffs and contracts, and to win public sympathy for business through the Press. The most important of these unions was the St. Petersburg Society of Factory-owners and Manufacturers (O.Z.F.), formed from an earlier organisation called the Society for Co-operation in the Improvement and Development of Factory-manufacturing Industry. In April 1906 an all-Russian organisation was created. It took the name of Congress of Representatives of Industry and Trade. It had a Provisional Council as its executive organ. Membership was to be not by individual firms but by "whole organisations of industrialists". In 1907 there were 48 members with the right of a vote and 101 advisory members. Fourteen of the 48 voting members were themselves "congresses". Examples are the petrol industrialists, glass-makers and millers. The first President of the Congress was N. S. Avdakov. The congress supported in principle the spread of education and the raising of peasant purchasing-power, both of which could be expected to raise the productivity of labour. It consistently opposed labour legislation.[2]

The intelligentsia also organised itself during the year. Unions of the chief professions were formed. The most important were the teachers (7,500 members), engineers (4,000), lawyers (2,250) and doctors (2,000). Others included university teachers, railway

[1] O.D., Vol. II, Part 2, pp. 48–9.
[2] O.D., Vol. II, Part 2, pp. 86–96. P. A. Berlin, *Russkaya burzhuaziya v staroe i novoe vremya* (SPB, 1922), chapters VI–VII.

officials, zemstvo agricultural experts and statisticians, veterinaries, pharmacists and writers. These unions in May 1905 held a congress in Moscow, at which they formed a central body, the Union of Unions, with an executive Central Bureau, composed of two delegates from each member Union. The Union of Unions supported the demand for a Constituent Assembly based on "fourfold formula suffrage"[1] and it supported the workers' movement. After the autumn it lost importance. Its members transferred their activity to the purely political field. Most supported the newly formed Cadet Party.[2]

The attitude of the small bourgeoisie—shopkeepers, minor officials, etc.—was not uniform. Some followed the intelligentsia, and were later drawn into support of the Cadets. Some on the other hand followed the demagogues of the Extreme Right, and provided the organisers of the "black hundreds" and pogroms.

The peasant disorders were economic in origin. The main reason seems to have been the rise in rents. This view is supported by the contents of the petitions sent to the Tsar after the *ukaz* of February and by the evidence given by peasants before tribunals in 1906. The first two demands usually made by peasants were reduction of rents and exclusion of rich tenants in favour of land-hungry smallholders. Only after these came the demand for a partition of landlords' estates.[3] The discontent of the peasants provided ground for agitation by the revolutionary parties. The Social Democrats were most successful in the Caucasus. They made some progress also in the Urals, in the south-west provinces and in the Baltic. In the first of these areas they won a following in mining villages, in the other two among the landless labourers employed by sugar-beet planters or by German landlords with farms of a modern capitalist type. Elsewhere the Socialist Revolutionaries won the peasants. Their special strongholds were the central black-earth belt and the Volga—the first a region of capitalist farming, the latter of subsistence smallholder renting.

In May 1905 a congress of peasant delegates was held in Moscow, which decided to set up an All-Russian Peasant Union. This was to be based on canton organisations of not less than five members, district organisations of at least five from each district and a central body of five delegates from each province. The formal founding congress opened on 31st July/13th August, and was attended by

[1] *O.D.*, Vol. II, Part 2, pp. 170–82. The "fourfold formula" meant direct, equal, secret and universal suffrage.
[2] See below, pp. 247–8.
[3] *O.D.*, Vol. II, Part 2, pp. 229–33 (article by P. P. Maslov).

delegates from twenty-two provinces. The new Union set up two central organs, a Chief Committee composed of peasants and a "Bureau of Co-operation" consisting of revolutionary intellectuals. Corresponding organs were to exist also at provincial level. A second congress was held in November, with 187 delegates from seventy-five districts and twenty-seven provinces. At this congress a divergence was noted between "peaceful" and "violent" sections. The latter, who defended the use of agrarian outrages, were in a minority but were especially strong in the Saratov region. The congress demanded the transfer of all land to the general ownership of the nation, to be used only by those working it, either with their families or in communities. It also called for a constituent assembly, and urged the Peasant Union to co-operate closely with the workers' trade unions and with any organisations "defending the interests of the toiling people". Meanwhile, members of the Union were to refuse to buy land from landlords, and if peasant demands were not satisfied, there was to be a strike of all agricultural labour. In the event of governmental repression of the Union, taxes and military recruits were to be withheld and savings deposits withdrawn. The Peasant Union encouraged the risings of the autumn. According to official figures damage in these risings amounted to not less than 29 million roubles, including 9 million in Saratov province, 4 million in Samara, 3 million each in Chernigov and Kursk.[1] In 1906 the Union declined. Its "Bureau" was arrested, and police were specially instructed to look for Peasant Union agitators. The political aspirations which were previously reflected in the Union were thereafter represented by the Trudovik and Socialist Revolutionary deputies in the first two Dumas.[2] But though the Peasant Union had not achieved its programme, and even at its best had been a much weaker organisation than the Workers' Soviets, yet it was an important phase of political experience for the peasantry.

The landowners' attitude changed markedly during the year. At the beginning, most supported the zemstvo constitutional movement. The Bulygin Duma proposals split them, when the followers of Shipov declared themselves satisfied. The October Manifesto carried the split further. At the same time the peasant risings created panic, and drove the landowners into reliance on the authorities. By the end of the year the land-owning class was divided into three political groups. Only a minority followed the Cadets, and still demanded a Constituent Assembly. A large part, the conservative parliamentarians, supported the newly created

---

[1] O.D., Vol. II, Part 2, p. 260.   [2] See below, pp. 249, 257.

Octobrist Party.[1] The third group supported the Extreme Right,
organised "black hundred" detachments, and actively encouraged
abuse and violence against Jews, intellectuals, rebellious peasants
and striking workers.

Two points are worth stressing as examples of the landlords'
changed attitude. One is the reaction against the "third element"—
teachers, doctors, engineers and especially statisticians employed
by the zemstvos. These were now dismissed in large numbers on
the grounds that they had instigated the peasant outbreaks. The
second point is the widespread loss of faith in the village commune.
In the past, conservative landlords had idealised the commune as
the repository of the fine old Russian traditions of the peasantry.
Now, when they saw the peasants rising together against themselves, and setting up the Peasant Union, the landlords began to
believe the *Narodnik* theory that the commune was a potential
basis of socialism. They therefore turned against this institution,
and began to agitate for the strengthening of peasant private
property and the dissolution of the commune.

A meeting of "Marshals of the Nobility" held in January 1906
advocated "strong government", a reduction in the interest rate of
the Peasants' Land Bank, abandonment of the commune in favour
of private holdings, and transfer to the peasants of State and Crown
lands. It did not however favour any transfer of nobles' land. A
growing section of the nobility denounced the Duma, advocated its
dissolution and a new electoral law, and greeted the decree of
August 1906 on "military field courts".[2] Zemstvo assembly
members who had signed the Vyborg manifesto[3] were in many
cases excluded from their zemstvos on their return. The Kostroma
provincial assembly of the nobility was almost unique in taking a
liberal attitude to Vyborg signatories from its ranks.[4]

The Nationalities in 1905

During the revolutionary year, political movements grew rapidly
among the non-Russian nationalities. There were important
developments in Poland, the Ukraine, Finland, the Baltic provinces and the Caucasus. Even among the Moslems and in eastern
Siberia the Russian revolutionary movement awoke an echo.

In Warsaw the First of May was celebrated by mass demonstrations, which clashed with the police and caused 150 casualties.
A month later, in mid-June, in the textile centre Łódź, a funeral

---

[1] See below, p. 248.   [3] See below, p. 256.
[2] See below, pp. 256–7.   [4] *O.D.*, Vol. II, Part 2, pp. 21–4.

procession for some workers killed in an earlier demonstration was attacked by the police, and this led to five days of street fighting with barricades. There were strikes and demonstrations also in other Polish cities.

Of the two main Polish parties, the National Democrats were against revolutionary action, while the P.P.S. favoured it. In this respect it may be said that Dmowski was the successor of the Realists of the eighties while Piłsudski took up the tradition of the nineteenth-century insurrections.

There were still two opinions within P.P.S. on collaboration with Russian revolutionaries. The right wing's thesis, that Russian revolutionaries are not to be taken seriously and that all Russians are bad, was discredited by events. The Russian workers showed by their actions that they were a real force. Piłsudski had gone to Japan when war broke out, to plan co-operation of Poles against Russia's war effort. Dmowski, who preferred to use Russia's troubles to force the government into concessions to the Poles as loyal subjects, also went to Tokyo, and tried to dissuade Piłsudski. Within Poland, the left wing of P.P.S. gained ground, and began to favour co-operation with the Social Democrats of Roza Luxemburg (S.D.K.P.L.). Both Polish socialist parties took part in the strike and demonstration movement of 1905, in co-operation with Russian Social Democracy. At the Eighth Congress of P.P.S., held in March 1905, the left wing had a majority, and passed a resolution in favour of "co-ordination of the revolutionary movement of the whole proletariat in all parts of the Russian Empire". The party now demanded a Constituent Assembly for the whole Russian Empire, and another Constituent for Russian Poland, the two to operate in close conjunction. Thus in the tactical situation of 1905 P.P.S., S.D.K.P.L. and R.S.D.R.P. had a good deal of common ground.[1]

In the First Duma the majority of Polish members were National Democrats. P.P.S. and S.D.K.P.L. boycotted the elections. The Polish Duma fraction, led by Dmowski and numbering fifty-one, brought forward a project for Polish autonomy. This would have reserved to the Imperial Government matters affecting the Court, foreign affairs, defence, customs, posts and all rail communications with foreign countries, but would have left all else to the Polish

---

[1] The article by K. Zalevski in *O.D.*, Vol. III, pp. 241–60, is written from a point of view favourable to S.D.K.P.L., but contains much useful information. See also Feldman, *op. cit.*, pp. 359 ff. Two further works of interest are Res (Feliks Perl), *Koordinacja czy utożsamienie* (Krakow 1906); and Rosa Luxemburg, *Kwestja polska a ruch socjalistyczny* (Krakow, 1905).

authorities. Like most other legislation of the First Duma, it did not become law. Dmowski's tactics in the Duma were entirely opportunist. For instance, though counting on the sympathy of the Cadets and the Left in his claim for Polish autonomy, he voted against the proposals from the Left for land reform. In the Second Duma there were forty-seven Poles, again under Dmowski's influence.

Though the political demands of the Poles were not achieved, something was gained in the cultural field. A decree of 19th June/2nd July 1905 allowed the use of the Polish language for instruction in State schools in two subjects only—Polish literature and Catholic religion. Permission was given to create from private funds schools in which all teaching would be in Polish. An organisation called *Macierz szkolna polska* (Mother of the Polish School) was set up for this purpose, and was extremely active. No Polish university was allowed, and the Russian university of Warsaw remained in existence.[1]

In the Ukraine, both strikes and peasant revolts took place on a large scale. But the industrial working class of Ukrainian cities was ethnically mixed, including many Russians and smaller numbers from the other nationalities. The strikes did not have a specifically Ukrainian nationalist character. There was perhaps more nationalism in the peasant revolts, which were especially violent in the provinces of Chernigov and Poltava.

In 1905 there were four Ukrainian political parties. On the Right was the People's Party. This was uncompromisingly nationalist. It demanded an independent Ukrainian state, whereas the other parties stood for varying degrees of autonomy. It corresponded to the Polish National Democrat Party, or to the Narodovsti in Galicia.[2] A pamphlet published by this party in 1904 entitled *Ten Commandments* stated: "Muscovites, Jews, Poles, Hungarians and Roumanians are enemies of our nation." Obviously it could look only to German help to achieve its aims. To its left was the Radical-Democrat Party, which came nearest among the Ukrainian groups to the Russian Cadets.[3] It stood for progressive labour legislation, full political rights for the whole population, and land

[1] A general survey of the effect of the years 1905–6 in Poland is given in *O.D.*, Vol. IV, Part 2, pp. 152–79.

[2] See above p. 190.

[3] The article by Zalevski in *O.D.*, quoted above, gives an account of Ukrainian parties (pp. 294–303). The general development of the Ukraine during the year is surveyed in *O.D.*, Vol. IV, Part 2, pp. 197–206. See also works cited earlier by Hrushevski and Krupnyckyj, also *Velika Istoriya Ukrainy* and *Narys istorii Ukrainy*.

reform. It was not anti-Semitic. It took part in the elections to the First Duma. Third was the Ukrainian Social Democratic Party. Its position was similar to that of P.P.S. in Poland. It was a socialist party which put national autonomy first. Last was the Ukrainian section (*spilka*) of R.S.D.R.P., which fully accepted the programme of Russian Social Democracy, inclining rather to the Mensheviks than to the Bolsheviks. In June 1905 the People's Party and the Radical Democrats held a joint congress, which adopted a resolution calling for a legislative assembly (*Sejm*) in Kiev. This assembly should have full powers to make laws on matters affecting only the Ukraine. The powers reserved to the central government in St. Petersburg should be limited to defence, customs, foreign affairs, commercial and political treaties, and financial matters of joint interest to the Ukraine and the rest of the empire. The congress also demanded that the Ukrainian language should be used in all schools and official institutions in the Ukraine. In the First Duma there were deputies of Ukrainian parties, the most numerous being Radical Democrats. They first joined the *Trudovik* group in the Duma, but then decided to form a group of their own, which was called *Ukrainska Hromada*, and published its own paper *Ridna Sprava* ("The Country's Cause").

An important gain for the Ukrainians was the declaration by the St. Petersburg Academy of Sciences, in March 1905, that in its opinion Ukrainian was not a dialect of Russian, but an independent language. During the year there was feverish cultural activity in the Ukraine. An organisation called *Prosvita* ("Enlightenment") was set up, modelled on the organisation of the same name founded by the Ukrainians of Austrian Galicia.[1] It published books, periodicals, and newspapers in the Ukrainian language, set up libraries, bookshops and public reading-rooms, and offered prizes and scholarships both for students and for adult writers and scientists. It was disliked by the Russian authorities, but at first they did not interfere with it. In the year 1905–7 it opened branches in fifteen towns, of which the most successful were in Kiev and Kamenets-Podolsk.

During 1905–6 appeared the first signs of political activity among the White Russians of the western provinces.[2] The White Russian language had little literature, but it had something of a history. It had been the language of the ruling class of the Grand Duchy of Lithuania in the fifteenth century. After the Union of Lublin, of 1569, when Poland and Lithuania, previously united only in

[1] See above, p. 190. [2] *O.D.*, Vol. IV, Part 2, p. 206.

the person of the monarch, had been combined in a single state, the educated class of these lands had become polonised, but the peasants had retained their language. When the western provinces came to Russia, the St. Petersburg authorities had treated White Russian as a dialect of Russian. In 1867 its use in official business had been forbidden. At the end of the nineties however some intellectuals in Minsk had formed study groups to develop the language. In 1902 was formed a "Society of White Russian popular education". In the following year appeared the first political organisation, the White Russian Gromada, which later added the word "socialist" to its title. In 1906 was founded a Peasants' Union, and in 1907 a Teachers' Union was created at a congress held in Vilna. These organisations demanded that White Russian be the language of instruction in local schools, and the first two also came out for White Russian autonomy within a federal Russia. Two White Russian newspapers appeared in 1906–7, but were then suppressed. The political activity thus produced no result at all, but the literary revival had its two poets, Yakov Kolas and Ivan Kupala.

The Roumanians of Bessarabia, who according to the census of 1897 numbered 47·5 per cent of the population of that province, and far exceeded any other single nationality,[1] also showed some sign of political activity. Their weakness was that they consisted almost entirely of peasants. The landowners were more or less russified, the bureaucrats were Russians, and the commercial class were Jews. The Roumanian language was publicly preserved only in church services and church schools. Dmitri Tolstoy and Pobedonostsev had made efforts to stop this. From 1871 to 1882 Archbishop Pavel Lebedev of Kishinyov pursued a policy of russification. He removed a number of priests who could not speak Russian, and in certain cases closed churches when no Russian-speaking priest could be found. The introduction of zemstvo institutions in 1869 was of less value to the Roumanian population than to the Russian. The annexation of southern Bessarabia in 1878 however strengthened the national spirit, as the population of the new region, having for a time experienced Roumanian rule, were more conscious of their nationality.

In 1905 a noble named Dicescu founded a Moldavian Cultural Society, and formally asked the St. Petersburg authorities to set up Moldavian schools in Bessarabia. There was no reply to his request. In 1906 a Democratic Party was founded by Emanuel

[1] Pelivan, *La Bessarabie sous le régime russe* (Paris, 1919).

Gavrilitsa. Several papers were published in Roumanian. The Roumanian language was introduced as a subject of instruction at the theological seminary and girls' school of Kishinyov. These modest gains were lost in the following years. Under the leadership of Archbishop Serafim Chichagov of Kishinyov (1908-13), and with the help of the Russian nobility of the province, russification was resumed. More Roumanian priests were dismissed, the teaching of Roumanian in the higher schools was again stopped, the Roumanian printing press was confiscated, and the authorities fiercely attacked "Moldavian separatism".

The Baltic provinces were the scene of a fierce revolutionary struggle in 1905-6. Strikes were organised in Riga and other Latvian towns by the Latvian Social Democratic movement. The Latvian party had been formally founded in June 1904, and had close relations with R.S.D.R.P.[1] The October strike movement in the Russian cities was reflected also in Latvia. The Social Democrats put themselves at the head of the movement of revolt not only of workers but of peasants and of a part of the middle class. In December 1905 a teachers' congress, held in Riga, adopted resolutions in support of the socialists. A few days later a peasants' congress was held. It also supported socialism, and recommended the formation in the villages of peasants' councils. Many of these were actually set up. They took over the estates of landowners who had fled, and paid the wages of labourers for months ahead. Some landlords were killed, and some manor houses were burned. The landowners organised armed detachments and attacked the villages. This action in many cases turned against them not only the labourers who were the main force behind the unrest but the peasant smallholders as well. A regular civil war developed in the countryside. During 1906 Russian troops were sent to pacify the provinces. Hundreds of peasants were killed fighting and some were executed. In the towns too repression was severe. Many workers were arrested and maltreated, and some were hanged.[2]

Besides the revolutionary Social Democrats four other Latvian political groups appeared. The Latvian Constitutional Democratic Party corresponded to the Russian Cadets. It asked for civil liberties including the right to strike, land reform and the abolition of all privileges of the Baltic nobility. It demanded the use of the

---

[1] See also below, p. 250.
[2] For the revolutionary movement in 1905-6, see Ames, *The Revolution in the Baltic Provinces* (London, 1907), and Kalnins, *De baltiska Staternas Frihetskamp* (Stockholm, 1950). For the agrarian background, Schwabe, *Agrarian History of Latvia* (Riga, 1930).

Latvian language in administration and the schools, and municipal and provincial self-government. To its left was the Latvian Democratic Party, which paid somewhat less attention to the national issue and laid greater stress on social reforms. Its agrarian programme was more detailed, and it was interested in the organisation of co-operatives and savings accounts for peasants. The Latvian Social Democratic League (quite distinct from the Social Democratic Party which co-operated with R.S.D.R.P.) was, like the Polish P.P.S., strongly nationalistic. Its minimum aim was a federal Russian state, its optimum an independent Latvia. The Latvian People's Party represented the more conservative of the forces formerly grouped round the old Riga Latvian Society. It was strongly nationalist, against universal suffrage, and lukewarm about social reforms. The Constitutionalists, Democrats and People's Party formed a block in the elections to the First Duma, and had a majority of the deputies from the Latvian provinces.[1]

In Esthonia agrarian disorders were less violent and less widespread than in Latvia. Two Esthonian parties made their appearance during the year. The more conservative was the Esthonian Free-thinking Progressive Party. It was supported by a large part of the peasantry and of the Lutheran pastors. Its demands included introduction of the Esthonian language in the schools and administration, and the transfer of the Church lands held by German landowners. The second party was the Esthonian Democratic Party, which appealed mainly to the urban middle class. In November 1905 an "All-Esthonian Congress" was held in Reval, with the approval of the Russian government, which hoped thus to enlist support against the agrarian revolution. The majority of the members of the congress held more or less radical opinions. The Free-thinking Party was in the minority. Its leaders co-operated with the landowners in suppressing insurgent peasants. In the First and Second Dumas, the representatives of both Esthonian parties supported the Russian Cadets.

The German element in the Baltic provinces was represented by the Baltic Constitutional Party, officially founded in October 1905. Though a middle-class rather than an aristocratic organisation, it showed little interest in reforms that challenged the privileges of the nobility. Its ideology may be compared with that of the Russian Octobrists. It denounced russification, demanded the right to

---

[1] Latvian parties are described in *O.D.*, Vol. III, pp. 271–8, Esthonian in the same volume pp. 281–3, and German Baltic pp. 278–80. General political development in the Baltic provinces in *O.D.*, Vol. IV, Part 2, pp. 190–9.

school instruction in their own language for all nationalities in the
Baltic provinces, and also stood for civil liberties. It attempted to
enlist Latvians and Russians in its ranks, but with little success. In
the elections to the First and Second Dumas, it polled more than
one-third of the votes in Riga, but failed to get a member elected. In
the Third Duma it had two seats, thanks to the electoral support
received from a new right-wing Latvian group, the Latvian Reforming Party.

In Lithuania there were two non-socialist parties.[1] The more
important was the Lithuanian Democratic Party founded in 1902
and led by Dr. Basanovicius. Though its leaders hoped for ultimate
independence, their immediate aim was autonomy within the
Russian Empire, which they felt was a necessary stage for the
political education of the Lithuanian people. Their programme was
democratic. It included separation of Church and State, secular-
isation of schools, and agrarian reform, besides the usual civil
liberties. In 1906 a Peasant Union was formed under its influence.
In the First Duma the Democratic Party had four members,
while three more Lithuanian deputies were strongly influenced by
it. In the Second Duma its membership fell to two, owing to the
competition of the socialists, who had boycotted the First Duma
elections. The second party was the Lithuanian Christian Democratic League, founded in 1905 and strongly influenced by the
Catholic clergy. Its programme was democratic, but its main
interest was in the maintenance of Church influence over the
schools. Its chief reason for opposition to St. Petersburg was the
latter's hostility to Catholicism.

In November 1905 a Lithuanian National Congress was held in
Vilna. It was a body of 2,000 members, of whom half had been
elected by some sort of community. Most of its members supported
the Democratic Party. The Congress demanded autonomy for
Lithuania within its ethnographic limits, and called on Lithuanians, until this was granted, to boycott Russian courts and institutions, schools and military service. Agrarian riots in Lithuania
were not on the same scale as in Latvia.

Lithuanian social democracy dated from 1896, when its first
congress had been held in Vilna. It was divided during the
following years between those who wished to achieve socialism
within an independent Lithuanian state, within a Polish-Lithuan-
ian federal state or within a socialist Russia. The second group

[1] Lithuanian socialism is described in *O.D.*, Vol. III, pp. 283-9, Lithuanian
bourgeois parties in the same volume, pp. 290-4, and general political development
in *O.D.*, Vol. IV, Part 2, pp. 179-90.

co-operated closely with the Polish P.P.S., the third with Roza Luxemburg's S.D.K.P.L. In 1905 Lithuanian socialists co-operated during the revolutionary months with R.S.D.R.P., S.D.K.P.L., and the Jewish Bund. The conflict between the nationalist and internationalist wings within their ranks continued. In June 1905 a Lithuanian socialist congress put forward the aim of a democratic Lithuanian republic, federally united with Poland, the Ukraine and other lands, united in the Russian state. A left-wing group, known by the name of its paper *Draugas*, seceded in the autumn of 1905, and accused the party of excessive nationalism and of neglect of the peasant question. In 1906 the party moved towards the point of view of this group, which then came back into its ranks. The party boycotted the First Duma elections, but took part in those for the Second Duma, in which it had five members elected.

The Caucasus was also the scene of serious disorders. The Armenians, firmly organised by the Dashnyaks, continued to ignore the Imperial authorities. The appointment of a new governor-general, Count Vorontsov-Dashkov, brought a better atmosphere. He revoked the decree transferring Armenian Church property to Russian administration. During 1905 there were bloody riots between Armenians and Tatars in Caucasian cities, especially in Baku. Between 6th/19th and 9th/22nd February 250 persons were killed, and between 20th August/2nd September and 26th August/8th September the casualties were even higher. It was generally believed that the Russian authorities had incited the Tatars against the Armenians, who, like Jews in other parts, were unpopular as shopkeepers and moneylenders. In rural districts where Tatars and Armenians lived side by side there was little sign of racial hatred.

During 1905 a split took place in the Dashnyak ranks. A radical group, known as the "Young Dashnyaks", favoured terrorist action and put forward a socialist programme of the Populist type. The Old Dashnyaks, deriving their support from the Armenian town middle class and more prosperous peasants, were more cautious. Whereas the Young Dashnyaks demanded the abolition of the autocracy and federal autonomy for Armenia within a democratic Russian state, the Old Dashnyaks still placed some hopes in the Tsar as deliverer of the Armenians suffering under Turkish rule.[1]

[1] Armenian parties are described in *O.D.*, Vol. III, pp. 313–16, and general development in *O.D.*, Vol. IV, Part 2, pp. 227–32. For the policy of Vorontsov-Dashkov, see his correspondence with Stolypin, *Krasny Arkhiv*, XXXIV, pp. 184–221.

In the Georgian areas, and especially in Kutais province, a national and social revolt took place. The Mensheviks had the support of the Georgian peasants, and organised a successful boycott of the Russian administration, courts and schools. It was not until the summer of 1906 that Russian authority was restored, by a punitive expedition of Russian troops commanded by General Alihanov. The Georgian Socialist Federalist Party, which demanded a Transcaucasian Federation, itself to be federally linked with Russia, was weaker than the Mensheviks, who asked only for provincial autonomy within a Russian democratic republic, with equal status for all languages of the province. In the First Duma there were six Georgian Mensheviks and one Socialist-Federalist, who was elected with the support of the Cadets. The Socialist Federalist Party formally decided to boycott the election, but in practice allowed its members to stand.[1]

The political movement of the year affected also the more advanced among the Moslems. In August 1905 a meeting of Moslem delegates, held in a ship on the Oka at Nizhni Novgorod, created an All-Russian Moslem League. It declared its intention to unite all Moslems of the empire into a political movement, expressed agreement with the general aims of "progressive Russian society" and in particular with the demand for an elected legislature, and asked for the removal of all forms of legal discrimination against Moslems. It called on all Moslems to make the necessary sarcifices to set up schools, libraries and reading-rooms, and to organise local assemblies (*mejlis*) of Moslems. Its main support came from the Volga Tatars, among whom the most active element were the school-teachers. But there were also supporters among the Crimean and Azerbaijan Tatars, Bashkirs, Turkmens, Kazah, Uzbeks and Kirgiz. At the same time there was a movement among the Kazah of Central Asia for more schools, for the use of their own language and the Arabic alphabet (instead of Cyrillic, which was being forced on them by the Russian administration) in the Press of their homeland, and the prevention of Russians from acquiring land in their country. A second All-Russian Moslem Congress was held in January 1906 in St. Petersburg, and a third in August 1906 in Nizhni Novgorod. At the third congress opinion was divided as to whether a Moslem political party should be formed. A radical minority opposed this, on the ground that conflicts of class and ideology were too profound

---

[1] Georgian parties are described in *O.D.*, Vol. III, pp. 316–18, and general development in *O.D.*, Vol. IV, Part 2, pp. 222–7.

to allow political unity, though the cultural unity of all Moslems was a reality. In the First and Second Dumas there were thirty Moslem deputies. The majority formed a block with the Cadets. A minority of six formed a Moslem Labour Group, which sympathised with the Socialist Revolutionaries and *Trudoviks* but remained independent of them. The electoral law of 1907 deprived most Central Asiatic Moslems of a vote, and reduced Moslem representation to ten in the Third Duma.[1]

In the Russian Far East the Buryat Mongols put forward demands. In April 1905 was held a congress of Transbaikal Buryats, with 180 delegates for a population of 180,000. They asked for local autonomy, judicial reforms, the use of their language in the administration, and compulsory education in the Mongol language and alphabet for children between 7 and 12 years. In August 1905 a congress of Irkutsk Buryats was held, with 77 delegates each representing 1,500 people. It repeated the same demands, and further asked for the creation of an arbitration court to handle disputes between Russians and Mongols. For some months at the end of 1905 the Mongols boycotted the Russian administration, elected their own officials and obeyed them. There were no Mongol deputies in the Dumas, though three Mongol political parties were created—nationalists, progressives and populists. More important than any of them as a political force was the League of Buryat Teachers, formed in 1905 and representing sixty Mongol schools.[2]

There were even stirrings among the obscure Yakuts of eastern Siberia. This primitive people, numbering 250,000 and organised under a patriarchal regime, had been affected by political ideas preached by revolutionaries exiled in its midst. As in the case of the Moslems and the Buryats, the schoolteachers were the leading element. In January 1906 a congress of 400 persons was held in the town of Yakutsk. It demanded recognition that the land was the property of the Yakuts only, the introduction of zemstvos, representation for the Yakuts in the Duma, and an end to "police protection". The congress declared that all relations with the authorities would be broken off and no taxes be paid until these demands were satisfied. The leaders of the congress were arrested, and nothing came of its demands. But a little progress had been made

---

[1] For Moslem activity in 1905–6, see *O.D.*, Vol. IV, Part 2, pp. 232–7; Hoetzsch, *op. cit.*, pp. 165 *n.*, and 468–71; Mende, *op. cit.*, pp. 100 ff.
[2] For Buryat Mongol activities see *O.D.*, Vol. IV, Part 2, pp. 238–9, for Yakut, pp. 240–1.

in the cultural field as a result of this agitation. A bilingual news-paper, *Yakutskii krai* ("The Land of the Yakuts") was published, a few works appeared in the Yakut language and a Yakut national theatre was founded.

The revolutionary year caused the reversal in Finland of the policy of russification associated with Bobrikov. The Diet elected in the autumn of 1904 sent a petition to the Tsar, which was answered by a decree of March 1905. This repealed the con-scription law of 1901 and restored the principle of irremovability of judges. The Diet was content with this, and decided to postpone the issue of universal suffrage, urged by the socialists with wide popular support. During the summer of 1905 however acts of terror by members of the Activist Party against Russian officials continued. The crisis in Finland came with a general strike in October, organised by the Social Democrats and co-ordinated with the railway strike in Russia. The Social Democrats, like their comrades in Russia, demanded a Constituent Assembly, besides far-reaching labour reforms including an eight-hour day. The Constitutionalists were content with less than this, and were hesitant or hostile towards the class demands of the workers. A compromise was reached by which the Social Democrats agreed to abandon their insistence on a Constituent Assembly provided that the Constitutionalists insisted on the introduction of universal suffrage. On the basis of this compromise the general strike was conducted for a week with nation-wide support.

On 4th/17th November the Tsar issued a manifesto in general terms which the Constitutionalists treated as acceptance of their demands while the Social Democrats were suspicious. A "Con-stituent Senate" was set up to prepare a draft of the future powers of the reformed Diet. It included a Social Democrat, Kari, who was however repudiated and expelled by his party. The Social Democrats now returned to their former policy, demanding nothing less than a Constituent Assembly. They boycotted the elections to the new Diet. During 1906 there were several strikes in the metal-working and printing industries.

During the days of revolution two armed organisations had been created, a White Guard composed largely of students and middle-class people, and a Red Guard composed of workers and led by the Social Democrat Party. At first the two organisations were allies, but once the Tsar had yielded and the class issue began to over-shadow the national issue, their relations became tense. Members of the Red Guard were involved in the mutiny at Sveaborg in July

1906.[1] It was then made illegal, and its leader Kok escaped abroad. Later in the year repressive measures, officially justified by the continuing terror of the Activists, were directed also against socialist workers. The freedom enjoyed on Finnish territory in 1905–6 by Russian revolutionaries caused anger in St. Petersburg, which found effective expression in the ensuing period of Stolypin's government.[2]

In July 1906 the Tsar signed the new provisions for the Finnish Diet. There was to be a single chamber of 200, elected for periods of three years from sixteen constituencies, by proportional representation and almost complete universal suffrage of both sexes. Finland was thus the first country in Europe to give the vote to women. In the elections of 1907 the Social Democrats obtained the largest single number of seats (80 out of 200). The Old Finns remained the next largest party. The Swedes were united in a Swedish People's Party, formally founded at a congress held in May 1906. Its political views were liberal, but it had both a left and a right wing. A new party were the Agrarians, who represented the small peasants and were mainly interested in land reform. Before 1914 they did not succeed in winning a majority of the peasants. Many peasants voted as previously for the Old Finns while a large number, especially among agricultural workers, supported the socialists.[3]

Perhaps of all Russia's nationalities that which gained least from the events of 1905–6 was the Jews. In the Bulygin Duma project the Jews were not to be given the franchise, on the grounds that their civil disabilities disqualified them from the full rights of Russian citizenship. This point of view was later abandoned, and Jews received the vote under the regime of the October Manifesto. But this was all. The Pale of Settlement remained in force, and the *numerus clausus* in education was not removed. It seems likely that the personal antipathy of Nicholas II to the Jews, of which there is clear evidence in his correspondence, was at least partly responsible.[4]

In February 1905 a congress of Jewish leaders was held in Vilna, which founded the League for the Attainment of Equal Rights for Jews. This body united the main Jewish political

---

[1] On the events of 1905–6 in Finland, see works earlier quoted by von Törne, Schybergson and Paasivirta, also Kollontay, in *O.D.*, Vol. IV, Part 2, pp. 284–93. For the Sveaborg mutiny, see below, p. 256.
[2] See below pp. 307–9.   [3] Kollontay, *loc. cit.*, pp. 195 ff., and Paasivirta, *op. cit.*
[4] See for instance his letter to his mother of 14th/27th December 1905 and of November 1906; his correspondence with Stolypin of 10th–11th/23rd–24th December 1906 (*Krasny Arkhiv*, V, pp. 105–7); and entry in diary of Kuropatkin for 31st August/13th September 1903 (*Krasny Arkhiv*, II, p. 73).

groups other than the Bund. It identified the cause of Russian
Jews with that of the Russian liberation movement as a whole.
It belonged to the Union of Unions, and co-operated with Russian
democratic parties, especially with the Cadets. In the First Duma
twelve Jews were elected who accepted the League's aims, half of
these being Zionists and half liberals. In the Duma speeches were
made in favour of Jewish rights and against the series of pogroms
which took place during the preceding year. These had caused
several thousand fatal casualties and enormous material destruction.
In Białystok fifty Jews were killed and more wounded in June 1905,
and eighty killed in June 1906—while the First Duma was sitting.
The worst of all the pogroms took place in Odessa in October 1905,
when more than 300 Jews were killed. On this occasion Russian
troops and police stood by while "black hundred" hooligans
attacked Jews, but intervened when the Jews, who had organised
their own "self-defence" units, defended themselves with arms.[1]
The First Duma was dissolved before any legislation in favour of
the Jews' civil rights had been enacted.

The recovery of the regime during 1906 had the same effect on
the Jews as on other nationalities.[2] The all-Russian liberation
movement had achieved so little that co-operation with the Russian
people for democracy was to some extent discredited. Nationalism
regained ground. During 1906 the League lost its importance.
Instead, three political tendencies appeared among the Jews who
had supported it.

First were the Zionists, who fall into several groups. The
Russian Zionist Organisation held a congress at the end of 1906 in
Helsingfors. It gave first priority to the development of Palestine
as a home for Jews, and regarded the improvement of the lot of
Jews in Russia as a transitional task, in which co-operation with
Russian, Polish or other groups should be decided by local oppor-
tunist considerations. The Zionists took part in the Second Duma
elections, but had only one member.

There were three smaller Zionist groups which considered themselves socialist—Poale Zion, Zionist Socialists, and Jewish Workers'
Socialist Party (known as "Sickle" or "Seymists"). Both the first
two recognised Marxism, but wished to combine it with allegiance
to a Jewish state. There was little difference between them. Poale
Zion laid somewhat less emphasis on Palestine than the Zionist

---

[1] Dubnow, *op. cit.*, Vol. III, pp. 128–9.
[2] For the developments of 1905–6 in connection with the Jews, see *O.D.*, Vol.
IV, Part 2, pp. 209–21, and for Jewish political parties and groups, *O.D.*, Vol. III,
pp. 318–346.

Socialists, was more interested in the situation in Russia, had better relations with Russian socialist parties, and was more suspicious of the bourgeois Zionists. The "Seymists" were not Marxists. Their ideas were influenced by Russian Populism. They began as an intellectual group with a paper published abroad, *Vozrozhdenie*, in 1903. They became a political party in April 1906. They were more nationalist than the other two socialist groups, and wished to have autonomous institutions for Russian Jews, during the transitional period while Jews would still be living in Russia.

The anti-Zionist liberals, who had been the main force behind the League, called themselves after the collapse of the League the "Jewish People's Group". They insisted that the fate of the Russian Jews was linked with that of the Russian people. They demanded full political liberty, civil rights and economic opportunity for Jews within Russia. These rights should include the right of education for Jews in Yiddish. But they were against a separate Jewish school system, and against all projects of a Jewish parliament within Russia, on the ground that these would strengthen the antagonism between Jews and Russians, which they wished to diminish.

The Jewish People's Party ("Volkspartei") stood between the Zionists and the People's Group. It asked for autonomy for the Jews within Russia. It realised that freedom for Jews depended on freedom for Russians too, but maintained that this was not enough. It wished for Jewish autonomous communes, democratically elected by the Jewish population and represented in a central League, with an executive committee and periodic congresses. The communes should have the right to tax Jews for funds to be spent on Jewish schools, mutual aid for workers and internal migration and resettlement.

The Duma, the Parties and the Government

The legislature created by the October Manifesto consisted of two Chambers—the State Council and the State Duma.

The State Council, the upper chamber, was formed partly from the existing institution of that name[1] and partly from persons elected by various public bodies. There were 196 members. One half were nominated by the Tsar from the existing State Councillors. Each of these appointments could be confirmed or revoked yearly. The other half were elected as follows. The Church chose six members, of whom three were elected by the monks and three

[1] See above, p. 13.

by the ordinary clergy. Provincial zemstvos—or in provinces where zemstvos did not exist, provincial congresses summoned by the governors—elected fifty-six. The nobility elected twelve, the universities and Academy of Sciences six, and trade and industry twelve. The old State Council continued its former duties, with personnel appointed by the Tsar for the purpose, and distinct from those who sat in the upper chamber.

The State Duma was elected indirectly, through electoral colleges based on social classes. The franchise was granted to all who owned immovable property, or paid house tax or business tax. In each country district separate elections were held by large land-owners, small landowners, and peasants. In the five cities of St. Petersburg, Moscow, Odessa, Kiev and Riga two colleges (one for those who paid a high tax or had valuable house property, the other for the rest), directly elected their Duma representatives. In all other cities and in all rural areas elections were indirect. Here the voters elected electors, who assembled on an appointed day in the chief city of their province and there elected their Duma representatives. Representatives of the peasants were elected in a more indirect manner than those of other classes. They were chosen by electors elected by canton assemblies, which were themselves elected by the householders in the canton. Peasants who were not householders, and members of householders' families, had no vote at all. The number of electors allotted to the different colleges and to the different cities and provinces, was decided by special regulations. It was on the whole proportional to the size of the populations represented. In general the authors of the electoral law aimed at giving an especially large representation to the peasants, believing them to be a naturally conservative element. Nevertheless, this complicated electoral system was much less unrepresentative than it sounds, as can be seen from the fact that in the first two Dumas the radical parties had large majorities.

The Manifesto had stated that the principle of autocracy remained untouched, and this was confirmed in the "fundamental laws" of May 1906. Ministers were appointed by the Tsar, and held office as long as they possessed his confidence. They were not responsible to the Duma. Members of the Duma were able to put questions to the President of the Council of Ministers or to individual ministers, but the explanations given by the ministers in answers to questions did not require the Duma's approval. The Duma could not over-throw ministers by motions of confidence or censure: it could only vote its displeasure, a moral gesture without political effect. The

Duma's control over the budget was ineffective, as the military and naval estimates and the expenditure of the Ministry of the Court were altogether excluded from it. Control of the execution of the budget was, as previously, entrusted to the State Comptroller, who had the rank of a minister. His report was presented to the Duma, for its information, but it had no means of checking it. The President of the Duma—whose office corresponded to that of Speaker of the House of Commons—had the right to make personal reports to the Tsar, and could use this to bring to the Tsar's notice the views of the Duma. But the Tsar had absolutely no obligation to take action on these reports.

Both chambers were entitled to initiate legislation. No law could come into effect unless passed by both chambers and signed by the Tsar. The Tsar had the right of veto. In practice the powers of the Tsar and the Council of State were used to stop the Duma's projects, but the Duma's right to veto the government's projects was avoided by the use of article 87 of the Fundamental Laws, which allowed the government to issue decrees when the Duma was not in session. The article provided that any decree passed in this manner must be submitted to the Duma within one month of the opening of the next session. This provision was avoided in the case of the first two Dumas by their dissolution, and ignored on certain occasions in the case of the more docile Third Duma.[1]

By the time that the election campaign began, the main political parties had taken definite form.

The most important liberal party were the Constitutional Democrats, popularly known by the shortened name of "Cadets".[2] The party was created by uniting most supporters of the League of Liberation, the Union of Unions, and the zemstvo constitutionalists. After the July zemstvo congress and the August congress of Liberation, the two organisations formed a joint commission, which later turned itself into the provisional committee of the new party. The foundation congress was held at the end of October 1905, and was in session when the October Manifesto was proclaimed. Its programme was more clearly defined at its second congress, held from 18th/31st January to 24th January/6th February 1906. Besides universal suffrage and full civil liberties, it demanded land reform with compensation to landlords, a progressive income tax, health insurance of workers at employers' expense, and the inclusion

[1] See below, p. 268.
[2] This name was derived from the first two initials of the party's title, K.D.—Ka De.

in factory inspectorates of men elected by the workers. The party had at first demanded a Constituent Assembly. At the second congress however it decided to take part in the elections to the Duma, but to insist that the Duma be given the "constituent" function of drawing up the fundamental laws of the State. Most of its supporters wished to preserve the monarchy, provided that it became genuinely constitutional. The Cadet leaders included Struve and Milyukov of Liberation and Petrunkievich and V. Maklakov of the zemstvo movement.

To the right of the Cadets was the League of 17th October, or Octobrist Party. It took its stand on the October Manifesto. It did not absolutely oppose land reform, but insisted that nothing should be done to lower the productivity of agriculture—an argument which, though no doubt largely justifiable on economic grounds, could easily be used against any subdivision of large estates among smallholders. It was in favour of decentralisation but against federalism, and unwilling to make concessions to the nationalities which might endanger the supremacy of the Russian nation. It was vague about civil liberties, and favoured residential restrictions on the franchise in cities and indirect election in small centres of population. The Octobrists drew their support from three directions. The most important was the right wing of the zemstvo movement, led by Shipov and Stahovich. The second was the business class, especially in the two capitals, which in the autumn of 1905 formed several political organisations which later became submerged in the Octobrist movement. The third source of support was the more liberal section of the bureaucracy, which found the Cadets too radical yet disliked the excesses of the extreme Right.

During 1905 several right-wing parties sprang up. In April was formed the Russian Monarchist Party, led by the editor of the reactionary newspaper, *Moskovskie vedomosti* ("Moscow Gazette"), Gringmut. It denounced West European institutions and insisted on the property rights of landowners. It urged the Tsar to resist all requests for popular representation. About the same time was formed the Union of Russian Men, led by the brothers Sheremetiev and supported by Metropolitan Vladimir of Moscow. It favoured a *zemskii sobor* of the Slavophile type. It set before itself the task of bringing Tsar and people closer together. It fiercely attacked the whole intelligentsia and was strongly anti-semitic. During the summer various local right-wing groups sprang up, connected with the "black hundred" gangs. In October 1905 a more ambitious right-wing group was founded—the Union of the Russian People, led by Prince Gagarin, Dr. Dubrovin and V. M. Purishkievich. It tried to appeal to a larger section of the people. It denounced the bureaucracy as a barrier between emperor and people, and launched demagogic slogans to workers and peasant smallholders. It tried, with some success, to divert social discontent against the Jews. Its members were prominent in the autumn pogroms. It laid great stress on its loyalty to the Tsar. Nicholas received a deputation of its leaders coldly on 1st/14th December 1905, but later became more friendly. On 16th February/1st March 1906 he told a deputation from Ivanovo, "My autocracy will remain as it was in old times".

The extreme Left was formed by the Socialist Revolutionaries and Social Democrats, the latter still divided between Mensheviks and Bolsheviks. All three groups were hostile to the bourgeois parties and sceptical about the Duma. They maintained their insistence on a Constituent Assembly and still urged an armed uprising to achieve it. But their practical attitude to the Duma elections now had to be decided. The armed rising might be the desirable aim, but opinions differed in the revolutionary ranks as to its imminence. If it was an immediate possibility, then clearly it was best to boycott the elections to a body which the rising would at once abolish. If however the prospect of revolution was receding, it might be worth while to take part in the elections, and see what use could be made of the Duma.

The Socialist Revolutionaries held their congress in January 1906.[1] They decided that the rising was possible in the near future, and so told their followers to boycott the elections. The boycott was not in practice effective. Most peasants used their vote. Many gave their support to the Cadets for lack of a more radical party. Others returned persons of a Socialist Revolutionary outlook who did not feel bound by the decisions of the party. Thus in the First Duma there was a strong group of deputies of Socialist Revolutionary outlook who did not however officially represent the party. It became known as the Labour Group (Trudovik).

The Social Democrats discussed the questions of the rising and the elections at their congress, held in Stockholm in April 1906. This became known as the "unifying congress", as the Mensheviks and Bolsheviks were formally reunited. In the debates of the congress, the Bolsheviks argued that the situation was still revolutionary, and that the main task was to organise an armed rising.

[1] See above, pp. 156–7.

The Mensheviks did not deny this, but insisted that there must not be a premature rising in unfavourable conditions. They also objected to what were known as "partisan actions". These were attacks by armed bands on official or private persons and property, including in some cases acts of sabotage or robbery. The Mensheviks argued that such actions only discredited the party, demoralised its members, and opened its ranks to criminals. Lenin admitted that abuses had occurred and must be prevented, but defended partisan actions in principle. On both these points, the congress adopted essentially the Menshevik view. No formal resolution was taken on whether to boycott the Duma. In practice the party took no official part in the elections in the greater part of Russia, but some individuals of Social Democrat views were elected. The congress decided, against Bolshevik opposition, to approve the formation from these individuals of a Social Democratic Duma group, to "work under the constant direction of the central institutions of the party". The elections had not yet however been held in the Caucasus. Here the Social Democrats were extremely strong in Georgia, and belonged to the Menshevik faction. The congress decided that in the forthcoming Caucasus elections the party might officially take part. This was opposed by the Bolsheviks, with the single exception of Lenin himself, who voted in favour of the decision.[1] The Stockholm congress also re-admitted the Bund into R.S.D.R.P. by an unconvincing compromise, and admitted the Lithuanian and Lettish Social Democratic organisations.

The most successful party in the elections were, as was to be expected, the Cadets. They and the minor groups who sympathised with them had 179 candidates elected, about half of those who took their seats. The Labour group of unofficial socialist revolutionaries had ninety-four and the Social Democrats eighteen. The Russian right-wing parties had only thirty-two, of whom seventeen were Octobrists. The rest of the Duma was composed of representatives of the nationalities or of persons of undefined views.

When the Duma met, Witte was no longer Premier. From the beginning of his ministry his relations with the Tsar had been strained. Nicholas believed that by granting the October Manifesto he had violated his promise to his father and his obligations as an autocrat. His wife, an enthusiastic convert to Orthodoxy, felt even more strongly about this than he did. Both regarded Witte as the

[1] For the proceedings of the congress, see *Protokoly ob'yedinitelnovo s'yezda R.S.D.R.P.*, (Moscow, 1926), ed. O. A. Varentsova.

man who had forced his emperor to commit sacrilege. During the crisis of October 1905 Nicholas had consulted Witte, who at that time held the post of President of the Committee of Ministers, and whose prestige stood high as a result of his success at the Portsmouth peace conference and his international connections both political and financial. The Tsar on 13th/26th October asked Witte to "co-ordinate the work of the ministers"—a step towards the formation of a united cabinet in place of a number of independent departmental chiefs responsible only to the Tsar. Witte expressed the opinion, on the 9th/22nd and 16th/29th, that there were only two possible courses of action—to grant a constitution, or to establish a military dictatorship. Witte favoured the first alternative and submitted concrete proposals in that sense. At the same time Nicholas was conducting discussions with Goremykin,[1] who urged the maintenance of bureaucratic rule, and kept this secret from Witte. The Tsar's own inclination was towards dictatorship, but it was not easy to find a suitable dictator. The loyalty of the armed forces was uncertain if they were to be used to repress disorders throughout the country. It seems probable that the decisive factor which made Nicholas grant the Manifesto and appoint Witte was the attitude of the Grand Duke Nikolai Nikolaievitch. According to the account given to Witte by the Minister of the Court, Baron Fredericks, the Grand Duke told the Baron on the morning of 17th/30th October that he was going to tell the Tsar that if he did not accept Witte's programme he would shoot himself on the spot. As the Grand Duke was the Tsar's choice as dictator, and refused the task so brutally, the Tsar had no choice but to surrender.[2] His preference for repression, and his bitter shame at defeat, appear in the letters which he wrote to his mother at this time. On 1st November he told how he had given command of St. Petersburg to Trepov, with orders that the troops should at once fire if attacked. There were "two ways out . . . to find an energetic soldier and crush the rebellion by sheer force . . . or to give the people their civil rights, freedom of Press and speech, also to have all laws confirmed by a State Duma—that of course would be a constitution. Witte defends this very energetically." He added that "almost everybody" agreed with Witte, and that he had "no one to rely on except honest Trepov". "There was no other way out than to cross oneself and give what everyone was asking for."[3]

[1] Witte, *op. cit.*, pp. 218–19.　　　　[2] Ibid., p. 219.
[3] *Letters of Tsar Nicholas and Empress Marie*, pp. 187–8.

For all this humiliation and mental anguish, Nicholas blamed Witte. Though he had granted the Manifesto, he continued to press for "strong measures" against "sedition". He disliked Witte's attempts to pacify by negotiation. On 10th/23rd November he wrote to his mother, "I keep on trying to force them—even Witte himself—to behave more energetically". On 1st/14th December, "Witte understands that the well-disposed elements in the country are not pleased with him and are getting impatient at his inaction". On 12th/25th January 1906, he wrote that Witte was now in favour of repression—"I have never seen such a chameleon of a man. That naturally is the reason why no one believes in him any more. He is absolutely discredited with every-body except perhaps the Jews abroad."[1]

The Tsar's dislike of Witte was exploited by irresponsible advisers who had access to the court. They made good use of his fear that Witte was building for himself the position of a British Prime Minister, and that the emperor would soon be no more than a figurehead. One of the chief intriguers was Prince Mesh-cherski, an elderly aristocrat who had once been a friend of Alexander III. He directed a paper *Grazhdanin* ("The Citizen") of extreme conservative views and with a taste for scandal. Nicholas was personally devoted to him, treated him as a sort of uncle and sought his advice on political and personal matters. Perhaps still more important was General Trepov. When Witte became Premier he insisted on Trepov's dismissal from the post of Governor-General of St. Petersburg. His instruction to his troops "not to spare the bullets" had become a byword, and made him one of the most hated men in Russia. But Nicholas then appointed Trepov Commandant of the Palace, in which post he had permanent access to the Tsar. In a letter to his mother of 8th/21st February 1906 Nicholas wrote, "Trepov is absolutely indispensable to me; he is acting in a kind of secretarial capacity. He is experienced and clever and cautious in his advice. I give him Witte's bulky memoranda to read, then he reports on them quickly and con-cisely."[2] A third adviser was P. N. Durnovo, the Minister of Interior. Though appointed by Witte, he did not scruple to intrigue against him. He enjoyed the confidence of the Tsar. In the same letter to his mother of 12th/25th January in which he spoke of Witte as discredited, Nicholas wrote "Durnovo is doing splendid work".

Witte remained in office until the conclusion of the French loan, so essential to the stability of the regime and so dependent on Witte's prestige abroad.[1] On 27th April/10th May Witte wrote to the Tsar to request that he be relieved of his duties. The reasons given in the letter included his disagreements with Durnovo and the disunity within the cabinet on the Jewish and agrarian questions and religious policy. His resignation was accepted by the Tsar and published on 5th/18th May. His successor was Goremykin. To his surprise and disappointment, Durnovo did not keep the Ministry of the Interior. He was replaced by P. A. Stolypin, who had attracted the Tsar's attention by his firm handling of the agrarian riots in 1905 in the province of Saratov, of which he was then Governor.

Thus the comparatively enlightened elements in the bureaucracy represented by Witte, who had been prepared to improve the status of the Jews and minor religious groups and to consider some redistribution of land in favour of the peasants, were defeated by the reactionaries. On the other hand the majority of the Duma consisted of people who were not satisfied with the October Manifesto, but demanded either a formal Constituent Assembly or the power themselves to draft far-reaching "Fundamental Laws" such as would determine the new constitution. In fact the Fundamental Laws were drafted by Witte's ministry and were published on 10th/23rd May, the day on which the Duma was opened by the Tsar with a speech delivered in the Winter Palace. They satisfied none but the extreme Right. Between this parliament and this government there could only be irreconcilable conflict.

Meanwhile the balance of power in the country was turning to the advantage of the government. Repression was more ruthless and more effective. The loyalty of the army was restored, though the navy continued to be unreliable. Punitive expeditions were sent to the most disaffected areas. Probably the most ferocious was the force led by General Orlov, who repressed the troubles in the Baltic provinces. The detachments of Alihanov and Krylov in the Caucasus earned a similar reputation. In Siberia two forces of loyal troops and gendarmes, led by Baron Meller-Zahomelski and Baron Rennenkampf, advanced along the railway from opposite ends and met in Irkutsk. Similar operations were carried out on the railways around Moscow after the December rising by units of the Semyonovski regiment under Colonel Min.[2] In all these

[1] For the importance of the loan in international policy see below, pp. 316–7. For Witte's account of the intrigues against him, see his memoirs, pp. 282–324.
[2] O.D., Vol. II, Part 1, p. 175.

operations the Tsar took a personal interest. He referred to the action in the Baltic as "splendid work". He also showed sympathy for the anti-Jewish pogroms. "Nine-tenths of the trouble-makers are Jews", he wrote to his mother in November 1905, "the people's whole anger turned against them. That's how the pogroms happened. It is amazing how they took place simultaneously in all towns in Russia and Siberia."[1] By the spring of 1906 repression had made good progress. In the middle of the year most Russian provinces were subject to some form of martial law, thirty-four provinces had "strengthened defence" and eight "exceptional defence". Many government officials suspected of liberal sympathies were dismissed. According to a contemporary source, in the Ministry of Communications 600 responsible officials were removed, while dismissals of government employees of all ranks exceeded 7,000.[2] Repression provoked an increase of assassinations of soldiers and policemen and of the "partisan actions" favoured by Socialist Revolutionaries and Bolsheviks. But the government was becoming master of the situation.

The Cadets dominated the First Duma, not only in number but in the quality of their orators. Muromtsev, a Cadet and former professor of Moscow university, was elected Speaker. The Duma's first task was to prepare an address in answer to the Tsar's opening speech from the throne. The address contained requests for a series of democratic reforms, including an amnesty for political offenders and a redistribution of the landed estates. It was accepted by all but seven Octobrists, who disagreed only with certain points, and did not vote against but absented themselves from the chamber when the vote was taken. Nicholas refused to accept the address from a deputation of the Duma and insisted that it should reach him through the government. The government's answer came on 26th May/8th June, when Goremykin with his cabinet appeared in the Taurid Palace (the former house of Potyomkin, the favourite of Catherine II, which had been placed at the disposal of the Duma), and read a speech. He rejected the proposals in the address, scolded the Duma, and described the demand for land redistribution as "inadmissible". This led to eloquent denunciations of the government by the Cadets Nabokov and Rodichev and the Labour leader Aladin. The most impressive of all the speeches was made by the Octobrist Count Heyden, who declared that Goremykin's words destroyed all hope of co-operation between government and

---

[1] *Letters of Tsar Nicholas and Empress Marie*, pp. 211, 190-1.
[2] *O.D.*, Vol. II, Part 1, pp. 175-7.

Duma. The Ministers withdrew in a body from the hall, and the debate ended with a vote of censure on the Goremykin government.

There now seemed only two alternatives. Either the government would resign, and be replaced by one which possessed the Duma's confidence, or the Duma would be dissolved, under the Fundamental Laws, and new elections held. The Tsar was no less determined than he had been to prevent the establishment of responsible government. But for two months he and his advisers could not make up their minds. Trepov at one time recommended to Nicholas the formation of a Cadet Ministry. Overtures were even made to Muromtsev and to the Octobrist leader Shipov. Izvolski, the Foreign Minister, favoured co-operation with the Duma, as this would create a good impression in France and Britain and assist his foreign policy. Stolypin was against a Cadet Ministry, but wished to form a government of "moderates" from both the Duma and the bureaucracy. Milyukov as leader of the Cadets was unwilling to share in a mixed cabinet. He and his party would assume office but would not be content with the outward forms of power only.[1] The failure of the contacts between Trepov and the Duma leaders convinced the Tsar and his advisers that dissolution was the only way out of the deadlock.

Meanwhile the Duma debated the great political issues of the day. Its speakers displayed detailed knowledge of problems, sincere patriotism and moving rhetoric, but their discussions were conducted in an unreal atmosphere. They talked as if the country were still in a revolution, but outside the gates of the Taurid palace reaction was triumphant. At the end of May began the debate on the agrarian question. The Cadet's expert on agriculture Herzenstein, proposed a bill for redistribution of the estates with compensation to owners, while the Labour group were for expropriation. On 8th/21st June Stolypin gave an unsatisfactory answer to a question about police complicity in the pogrom in Białystok. In the debate which followed, Prince Urussov, formerly Assistant Minister of the Interior and now a Cadet deputy, revealed that incitements to violence against Jews had been printed on the press of the Police Department. By the end of June the decision to dissolve had been taken. On 21st June/3rd July the government suddenly published a statement on its agrarian policy, in which it promised a further distribution of State lands, easier credits, and assistance for peasants emigrating to Siberia, but at the same time categorically refused forcible division of private estates. The statement repre-

[1] Pares, *Fall of the Russian Monarchy* (London, 1939), pp. 96–7.

sented the Duma's proposals to this effect as an attack on the rights of property of peasants as well as of landlords. The Duma felt obliged to reply to this statement, which gave a distorted account of its agrarian plans as well as accusing it of disloyalty to the Tsar. A moderately worded proclamation to the people was issued. It stated that the land question could not be solved without the co-operation of the Duma. It appealed to the people peacefully to await an agrarian reform by legislation. This proclamation was made the excuse for the dissolution of the Duma. The Tsar replaced the elderly Goremykin as Premier by the energetic Stolypin. On Sunday, 9th/22nd July, troops occupied the empty Taurid Palace, and a decree, dated the previous day, was published. It declared that the Duma had shown itself incapable of discharging its duties, and had exceeded its powers by addressing an unlawful appeal to the people.[1]

The Cadet and Labour deputies replied by crossing into Finland and publishing in Vyborg an appeal to the Russian people. This asked all Russian subjects to refuse taxes, to disobey the call to military service, and to withdraw deposits from savings banks, until the lawful Duma was restored. The appeal was not obeyed, but those who had signed it were made ineligible for future parliaments and, in many cases, for membership of zemstvo assemblies. The situation remained tense. There was a mutiny at the naval base of Sveaborg, and a few weeks later there were disorders among the sailors of Kronstadt. At the end of July Herzenstein was murdered at Terioki in Finland. The assassins were condemned by a Finnish court, but later pardoned and released by the Tsar. Investigation into the believed connection between them and the Union of the Russian People was suspended. On 12th/25th August Socialist Revolutionaries made a bomb attempt on Stolypin's life. He himself was uninjured, but twenty-seven persons were killed in his house and his daughter was wounded.

On 19th August/1st September, using the powers granted by article 87 of the fundamental laws to issue decrees between Duma sessions, Stolypin instituted "field courts martial". These were specially designed against peasant riots. They were supposed to pass sentence—which was often of death—within one day, and if approved by the local governor or military commander it was at once carried out. According to subsequent official statement,

[1] The basic source for the debates is the stenographic report of the proceedings of the First Duma, published SPB, 1906. There is a full survey in *O.D.*, Vol. IV, Part 1, pp. 275–392, and Part 2, pp. 1–148. Brief accounts are in Kizevetter, *op. cit.*, pp. 425–34, and Pares. *op. cit.*, pp. 94 ff.

between September 1906 and April 1907 683 death sentences were executed by these courts. The number was generally believed to have been higher.[1]

In the autumn Stolypin negotiated with Octobrists (Guchkov, Lvov, Heyden, Shipov, Stahovitch and others). As Stolypin was not prepared to give them enough seats in the new ministry to ensure that they could really influence policy, the discussions broke down.[2] The government decided however to hold elections to a new Duma, and not radically to alter the electoral law. Certain categories regarded by the authorities as potentially revolutionary were excluded from the franchise by various verdicts of the Senate. Nevertheless the poll was still large and fairly representative. The election took place in February 1907. The Social Democrats had decided to take part, and the Socialist Revolutionaries, in their second congress held in February 1907, did the same. The Second Duma was stronger at both extremes and weaker in the centre than the First. On the right there were thirty-two Octobrists and sixty-three extreme conservatives (including Purishkievich and the Bessarabian anti-semite Krushevan). In the centre were ninety-two Cadets. On the left the Labour group had 101 seats, the Socialist Revolutionaries thirty four, and the Social Democrats sixty-five.

It was clear that the government would be no more willing to co-operate with this Duma than with its predecessor. The extreme Right, led by Purishkievich, demanded its dissolution as soon as it met, and the same cry was taken up outside the Taurid Palace by assemblies of the nobility and by the Tsar's closest advisers. Stolypin however did not wish to hurry. He preferred to avoid making a martyr of the Duma. The Tsar was impatient, and repeatedly urged his Premier to action. He felt a growing sympathy for the extreme reactionary parties. "I have been constantly receiving messages from True Russian Men all over Russia", he wrote to his mother on 1st/14th March, "expressing their indignation at such disrespectful behaviour in the Duma." On 29th March/11th April he wrote, "I am getting telegrams from everywhere petitioning me to order a dissolution; but it is too early for that. One must let them do something manifestly stupid or mean, and then—slap! And they are gone!"[3] This condition was fulfilled, in the Tsar's view, when in the debate on the budget the Social Demo-

---

[1] *O.D.*, Vol. II, Part 1, pp. 175 ff.
[2] *Krasny Arkhiv*, V, pp. 101 ff.; Kizevetter, *op. cit.*, p. 439.
[3] *Letters of Tsar Nicholas and Empress Marie*, pp. 223, 228–9.

crat Zurabov bitterly attacked the army. He declared that the
army's task was not in fact to protect the Russian people against
foreign danger, but to massacre Russian workers and peasants.
After this "insult to the honour of the army", the Tsar clamoured
for dissolution. Meanwhile the Duma debated the abolition of the
field courts martial and expropriation of landed estates. Stolypin
ignored both demands. He did not intend to stop the repression,
and in the land question he had already begun to put his own policy
into practice by decree in the months between the Dumas.[1]

The alleged Social Democratic danger provided Stolypin with
the excuse for dissolution.

The Social Democrats had held their fifth congress in London
in May 1907. The Central Committee elected at Stockholm had
had a Menshevik majority: at London the Bolsheviks outnumbered
their rivals. The congress took a more strongly anti-liberal line. It
attacked the Cadets, and denounced their aim of responsible government as a "deal with the autocracy". It permitted local branches
of the party to co-operate with local Socialist Revolutionary
organisations provided there was no "retreat" from Marxist
policy and tactics. The congress showed a certain distrust towards the party's Duma representatives, and insisted strongly
on their complete subordination to the party. They must use the
Duma merely as a platform from which to denounce bourgeois
democracy and to point out the impossibility of securing political
freedom by other than revolutionary means. They must act in the
Duma as revolutionary propagandists, not as legislators. All these
points were gains for the Bolsheviks. Lenin favoured a measure of
co-operation with the Socialist Revolutionaries, because they were
genuinely revolutionary, and because their agrarian programme in
its immediate aims resembled his own, though his more distant
objectives and his ideological attitude to the peasant question
differed completely from theirs. The Mensheviks on the other
hand distrusted the peasants and disliked the Socialist Revolutionaries. They were more favourably disposed towards the
Cadets, partly because they believed a long period of bourgeois
democracy was inevitable, and partly because their own agrarian
programme of "municipalisation" was not irreconcilable with
the Cadets' programme.[2] On one point in the decisions of the
London congress the Mensheviks had their way. This was the

[1] See below, pp. 272-5.
[2] For the agrarian policy of the two Social Democrat factions, and of the Socialist
Revolutionaries, see below pp. 278-280,

condemnation of "partisan actions", which had persisted in spite of the disapproval of the Stockholm congress. At London not only were all partisan actions and "expropriations"[1] forbidden, but it was decided to disband the "fighting groups" of the party, which had been approved at Stockholm but had been found during the following year to be liable to abuse.[2]

Though the London congress marked a turn away from violence, it was now that the police announced the discovery of a Social Democratic plot against the life of the Tsar. On 1st/14th June Stolypin asked the Duma to cancel the parliamentary immunity of fifty-five Social Democratic deputies whom he alleged to be implicated in the plot, in order that they might be arrested by the police. The Duma decided to form a special commission of its members to examine the evidence for the prosecution. By the evening of the 2nd/15th it reported that it could not reach a conclusion until the following day. According to a member of the commission, the documents produced by the procurator of the chamber of justice Kamyshanski were far from justifying the sweeping assertions of Stolypin on the deputies' guilt.[3] The commission worked until 1 a.m. on the 3rd/16th and was due to continue its work on the next day. On the morning of 3rd/16th June however the deputies returning to the Taurid Palace found its gates closed and a notice to the effect that the Duma was dissolved.

Together with the dissolution order was published a decree changing the electoral law. This was of course a breach of the Fundamental Laws, by which the electoral law could not be changed without the consent of the Duma. The new law was designed to decrease the representation of the non-Russian nationalities, of the urban working and professional classes and of the peasantry. Election was, as previously, indirect. The allocation of electors between the main social classes was roughly as follows. One elector was chosen by every 230 landowners, 1,000 wealthy business men, 15,000 lower middle-class townsmen, 60,000 peasants and 125,000 workers.[4]

The *coup d'état* of 3rd/16th June was rightly felt as a victory by the extreme right in and outside the Duma. By this action the Tsar was able to satisfy the "true Russians" whose petitions had so moved him in the preceding months. On the same day as he

---

[1] Forcible seizure of property or money from State institutions, or even from private individuals, in order to provide funds for the party. See below, pp. 293-4.

[2] The proceedings of the congress are in *Pyaty s'yezd R.S.D.R.P.*, (Moscow, 1935), ed. E. Yaroslavski.

[3] Kizevetter, *op. cit.*, pp. 463-5.   [4] Hoetzsch, *op. cit.*, pp. 162-3.

dissolved the Duma, Nicholas sent a telegram to Dr. Dubrovin, leader of the Union of the Russian People, in which he approved of the Union's activities and said that he would rely on its support.[1]

[1] Witte, *op. cit.*, p. 170.

Chapter VIII

REACTION AND CONSOLIDATION

Tsar, Ministers and Duma

B Y the summer of 1907 the revolutionary movement had been
defeated, but the regime which emerged from the revolutionary years was not the same as the old regime. It was
neither an autocracy nor a constitutional system, but had elements
of each. Whereas in the past power had belonged only to the Tsar
and the bureaucratic machine which he commanded, now it was to
some extent shared by three social classes—the whole landed gentry,
a large part of the business class, and the upper layer of the
peasantry. Stolypin deliberately based his policy on the support of
these classes, and sought to collaborate with their representatives
in the Duma. His agrarian policy won the approval of a considerable section of the peasants, his conciliatory attitude in the Duma
won the respect and even the sympathy of the more conservative
liberals, and his nationalism in foreign policy and in the treatment
of the non-Russian subjects of the empire provided a common
ideology which could rally the somewhat heterogeneous elements
which formed the majority of the Duma.

The largest party in the Third Duma were the Octobrists, who
had 154 seats. The parties of the Right had 127. Their success
was to some extent at least due to the subsidies which they received from the government.[1] The Cadets now had only fifty-
four seats, and the Left thirty-three—of whom seventeen were
Social Democrats. The commissions of the Duma, of which the
most important were those on Finance and Defence, were dominated by Octobrists. Between them and Stolypin and his Finance
Minister, Kokovtsov, fairly good relations were established. The
Octobrists had a right and left wing, the former showing some
sympathy for the parties of the Right, the latter for the Cadets.
The extreme Right used the floor of the Duma to denounce the
institution itself, and to defend the Union of the Russian People and
"black hundreds" which from time to time committed lawless acts

[1] Count Kokovtsov, *Out of my Past* (Stanford University Press, 1935), pp. 280–4.

in the country and aroused the indignation of both Centre and Left in the Duma. In March 1910 the extreme Right speaker Purish-kievich made a violent speech, full of coarse personal abuse of liberals. The right Octobrist Homyakov, the Speaker of the Duma, did not call him to order, and this caused such indignation that he was forced to resign from his office.[1] He was replaced by the more progressive Octobrist, A. I. Guchkov, who pleased liberals but infuriated the Court and many of the ministers by ostentatiously describing Russia, in his first speech as Speaker, as a "constitutional monarchy".

One of the subjects most seriously discussed in the Duma was education. Here the revolutionary years had brought real progress. The new university statute of August 1905 had fully restored the freedom of the universities, whose professors and officials were to be freely chosen by academic bodies. In September 1906 the Inspectorate of the students was formally abolished. In June 1908 a new free university was set up in Moscow, from funds bequeathed by the liberal General Shanyavski. In 1909 a new State university was created in Saratov. But from 1908 a more reactionary spirit made itself felt once more. Schwarz, Minister of Education 1908–10, reintroduced the restrictions on Jewish university students, which had never been formally abolished but had not been applied since 1905. He was criticised, in well-documented and argued speeches, by the Octobrist deputy Anrep and by spokesmen of the Cadets and the Left. His successor Casso (1910–11) was still more reactionary. He began to interfere with the autonomy of the university of Moscow. When the university's Council protested, he dismissed the Rector. Several eminent professors then resigned. The death of the great writer Leo Tolstoy in November 1910 was the occasion of student demonstrations. There were riots in Odessa university. Casso repealed the rules which had been made in 1907 to permit the formation of student societies, and during 1911 expelled numbers of students from the universities.[2]

During these years elementary education made solid progress. Expenditure by both zemstvos and municipalities, as well as government grants, greatly increased. The proportion of literates among army recruits was 49 per cent in 1900 and had risen to 73 per cent in 1914.[3] In the older age-groups illiteracy was of course still widespread, but of the forward movement of Russian education there could be no doubt. Improvements in quality

---

[1] Kizevetter, *op. cit.*, p. 509.   [2] For further details, see Hans. *op. cit.*, pp. 200–4.
[3] Robinson, *op. cit.*, pp. 256–7.

were less satisfactory. The Duma made repeated attempts to cure secondary education of the maladies of the Dmitri Tolstoy era and to ensure better access to the poor, but none of its projects became law. During these years book publication was larger and more varied than ever before in Russia's history. The censors interfered little with either books or the Press. Even the revolutionaries were able to express their views with comparative freedom, at least when they avoided direct incitement to sedition or violence.

Religious reform and religious toleration were not achieved. During the revolutionary years there had been a genuine movement for reform within the Orthodox Church itself. It was strongest in the religious academies and seminaries, among both professors and students. Metropolitan Antony of St. Petersburg had some sympathy for reform, but Metropolitans Vladimir of Moscow and Flavian of Kiev were reactionaries. In December 1904 a conference of ministers invited Antony to express his views on reform. Witte, then chairman of the Committee of Ministers, recommended to the Tsar that an assembly (*Sobor*) of clergy and laymen should be held; that priests be guaranteed regular salaries; that parishioners be allowed to choose their priests and have some say in the conduct of parish affairs; and that the curriculum of Church schools be broadened. Pobedonostsev opposed these changes, and argued that the system created by Peter the Great should be left intact. The matter was referred to the Synod, which approved most of Witte's ideas. In January 1906 a "pre-*Sobor*" conference was appointed by the Tsar. It was attended by ten metropolitans and bishops and twenty-five professors of theology of religious academies and universities. There were no representatives of the lower clergy. The new Procurator, Prince Obolenski, who had succeeded Pobedonostsev in October 1905, also attended. The conference's proposals were as follows. The future *Sobor* was to consist of one layman and one priest from each diocese, to be chosen by the bishop from a list of persons elected by the diocesan congress. Only bishops however would have a deciding vote at the *Sobor*. The bishops themselves would be elected by assemblies to be held in the metropolitanates. The number of Metropolitans should be increased from four to seven. The Church should have a Patriarch, who was to preside at meetings of the *Sobor* and of the Synod. The powers of the Procurator should be reduced to those of an observer.[1]

---

[1] For a detailed account of projects of Church reform in and after 1905, see Curtiss, *op. cit.*, chapters 5 and 7.

No *Sobor* was in fact ever called. In 1912 the Synod announced that yet another pre-*Sobor* conference would be summoned, but this did not take place. The tercentenary of the Romanov dynasty, 1913, was expected to bring changes, but again hopes were disappointed. To questions in the Duma in 1913 and 1914 the Procurator, Sabler, gave evasive replies. Parish reform was discussed by the Council of Ministers in October 1908 and November 1910, but no legislation was passed. All that Sabler would say of diocesan reform was that it is necessary but "the question is, how to do it". The curriculum of seminaries remained as narrow as ever. The Synod abolished in March 1909 the provision that only 10 per cent of their pupils might come from non-priestly families, but this did not attract a noticeable increase of recruits. The flight of the best seminarists into civil life continued.

During the revolutionary years the Synod had urged bishops and priests to plead for civil peace and obedience to the Tsars. This was not however either meant or interpreted as unconditional opposition to the liberation movement and unconditional support of the forces of repression. A message of October 1905 of Metropolitan Vladimir of Moscow, which could be understood as an incitement to violence against revolutionaries, was condemned by the Synod. It exiled the abbot Arseni of Yaroslavl in February 1906 for anti-semitic agitation. By 1907 however the Synod's policy had become more reactionary. The liberal-minded bishop Yakob of Yaroslavl was transferred to the more remote diocese of Simbirsk in January. Especially in the south-western provinces the Church supported anti-semitism. The Pochaevskaya monastery in Volhynia became notorious for its anti-semitic *Listok*, edited by the monk Iliodor. In August 1907, in reply to a request from the Union of Russian People in Yekaterinoslav, the Synod agreed to give its blessing to the participation of the clergy of Yekaterinoslav in the Union as long as the Union's activity should "conform to the rules of the Orthodox Church". In March 1908 it instructed bishops to permit the participation of clergy in the All-Russian Congress of the Union of Russian People on similar conditions. In the same year a Missionary Congress, held in Kiev, resolved, with the approval of the Synod, that missionaries should co-operate with political parties which "inscribe on their banners the defence of the Orthodox faith, namely the Union of the Russian People and the Union of Archangel Michael". During the Beilis trial of 1913 Metropolitan Flavian of Kiev sent a laudatory telegram to the leading witnesses for the prosecution, and in 1914 received the approval of the Synod for building a church to commemorate the "martyr".[1] Priests took part in the Duma. In the First there were six, of whom four were liberals. In the Second there were eleven, of whom two were of the Right and nine were oppositional. In the Third there were forty-five, of whom thirty-two were of the Right, nine Octobrists and four Cadets.

The most important step towards religious toleration was a decree of April 1905, that any Russian subject might leave Orthodoxy for any other Christian faith without penalties or loss of civil rights. It still however remained a crime to proselytise the Orthodox on behalf of another faith. This was not changed before the Revolution. Old Believers were allowed to build new prayer-houses, and among the sectarians the Molokane received the same right. In 1906 the split between the "Austrian" and the other branch of Old Believers was ended. The Orthodox Church hoped that all the Old Believers would rejoin the Church, but this was never accomplished. In 1909 a Bill to implement the 1905 decree was brought before the Duma by the Minister of Interior. It was revised in a more liberal sense by the Duma. The amended Bill was denounced by the Synod as an infringement of the Fundamental Laws and was rejected by the Council of State. Another Bill initiated from the Duma, permitting the formation of Old Believer congregations, was also rejected by the Council of State.[2] Thus no legislation on this subject was in fact enacted.

The Duma attempted to make itself felt in questions of national defence. Whereas the first two Dumas had regarded the armed forces with simple enmity, as an instrument of the hated autocracy, the third wished to reform and modernise them in order that Russia should be strong. The chairman of the Defence Commission of the Duma, the Octobrist leader A. I. Guchkov, was a vigilant critic. He made himself unpopular in court circles by denouncing the irresponsible influence of the Grand Dukes in military and naval affairs. When in 1909, after the Bosnian annexation crisis had revealed the military weakness of Russia, Guchkov attacked the conduct of the army, the War Minister, General Roediger, did not deny his charges. For this he was dismissed by the Tsar. Both Stolypin and his Finance Minister, Kokovtsov, eager to enlist the support of the moderates in the Duma for the policy of "Greater Russia", established fairly good relations with Guchkov. The Assistant Minister of War, General Polivanov, was also his friend.

---

[1] Curtiss, *op. cit.*, p. 340. On the Beilis case, see below pp. 309–10. [2] Ibid,. pp. 324–6.

But the new War Minister, General Suhomlinov, regarded the Duma as a nuisance and Guchkov as an enemy. His dislike of civilian politicians also included his colleague Kokovtsov. Whenever any financial obstacles to his army plans appeared, he assumed that the Finance Minister was making difficulties for national defence.[1]

In this Suhomlinov was only reflecting a mentality widespread in high military and naval circles and shared by the Tsar himself. An example of the Tsar's attitude to the Duma in defence matters is the crisis which arose in 1909 about the reorganisation of the navy. A project for the creation of a Naval General Staff was, by an error in the Admiralty, incorporated with the text of an estimate for a credit to the navy for 1909. The Duma, eager to co-operate with the government in this, confirmed both measures. When the Bill came before the Council of State, one of its members, the reactionary former Minister of Interior P. N. Durnovo, pointed out that though the credit was subject to Duma approval, the project of reorganisation was an imperial prerogative. By confirming a measure on which it was not entitled to an opinion, the Duma had exceeded its powers. After much pressure from Stolypin, Kokovtsov and the Minister of the Navy, Admiral Grigorovich, all of whom were keen to avoid friction with the Duma, the Council of State passed the measure as it stood, on receiving an assurance that this excess of powers by the Lower House would not be repeated. But the Tsar refused to sign it.[2]

The defeat in the Far East had clearly shown that the army needed reorganisation. In June 1905 the Tsar was persuaded by the Grand Duke Nikolai Nikolaevich to create a State Defence Council to co-ordinate military and financial policy. The Grand Duke was made Head of the Council. The Council was to act parallel with the War Ministry, to which it was not subject. The Chief of General Staff was not subject to the War Minister, and had direct personal access to the Tsar. Several Grand Dukes, who held the posts of General Inspectors of various branches of the army, also had direct access. The Council proved in practice too large a body, and its members included too many irresponsible persons. It achieved little if any improvement, and was abolished in August 1908.[3] In November 1908 the Chief of General Staff was once more subordinated to the Minister of War.

[1] Suhomlinov's own views are expressed in his *Erinnerungen* (Berlin, 1924); Polivanov's in his *Memuary* (Moscow, 1924). Pares, *op. cit.*, supports the views of Polivanov and Guchkov.

[2] Kokovtsov, *op. cit.*, pp. 218–24.

[3] The Council is briefly discussed in Suhomlinov, *op. cit.*, pp. 197–9, and in General Y. Danilov, *Velikii knyaz Nikolay Nikolayevich* (Paris, 1930), pp. 66–71.

General Suhomlinov, War Minister from 1909 to 1914, had the vast task of reforming the army, which was made even more difficult than it need have been by the intrigues of his rivals and his own prejudices. The Grand Duke Nikolai was his bitter opponent. The other Grand Dukes who were General Inspectors were a nuisance to him, especially Grand Duke Sergei Mihailovich in the artillery. Suhomlinov distrusted his Assistant Polivanov because of his friendly relations with Guchkov, and Polivanov in fact lost little opportunity of intriguing against him. All these troubles were made worse by the irresolution of Nicholas II, who would agree with him in his presence and with his enemies a few days later, only to veer once more to his support. The most striking example of this occurred in 1912. Kokovtsov had spoken to the Tsar against Suhomlinov and believed that the Tsar would dismiss him, and even the Press was discussing his imminent fall, yet when the general returned from a journey in Central Asia and was received in audience, it was not Suhomlinov, but his presumed successor, Polivanov, who lost his job.[1]

In this atmosphere, important issues of national defence were liable to be discussed at the highest levels not on their merits but according to the personalities involved. Suhomlinov wished above all to strengthen the field army, and so proposed to abolish the special fortress formations along the western frontier, which tied down men needed with field units. He also believed that, as financial resources were limited, the first priority should be given to the equipment of the army, and only after this should expensive fortifications and railways be constructed. Kokovtsov and Guchkov, no doubt in good faith, interpreted this as sinister neglect of the defences of the German frontier. Suhomlinov succeeded in placing the existing fortresses, whose administration had been independent, under the authority of the General Staff. Units were recruited as far as possible on a territorial basis. Larger sums were devoted to military training colleges. Payment of officers was appreciably raised. General Staff officers were made to serve for longer periods with units, in order to increase mutual understanding between the Staff and the army. In 1914 the Russian army had thirty-seven corps, of two or three divisions each, and each division had a brigade of artillery. In 1914 the period of service was raised by six months to four years. A year's intake of recruits was estimated at 580,000 men.[2] The reforms were only beginning to have their effect when war came.

[1] Suhomlinov, *op. cit.*, pp. 289–90. [2] Ibid., pp. 330–48.

Stolypin served his Tsar well. But he could not escape the attacks which had ruined Witte, Nicholas II's other able minister. The Tsar was grateful to him for his firm and energetic repression in 1906-7, and approved his policy towards the peasants. But he began to resent the prestige acquired by Stolypin. Like Witte before him, Stolypin appeared to be obtaining a position similar to that of a British Premier—a position incompatible with the survival of the dogma of the Tsar's absolute autocratic power. Reactionaries at court made use of Nicholas' misgivings to turn him against Stolypin. In March 1911 a constitutional crisis occurred. In the preceding summer, Stolypin had passed through the Duma a project for the introduction of zemstvos in the western provinces. In March 1911 this came before the Council of State. The law was so designed as to favour the representation of the peasants and officials (who were Russian or White Russian) against the landowners (who were Poles) or the merchants (who were Jews). The Council of State objected to this, on the ground that the Polish landowners had proved loyal subjects, and that they would now be driven into needless opposition. The Council in fact took a conservative class point of view, while Stolypin took a Great Russian nationalist point of view. The leaders of the opposition in the Council of State were P. N. Durnovo and V. F. Trepov, personal enemies of Stolypin. The Premier asked the Tsar to adjourn both chambers, and to enact the law under paragraph 87 of the Fundamental Laws. This Nicholas did, although reluctantly. Great indignation was felt in the Duma, where a majority had supported the law but now objected to this treatment of the legislature. The paragraph had been intended to facilitate action when the chambers were not in session. Its present application was clearly an abuse. Guchkov resigned the office of Speaker on this occasion, and was replaced by a more conservative member of his party, Rodzyanko.

After the crisis was over, Nicholas' attitude to Stolypin cooled. In May 1911, despite Stolypin's protest, Durnovo and Trepov, who had been suspended from the Council, had their seats restored to them. Stolypin was aware that his influence was waning, and that the reactionaries detested him. He told Guchkov on one occasion that he believed he would be assassinated by a police agent.[1] On 1st/14th September 1911, at a gala performance

---

[1] Pares, *op. cit.*, p. 124. Pares' source for this information was Guchkov himself. For the aftermath of the Paragraph 87 affair on Stolypin's relations with the Tsar, see *Krasny Arkhiv*, XXX, pp. 80-8.

held in honour of the Tsar in the theatre at Kiev, Stolypin was shot by a certain Bogrov. This man had been both a Socialist Revolutionary and a police agent. He had obtained permission to enter the theatre with a police pass. An official commission of inquiry later recommended that certain high police officials should be put on trial in connection with the assassination. But the Tsar, apparently in a moment of gratitude at the recovery of his son from his illness, refused to punish anyone. Whether Bogrov acted on behalf of the revolution or of the police will probably never be known.

His successor as Premier was the Finance Minister, Kokovtsov. He represented the moderate, semi-constitutional trend in government circles. Though he had once infuriated the Duma in April 1908, during discussion of the Duma's demand for a commission of enquiry into the railways, by exclaiming "Thank God, we have no parliament yet", he was on the whole respected by the Octobrists and even by the Cadets. His first difficulty was with the appointment of his Minister of Interior. The Tsar suggested the governor of Chernigov, N. Maklakov, or the governor of Nizhni Novgorod, Hvostov, both extreme reactionaries. Kokovtsov was able to persuade him to accept a moderate official named Makarov.

In 1912 the Third Duma came to the end of its term, and elections were held for its successor. The Octobrists lost ground, winning only 121 seats. Guchkov himself was not re-elected. The Right increased to 145 seats, of which ninety-three were held by the Nationalists and fifty-two by the extreme Right. The Cadets and the similar-minded Progressives together had over 100, the Labour group ten, and the Social Democrats thirteen. During the last two years before the First World War, there was a notable change in the political atmosphere of Russia. The Lena goldfields shooting of April 1912 was followed by a wave of strikes. There were more strikes in 1913 than in 1912, and still more in the first six months of 1914.[1] The introduction of sickness insurance for workers in June 1912, one of the last acts of the Third Duma,[2] did not diminish the discontent. Nor did the restoration of Justices of the Peace, enacted in the same month, satisfy liberal opinion. Since the repressive action of Casso, student discontent had increased. In the autumn of 1913, at the time of the unveiling of a monument to Stolypin in Kiev, two congresses were held in that city at which liberal demands were strongly expressed. Municipal representatives deplored the inactivity of the legislature, the bad organisation of the bureaucracy and the abandonment by the government of the

[1] See below, pp. 291–2. [2] See below, p. 290.

principles of the October Manifesto of 1905. Agricultural experts demanded the creation of cantonal institutions on an all-class basis.[1] But the government paid no attention. The tercentenary of the Romanov dynasty in 1913 was celebrated by an amnesty for political offenders, but there were no reforms.

In these last years a new power had arisen in the land. On 1st/14th November 1905 the diary of Nicholas II contains the entry: "We have become acquainted with a man of God, Gregory, from Tobolsk province."[2] Gregory was the peasant Rasputin, mystic and debauchee, who impressed with his holiness several members of the Orthodox hierarchy, was patronised by the Montenegrin princess, Grand Duchess Militsa,[3] and at last obtained access to the imperial household. Rasputin appealed to the mystical side of the Empress, an enthusiastic convert to Orthodoxy. To the Tsar, who, surrounded by aristocrats and bureaucrats, had a genuine if naïf longing for contact with the peasantry, in whom he vaguely felt that the strength of Russia lay, Rasputin seemed to embody the profound spiritual gifts of the simple people. But Rasputin's power over both Nicholas and Alexandra was due above all to the hypnotic effect he had on the heir to the throne. Born in August 1904, the Tsarevich Alexei suffered from haemophilia. Rasputin was able to stop the bleeding, and seems more than once to have saved the boy's life. In their anxiety for their son, the Imperial parents were at the mercy of Rasputin's whims. The Empress would not tolerate, or allow the Tsar to tolerate, any criticism of the *starets*.[4]

Rasputin's influence grew from 1906 onwards. By 1911 he had obtained an ascendancy. His sexual and alcoholic orgies attracted ever greater scandal in St. Petersburg. One of his early protectors had been the monk Iliodor of the Pochaevskaya monastery, a violent anti-semite, whose excesses had incurred the displeasure of the Church hierarchy. It was only when Iliodor, and his patron Bishop Hermogen of Saratov, quarrelled with Rasputin, that the Synod was able to take disciplinary action against them. In 1911 Lukyanov, Procurator of the Synod, had been replaced by Sabler, who was subservient to Rasputin. In the days when Iliodor had been Rasputin's friend, he had given him some letters written to him by the Empress and by some of the Grand Duchesses. The

---

[1] Kizevetter, *op. cit.*, pp. 517–18.   [2] *Dnevnik Imperatora Nikolaya II*, p. 229.
[3] Wife of Grand-Duke Pyotr Nikolayevich, whose father was a younger brother of Alexander II.
[4] Literally "old man". A title of respect given by the faithful to leaders of some religious sects.

Empress used words of devotion which were capable of interpretation as physical attraction. Copies of the letters passed into
the hands of Guchkov, who circulated them privately. Both
Kokovtsov and Rodzyanko did their best to convince the Tsar of
the danger to the throne from the scandals caused by Rasputin:
they only incurred the hatred of the Empress and were unable to
break Rasputin's hold. The Press began in 1912 to write about
Rasputin's misdeeds. The Tsar secured an order forbidding
mention of his name or actions, thus violating the existing laws,
which had abolished the preventive censorship. Spurred on by his
wife, Nicholas became ever more hostile to the Minister of Interior
Makarov, who appeared unable to protect the *starets* from insults.
Makarov's career ended when, having recovered the originals of
the Empress's letters to Rasputin, he returned them not to her but
to the Tsar. In December 1912 Nicholas dismissed him and
appointed in his place the reactionary N. Maklakov.

Kokovtsov's own days were numbered. One of his most powerful enemies was Prince Meshcherski. Within the government he
was opposed by Suhomlinov and by Krivoshein, the Minister of
Agriculture. Krivoshein wished to increase his powers at the
expense of the Finance Ministry, which Kokovtsov held in addition
to the premiership. When his attempt in 1911 to transfer the
Peasant Bank to his Ministry was defeated, he became Kokovtsov's
enemy. He did not want the responsibility of the premiership for
himself, but wished to concentrate in his hands the conduct of
State economic policy, while nominal leadership was entrusted to
some nonentity.[1] Kokovtsov had also won the enmity of the
political parties of the extreme Right. During Stolypin's premiership, he had opposed the policy of official subsidies to these parties,
but from 1910 to 1912 he had been forced to grant 3,000,000
roubles to them. Among those who received money were Purishkievich and his Students' Academic Group, Dubrovin and his
paper *Russkoe znamya*, and a reactionary Duma member named
Markov. During the Fourth Duma election campaign Markov,
who had for three years received 200,000 roubles yearly, asked
for a further 960,000 roubles, which Kokovtsov refused. In May
1913 Markov accused Kokovtsov in the Duma of connivance with
Jewish financiers at the expense of the State. When Kokovtsov
replied, Markov shouted out "One must not steal".[2] In September 1913 Meshcherski's paper accused Kokovtsov of introducing

---

[1] For Kokovtsov's account of the intrigues against him, see *op. cit.*, pp. 434–47.
[2] Kokovtsov, *op. cit.*, pp. 284–5, 338–9, 365.

"West European innovations", and of too much friendship for
Guchkov and Rodzyanko. Kokovtsov remained in office until he
had concluded an important outstanding loan from France. This
was done in November 1913. A sum of 500 million francs yearly
for five years was granted for the construction of railways of
strategic value in the West. Like Witte in 1906, Kokovtsov,
having got his master the necessary funds, could be dispensed with.
He was dismissed in January 1914.

Kokovtsov's successor was the colourless Goremykin. His
appointment marks the triumph of Rasputin. Henceforth the first
qualification for high office in the Russian Empire was to be a
recommendation from "Our Friend".[1] The astonishing fact is not
that the Russian State collapsed in 1917, but that with such leadership it was able to wage for three years the greatest war in its history.

Agricultural Policy

The events of 1905 as we have seen had turned the landowners
and the bureaucracy against the institution of the village commune.
This change of view was reflected in legislation after 1907. The
most important measures introduced during the years of consolidation under the premierships of Stolypin and Kokovtsov were
the laws concerning peasant ownership of land. The main changes
were contained in the laws of 4th/17th March 1906, which set up
the Land Organisation Commissions; of 5th/18th October 1906
on personal rights of peasants; and of 9th/22nd November 1906
on tenure and re-allocation of peasant allotment land. This last
law was further extended by laws of 1911 and 1912.

The main changes in the peasants' personal rights may be summarised as follows. In future the choice of peasant representatives
in the zemstvo assemblies, from the list of candidates elected by the
peasants, was no longer left to the provincial governor. The candidates themselves were to meet and elect enough persons from
their number to fill the vacancies. Land Commandants were no
longer allowed administratively to imprison or fine peasants,
though they retained these powers over officials elected by the
peasants. Collective responsibility for taxes was abolished in those
regions where it still survived after the decree of February 1903.
The power of the communal assemblies to send to forced labour a

---

[1] This was how the Empress Alexandra described him in her correspondence with
the Tsar. For a thorough account of Rasputin's influence on the imperial family,
see Pares, *op. cit.*

peasant who had fallen behind in public obligations was abolished. Passports were no longer controlled by Elders or heads of households.[1] Peasants wishing to withdraw from a commune were not obliged to get themselves registered with another commune, but could be registered with the canton as "members-at-large". Those withdrawing from a repartitional commune now only had to give up non-consolidated hereditary land.

The law of November 1906 was designed to help the secession of individual peasants from the commune. In a commune where there had been no general redistribution of land since 1882 any householder might demand separate and permanent title to all strips in his possession at the time of publication of the law. In a commune where there had been a general redistribution during this period any householder might claim all land he held before the last redistribution, and might also obtain definite possession of any further land he had received by the last redistribution provided he paid the commune the original redemption price for that land. He was also guaranteed a quantity of meadow land equal to that in his possession at the time of publication. Under these provisions between 1906 and 1915 2,500,000 householders applied to secede, and by January 1916 2,000,000 of these had received legal titles.

The former right of any commune to do away with repartition by a two-thirds majority of its householders was confirmed, and in the same decade dissolutions thus carried out affected a total of 130,000 households.

The law of 1910 proclaimed the compulsory abolition, whether the peasants asked for it or not, of repartitional tenure in every commune where there had been no repartition since 1861. Under this law heads of households were recognised as hereditary owners of plough lands in their possession at the time of publication and as hereditary holders of a share of the commune's undivided meadow, pasture or forest lands. Up to 1915 legal confirmation of title had been issued to 470,000 households in this category. The number of families whose status was affected by the 1910 law was however much larger. Some authorities place it higher than 2,000,000.[2]

This gives a total by 1915 of somewhere between a minimum of 3,100,000 households and a maximum of more than 5,000,000. To these must be added about 3,000,000 already existing hereditary allotments (in 1905 there were 2,800,000). Thus by 1915 probably more than 7,000,000 peasant families possessed hereditary private holdings. The independence of many of these holdings was how-

---

[1] See above pp. 6–7, 43.   [2] Robinson, *op. cit.*, p. 214.

ever still limited by the fact that those which consisted of separate strips remained subject to the village assembly's decisions regarding the crop-cycle, and still usually shared in the communal forests, meadows and pastures.

Stolypin's legislation was also designed to encourage consolidation of holdings.

In hereditary tenure communes, consolidation by one holder still required the consent of every other holder whose land was to be displaced in the process. But procedure for a decision by the whole commune in favour of a general consolidation was made simpler and easier. The 1906 law allowed this if a two-thirds majority of the village assembly desired it. Under the 1910 law the same procedure was extended to cover not only arable but also the undivided pasture and meadow lands.

In the case of repartitional communes, the 1906 law provided that any householder who obtained separate title to his land, might at any time demand consolidation of his strips in one place. The commune was obliged either to grant his request or to pay him compensation in money. The 1910 and 1911 laws extended this right to those who had not already obtained separate title, provided this was recommended by the Land Organisation Commissions. The 1911 law gave the further right to demand a share of meadow or other undivided land. Should the new owner wish to move his home from the village to his new holding, he was entitled by the law to demand from the commune, in exchange for the site of his former house, an additional piece of land on which to build a new house beside his consolidated holding. A general consolidation of all holdings in a repartitional commune required a two-thirds majority of the assembly under all three laws.[1]

In order to deal with the various problems, such as differences in quality of land, which were bound to arise in cases of consolidation, the Land Organisation Commissions were set up. The 1906 law provided that they should give decisions when asked by peasants to do so. The 1911 law went further, and entrusted them with the execution of the law regardless of a request from an individual. The Commissions were in practice controlled by representatives of the landowning gentry and of the bureaucracy. District commissions had twelve or thirteen members, of whom three or four were elected by peasants and the remainder appointed by the authorities or elected by the district zemstvo. The provincial commissions had fifteen or sixteen members (later reduced to ten) of which six (later

[1] Robinson, *op. cit.*, pp. 220–3.

two) were elected by the provincial zemstvo. Half those elected by zemstvos must be peasants. In practice the commissions definitely favoured individual as opposed to communal tendencies. Through the commissions the Government made, up to the end of 1915, 300,000 loans averaging 100 roubles, and 58,000 grants averaging 22 roubles, to individual farmers engaged in consolidating their holdings. The commissions made use of trained agricultural engineers and of model farms, which gave expert advice to peasants.[1]

By the end of 1915 about one-tenth of the holdings in European Russia had been consolidated. The commissions had made changes which affected 2,400,000 households, and half of these had been consolidated. Two types of consolidated holding emerged from the application of this policy. The *hutor* had its buildings on its own land, away from the village. The *otrub* was a holding whose land was concentrated but whose house was still in the village street, and which still took its share of the communal meadow and pasture land. Despite these changes however the repartitional commune remained the most widespread form of land tenure in Russia.

Purchase of land by peasants between 1906 and 1914 somewhat exceeded 9,500,000 *desyatin*. During the same period State lands were reduced by 240,000, imperial estates by 1,260,000 and nobles' land by 10,200,000. The Peasants' Bank had in its possession in 1914 about 2,000,000—which accounts for the difference between the amount sold and the amount acquired by peasants. In 1914 the land held (to the nearest million *desyatin*) by the main categories was:

Peasants	170
Nobles	40
State and imperial family	144
Peasants' Bank	2
Others	32

The State and imperial land was almost wholly non-arable. "Others" includes the Church, monasteries, townspeople, and "mixed collectives" (most of whose members were peasants).[2]

On the eve of the war Russian agriculture was still extremely backward. The three-year cycle of winter grain, spring grain and fallow still prevailed. More valuable fodder or industrial crops were little cultivated. Only 2 per cent of the arable area was under forage plants, 2 per cent under flax, and 3½ per cent under potatoes. More than half the peasant holdings were without an iron plough.

[1] Robinson, *op. cit.*, pp. 222–5. [2] Ibid., Appendix II, pp. 270–2.

Subsidiary earnings played an important part in the income of peasants living north of the forest line and in the northern black-earth provinces, but were much less important in the south. It is not clear from the evidence to what extent craft industries had declined. The zemstvos continued to make efforts to preserve or revive them in the central provinces. Enquiries made respectively by the Ministry of Finance and the Ministry of Agriculture into the condition of craft industries produced completely contradictory results.[1] Factory industry continued to receive a large influx of workers from the villages. Though the proportion of completely urbanised and skilled workers in the industrial labour force was now much greater and much higher than thirty years earlier, contact between factory workers and villages was still important. For instance on the eve of war even in the Moscow printing trade—one of the most highly skilled—it was reckoned that 46 per cent of the workers were still to some extent engaged in farming and 16 per cent still had a house in a village.[2]

Between 1906 and 1912 the money wage of agricultural labourers increased. Agricultural labourers were still subject to heavy penalties for "breach of contract". Food prices also rose appreciably during these years. This was an advantage to peasants in the main food-producing areas, but harmed those who lived north of the steppe–forest line, who were buyers rather than sellers of food. As a result of high costs of production, industrial prices were considerably higher in Russia than in Western Europe, while agricultural prices were about 30 per cent lower. This disproportion, which was to become known to Soviet economists in the 1920's as "price scissors", worked to the disadvantage of the majority of the peasantry.

Immigration to the Asiatic provinces was much greater than before 1905. The highest number to immigrate in one year was 650,000 in 1907. By 1911 the number had fallen to 200,000. It rose slightly in the following years. Every year there was also a reverse movement of those who returned discouraged, particularly by the repeated failure of the authorities who had encouraged the migration to provide any living accommodation for them. This

[1] Robinson, *op. cit.*, pp. 246–7.
[2] Ibid., p. 249, quoting Milyutin, *Selsko-hozyaistvennie rabochie i voina* (SPB., 1917). I have not been able to consult this work. The contrast between these figures and those of the Moscow factory inspectors at the end of the nineteenth century (see above, p. 123) is striking. The truth is that the question of the composition of the working class, and its relation with the peasantry, is too much confused by the controversies between Marxists and non-Marxists for a clear picture to be obtained.

reverse movement was never less than 20,000 in any year from 1907–13. In 1910 it was as high as 76,000.

The last years before the war brought a striking increase of co-operatives. The membership of co-operative credit and savings associations multiplied nine times. In 1914 there were 8,000,000 members throughout the empire. These organisations made loans for the purchase of land, livestock, tools and fertilisers. Marketing co-operatives were less developed. In the northern provinces there were co-operative creameries and hunting and fishing co-operatives, and there were artels to look after the welfare of seasonal labourers. Consumers' co-operatives had in 1914 about 800,000 peasant members in European Russia. There were a few cases, in the provinces of Tula, Penza, Tver and Poltava, of peasants sharing agricultural machinery, but this was unusual.[1]

Schools increased in the period, from about 100,000 to 150,000. The results are shown in the contrast between the literacy of army recruits in 1900 and 1913.[2] Purchases of printed matter by peasants were small, considerably less than the sums spent on oil for ikons.

To sum up, Stolypin's policy improved the efficiency of Russian agriculture, both on the big landed estates and on-peasant holdings. The most efficient of the noble landowners turned their estates into modern capitalist enterprises. Those who were not interested in their land sold it, through the Peasant Bank or otherwise, to the peasants. Among the peasants a class of prosperous medium farmers (*kulaks*) emerged. They too were efficient producers, and increasingly used modern capitalist methods. Their prosperity gave them an incentive to support the government. But they were only a minority of the peasants, perhaps 15 per cent. For the great majority, Stolypin's policy provided no solution. Over-population, under-employment and poverty were hardly affected. With each year the annual increase in the villages was bound to make them more, not less acute. Yet it is perhaps unfair to blame Stolypin for failure to solve a problem with which in the last forty years many other governments in Europe and Asia have found themselves unable to cope.

It is worth while at this point to summarise the views of the political parties on the peasant question on the eve of the war.

The extreme Right stood consistently for the complete supremacy of the landlord in the Russian village. They were against any measures which would facilitate the transfer of land from nobles to peasants. The attitude of the Octobrists was less clear. The party

[1] Robinson, *op. cit.*, pp. 255–6.   [2] See above, p. 262.

drew its support partly from landlords and partly from business men. Among the latter there was still some animosity against the landed class. The mild liberalism of the Octobrists would not allow them to reject the notion of land reform, but their opposition to infringement of property rights of any kind prevented them from supporting radical measures. The Cadets favoured a far-reaching reform. They did not object to the disappearance of the land-owning class as such, and the transfer of all arable to the peasants. As liberal democrats however they respected property rights, and insisted that landowners should be given fair compensation.[1]

Socialist Revolutionaries and Social Democrats were for the expropriation of landowners, but disagreed as to what should then be done with the land. The Socialist Revolutionaries proposed to "nationalise" all land, including that which already belonged to smallholders, and then to grant to individual peasants the use of such land as they required for their families' needs, on the principle of "labour ownership".[2] Once "labour ownership" had been introduced, socialism could be built in the Russian village: the purpose of the revolution would be achieved. The Social Democrats on the other hand considered the peasants a part of the "small bourgeoisie". They did not believe that if land were given to peasant smallholders the latter could thereby be converted into socialists.

In 1903 the second congress of R.S.D.R.P. had accepted the Agrarian Programme drafted by Lenin in the previous year.[3] This proposed various reforms with regard to rent and taxes, and also demanded that the *otrezki*[4] be restored to the peasants and the redemption payments be paid back to them. The events of 1905 however showed that the division of landlords' estates among the peasants had become a practical possibility. The party was bound to adopt a more radical programme. It was at this point that the views of Mensheviks and Bolsheviks on the agrarian question diverged. The chief Menshevik agrarian expert, P. Maslov, pro-posed that when the landlords' estates were seized they should be handed, not to the individual peasants as their property but to popularly elected local authorities, who should administer them on behalf of the peasants, their electors. This policy, known as

[1] For the Cadet project of agrarian reform, see the Proceedings of the Duma, *Gosudarstvennaya Duma, Stenographicheskie otchoty Goda 1906*, pp. 248–50, and the subsequent debates in the same volume.
[2] See above, p. 157.
[3] Lenin, *Sochinenia*, 3rd edition, Vol. V, pp. 87–122. First published in *Zarya* in August 1902.
[4] See above, p. 44.

"municipalisation", was accepted by the fourth congress of R.S.D.R.P. in 1906 against the opposition of Lenin. Lenin urged that if as a result of the expected bourgeois revolution "a republic and a completely democratic state machine is created", the party should "work for the abolition of private ownership of land and for the transfer of all lands to the public ownership of the whole people".[1] His ideas were later more fully expressed in his work *The Agrarian Programme of Social Democracy in the First Russian Revolution*, written in November–December 1907.[2] Thus Lenin now in effect supported the "nationalisation" slogan of the Socialist Revolutionaries.

Lenin of course rejected the ideas and programme of the Socialist Revolutionaries, and supported their slogan only because he believed that its achievement would lead to results quite different from those which they anticipated. Lenin aimed to remove the last remnants of feudalism from the villages, and so to give free play to the forces of capitalism. This would, he believed, accelerate the differentiation of the peasantry into classes. The differentiation had already made some progress as early as the 1890's, and was being speeded by the agricultural policy of Stolypin. Stolypin, in fact, was contributing to the process desired by Lenin. But Stolypin's method was what Lenin called "the Prussian way", designed to strengthen the more efficient landowners and the *kulaks*. Lenin preferred what he called "the American way", the removal of all traditional privileges and the opening of equal opportunities to all. Lenin did not believe that equality of opportunity to all peasants would lead to socialism, but that it would clear away obstacles to class differentiation and class struggle in the countryside. Soon a small section of the peasants would win control of the greater part of the redistributed land, while the majority would grow steadily poorer. When this process had operated for some time, a strong and politically conscious rural proletariat would be created. This proletariat would be an essential force in the ultimate struggle for power. The alliance of the rural proletariat with the industrial proletariat, against both the rural and the urban bourgeoisie, would make possible the advance towards the socialist revolution. Moreover the transition from bourgeois to socialist revolution could be shortened if the bourgeois revolution were carried out not by the bourgeoisie but by a "democratic dictatorship of workers and

[1] Lenin, *Sochinenia*, 3rd edition, Vol. IX, p. 75. From a pamphle *Peresmotr agrarnoy programmy rabochey partii*, published in St. Petersburg in April 1906. *Loc. cit.*, pp. 55–76.
[2] Lenin, *Sochinenia*, 3rd edition, Vol. XI, pp. 333–498.

peasants".[1] In order to win the peasants to partnership in this dictatorship, the workers—that is, the Bolshevik party—must support the demand of the peasants for redistribution of land.

Mensheviks and Bolsheviks agreed that the next stage in the political struggle would be the bourgeois revolution, and that after its victory the fight for socialism must be pushed ahead to the socialist revolution. In this they differed from the Cadets, who wished to go no further than the bourgeois revolution, and from the Socialist Revolutionaries, who believed that when they gave the land to the peasants they would be making a socialist revolution.

But though theoretically agreed on the long-term issue, Mensheviks and Bolsheviks were tactically nearer to one or other of the non-Marxist parties than to each other. The Mensheviks were nearer to the Cadets, the Bolsheviks to the Socialist Revolutionaries.

The Cadets wished to create a bourgeois democracy in Russia. So did the Mensheviks, in order to give the working class the opportunity to build itself into an economic and political force strong enough ultimately to overthrow the bourgeoisie. The Mensheviks were not much interested in the situation of the peasants in the period between the bourgeois and the socialist revolutions. No doubt a large part of the peasantry would enter the industrial working class. The important thing was that the economy should develop well and rapidly, in order that the workers might become an ever-greater force. Redistribution of land to the peasants would disorganise the economy and retard the economic process on which the future of socialism depended. Mensheviks and Cadets agreed in wishing to minimise disorganisation.

The Socialist Revolutionaries wished at once to distribute the land to the peasants who tilled it. So did Lenin, in order, even at the price of dislocation, to win the peasants as allies of his party, and in order in the longer term to help that sharpening of the class struggle in the villages which, he believed, would later enable the "workers' vanguard", backed by the industrial and rural proletariats, to sweep away the "petty bourgeois utopia" of the Socialist Revolutionaries, and to achieve a socialist revolution.

General economic development

As Russian industry was completing its recovery from the slump of 1899–1902, it was plunged once more into difficulty by the war with Japan, followed in turn by the disorders of 1905–6. The losses

[1] See above, p. 153.

caused by strikes, lock-outs and riots were serious, and further recovery was slow. Only from 1908 did the economy once more expand. Then progress was rapid, until a new war brought the collapse of the whole regime. Some impression of the economic progress in the last years before the First World War can be given by output figures for certain major industries. We will take coal, iron ore, pig-iron, petrol, cotton textiles and sugar.

The Donets basin continued to be Russia's main source of coal. In 1913 it produced 55 per cent of the coal consumed in the empire, while 29 per cent came from other fields within the Empire and 16 per cent was imported. The Donets basin produced 83 per cent of the coke consumed, while 17 per cent was imported. Imported coal and coke were used in St. Petersburg and the Baltic provinces, where it was cheaper to bring them by sea from abroad than by rail from the south. Coalfields of small but growing importance were exploited in the Urals, Siberia, Turkestan and the Moscow region. Output in the two principal areas, the Donets basin and the Polish Dombrowa region, was as follows (in millions of tons):[1]

	Donets	Dombrowa
1900	11	4·6
1908	18	5·6
1913	25	7

In iron ore production, the south had far outstripped the Urals, and maintained its lead. Figures are as follows (millions of *pud*. 62·2 *pud* = 1 ton):

	South Russia	Urals
1905	189	83
1913	402	105

In output of pig-iron the lead of the south was rather smaller, but still overwhelming. Figures are as follows (millions of *pud*. 62·2 *pud* = 1 ton:[2]

	South Russia	Urals	Poland
1905	103		
1910	126	45	15
1913	189·7	56	26

[1] See Margaret Miller, *The Economic Development of Russia, 1905–1914* (London, 1926), pp. 258–60, 289.

[2] Miller, *op. cit.*, pp. 291, 288.

The oil industry suffered especially heavily from the 1905 disorders, including both strikes and Armenian-Tatar massacres. When order was restored, it was found that the resources of the Baku region were diminishing. The decline of the Baku fields was partly compensated by the development of new areas in the neighbourhood. The most important new centre was Grozny. The next most valuable was Surahany. Output in these areas was as follows (in millions of *pud*. 62·2 *pud* = 1 ton):

	Baku	Grozny	Surahany
1910	481		10
1911	431		
1912	434	65	
1913	407		
1914		98	51

The total Russian output of crude oil rose from 456 million *pud* in 1905 to 550 million in 1914, but this was well below the peak year 1901, with its output of 706 million. When trade recovered from the damage of 1905-6, Russian oil had been driven from the Indian market by the oil of Burma and the Netherlands East Indies. The Russian share in world production had been 37 per cent in 1900, but fell to 22·5 per cent in 1910 and 16 per cent in 1913.[1]

Consumption of cotton textiles in 1905 was 602 million pounds, of which 246 million were produced in Russia and 355 imported. In 1910 consumption was 797 million pounds, of which 405 were home-produced and 391 imported. Cotton produced within the Russian Empire had provided 25 per cent of the raw cotton used in the Russian textile industry in 1890: in 1910 it provided 51 per cent. In 1909 the value of imports of raw cotton into Russia was estimated at U.S. $10,900,000 (of which a little less than half was from Germany), while the value of exports of cotton yarn and cloth from Russia was U.S. $12,440,000 (of which a little more than half went to Persia and nearly a quarter to China). In the year 1910-11 Russian exports of cotton goods to Persia were slightly behind British, while in 1912-13 they had surpassed them. Before 1914 the area under cotton cultivation in the Russian Empire was 1¼ million acres in Turkestan and 323,000 acres in Transcaucasia. Consumption of cotton cloth per head in Russia was still extremely low, having increased from 2·31 pounds in 1890 to 4·56 pounds in 1910. The contrast between the poor development of the home market and the relative success

[1] Miller, *op. cit.*, pp. 261-7, 291-2; Lyashchenko, *Istoria narodnovo hozyaistva S.S.S.R.* (Moscow, 1948), Vol. II, p. 410.

of export trade is a good example of the low purchasing power of the Russian masses and the distorted nature of the Russian economy.[1]

Output of sugar was as follows (in millions of *pud*):[2]

1900	..	..	..	..	.. 48
1905	..	..	..	..	.. 53
1910	..	..	..	..	.. 117
1913	..	..	..	..	.. 92

Russia had the second largest number of sugar refineries in Europe (288, to 342 in Germany). Half of these were in the south-west (Kiev province alone had more than a quarter of the empire's refineries), a quarter in Poland, and most of the rest in south central Russia. Output of sugar-beet per unit of land under cultivation was low. The Russian yield in 1912–13 was 125 *pud* of refined sugar for every *desyatin* of sugar-beet. Comparable figures for other countries are Germany 296, France 256, Holland 272.[3]

Consumption of sugar per head in Russia was 4·7 kilogrammes, in contrast to 30 in Great Britain. This was a result of the high price, itself largely due to heavy taxation. Since 1887 the sugar industry had been highly organised. A syndicate formed in that year, and including 206 out of 226 refineries, had established a system of quotas for each member. In 1895 the government took over the regulation of quotas, and membership of the syndicate was made compulsory for sugar refineries. The revenue from the sugar tax was partly used to subsidise export at low prices. Money in fact was taken from the poorest classes and given to the sugar manufacturers. This is strikingly illustrated in figures. In 1895–6 the tax per *pud* of sugar was 1·75 roubles, and the cost of production of the same quantity was 3·25. In 1900 the retail price of refined sugar to the Russian consumer was 6·15 roubles per *pud*, while a *pud* of Russian sugar was sold in London for the equivalent of 2·38 roubles. This state of affairs remained unchanged up to 1914.[4]

These years were marked by a notable growth of industrial combinations. The most important was *Prodameta*, formed in 1902. It included the main metallurgical factories of the south. In 1910 its member firms produced 74 per cent of the pig-iron of the Russian Empire, 78 per cent of the sheet iron, and 46 per cent of the rails. Its five largest members produced 41 per cent of the empire's pig-iron output.[1] It distributed contracts among its members according to quotas, and made contracts on their behalf with merchants and with other industries. It strongly urged the maintenance of high protective tariffs, and kept internal prices high. The factory price of pig-iron in 1902 was 40-41 kopek per *pud*, in 1909-10 47, in 1911-12 65. During this period the import duty on a *pud* of pig-iron varied between 45 and 52 kopek. The high cost of metallurgical products led to a shortage of iron in the last years before the war.

The most important customer of the metallurgical industry was the government, which found it convenient to buy from the big producers and did not object to paying high prices. The government therefore gave little support to those interests which tried to resist the price policy of *Prodameta*. One of these were the zemstvos, which bought ironware at lower prices from non-members of *Prodameta*, and sold cheaply to peasants. *Prodameta* replied by boycotting the zemstvos, and selling only to commercial firms. Another opponent was the Congress of Manufacturers of Agricultural Machines and Instruments, which in 1910 and 1913 asked "Prodameta" to reduce the prices of iron and steel goods and was refused. It also unsuccessfully asked the government in 1912 to intervene in its favour. From 1910 onwards the biggest metallurgical firms made several attempts to acquire direct control of their ore and coal supplies. In 1908 there was a project to form a "vertical" trust, to control several stages in the process of metallurgical production. The project had French financial backing, but was fiercely attacked in the Duma by the Octobrists. A conference appointed by Stolypin expressed no objection in principle to the creation of a trust, but the project was abandoned.[2]

Another important combination was *Produgol*. Founded in 1904, this included the eighteen largest coal-mines of the Donets basin. In 1907-8 the Siberian and Transbaikal coal-mines also joined, and "Produgol" then controlled 75 per cent of the empire's coal output. As in the case of the metallurgical combination, prices were kept high. Non-member firms continued to sell coal at lower prices, and were able to resist cut-throat competition from *Produgol*. But government contracts still went to the big producers of the Donets basin in *Produgol*, though this involved the State in additional expense. A similar organisation was *Pro-*

[1] These were the New Russia Co., of Yuzovka; South Russian Dnieper Co.; Donets-Yuryevsk Metallurgical Co.; Bryansk Co.; and Russo-Belgian Co., of Petrovsk. *Prodameta* is discussed at length in Lyashchenko, *op. cit.*, pp. 294-324.
[2] Lyashchenko, *op. cit.*, pp. 321-3.

darud, founded in 1907, which included the six main producers of iron ore in the south, and so controlled 80 per cent of the empire's iron ore output. Almost the whole output of wagons was controlled by thirteen firms, which in 1904 formed a combination called *Prodvagon*. A copper syndicate was formed in 1907 under the name *Med*, and was closely linked with the German merchant house of Vogau in Moscow. In the textile industry combination was less developed. But a beginning was made with the formation in 1908 of the syndicate of cotton manufacturers of Łódź, soon followed by the Society of Cotton Manufacturers of the Moscow region, which included forty-seven firms with about 40 per cent of the capacity of the region.[1]

Railway development continued, though at a slower rate than in the last decade of the nineteenth century. Between 1897 and 1901 new lines constructed had totalled 15,000 versts, between 1902 and 1906 the figure was 6,350, between 1907 and 1911 3,400. From 1908 onwards the railways began to pay their way. But the substantial excesses of revenue over expenditure on government railways were less important than appeared. Against them had to be set debts for construction which were estimated at about 5,000 million roubles. There was much well-informed criticism in the Third Duma of government railway management, and this led to improvements. Revenue rose from 512 million roubles in 1908 to 813 million roubles in 1913. Private companies continued to operate. A law of June 1905 improved the conditions for private railway concessions. The cost of the private lines was appreciably lower than that of the government lines—87,000 roubles per verst of line, as compared with 107,000 in 1908.[2]

In these years the importance of foreign capital in the Russian economy increased. Estimates of its amount vary appreciably. The total value of foreign loans to the Russian State was probably over 6,000 million roubles, of which at least 4,000 million came from France.[3] The total value of foreign investments in Russian enterprises in 1914 was probably not less than 1,200 million roubles.[4] The proportions originating in the chief investing countries were: France 32 per cent, Great Britain 22·5 per cent to 25 per cent, Germany 16 per cent to 20 per cent, Belgium 15 per cent, and the

[1] Lyashchenko, *op. cit.*, pp. 324–6, 327, 329, 330–8.
[2] Miller, *op. cit.*, pp. 182–201.
[3] Ischchanian, *Die ausländischen Elemente in der russischen Volkswirtschaft* (Berlin, 1913).
[4] Lyashchenko quotes two Soviet writers who estimate respectively 1,340 million and 1,282 million for 1914. Ishchanian's figure for 1913 is Reichsmark 2,370 million (*c.* 1,185 million roubles).

United States 5 per cent to 6 per cent.[1] Foreign investments amounted to about one-third of the total share capital invested in Russia. Somewhat more than half the foreign capital was in metallurgy and mining. As at the turn of the century, French and Belgian capital was mainly in the southern metallurgical industry. German capital was partly in Polish textiles and partly in copper mining and electrical industry. British capital in the Caucasian oilfields notably increased in the last years before the war. Foreign interests were also strongly represented in the foundation capital of the main Russian joint stock banks. In the eighteen chief banks in 1914, 42 per cent of the foundation capital was foreign (17 per cent German, 22 per cent French and 3 per cent British). Examples are the Siberian Bank (40 per cent French and a further 20 per cent other foreign holdings) and the Riga Commercial Bank (50 per cent German).[2]

The last decade before 1914 saw a striking increase in bank deposits. The value of deposits in private banks was as follows:

1900	..	..	..	1,165 million roubles
1909	..	..	..	2,175 ,,
1911	..	..	..	3,206 ,,
1912	..	..	..	3,952 ,,

Savings bank deposits were:

1903	..	..	..	860 million roubles
1908	..	..	..	1,207 ,,
1912	..	..	..	1,594 ,,

In 1910 there were thirty-one joint stock banks in Russia, of which ten were in St. Petersburg, four in Moscow and seventeen in the provinces. The four biggest St. Petersburg banks[3] had 40 per cent of the total of capital and deposits in private banks. Between 1910 and 1914 the number of joint stock banks increased from thirty-one to forty-seven (with a total of 743 branches throughout the empire), and their foundation capital from 332 million roubles to 836 million roubles.[4]

The currency remained stable in spite of the disorders of 1905–6. The gold reserves of the State Bank remained very large. The State

---

[1] The higher figures for Great Britain and the United States come from the American writers Pasvolski and Moulton, the higher figure for Germany from the Soviet writer Ol. Both are quoted in Lyashchenko, *op. cit.*, p. 376.

[2] Lyashchenko, *op. cit.*, p. 362.

[3] St. Petersburg International; Volga-Kama; Azov-Don; and Russian Bank for International Trade.

[4] Miller, *op. cit.*, pp. 102–4, 160; Lyashchenko, *op. cit.*, pp. 356–7.

Bank continued to be closely controlled by the Ministry of Finance, and continued to make loans to industry. The Bank was thus, as in the previous period, one of the main channels through which the government influenced industrial development, and also through which *industrialists influenced the government. Critics of the regime argued that it enabled individual officials of the Ministry of Finance to favour individual firms to their personal advantage; that industry was encumbered by the interference of State Bank or Ministry officials who sat on managing boards; and that credit to agriculture was neglected.

Russian foreign trade policy continued to be protectionist.[1] In the years 1905–12, tariffs averaged the fabulously high rate of 30–38 per cent of the total value of imports. Comparable percentages for other countries were: Great Britain 5·7, Germany 8·4, France 8·2, United States 18·5. The items which yielded the largest tariff receipts were tea (15 per cent of the total value), raw cotton (12 per cent) and machines and spare parts (10·6 per cent). Taxation of tea, a drink widely consumed in Russia, principally hit the poorest consumers, taxation of raw cotton hit the textile industries of Poland and St. Petersburg, while taxation of machinery affected many branches of industry. Foodstuffs continued to be the main Russian export, though their share decreased from an average of 60 per cent in the decade 1904–13 to 55 per cent in 1913 and 1914. Less than 3 per cent was exported by rail, and 5 per cent by Baltic ports. The rest went from the southern ports. The distribution of trade between these ports changed to the advantage of Rostov-on-Don in the Sea of Azov (increase from 13·5 per cent in 1909 to 18 per cent in 1914) and Novorossiisk on the Kuban coast (from 10 per cent to 17 per cent). The share of raw materials in Russian imports remained almost unchanged at about 49 per cent between 1904–8 and 1913, while foodstuffs fell from 23 per cent to 17 per cent and manufactures rose from 28 per cent to 33 per cent. Russia's two best customers remained Germany and Britain. Trade with Germany was regulated by the renewal in 1904 of the treaty of 1894, under which duties were somewhat higher on both sides. Russian opinion was that the treaty was more damaging to Russian exports of grain and raw materials than to German exports of manufactures. The figures for trade with the two countries in the last years are as follows (in millions of roubles):

[1] The figures in the following paragraph come from Miller, *op. cit.*, pp. 70–8. They are mostly derived from the official publication *Vestnik Finansov*.

		1909	1911	1913
Germany	(exports to Russia)	355	477	643
	(imports from Russia)	387	490	453
Britain	(exports to Russia)	128	154	170
	(imports from Russia)	289	337	267

The sources of government revenue remained much the same. Income from the main direct taxes doubled between 1903 and 1913, but was still far behind that from indirect taxes. Of these the sugar and match taxes increased most rapidly. Customs receipts increased nearly by half, while the spirits monopoly and the State railways brought in respectively 65 per cent and 80 per cent more revenue. The following figures show the changes in the main items:[1]

(millions of roubles)

	1903	1913
Direct taxation		
Land tax	49	87
Business tax	67	150
Money capital tax	17	35
Indirect taxation		
Alcohol*	34	53
Tobacco	49	78
Sugar	75	149
Petroleum products	32	48
Matches	8	20
Cigarette tubes	none	4·8
Stamp duties	107	231
Customs	242	353
State property		
State forests	62	92
Railways	453	813
Post, telephones, telegraphs ..	58	120
Spirits monopoly	542	899

* Excluding proceeds of the Spirits monopoly, which are given below under "State property".

Total State expenditure was divided into two categories, "ordinary" and "extraordinary". Ordinary expenditure amounted in 1903 to 1,883 million roubles and in 1913 to 3,070 million. It included military and naval expenditure, which was 466·3 million

[1] For a discussion of the budget, see Miller, *op. cit.*, chapter 7. The complete figures are in Raffalovich, *Russia: its Trade and Commerce* (London, 1918). I have left out some minor items, and have made the table as far as possible comparable with that on pp. 121-2 above.

roubles in 1903 and 866 million in 1913. The extraordinary expenditure for the period 1903–13 totalled 4,476 million roubles. Of this sum 2,242 million were spent on the war with Japan, 455 million on "State defence" (police), 403 on harvest failure relief, and 763 on railway building. The expenses arising out of the Japanese war and the internal disorders were largely covered by foreign loan. In peace years however the extraordinary budget was mainly covered by the so-called "Treasury free balance" of ordinary revenue over ordinary expenditure. The official justification of this practice was that it was useful to have a reserve to meet harvest fluctuations and to strengthen the government's bargaining power in negotiating foreign loans. The objection to it was that it made the government more independent of the Duma in its choice of objects of expenditure—for instance, on police activities.[1]

The percentages of expenditure in the ordinary budget on the main items in 1903 and 1913 were as follows (in millions of roubles):

		1903	1913
"General administration"	..	17·4	16·4
National debt	.. .. ..	15·3	13·1
Armed forces	.. .. ..	24·8	26·6
"Productive expenditure"	..	11·5	16·9
State enterprises	.. ..	31·2	27

Despite the restrictive law of 1900, zemstvo revenues and expenditure greatly increased during these years. Provincial governors and the Ministry of Finance frequently allowed zemstvos to exceed the limits set by the law. In May 1908 a Treasury loan of 6·9 million roubles was made to zemstvos which had difficulty in maintaining or developing education. In May 1911 a yearly credit of 7 million roubles was added, and a special grant of 4 million roubles was made for measures against cholera and plague. In June 1912 a special State Board for credits to zemstvos and city councils was created. In 1913 about 63 per cent of zemstvo income came from taxes on immovable property and 21 per cent from government grants. Income from zemstvo taxes was as follows (in millions of roubles):

1900	..	..	..	88
1910	..	..	..	168
1912	..	..	..	220
1913	..	..	..	254

[1] Miller, *op. cit.*, pp. 130–6.

The share of the main items in zemstvo expenditure in 1913 was: Education 31 per cent, Health 24·6 per cent, Roads 7·4 per cent, Administration 6·8 per cent, Veterinary services 2·8 per cent. Execution of tasks on behalf of the central government, which had been so heavy a burden on the zemstvos' resources in the past, now formed only 4·2 per cent of their expenditure. It had been further reduced by a law of December 1912, by which the State took over all expenses arising out of travel of government officials and the administration of prisons.

Municipal revenue was as follows (in millions of roubles):

1904	..	..	..	131
1910	..	..	..	200
1913	..	..	..	276

Direct expenditure on health and education was proportionately smaller than in the case of municipalities than of zemstvos, but considerable sums were spent on water, lighting and transport. In general, expenditure by local government on social services, though miserably small in comparison with the needs, was increasing at an impressive rate.[1]

In labour policy the most important development of these years was the introduction of health and accident insurance. A law of 10th/23rd June 1912 set up a "hospital fund" in every factory employing 200 or more workers, and laid down that smaller establishments should share such a fund between them. From the funds, sickness benefit was to be paid to sick workers. The funds' resources included a contribution from wages (usually not more than 2 per cent and a maximum of 3 per cent) and from employers. The funds in some cases also received gifts or possessed other property. Disputes arising out of claims for sickness benefits were settled by an Insurance Board, which was set up in each province, and was composed of the provincial Procurator, two representatives each of employers, workers and zemstvos, and one representative each of city councils and the Ministry of the Interior. Insurance against accidents was instituted by a law of the same date. The whole cost was in this case placed on the employer.[2]

The number of industrial workers grew during these years. Official figures for workers employed in mines and factories are as follows:

---

[1] Miller, *op. cit.*, pp. 139-46, 168-70.
[2] This superseded the law introduced on the recommendation of Pleve in June, 1903 (see above, p. 128). For details of the 1912 laws, see Raffalovich, *op. cit.*, pp. 156-9.

1890	..	..	..	1,425,000
1900	..	..	..	2,373,000
1908	..	..	..	2,680,000
1912	..	..	..	2,931,000

These figures exclude railwaymen and various other categories of workers. Of the 1908 total, 823,000 were employed in the textile industry, 552,000 in metallurgy, and 388,000 were miners.[1]

The limits set to trade union activity by the law of 1906[2] were extremely narrow. Strikes were illegal as before, and unions were forbidden to make preparations for them. From 1907 onwards the provincial and city authorities used various excuses to prevent the formation of new unions and to close existing unions. A decision of the Senate of 16th/29th May 1907 refused the right to unions to organise any sort of public meeting, and another of 6th/19th June 1907 forbade unions to hold concerts or public spectacles. Unions were nevertheless able to do their members various services. Before the introduction of health insurance they gave some sickness benefit. Some gave unemployment relief for brief periods, acted as primitive labour exchanges and provided the cost of transport for members to centres where jobs were more numerous. They gave some help to families of arrested or exiled members (though this was of course forbidden), and provided legal assistance to members in cases arising out of disputes with employers concerning contracts, or conflicts with the police "in the field of economic struggle or activity on behalf of trade union interests". Unions also collected small libraries, organised reading-rooms for members, and occasionally arranged lectures. In general the legal trade unions were of small value as weapons in the struggle with employers, but were valuable as a means of increasing the workers' sense of solidarity and of training leaders.[3]

There were few strikes in the first years after 1907, but in 1912 the number greatly increased, and rose up till 1914. An important landmark was the strike of April 1912 in the British-owned Lena goldfields. A crowd of workers, protesting at the food supplied by the management, were fired on by order of a gendarmerie officer, and more than a hundred were killed or wounded. The next two years saw a rapid growth of political strikes. These were most numerous among metal workers, and the main centre of political strikes was St. Petersburg. But other branches of industry, including the relatively "backward" textile workers, and other industrial

---

[1] Raffalovich, *op. cit.*, p.107. See also above p. 123.
[2] See above, p. 226.   [3] Grinevich, *op. cit.*, chapters 4 and 5.

regions, were also affected. The number of workers on strike in 1912 was 725,000 (of whom 550,000 were "political"), in 1913 887,000 (of whom 502,000 were "political"), in 1914 (January–July) 1,450,000 (of whom 1,030,000 were "political").[1]

The Revolutionaries

The repression which followed the dissolution of the Second Duma made it dangerous for the leaders of the revolutionary parties to remain in Russia. The local organisations did their best to maintain political activity, the party newspapers appeared irregularly, often slashed by the censors, and the Social Democrat and Trudovik deputies in the Duma made speeches on party lines. But the best-known leaders, including Martov, Plehanov, Lenin, Akrelrod and Dan among the Social Democrats and Chernov and Avksentiev among the Socialist Revolutionaries, returned to exile.

Emigration is a frustrating and demoralising experience. The advantages of free expression and wider perspective barely compensate for the sense of isolation and long periods of idleness. The exiled revolutionaries busily produced their articles and pamphlets, organised supply routes into Russia and received clandestine correspondence. But these tasks could not fully occupy them. There were days or weeks with nothing to do but quarrel and intrigue. To anyone so naturally quarrelsome and predisposed to intrigue as Lenin the atmosphere of exile was especially harmful. Besides, real differences on policy and tactics divided the exiles, especially the Social Democrats.

Meanwhile in Russia both workers and peasants were growing tired of revolutionary slogans and conspiracy. These seemed to have got them nowhere. They only diverted the attention of the workers from practical tasks, and gave the police excuses to persecute peaceful people. The new regime was very far from democratic, but at least it granted more freedom than in the past. Workers could at least meet in unions, and could put forward demands without automatic punishment. Peasants could have some hope of acquiring more land. In the Duma the voice of workers' and peasants' representatives could be heard, and was not always ignored. The views once held by the "Economists" therefore reappeared in a new form. Some of the workers' leaders inside Russia argued that the old party had been a failure, and should now be "liquidated", that conspiratorial methods should be abandoned,

[1] *Krasny Arkhiv*, XXXIV, pp. 95–125.

that less emphasis should be put on political issues, and that the workers' organisations permitted by law should be built up until they were strong enough to do what the government and the employers wished to prevent them from doing—effectively defend the economic interests of the working class.

This point of view was received with sympathy by some of the Menshevik leaders, including Martov. To Lenin it was pernicious heresy, a repudiation of all that he had stood for. He remained true to the principles of his "What is to be done?" The new point of view he bitterly denounced as "Liquidatorism". The party, he argued, must remain centralised and conspiratorial, and discipline must be rigid. But it soon became clear that these principles were valid for him only as long as the orders given from above were acceptable to him. As soon as the party took a decision with which Lenin disagreed, he regarded himself as exempt from the obligation of unconditional obedience on which he insisted so strongly where others were concerned. Despite the formal "unification" of the party at Stockholm, and the formal maintenance of unity at London,[1] the separate Bolshevik centre remained in existence. Lenin created his own party within the party. Its members were to be unconditionally devoted to him. When hesitation or heresy appeared within his own ranks, they were purged. Thus was the attempt made to build the steel-hard monolithic party which was to embody Lenin's ideal of a vanguard of professional revolutionaries, the only reliable instrument of revolution.

Lenin's twisted manœuvres and intrigues in the following years can only be understood if it is realised that he considered all the principles of organisation and obligations of party membership of which he talked as applicable only within his own faction. Members of his group must be unreservedly loyal to him: he would be equally loyal to them as long as they accepted his policy. Those outside his party were enemies. The Mensheviks were not comrades. The nominal R.S.D.R.P. was not "the party" at all. The Mensheviks felt loyalty to the whole party, and felt obligations to Lenin as a comrade: Lenin recognised no loyalty either to the wider party or to the Mensheviks. Any promise made to them was a tactical concession, to be withdrawn as soon as convenient.

Among Lenin's broken promises was suppression of partisan actions. The London congress was hardly over when a daring bank robbery took place in Tiflis on 13th/26th June 1907. It was carried out by an Armenian named Terpetrossian and known by the

---

[1] See above pp. 249–50, 258–9.

conspiratorial name of Kamo. Its organiser was a Georgian Bolshevik named Djugashvili, who at this time used the conspiratorial name Koba, and later took the name Stalin. The loot, 400,000 roubles in notes, was smuggled out of Russia to the Bolshevik exiles. Unfortunately one of Lenin's trusted men, responsible for its distribution, was a police spy. On his information the French, German and Swedish police were able to arrest the distributors. The facts became generally known, and shocked the Second International. The Mensheviks were furious that the Russian party should be so dishonoured. They also discovered that Lenin had given his approval to partisan actions in the Urals by a band led by a certain Lbov. A further scandal concerned some money promised to the party by an industrialist sympathiser. Two sisters had legally inherited the money. Lenin sent a Bolshevik to marry one sister, a second to make the other his mistress, and a third to marry her. The first husband, who wanted to keep the money for himself, was forced by threats to give it up. All the loot then went, not to the party, but to the Bolsheviks.[1]

The original justification of partisan actions had been that they gave workers battle-training, and of expropriations that they provided the means of acquiring further arms. But by 1908 it was clear that armed risings had no chance of success, and Lenin unashamedly used the proceeds of these actions for his factional struggle. They provided his professional revolutionaries with a living, and paid for propagandist literature directed not against the "class enemy" in Russia but against Mensheviks, Liquidators, dissident Bolsheviks and other heretics within the movement. These funds also helped Lenin to maintain better contact with Russia than the Menshevik exiles with their slender resources could achieve, and to give financial assistance to those organisations of the party within Russia which accepted Lenin's lead.

The party in Russia did not of course know much of the quarrels among the exiles. Lenin seemed to many Social Democrats at home to be the best leader because he was the most efficient and the most helpful. In so far as they heard of the disputes abroad, they deplored them and urged conciliation. Thus Bolshevism inside Russia was a genuine workers' revolutionary movement, while Bolshevism outside Russia was a warring sect led by an autocratic and infallible leader. But in his sectarian battles abroad Lenin

---

[1] The Menshevik case against Lenin in these affairs is Martov's pamphlet, *Spasiteli ili uprazdniteli* (Paris, 1911). See also *Pisma P.B. Akselroda k Yu. O. Martovu* (Berlin, 1924). A recent work is B. D. Wolfe, *Three Who Made a Revolution* (New York, 1948).

derived prestige from the undoubted fact that he commanded support and admiration inside Russia.

As long as the Bolsheviks in Russia recognised him as the leader, Lenin did not demand from them specific acceptance of all his tactical dogmas on the sectarian front. But Bolsheviks abroad were of course expected to obey in all things. There were two main dissident tendencies among exiled Bolsheviks, against which Lenin fought ruthlessly. One was "conciliationism"—the heresy of regarding Mensheviks as party comrades with whom one should seek reconciliation, rather than as enemies to be politically destroyed. The other was "recallism"—the extreme Left position of those who after June 1907 wished completely to boycott the Duma and to "recall" the party's representatives from it, rather than make use of its facilities for party propaganda, as Lenin urged. A prominent conciliationist was Rykov, later Prime Minister of the Soviet Union. Among the extreme left wing were the philosopher Bogdanov and the writer Lunacharsky. Though his quarrel with these two was essentially tactical, Lenin chose as his battle-ground their philosophical doctrines. He attacked them as "God-seekers" and as critics of materialism. His own views were expounded in his *Materialism and Empiriocriticism*. It was Lenin's only incursion into the field of pure philosophy. The subject as such did not interest him: he only needed an intellectual weapon with which to beat his tactically unreliable followers. But an unexpected result of Lenin's dispute with Lunacharsky and Bogdanov has been that Lenin's book has received in the Soviet Union the same degree of dogmatic infallibility as his political writings, and is compulsory for all Soviet philosophers.

During 1909 indignation against Lenin's methods grew in exiled Russian and in international socialist circles. Though he fought back, and hurled abuse at Mensheviks and "Liquidators", he was forced to yield. At the end of the year was held a plenary meeting of the still nominally united R.S.D.R.P. Central Committee. Though some Mensheviks now considered Lenin unreformable, and wished to expel him and his group from the party, they were restrained by moderates who hoped that gentle treatment of Lenin would win over the more reasonable Bolsheviks, that thus Lenin's influence within the Bolshevik faction could be reduced and ultimately true unity of the party be achieved. Expulsion of Lenin would, they believed, force all Bolsheviks from loyalty to support Lenin, and so deprive the party for good of valuabe members. These views were held by Plehanov, by Trotski and by the Bund.

The conclusions of the plenary meeting appeared a success for moderation. A compromise was made. The Bolsheviks insisted that the distribution of seats between the factions on the editorial board of the party newspaper should be the same as after the London congress—which favoured Bolsheviks rather than Mensheviks—and won their point. On the other hand the Bolsheviks promised to dissolve their separate organisation, to hand over to the party the funds belonging to it which they had wrongfully acquired, to recognise as the supreme leadership of the Party a "Russian College of the Central Committee" which was to be formed inside Russia, and to help found a legal party newspaper in Russia whose editorial board was to include people whom Lenin had earlier attacked as "Liquidators". The effect of these concessions would be, the Mensheviks hoped, to give more influence over party policy to the real workers' movement inside Russia, and less to the warring factions in exile.

But once again, Lenin broke his promises. The Bolshevik centre was not dissolved. Lenin made excuses to postpone the delivery of his funds to the party. He agreed to the calling of a conference with the "Liquidators" from Russia. But when the three "Liquidator" leaders who were invited to attend (Garvi, Yermolaev and Issuf) refused, as they would have nothing to do with the conspiratorial Bolsheviks in exile, Lenin announced in the name of the Central Committee that all relations with the Liquidators were broken. Martov protested that the refusal of these three men need not prevent eventual co-operation with the legal movement in Russia, but Lenin, who controlled the party paper, refused to print an article by Martov to this effect. Martov appealed to the Foreign Bureau of the Central Committee against this action, which was a violation of the conditions on which it had been agreed by all that the paper should be managed. Lenin, with the support of the Polish Social Democrats, then declared the Foreign Bureau dissolved, and set up instead an "Organising Committee" run by himself and the Poles. Martov and Dan then resigned from the editorial board of a paper in which they were prevented by their colleagues from expressing their views. Soon after this Lenin quarrelled with the Poles, declared his new committee dissolved, and set up yet another, now called the "Russian Organising Committee" and entirely controlled by his faction.[1]

[1] Martov and Dan, op. cit., pp. 232-50; Dan, Proiz'hozhdenie Bolshevizma, pp. 438 ff.; Wolfe, op. cit., pp. 475-557. The Bolshevik view during these years is best found in Lenin, Sochinenia, Vols. XIV-XVI. The current Stalinist view is found in Short History, pp. 127-38.

The formal declaration of a split which had long been a fact took place in January 1912 in Prague, in the "People's House" or head-quarters of the Czech Social Democrats.[1] Here the Bolsheviks declared themselves to be "the party" and the Mensheviks, Liquidators, Trotski and the rest to be renegades. A new Central Committee was elected, which included such later leaders of the Soviet Union as Ordjonikidze, Sverdlov and Zinoviev. The dele-gates also included a young man named Scriabin, who later achieved some notoriety under the name of Molotov. The con-ference gave the new Central Committee power to co-opt members, and this power was soon afterwards used by Lenin to add the young Georgian Djugashvili, with whom he had been in corre-spondence and whom he had met three times. Djugashvili was at this time in "administrative exile" in Siberia.

Now Lenin had what he had been working for, a small docile group of professional revolutionaries, purged of all waverers and unreservedly devoted to him. The "steel-hard cadres" of the "monolithic" Bolshevik party were there: it still remained to make the party a force in Russia. And here circumstances began to favour Lenin. From the Lena goldfields strike of April 1912 onwards, the labour movement in Russia entered a new offensive phase. Strikes grew, and social and political unrest affected a growing number of workers in all the main industrial centres. The disillusionment and pessimism of the Stolypin years gave way to a new revolutionary spirit. And at this time the son of a rich Kazan merchant named Tihomirov presented Lenin with 100,000 roubles. The money was used to found a daily paper *Pravda* which appeared legally in St. Petersburg.

During the last two years before the war, the Bolsheviks made good use of the legal opportunities allowed to them. In the Fourth Duma elections thirteen Social Democrats were returned, of whom six were Bolsheviks. Though Bolsheviks and Mensheviks were now separate parties, the Duma group was not at first split. *Pravda* did not satisfy Lenin. Both in its columns and in the conduct of the Bolsheviks in the Duma was reflected the desire of the Russian workers for a united party. The heresy of "conciliationism", which Lenin had at last purged from the Bolshevik ranks in exile, was still strong within Russia. In order to ensure a "steel-hard" attitude among the Bolsheviks at home, Lenin summoned Djugash-vili to meet him in Cracow to be instructed. It was during this visit

[1] The proceedings of the conference are summarised in *Vserossiiskaya kon-ferentsia R.S.D.R.P. 1912 goda* (Paris, 1912).

to Austrian territory—which included a short trip to Vienna—that the future "teacher of genius of all progressive humanity" made, at Lenin's request, the study of the problem of nationalities which led to his famous publication *Marxism and the National Question*.[1] Lenin sent Sverdlov to Russia to "correct" the "line" of *Pravda*, but after a few days he was arrested. When Stalin returned from Cracow to St. Petersburg, he too was arrested. Lenin's third emissary, Kamenev, was only saved from the same fate by an amnesty granted to all "literary political" criminals in honour of the third centenary of the Romanov dynasty. After Kamenev took over, *Pravda*'s attitude became more factional, and Lenin was satisfied. At the same time the Bolshevik Duma group, led by Malinovski, began to quarrel with the Mensheviks, and in the autumn the Social Democrat Duma group was finally split.[2]

During these years the Menshevik exiles made further attempts to unite the party leadership. In August 1912 a conference was held in Vienna of representatives of the three groups of Martov, Trotski and the "Liquidators". A common front was formed under the name of "August block". Its views were expressed inside Russia by a legal daily called *Luch*. Between the two camps however there was no prospect of unity. Among the masses there was little difference between Bolsheviks and Mensheviks. Even among the leaders on both sides there was still support for reconciliation, but the iron will of Lenin was inflexibly opposed to compromise. From his place of exile he kept his hold over the Bolshevik organisation inside Russia, and as in the last resort the masses of each faction obeyed their leader, reconciliation was impossible. In May 1914 the Second International tried to intervene, and called a conference of all Russian Social Democrat groups in Brussels. But war made this impossible. On the eve of war, the Mensheviks were stronger than their rivals in the Caucasus, Odessa, Harkov and the Donets, the Bolsheviks in the Urals and the Moscow region. In St. Petersburg both were strong. The Bolsheviks were the better supplied with funds, while the Mensheviks probably had more support from the skilled and educated workers.

This brief account should have made clear that the quarrel

[1] The essential contribution was an article entitled "The national question and social democracy", written at Lenin's request for the Bolshevik periodical *Prosveshchenie* in the spring of 1913. It consisted of a polemic against the doctrines of the Austrian Marxist experts on the National question, Bauer and Renner.

[2] For a Bolshevik account of the group's activities, see Badaev, *The Bolsheviks in the Tsarist Duma* (London, 1929). Some information can also be found in Liubov Krassin, *Leonid Krassin, his Life and Work* (London, 1929). On Malinovski, see also below, p. 302.

between Mensheviks and Bolsheviks was largely personal. Lenin's conviction of his infallible revolutionary sense, and his implacable opposition to all who questioned his tactics, are essential factors in the split. But it is also true that there were important differences of policy between the two groups. These have already been described,[1] and did not notably change after 1906–7. They all derive from the basic difference on the organisation of the party. Once the doctrine of the conspiratorial vanguard of professional revolutionaries is accepted, everything else follows from it. Lenin's views on the relationship of the party to the Duma, to trade unions, to the agrarian problem and to the preparations for armed action are all a logical consequence of his view of the party. The Mensheviks denied the conspiratorial conception, and their views of the same four problems follow inevitably from the denial. Neither side can be proved absolutely right. The correctness of tactics depends on the situation in which they are to be applied. The political and economic evolution of Russia between 1906 and 1914 definitely supported the Menshevik view, but the situation of Russia in 1917 equally supported the Bolsheviks, theoretically as well as in practice. The Russian professional revolutionary is essentially the product of a society in which the nineteenth- or twentieth-century intellectual is driven to revolutionary action by the spectacle of his people living in the Middle Ages and unable to climb out of them, a situation in which the links between the intellectual and the people are, and can be, only very tenuous. Russia was such a country in the days of People's Will, but she was ceasing to be in 1914. A large industrial working class, with a considerable education, skill and class consciousness, was becoming a real force. So was a bourgeois middle class. Russia was drawing rapidly nearer to Western Europe. In such conditions the conspiratorial revolutionary was becoming an anachronism, and was so regarded by a growing number of Russian Marxists, both among workers and among intellectuals. To them Lenin, passionately defending the earlier type of organisation, seemed a utopian reactionary. Yet in 1917 Lenin's tactics were better suited to the facts than those of his opponents. Military defeat, economic chaos and famine in the cities had reduced Russia to a condition more primitive even than in the days of Alexander II. In this situation a group of resolute conspirators, clearly understanding what they wanted, and inhibited by no scruples from the use either of terror or of demagogy, were a match for any party modelled on the mass movements of Western

[1] See above, pp. 152, 153–4, 278–80.

Europe. Lenin in 1917 came into his own. Yet if history had not made him a present of chaos his talents might have been wasted in the frustration and intrigues of exile. Chaos of course resulted from defeat in war, which some had predicted, and war resulted from international conflicts which many, whether Marxists or not, had long felt to be incapable of peaceful settlement. But the fact that Lenin had anticipated war, and had foreseen the possibility of Russia's defeat, already before 1914, proves nothing. Lenin had not foreseen, and no one could have foreseen, the way that Russia and other countries would be affected by these events. The course of military events in 1914–17, and the proved suitability of Lenin's revolutionary tactics to the Russian developments in 1917, do not prove retrospectively that the Bolshevik "line" from 1903 onwards was "correct", "scientific" or historically predestined.

.   .   .   .   .

The development of the Socialist Revolutionary Party after 1907 is less interesting than that of the Social Democrats, partly because its leaders in exile were less gifted and able politicians, and partly because the party machine within Russia, dependent on the scattered peasants rather than the concentrated urban workers, was less effective. But several of the old problems of revolutionary policy, familiar from the experience of the Marxists, also beset their ideological rivals.

There were the same debates over a centralised or a less central-ised party, the use of political action in general and parliamentary action in particular, and the value or harm of terrorism as a revolu-tionary weapon. The Socialist Revolutionaries, like the Social Democrats, had their left and their right wings. They were embarrassed by the activities of the terrorist "Maximalists" just as their rivals were embarrassed by the activities of the "partisan bands" of Lbov, Djugashvili and their like.[2] The relations between the Battle Organisation and the Central Committee were seldom as smooth as they should have been.

A most serious crisis in the party came when the head of the Battle Organisation, Yevno Azeff, was accused during 1908 of working for the police. His chief accuser was Vladimir Burtsev, the party's security expert, and a kind of self-appointed adviser on conspiratorial technique to all revolutionary parties. Burtsev pieced together evidence which showed there must be leakages in the party, and finally traced their source to Azeff. His crowning

---

[1] The Maximalists were responsible for a series of outrages during 1906, including the bomb in Stolypin's villa. See Spiridovich, *op. cit.*

piece of evidence was the admission by a former head of the political police that Azeff had been his agent. The accusations were at first indignantly rejected not only by Azeff himself but by the party leaders, who regarded him as one of their great heroes. But the evidence was overwhelming, and a party "court of honour" in January 1909 found Azeff guilty. He succeeded in escaping and changing his identity. He died in 1918 in Germany, after spending some years in internment as a Russian subject and a terrorist during the World War.[1]

The case of Azeff has never been satisfactorily explained. There is no doubt that he offered his services at an early age to the secret police, and received regular pay from them. He began as an informer on Russian students abroad, on whom he sent reports to St. Petersburg while building his reputation as a revolutionary. He was one of the founders of the Socialist Revolutionary Party in 1902, and became chief of the Battle Organisation when Gershuni was arrested. All this time he was supplying the police with information. Yet in 1904, shortly after betraying to the police the plans of another group to assassinate Pleve, he himself organised the assassination and did not betray it. Again, in February 1905 he organised the assassination of the Grand Duke Sergei. Azeff's career cannot be completely explained by either mercenary or political motives. Love of power and secrecy must have been his strongest passions, But he remains an unexplained mystery.

The Azeff scandal demoralised many supporters of the party. Inside Russia the best organisers had suffered from the repression of 1906–8. Small local groups continued to exist, but the party was not an effective force. Yet much had been gained from the two years of opportunity. The peasants had seen something of the importance of politics and of organisation. They had heard the slogans of the Socialist-Revolutionaries. Even in the years of Stolypin, party organisers stressed this great increase of political consciousness among the peasants as a permanent gain.[1] It was not until 1917 that the peasants again had a chance to express themselves politically without restriction and without fear. The fact that they then gave their votes overwhelmingly to the Socialist Revolutionaries shows that in the earlier years the party had not entirely wasted its time.

Police provocation was not confined to the Socialist Revolution-

[1] On Azeff see Nicolaevsky, *Azeff the Russian Judas* (London, 1934). Another valuable source is Burtsev, *Borba za svobodnuyu Rossiyu.*

[2] *Protokoly pervoy obshchepartiinoy konferentsii Partii Sotsialistov-Revolyutsion-erov* (Paris, 1908).

aries. In 1914 a scandal of equal proportions was revealed in the Bolshevik ranks. The worker Roman Malinovski, who headed the Bolshevik faction in the Fourth Duma, was a police spy. He first gave information to the police in 1906, and was a regular agent from 1910 onwards. He betrayed the hiding-places of such prominent Bolsheviks as Sverdlov and Djugashvili on more than one occasion. Thoroughly informed by him of the factional struggles within the Marxist movement, the police decided to encourage them. Advised by Malinovski, they took various steps to make things easier for Lenin in his intrigues. For instance, in 1912 they arrested three intended delegates to the Prague conference of the Bolsheviks, whose presence was expected to embarrass Lenin. In the elections to the Fourth Duma, Malinovski's candidature was actively helped by the police Defence Section ("Ohrana"), both by funds and by interference with rival candidates. The final split in the Social Democratic Duma faction was carried out under simultaneous instructions from Lenin and from Ohrana headquarters. At the end of 1913 however the authorities became displeased with Malinovski, who continued to make violent revolutionary harangues, and even denounced the practice of provocation by the police in one of his Duma speeches. The police therefore revealed his activities to Rodzianko, the Speaker of the Duma and an Octobrist. Malinovski suddenly resigned his seat in the Duma and left Russia. Lenin received him with enthusiasm in Galicia, and long refused to admit his guilt. It was ultimately proved in detail by the evidence given before the Commission on the fall of the imperial regime in 1917.

Just as dictatorship by the police breeds conspiratorial sects, so conspiracy breeds provocation. The Russian police were skilful organisers of provocation, but whether it benefited them is doubtful. An interesting feature of most secret police organisations is the conflict of interest between the "intelligence" branch and the "operational" branch. The former is interested in information, and so wishes to leave at liberty revolutionaries of whose activities it is informed: the latter wishes to break up the revolutionary organisations. The efficiency of the Russian police's information and provocation services to some extent paralysed its will to action, and so benefited the revolutionaries. Lenin was duped by Malinovski, yet Malinovski's contacts with the Ohrana may in fact have helped Lenin more than they helped the Ohrana. If this be so, it is of course no ground to admire Lenin's wisdom. It only shows that too much subtlety may be as dangerous as stupidity.[1]

[1] On police methods, see Laporte, *op. cit.*, Zavarzin, *op. cit.*

The Nationalities

The years of consolidation under Stolypin and Kokovtsov were a period of Great Russian nationalism.[1] The concessions made to the non-Russian nationalities under pressure of the revolutionary movement of 1905 were mostly withdrawn. In Poland, the Ukraine and the Caucasus the situation in 1914 was little better than in 1904: in Finland it was on the whole worse.

The electoral law of 1907 was planned to discriminate as much against the nationalities as against the Russian Left. The greatest number of seats that Poles could now hope to win was eleven in the "Vistula provinces" and four in the western. The franchise was also weighted in favour of the landowners. Since the aristocratic romantic nationalism of the nineteenth century had given place to the bourgeois nationalism of the twentieth, the Russian authorities, who had once favoured the bourgeoisie of Poland against the land-lords, now preferred the landlords. And in fact, part of the Polish rural vote was given not to the National Democrats but to the "Party of Realpolitik", lead by Staszewicz, which stood for closer co-operation with the imperial government.[2]

The first important measure of Stolypin's regime against the Poles was the suppression of the *Macierz Szkolna* in December 1907. It was followed by other blows. In 1911 Stolypin introduced zemstvo institutions into the "western provinces". This was accompanied by a system of franchise which weighted representation in favour of the Russian element and against the Polish. It was this measure which caused the conflict between Stolypin and the legislative chambers already mentioned.[3]

In 1912 a new province of Cholm was formed out of the two Polish provinces of Lublin and Siedlce. Its purpose was to take away from Poland an area which had a strong Ukrainian element and thus to reduce the amount of Polish territory within the empire. In 1913 city councils were introduced in the "Vistula provinces". The system was modelled on that prevailing since 1870 in Russia proper, but there were three electoral colleges, based on nationality—Polish, Jewish and Russian. It was so arranged that the small number of Russian bureaucrats were greatly over-represented. Though in practice this was done rather at the expense of the Jews

---

[1] For an expression of Russian right-wing nationalism, anti-Semitic, anti-Polish and anti-Finnish, see P. I. Kovalevski, *Russkii natsionalizm i natsionalnoe vospitanie* (SPB., 1912).
[2] This party is briefly described in *O.D.*, Vol. III, pp. 260–7.
[3] See above, p. 268.

than of the Poles, indignation was caused among the Polish population. Official business in the new councils had to be done in the Russian language. Another most unpopular measure was the acquisition in 1913 by the State of the Warsaw–Vienna railway, which had previously belonged to a Polish private company. It was followed by the introduction of Russian workers and technical personnel in place of Polish.

The Ukrainians had no specific representation at all in the Third and Fourth Dumas. The Ukrainian political parties as such more or less ceased to exist, though their ideas still had a following among the people. In their place was formed in 1908 a new secret organisation, the Society of Ukrainian Progressives (T.U.P.), a non-Marxist radical group with some socialist sympathies. Many Ukrainian workers gave their votes to candidates of the R.S.D.R.P. The Mensheviks were probably the stronger of the two Marxist factions in the Ukraine. In Harkov however the workers' "curia" returned a Bolshevik to the Fourth Duma.[1]

From 1907 onwards Ukrainian cultural activities became very difficult. The Kuban branch of *Prosvita* was closed by the administration and the Chernigov branch was forced to shut down as a result of repeated interference by the authorities. In 1908, when permission was refused to open a branch in Poltava, and the population appealed to the Imperial Senate, the reply was that a *Prosvita* organisation would "not be desirable". Stolypin in the Third Duma stated that he was against all movements that "weakened the unity of the Russian people", and made it clear that under this heading he included all Ukrainian nationalism. In 1910 *Prosvita* was finally closed.[2]

Use was made of the years of freedom to organise a rural co-operative movement in the Ukraine. In 1904 there were three of these in Kiev province, in 1908 450, and a further 200 in Poltava province. In 1908 a co-operative congress was held in Kiev, at which all business was publicly transacted in the Ukrainian language. In the years after 1908 discontent was growing in the Ukraine. The failure to deal with the land problem was especially important. Stolypin's reforms were calculated, as we have seen, to destroy the Russian village commune and to enable peasants to create consolidated holdings of their own. But this was of little value in the Ukraine, where the village commune had hardly existed. Here the peasants' shortage of land was directly due to the existence of large private landed estates. State land was of

---

[1] *Narys istorii Ukrainy*, p. 148.   [2] *O.D.*, Vol. IV, Part 2, p. 206; Krupnyckyj, *op. cit.*

less importance than in the north. At the time of the emancipation of 1861 the landowners in the Ukraine had passed on the cost to the peasants not, as in the north, by high redemption payments, but by granting them as their own property less land than they had previously been in the habit of cultivating under serfdom.[1] Stolypin's remission of redemption payments was of little value to the Ukrainian peasants, who were however bitterly disappointed at the failure of the revolutionary years to bring a redistribution of landlords' estates. When we add that the landowners in the Ukraine were an ethnically alien element, Russians or Poles or russified Ukrainians who no longer spoke their language, it is easy to see why Ukrianian nationalism should despite persecution gain ground among the discontented peasants.

In the Baltic provinces official policy became more hostile to the Baltic nations and more tolerant to the Germans. Latvians and Esthonians were clearly more affected by revolutionary ideas than Germans. Though the latter might be the eternal enemies of Slavdom, they had shown themselves loyal subjects of the Tsar. The maintenance of their economic privileges linked them to the established order. After 1906 a number of German secondary schools, closed in the preceding years, were reopened with government consent. These included the famous Domschule in Reval and the Albertschule in Riga. The university of Dorpat was not however regermanised. In the provinical Diets the Germans predominated up to 1914. German ownership of land was also maintained. Some German landowners were even allowed by the Russian authorities to buy additional land and settle it with German peasants from other parts of Russia, especially from Volhynia. The Manteuffel and Broderich families between 1908 and 1913 settled 15,000 German farmers on some 160,000 acres of land thus acquired.[2]

Nevertheless the loyalty of the Baltic Germans to Russia had suffered a heavy blow. Even if the authorities were less hostile to them, their ability to protect them from the rage of the Latvian and Esthonian peasants was in doubt. The attraction of a more powerful protector, the German Empire, increased. Contacts between Baltic Germans and the Pan-German League grew during the last years before 1914.[3]

---

[1] See above p. 44.
[2] Schwabe, *op. cit.*, p. 117.
[3] For further details on this, and bibliographical references, see C. L. Lundin, "The Road from Tsar to Kaiser: changing loyalties of the Baltic German, 1905–1914" in *Journal of Central European Studies*, Oct. 1950.

In the Caucasus Russian policy was somewhat uncertain. The government in St. Petersburg was on the whole hostile to all Caucasian national movements, though perhaps less so to the Moslem Tatars than to the Christian Georgians and Armenians. The Governor-General of the Caucasus, Count Vorontsov-Dashkov, showed some sympathy to the Armenians. He regarded them as a useful weapon against Turkey, with whom he assumed that conflict was inevitable. Stolypin saw in the Dashnyak party only a pernicious revolutionary movement. He protested in correspondence with Vorontsov-Dashkov against the latter's toleration of the Armenians. The Governor-General replied that he was doing the best he could with inadequate numbers and low quality of police and troops, and that the Premier was misinformed as to the state of affairs in the Caucasus by the gendarmerie, who were considerably more incompetent than the local police. He pointed out that the Dashnyaks had been divided since 1905, and that the stronger and more conservative section was loyal to the empire.[1] Again, in 1912, in a letter to the Tsar, Vorontsov-Dashkov strongly recommended a friendly policy towards the Armenians. He claimed that as a result of his administration in the Caucasus the Armenians within Russia had become a loyal element while those in the Ottoman Empire looked to Russia for protection.[2]

The main area of Moslem political activity remained the Volga region, with Kazan as its centre. During the last years before the war many Tatars who had become Christians were reconverted to Islam, and Tatar Moslem propagandists had great success among neighbouring non-European peoples. The fact that Islam was gaining ground on Orthodoxy, and that the Tatars were winning political leadership of the minor nationalities in eastern Russia, alarmed both the Church hierarchy and the civil administration. It was also of grave concern to Stolypin, who called several special conferences of experts to plan counter-measures.[3] Financial contributions by the government to the Church were increased, and renewed efforts were made to encourage Russian priests, teachers and officials to learn the local languages in order to compete with the Tatar Moslem propagandists. But little progress was made. The Tatars were often better educated than the Russians who lived in their midst. The Tatar middle class in

---

[1] The correspondence is published in *Krasny Arkhiv*, XXXIV, pp. 184–221, and XXXV, pp. 128–50.
[2] *Krasny Arkhiv*, XXVI, pp. 97–128.
[3] *Krasny Arkhiv*, XXXV, pp. 107–27, and XXXVI, pp. 61–83.

town and village and the Tatar intelligentsia were becoming a
serious force. At the same time the economic condition of the
peasants of the minor nationalities made them willing listeners
to the anti-government and anti-Russian propaganda of the
Tatars.

The Russian authorities at this time were greatly alarmed by
the growth of what they called "Panislamism". But in fact the
political movement among the Moslems of Russia was not so much
Panislamic as Panturk. Whereas the Moslems of the Ottoman
Empire included Albanians and Arabs, those of the Russian
Empire almost all belonged to some Turkic language group—the
Iranian Tadjiks, numbering about one million, were the only
important exception. The ideology of Panturkism, or Panturan-
ianism, was popular among the Moslem intelligentsia in Russia
earlier than in the Ottoman Empire. It was not until the loss of
the Balkan and Arab territories that the Turks of Anatolia began to
follow the doctrines of Turkish nationalism, propounded at first
with little success by the writer Zia Gök Alp. The Russian Moslems found little sympathy in Ottoman Turkey for their Panturk
ideas. The Ottoman rulers—first Sultan Abdul-Hamid, then the
Young Turks—had too many commitments in too wide an area
to bother about helping the Turks of Russia. The Russian Government's fears of Ottoman Turkish intrigues were greatly exaggerated.
If it had devoted less energy to looking for Ottoman spies, and
more to improving religious tolerance and economic conditions
in the Tatar and other Moslem areas, it would have had more
loyal subjects.[1]

In Finland part of the gains of 1905–6 were maintained and part
were lost. The reform of the constitution remained a fact. The
Social Democrats remained the strongest party in the Diet, with
eighty seats or more. The Old Finns were second, with an average
of about fifty. The Young Finns and the Swedes usually each had
about twenty-five seats, and the Agrarians about half as many.[2]

The Social Democratic vote was much larger than the total
number of factory workers. Considerable numbers of poorer
peasants, especially of the small tenant farmers, voted socialist.

[1] Mende *op. cit.*, pp. 71–90.
[2] Distribution of seats in four elections was as follows:

	1907	1908	1909	1910
Social Democrats	80	83	84	86
Old Finns	59	54	48	42
Swedes	24	25	25	26
Young Finns	25	27	28	28
Agrarians	10	9	13	17

As the socialists never had a clear majority, government was carried on by a coalition of Old Finns and Swedes with support in the Diet also from Young Finns or Agrarians. Social Democrat pressure in the Diet was able to secure a number of social reforms, in regard to land rents and labour conditions in industry.

In relations between Finland and Russia the achievements of the revolutionary year were lost. Conflict between the Finnish Diet and the Russian government began in 1907 with the opposition of the Diet to a contribution of 20 million Finnish marks to imperial defence, demanded by St. Petersburg. Further points of controversy were the laws on Press and associations, and the use of Russian language in official business in Finland. Pressure for the abolition of Finland's autonomy came from the Nationalists in the Third Duma. Stolypin showed his support of the Russian nationalist point of view in a speech to the Duma in May 1908. A mixed Russo-Finnish commission was set up under Haritonov to establish principles for the differentiation of matters of "imperial significance" from those of purely Finnish interest. The commission could not reach agreement. In February 1909 the Diet was dissolved a few days after it met, because of a speech by the Young Finn Svinhufvud, which expressed anxiety at recent developments in government policy. In March 1910 the Duma passed a law on the basis of the recommendations of the Russian members of the Haritonov commission. It so defined matters of imperial interest— reserved to the imperial Duma—as to reduce the powers of the Finnish Diet to those of a provincial assembly. Finnish independence was over, and the policy of Bobrikov had triumphed.

The Diet was dissolved in 1910, but the new Diet was no more accommodating. It met in September, and on the motion of Svinhufvud refused to consider the agenda submitted from St. Petersburg as this was based on Duma laws which the Diet did not consider legally binding in Finland. In October the Diet was dissolved.

The new regime was enforced by Governor-General Seyn, a former assistant of Bobrikov, appointed in November 1910. The Senate was composed of Finns willing to carry out Russian orders. Russians were introduced into the police, and some were made provincial governors. The pilot service in the Gulf of Finland was brought under Russian control, which resulted in the resignation of 500 out of its total membership of 700. Russian nationalist opinion, and especially the paper *Novoe Vremya*, began to agitate for the annexation of Vyborg to Russia. In August 1911 the Russian government decided to annex two municipalities on the border towards Vyborg, but Finnish protests caused the matter to be postponed indefinitely. In November 1911 a law of the Duma placed Russian subjects on an equal footing with Finns for employment and business in Finland. This caused great rage in Finland. The town magistrates of Vyborg refused to accept notice of the intention of Russian subjects to open business in the town. Other towns followed their example. In December 1912 twenty-three Vyborg officials were brought for trial to St. Petersburg and sentenced to seven to nine months' prison and ten years' disqualification from public or municipal employment. On the eve of the war it was clear that the russification of Finland was to be ruthlessly pursued, and that the Finns, once loyal subjects of the Tsar-Grand Duke, were ripe for rebellion.

The new franchise for the Third Duma deprived of most of its value the only important gain which the revolutionary years had brought to the Jews. Those Jews whom the Pale regulations allowed to live in the rest of Russia, benefited as individuals from the greater freedom of expression as compared with the years before 1905. There was a noteworthy development of Jewish literature and learning. The Jewish Literary Society, founded in St. Petersburg in 1908, and the Jewish Historical-Ethnographical Society, which published from 1908 a quarterly, *Yevreiskaya Starina*, were its most outstanding examples.

Within the Pale, however, the situation of the Jews was as insecure and humiliating as ever. There were no more pogroms. But in 1910, 1,200 Jewish families were suddenly and brutally expelled from Kiev. In 1911 restrictions on education were made more severe. Hitherto Jewish children who were not able to attend secondary schools, but studied at home, had been allowed to take school examinations and so obtain a recognised educational qualification. Now the *numerus clausus* was extended to this category of "externs" as well. The most striking indication of the attitude of the Russian government to the Jews was given by the Beilis case.[1] A Jewish workman in Kiev, named Mendel Beilis, was arrested on a charge of ritual murder of a Christian child. When a judicial inquiry produced no evidence of Jewish complicity in the death of the child, the Minister of Justice, Shcheglovitov, ordered a second inquiry, with new selected personnel. The case dragged on for two years, until the trial of Beilis took place in October 1913. He was acquitted but in the most humiliating manner possible, on the ground that

[1] For documents relating to the Beilis case, see *Krasny Arkhiv*, LIV, pp. 162–204.

evidence was insufficient. The case raised a storm of protest from democratic Russians, especially from the legal profession and the Press. The government, having failed to get a conviction, revenged itself by lawsuits against newspapers which had criticised its conduct of the affair.

Chapter IX

THE COMING OF THE WAR

Russia, Germany and France

THE defeat of Russia in the Far East was also a defeat for German foreign policy, which had encouraged Russia to expand in Asia. At the turn of the century Anglo-Russian rivalry had seemed the most serious of all international conflicts. Germany had sought a middle position between the two rivals. Believing that they could never be reconciled, and that each when need arose would pay dearly for her favours, she believed that she need commit herself to neither. William II enjoyed playing the role of friend of each in turn. It was pleasant to feel that the two other greatest states in Europe were competing for his favours, and that he held the balance in his hands. But this position, which promised so much prestige and so much advantage, was not compatible with intimate relations with either Power. Therefore in the years before the Russo-Japanese war both Russian and British overtures had been received with reserve.

In April 1899 the Russian ambassador in Berlin had proposed a written agreement, by which Germany should guarantee to respect Russian interests in the Straits while Russia would give Germany a free hand in economic penetration of Anatolia. Holstein advised against acceptance, both for the formal reason that it was not compatible with the renewed Triple Alliance, and on the general grounds that closer relations with Russia would make Britain the enemy of Germany. A further overture was made in June by Muraviev to the German ambassador in St. Petersburg, but without result.[1] The Russian government however continued to attach great importance to an agreement with Germany about the Straits. It was mentioned in a memorandum by Muraviev to the Tsar of 7th/20th February 1900 and strongly supported by Kuropatkin in a comment dated 29th February/11th March.[2] But no progress was made.

The isolation of Britain in the Boer War had suggested to

---

[1] Meinecke, *op. cit.*, chapter 7. GP. Vol. xiv, Part II pp. 533–63.
[2] *Krasny Arkhiv*, XVIII, pp. 4–18, 22.

Muraviev a more ambitious project of joint action with France and Germany against Britain. The Russian ambassador in Berlin, Count Osten-Sacken, had a conversation on 13th January 1900 with William II. According to the emperor's own account, he had stressed the neutral position of Germany, which would neither support the Dual Alliance in East Africa nor help Britain to maintain her security in India. Osten-Sacken however seems to have interpreted William's remarks in a sense more favourable to his country, for Muraviev took up the question again. On 25th February 1900 he proposed to Bülow, the German Chancellor, a joint Russo-Franco-German mediation between the British and the Boers. Bülow replied with the proposal that the three Powers should first guarantee each other's frontiers—that is, that France should formally and voluntarily accept the loss of Alsace-Lorraine. Bülow's reason for this reply is hard to see. If he really thought that France could accept this, or that Russia would be willing to press her, he was curiously ignorant of French politics. If however he was merely looking for a pretext to turn down the whole Russian proposal, he could have found a better one than this. His reply reached London from Paris in somewhat distorted form. On 3rd March William II informed Edward VII by letter of the Russian suggestion and of his own refusal. As a fuller version of the facts was already known in London, there was less gratitude than William may have expected. What he was keen to represent to his uncle as a disinterested service looked instead like a clumsy and unsuccessful attempt to gain material advantages for Germany at Britain's expense.[1]

Germany's failure to establish closer co-operation with Russia during these years was of undoubted advantage to Britain. But Germany failed to turn the situation to her own advantage by improving her relations with Britain. Just as she was unwilling to win Russian friendship at the price of antagonising Britain in African affairs, so she refused to buy Britain's friendship by opposing Russian action in Manchuria. This was perhaps the main cause of the failure of Anglo-German negotiations in 1901.

Russian hostility to Britain in the Dogger Bank crisis,[2] and the widespread if unjustifiable Russian belief that France had proved a poor ally, gave Germany another opportunity to strengthen her relations with her eastern neighbour. This seemed the more

---

[1] Meinecke, op. cit., pp. 154–61. GP. Vol. xv, pp., 516–7, 519– 20, 523–4, 528–9, 534, 540–2.
[2] See above, pp. 215–6.

necessary in Berlin as the German naval programme was now beginning to alarm Britain, and the Anglo-French *entente* of April 1904 had been an unwelcome surprise for Germany.

On 27th October 1904 William II suggested, in a telegram to the Tsar, a Russo-Franco-German combination against Britain. The proposal was justified on the ground that the British Press was using threatening language about German supplies of coal to the Russian fleet on its way to the Far East. Lamsdorff, the Russian Foreign Minister,[1] was sceptical of the Emperor's suggestion, seeing in it an attempt to make trouble between Russia and France. He was against pressing France, as France had not put any pressure on Russia during the Fashoda crisis with Britain of 1898–9. But Nicholas was extremely pleased by the proposal which, he believed, would "deliver Europe from the unmeasured impudence of England". He asked William at once to prepare a draft agreement. "As soon as it is accepted by us, France will have to join with her ally."[2] Meanwhile the Russian ambassador in Berlin, Osten-Sacken, was approached by Holstein and Bülow on the same lines. On 12th November William sent a draft in a letter to the Tsar. The first article provided that the two Powers would give armed help to each other if either were attacked by a European Power, and would take common action to remind France of her obligations under the Franco-Russian alliance. Both Lamsdorff and Osten-Sacken were sceptical of German aims. In the following two weeks modifications of the draft were suggested on both sides. Lamsdorff however persuaded the Tsar to ask William for permission to inform France of the terms of the treaty before signing it. Thus there could be no question of a humiliating demand for France to accept a treaty on which she had not been consulted. But William would not agree to this. He argued that if France were informed, she would inform Britain, and the British and Japanese fleets would then suddenly attack Germany. He suggested that if his draft was not compatible with Russia's obligations to France, it would be better not to make a treaty at all. The secret would be kept, and German-Russian friendship would remain as before. Lamsdorff made final counter-proposals, but William persisted in his refusal in a letter of 21st December. The project was then dropped.[3]

---

[1] Count Lamsdorff had served most of his career in the Ministry of Foreign Affairs in St. Petersburg. From 1882 to 1886 he had been Director of the Chancellery. He had become a Senior Counsellor. From 1897 to 1900 he had been Assistant Foreign Minister. In 1900 he succeeded Muraviev as Foreign Minister.

[2] *Krasny Arkhiv*, V, p. 9. The correspondence relating to these proposals is on pp. 6–24.

[3] Ibid., p. 24.

The second attempt was made in July 1905. William II and Nicholas II met on the Tsar's yacht in Björkö bay in the Gulf of Finland on 23rd–24th July. The isolation and weakness of Russia, the defeat in the East and the disorders at home, were good reason for the Tsar to be depressed. In this mood, and with no competent adviser on board, he fell a victim to William's charm and friendliness. For his part William, having reluctantly accepted his Chancellor Bülow's policy of pressure on France in the Moroccan question, was eager to secure better relations with Russia. At breakfast on the second day. William produced a draft treaty, which he "happened to have in his pocket", and the Tsar signed.[1] The first article stated: "If one of the two Empires is attacked by a European Power, its ally will aid it in Europe with all its forces on land and sea." The fourth article obliged the Tsar, "after the coming into force of the treaty", to take steps to "initiate France into the accord and associate herself with it as an ally".

When the two Emperors returned home and informed their ministers, they found that the problem could not be so easily settled.

Bülow objected to the fact that the action was confined to Europe. He wished Russia to be committed to help Germany against Britain by land in Asia. This objection was not shared by the experts of the German General Staff. They did not believe that Russia could do much in Asia, and valued the treaty above all because it would give Germany security on her eastern frontier, and enable her, in the event of war, to throw all her forces against France or Britain or the two together. Bülow however threatened to resign, and thus reduced the Emperor to a state of hysteria.[2] When Bülow saw that his master was completely dependent on him, and his own personal position was impregnable, he gracefully consented to remain in office. He also decided that, for all its faults, the treaty was too valuable to risk, and agreed with Holstein that for the time being it should be accepted, and improvements not be suggested until later.[3]

The objections on the Russian side were more serious. Lamsdorff

[1] William's own account is in *Grosse Politik*, Vol. XIX, pp. 458–65, that of Tschirschky, who countersigned the treaty, on pp. 454–6.
[2] *G.P.*, XIX, pp. 496–8.
[3] Ibid., pp. 501–2. For a good survey of the crisis of 1905, including the Björkö treaty, see Anderson, *The First Morocco Crisis* (Chicago University Press, 1930). A German monograph is Dr. W. Klein, *Der Vertrag von Bjoerkoe* (Berlin, 1931). The Moroccan aspect of the crisis is outside the scope of the present work. It is therefore only mentioned where it affects the policy of France and Germany towards Russia.

was not informed by the Tsar until 30th August. He was then most alarmed by the treaty, which he at once realised was incompatible with the Franco-Russian alliance. He was however obliged to instruct Nelidov, now Russian ambassador in Paris, to sound the French government on the idea of a Russo-Franco-German "continental" grouping. On 21st September Nelidov brought the matter up hypothetically in conversation with the French Premier, Rouvier. The Premier opposed the idea, on the grounds that the Continent was in no need of protection from Britain; that hostility to Britain was undesirable for France as it would place the French overseas empire at the mercy of the British navy; and that France did not require more than one formal ally—Russia—to whom she remained loyal. Nelidov gave his own opinion that the project was impossible, and instead recommended a rapprochement between Russia and Britain. The Tsar however instructed Lamsdorff to order Nelidov to explore the matter further. In addition to his official despatch to this effect, Lamsdorff sent Nelidov a private letter through a personal friend.[1] In this letter he spoke of the Björkö visit as a "disastrous meeting", and deplored the fact that "our dear emperor" had succumbed to the "sly flattery" of William. On 5th October Nelidov reported a further conversation with Rouvier, in which he had asked him about the prospects of Franco-German friendship. Rouvier replied that in view of past sufferings and the present German behaviour in the Moroccan question, "our people would not endure a closer relationship to Germany". This was the end of the Björkö treaty. Realising that it could only be achieved at the cost of breaking the alliance with France, the Tsar asked for modifications of the text which deprived it of value for Germany. By the end of November it was clear that it had failed.[2]

It may be asked why, if forced to choose between France and Germany, Russia should not have chosen Germany and abandoned France. One reason is that diplomats are naturally unwilling to throw over alliances which have been secured with some trouble and still seem likely to be useful. The Russian Foreign Office was on the whole pro-French, and Lamsdorff was especially so. Another reason is that friendship with Germany was likely, as in the past, to be made difficult by Germany's connection with Austria. Panslavism, though less vocal now than it had been or was to become, was still a force in Russia. But perhaps the decisive factor was financial. Russia was in desperate need of financial

---

[1] *Krasny Arkhiv*, V, pp. 35–7.   [2] Ibid., pp. 46–8.

help to recover from the losses of war and internal disorder. France had provided loans in the past, and was the most promising lender now. If Germany had offered financial assistance on a massive scale, she might have been able to outbid France and to persuade Russia to change her partner. But just as Bismarck in 1887 had failed to understand the political importance of loan policy,[1] so now William II and his diplomatic advisers appear to have ignored the financial factor.

Nicholas II had chosen Witte as his first Premier, largely because of his connections with west European banking houses. Witte's most important task was to get a great loan for Russia. Witte wished the loan to be international. In particular, he wished German and American banks to participate as well as French. He had discussed the matter in the United States and France after the Portsmouth conference. In December 1905 he sent Kokovtsov, his Finance Minister, to Paris and Berlin. The French bankers and the French government expressed themselves willing to give Russia a loan, but pointed out that the resistance of the regime to the democratic movement in Russia and the pogroms against Jews had created a bad impression on the French public as a whole, and especially in financial circles where Jews were influential. Moreover, though willing in principle to grant a loan, both bankers and politicians in Paris insisted that little could be done until the Moroccan crisis was over.[2] The most that Kokovtsov could achieve was an advance to the value of 100 million roubles. It was clear in fact that the French condition for a loan was Russian diplomatic support during the impending conference on the Moroccan question.

The year that ended with the Algeciras conference on Morocco was thus disastrous for German policy. Germany had hoped by pressure in the Moroccan problem to break the new Anglo-French entente and to force France into submission to Germany. This situation was then to be used either to draw France, through Russia, towards Germany or to break the Franco-Russian alliance. Germany had scored initial successes with the resignation of Delcassé on 6th June 1905 and with the signature of the Björkö treaty by the Tsar. But the fall of Delcassé proved not to have tamed but to have bitterly antagonised France, and the Björkö plan did not in the end prove sufficiently attractive to induce

---

[1] See above, pp. 177-8.
[2] The correspondence of Kokovtsov relating to the loan negotiations is in *Krasny Arkhiv*, X, pp. 9-40.

Russia to risk the loss of the alliance with France. France was driven closer to Britain and Russia was driven closer to France. At Algeciras the French, British and Russian representatives supported each other.

When the conference was concluded, substantially to French satisfaction, the loan to Russia was quickly arranged. On 3rd April 1906 Kokovtsov signed the agreement in Paris. Russia received a sum of 2,250 million French francs, the largest loan yet made to a government. The German government, infuriated by the failure of Björkö and the Russian attitude at Algeciras, forbade the German firm of Mendelssohn to take part. The loan was thus predominantly French, with small British and Dutch participation.[1] Dire financial need forced Russia to accept French wishes at the cost of German friendship. Dire diplomatic and military need forced France to give money to the Tsar to suppress democracy in Russia, despite the indignation of the French Left. The episode shows the importance of the financial factor in foreign policy. It does not, however, show that foreign policy is "made" by financiers, by farsighted Machiavellian capitalists seeking to conquer markets. The French bankers made good business out of the Russian loans, the interest on which was punctually paid until the Bolshevik Revolution. But their decision to grant the loan was substantially affected by the advice—not of course the orders—of the French government, whose motives were not economic but political and strategic. The French loans to Russia are an example of a powerful economic instrument used for political ends, not of political action determined by economic interests.

Russia, Austria and Neoslavism

After 1907 the Slav factor again became important in Russian foreign policy. An obvious reason is that Russia, beaten in the Far East, sought compensation in her traditional field of interest, the Balkans. But there is also another reason, which arises from Russian internal politics. The changes in Russia's political system had not given power to the people, but they had appreciably extended the basis of power. The views of those elements whom the Third and Fourth Dumas represented—the landowning nobility, business men, the prosperous minority of the peasantry, and even a section of the professional class—now mattered. The government was more dependent than before on public opinion, even if this was only a restricted public opinion. If there was one idea which rallied these

[1] Witte, *op. cit.*, pp. 271–4.

different social elements, it was nationalism. And the direction in which these elements wished Russian nationalism to be effective was the Slav world.

It is a convenient and helpful over-simplification to divide Russian foreign policy since the 1870's into four main periods. Under Alexander II public opinion, though extremely limited, was a force, and at the end of the reign acquired a strongly Panslav character. The eighties saw a return to conservative and diplomatic methods, with public opinion not entirely excluded but certainly discouraged. The nineties were a period of economic imperialism, capitalist development within Russia being accompanied by expansion in the Far East. At the beginning of the new century, this policy got out of hand, control passed to adventurers or incompetents, and disaster followed abroad and at home. The fourth period began with the stabilisation of the Stolypin regime and the Third Duma. Once more public opinion was a force, and the Slav policy abandoned after 1878 was revived.

But Panslavism was now a different force from the Panslavism of the seventies. For a short time a democratic, liberal form made its appearance. It was known as "Neoslavism". Like the Greater German idea of 1848, Neoslavism stressed the will of peoples rather than of dynasties. Just as the Greater Germans had welcomed within the fold all Germans, Catholic or Protestant, so the Neoslavs welcomed all Slavs, Orthodox or Catholic. In a sense the Neoslavs were the heirs of the revolutionary champions of Slav brotherhood, Bakunin and Shevchenko. But the Neoslavs tried to be not utopians but practical politicians. They saw that a federal republic of Slav nations was not practicable. Instead they aimed at close friendship between great and small Slav states— Russia, Serbia, Bulgaria, and—Austria. Austria could be regarded as either the second German Power or the second Slav Power. At present she was the former: the Neoslavs must turn her into the latter. In order that the two Powers might become friends, and might together pursue a Slav policy, both must undergo internal reforms. In Austria, the predominance of Germans and Magyars must be broken, and the Slav peoples have a completely equal status. The Slavs already formed nearly half the population of the empire. If, as was to be expected, the Roumanians of Transylvania, victims like the Slavs of Magyar arrogance, would give them their support, they would have a majority as soon as political democracy was introduced and cultural opportunities were equalised. Russia for her part must stop all oppression by Russians of non-Russian

Slavs. The Ukrainians, White Russians and above all the Poles, must have the self-government for which they asked.

Within Russia this programme had its supporters among the Cadets, and to some extent among the Octobrists. It had some sympathisers among minor groups of the Left, but was rejected by the Social Democrats on principle. In Poland, it was supported by Dmowski and the National Democrats in both Russian and Austrian territory. In Austria, its chief spokesman was the Czech leader Kramář. It was well received by the moderate democrats among the Catholic Slavs, but the right wing clericals among Croats, Slovaks and Slovenes had little use for it. The young Peasant Party of Croatia, led by the Radić brothers, shared some of the ideas of the Neoslavs, but would not have been content with less than a republic. The Orthodox Slavs of Austria were less interested, as their sympathies went to Serbia and to Russia, and they had grounds for believing that, being both Slav and Orthodox, they were more likely to receive Russian patronage than their Catholic neighbours. Nevertheless the Serbian elements which supported the Serbo-Croat coalition in Croatia[1] were favourable to Neoslavism.

The Neoslav policy was not achieved, and in the light of all that has happened in the last forty years one must doubt whether it could ever have been achieved.

On the Austro-Hungarian side, neither the Germans of Austria nor the Magyar ruling class of Hungary would have surrendered their position without a fight. And until the fight started, they held the power. An internal reorganisation of the empire might have been attempted by Archduke Francis Ferdinand, had he ever succeeded his uncle Emperor Francis Joseph. But the Archduke's ideas were limited to an attack on the power of the Hungarian ruling class, which he disliked not because it was aristocratic or reactionary, but because it was insufficiently submissive to the dynasty. His aim was to strengthen and unify the empire, to make it once more a Great Power, and to revive the Alliance of Three Emperors. He was a devout Catholic, and hated the enemies of the

---

[1] This was a combination of Serbian and Croatian political leaders, which did not include either the Croatian clerical nationalists or the extreme Panserbs. It demanded the union of Dalmatia (which was part of Austria) with Croatia (which was part of Hungary), and more self-government for both Croats and Serbs within the dominions of the Habsburgs. It was strengthened by the Hungarian Railway Act of 1907, which made the Magyar language obligatory in the railway administration through the whole Kingdom of Hungary. From 1907 there was a growing tendency for Croats and Serbs to subordinate their many differences to the needs of common resistance to Hungarian official policy.

Vatican, be they the Italian government or the Orthodox Serbs. He wished the friendship of Russia, but on a dynastic, not a popular basis, and without sacrificing the alliance with Germany.[1]

By the turn of the century both the public opinion and the economic interests of Germany and Austria had become inextricably connected. In the years when the Habsburg dynasty and aristocracy and the Hohenzollern dynasty and Prussian Junkers really ruled their respective states, it was possible for either to break away from the other and make its terms with Russia. But once a single German nationalist public opinion had been created, differing little between Hamburg and Graz, Reichenberg and Essen, and once Pangermanism, a bastard offspring of the Greater and Lesser German ideas, had been born, the choice was no longer there. The relative democratisation of the German Empire and of German Austria, by which the aristocracy first shared its power with the bourgeoisie and was then surpassed by it, made not for a more pacific but for a more imperialist attitude of both German states towards the Slavs.[2]

The obstacles to Neoslavism on the Russian side were no less strong. As we have seen, Stolypin refused to placate either the Poles or the Ukrainians.[3] Eminent Russians, even including members of the Foreign Office, pleaded for Russian-Polish friendship without effect.[4]

Dmowski urged his countrymen to support Russia, as the German danger to the Polish nation was fundamentally greater than the Russian. He admitted that Austria treated her Poles well, but pointed out that Galicia was less than a third of Poland, and that in the relationship between Germany and Austria the former was the dominant partner. In Germany, Bülow's treatment of the Poles was worse than that of Bismarck. In 1901 German was made compulsory as the language of instruction in all schools. The use of Polish at public meetings was drastically restricted by law. From

[1] For the life and views of the Archduke, see von Chlumecky, *Erzherzog Franz Ferdinand* (Berlin, 1929). An interesting work, proposing the reorganisation of the empire into fifteen federal units, is Aurel Popovici, *Die Vereinigten Staaten von Grossösterreich* (Lepizig, 1906). Popovici's ideas found some support in the Archduke's circle. Another possible solution, to which Francis Ferdinand was probably more inclined, was "Trialism"—the third unit to consist of the South Slav provinces, in which the Croats in general and the Croatian clericals in particular would have predominated.

[2] The Pan-German League was a middle-class, not an aristocratic, organisation. Its supporters were bureaucrats, business men, and above all intellectuals. See Werner, *op. cit.*

[3] See above, pp. 303-4.

[4] Prince G. Trubetskoy, *Russland als Grossmacht* (Stuttgart, 1913), is an example.

1908 onwards large sums of public money were granted for compulsory purchase of land held by Poles. The Polish population stubbornly defended their land, religion and language, but the pressure was becoming very heavy.[1]

In view of this increasing German danger, therefore, Dmowski urged Poles to support Russia, in spite of Stolypin's russification policy, hoping that in time liberal views would prevail, and that the influence of Russia's ally France and her new friend Britain would help the Polish cause.[2] But the complete lack of concessions from St. Petersburg alienated the majority of Poles. In Galicia, the anti-Russian group was stronger than the pro-Russian. It was reinforced by socialist exiles from Russian territory, led by Piłsudski, who began with the consent of the Austrian authorities to train Polish riflemen on Austrian soil. Within the P.P.S. on Russian territory, the Right or nationalist wing, known as the "Revolutionary Fraction", recovered ground at the expense of the Left and of the Polish Social Democrats of Roza Luxemburg.

If the Poles were disillusioned with Neoslavism, the Ukrainians had never supported it. The only government which gave Ukrainians political rights was the Austrian. In the German Empire there was some sympathy in intellectual circles for the Ukrainian cause. German nationalism, whether Prussian or Austrian, had no quarrel with the Ukrainians, and the Ukrainians had no cause to hate the Germans. They were therefore unwilling to be drawn into any anti-German movement, even if it expressed as much devotion to democracy and to national equality as did Neoslavism.

The official Russian view that Ukrainians are "Little Russians" and not a distinct people had, it is true, its followers among the Ukrainian population of East Galicia. These were the so-called "Moscalophiles", led by Markov. They wished East Galicia to be simply incorporated in the Russian Empire. Within Russia this aim was put forward by a section of the extreme Nationalists in the Third and Fourth Dumas. The Moscalophiles were bitter enemies of the Ukrainian nationalists, who were supported by the majority of Galician Ukrainians. A curious community of interest developed in East Galicia between the Moscalophiles and the Polish great landowners, the "Podolian Conservatives". Both feared Ukrainian nationalism, and to these Poles union with Russia might be acceptable if it involved the suppression of Ukrainian nationalism and the guarantee of their estates. This Polish group was of course a small

---

[1] *Cambridge History of Poland*, Vol. II, pp. 427–31.
[2] Dmowski, *La question polonaise* (Paris, 1909) expounds his views at this time.

minority of Galician Poles. Its attitude to Russia was opposed by
the socialists and by the landowners of the western provinces, the
so-called Cracow Conservatives. The National Democrats disagreed less fiercely with the international orientation of the Podolian
group, but were their opponents in social and political questions.
The bulk of Polish political opinion in Galicia, though hostile to
Ukrainian nationalism, disliked it less than Russian.

Thus in the triangular relationship between Russians, Poles and
Ukrainians, a common front of Poles and Ukrainians against Russia
was less difficult than one of Russians and Poles against Ukrainians
or of Russians and Ukrainians against Poles. With regard to the
German-Slav problem, the Poles were divided between those who
sought in Austria a protector against Russia and to some extent
against Prussia, and those who considered Austria too weak as a
protector and therefore sought co-operation with Russia against
Prussia. The majority of Ukrainians were pro-German. Polish-
Ukrainian co-operation was possible only in collaboration with the
German Powers, and with the rejection of Neoslav ideas.

Though the new Russian electoral law of 1907 showed that
Stolypin had no intention of satisfying the Poles, and the reconciliation of the Magyar nationalists with Francis Joseph in 1906
put an end to talk of universal suffrage in Hungary,[1] Neoslav hopes
lingered on. In 1908 Kramař visited St. Petersburg, conferred
with Russian Neoslavs, and was received by Stolypin. There was
still talk in the Russian capital of Russo-Polish friendship. In
July 1908 a conference was held in Prague. Poles from Prussia and
Slovaks and Serbs from Hungary were prevented by their governments from attending, and Ukrainians were represented only by
Moscalophiles. But Russians, Poles, Czechs, Slovenes, Croats and
Bulgarians were well represented. Among those present were such
radicals as the Czech Professor T. G. Masaryk, and the Croatian
peasant leader Stepan Radić. The most progressive of the Russians
at Prague was the Octobrist Stahovich. The delegation also

[1] From 1903 to 1905 there was a conflict between Francis Josef and the Hungarian
parliament, which sought to make Magyar the official language of the Hungarian
army instead of German. In 1905 the king appointed General Fejérváry as Hungarian Premier. In October the general declared his intention of introducing
universal suffrage in Hungary. This would have enfranchised the Magyar peasants
and the non-Magyar nationalities. The threat was enough to bring the Magyar
ruling class to heel. In April 1906 the Hungarian leaders came to terms with the
monarchy. The claim for Magyar as the "language of command" was dropped,
and universal suffrage was indefinitely postponed. The alliance between the throne
and the Magyar landowning class was renewed. Once again the Habsburgs had
betrayed the Magyar masses and the non-Magyar nationalities. For a brief account
of this crisis, see Taylor, *op. cit.*,

ıncluded nationalists of the Right such as Count Bobrinski. Among the Poles were Dmowski and Balicki.

. . . . . .

The Bosnian crisis of 1908[1] naturally turned Slav attention to the Balkans. At the next Slav conference, held in 1909 in St. Petersburg, the Polish question received little attention and the Polish representation was weak. The 1910 meeting, the only one which received the official title of "congress", and the last to be held, took place in Sofia. The internal conflict which this congress sought, in the interests of Slav solidarity, to remove, was no longer the Russo-Polish—now regarded as practically incurable—but the smaller, though no less intractable, antagonism between Serbs and Bulgars.

Brotherhood of Balkan Slavs, and closer relations between them and their Russian big brother, were causes not only dear to the heart of conservative Panslavs in Russia, but wholly acceptable to Stolypin and the Russian government. By 1910 the original democratic Neoslavism had gone: in its place was a new version of the narrow Panslavism of the seventies.[2] Just as the Lesser German idea had been principally directed towards Protestants, and had relied on the power of the Prussian dynasty and state, so the narrow Panslavism appealed almost entirely to Orthodox Slavs, and relied on the power of the Russian dynasty and state. The narrow Pan-slavism was easily compatible with Russian imperialism, with the aspirations of those elements in Russian society on which the Third and Fourth Dumas rested, and with the programme of Greater Russia which Stolypin had proudly proclaimed.

Russian foreign policy in the last years before the war is thus dominated by the conflict with Austria. But this conflict, which might have extended to the Czech, Polish and Ukrainian questions, was in fact concentrated on the South Slav question.

The purely Balkan and Ottoman aspects of the South Slav question have already been discussed.[3] Here a few words are needed on the Austrian aspect.

Both Croats and Serbs (speaking the same language, but differing in religion, historical background and sense of nationality) were to be found in both the Austrian and the Hungarian portions of the Habsburg Empire. In Croatia, which enjoyed a decreasing measure of autonomy under the Hungarian Crown, the Croats were a majority and the Serbs a considerable minority. In Dalmatia, which was an Austrian province, the same was true. In southern Hungary

[1] See below, pp. 341–4. [2] See above, pp. 91–2. [3] See above, pp. 192–4.

the Serbs were the most numerous element of a highly heterogeneous population. In Bosnia-Hercegovina, jointly administered by Vienna and Budapest, nearly half the population were Serbs, about a fifth were Croats, and the rest were Moslems.[1]

Among these South Slavs of the Habsburg Empire three trends can be distinguished in regard to foreign policy. Firstly, the Croatian nationalists, who were also clericals and conservatives, wanted a Great Croatia, to include all Bosnia-Hercegovina and Dalmatia. They were anti-Serb, anti-Hungarian and anti-Italian, but much less anti-German. They hoped to achieve their aims with the help of Vienna, and placed some hopes in the Archduke Francis Ferdinand. Secondly, the Serbian nationalists wished to join all Habsburg territories of Serbian population to the Kingdom of Serbia. This point of view, which was known as Great Serbdom (*velikosrpstvo*) had strong support in Bosnia and in the Kingdom of Serbia. Its most fanatical exponents were found among army officer groups, in Serbia, and in more moderate form it was the aim of the eminent Serbian politician Nikola Pašić, leader of the Radical Party in the kingdom.[2] The third point of view was the "Yugoslav idea". This idea, which had support from some Croats and some Serbs, was unity and equality of all South Slavs. The maximum programme was a single, federal South Slav state, from the Alps to the Black Sea, to include Slovenes and Bulgarians as well as Croats and Serbs. The minimum programme was self-government for Croats and Serbs, on a footing of equality, within the Habsburg Empire, and close friendship between a democratic Habsburg Empire and a democratic Serbia. The Yugoslav idea had strong support among the Croatian middle class of Dalmatia and among the Serbs of southern Hungary. It was also supported, though in a radical and republican form, by the Croatian Peasant Party. The restricted franchise in Croatia prevented the Peasant Party from being a strong force. But the Yugoslav idea was represented in the Croatian Diet at Zagreb by the "Serbo-Croat coalition".[3]

The divisions among the Austro-Hungarian South Slavs thus have certain analogies with the divisions in the wider Slav field. The Yugoslav idea, with its emphasis on democracy and national equality, corresponds to Neoslavism. The Greater Serb idea corresponds to narrow Panslavism, and is easily reconcilable with the Great Russian, Orthodox, imperialism of Stolypin. The Greater Croat idea, like the anti-Russian form of Polish nation-

---

[1] See above, p. 97.   [2] See above p. 168.   [2] See above p. 319 and n.

alism represented by Piłsudski, and like Ukrainian nationalism, was compatible with, and could only be achieved with the help of, Austro-German imperialism.

This then was the background to the series of diplomatic crises produced by Austro-Russian conflict in the Balkans between 1908 and 1914. But when the first of these crises began, the general international position of Russia had already been strengthened by the removal of conflicts in Asia, in the south with Britain and in the east with Japan. The agreements with these two Powers, and their effect on Russia's relations with Germany, must now be considered.

Russia, Britain and Germany

The conference of Algeciras, and the subsequent French loan to Russia, had consolidated Russo-French relations. The conference had also strengthened Anglo-French co-operation, and had thus brought Russia and Britain together in support of France. It was clearly desirable to French statesmen that this passive co-operation between their old ally and their new friend should be further developed. Britain, increasingly alarmed by German policy and German naval armaments, was well disposed to take up once more the project, first raised by Salisbury in the nineties and cautiously repeated by Lansdowne in 1903, of an entente with Russia. For their part, the Russian leaders understood that they could not afford to be on bad terms with several Great Powers at once. As the Björkö treaty had failed, relations with France were closer, and the future policy of the German Powers was uncertain, it seemed prudent to come to terms with Britain. At the same time however the Russian government was anxious to avoid any action which might unnecessarily antagonise Germany.

Anglo-Russian conflicts had long lain in Asia. There had been three main regions—Turkey, the Indian frontier, and the Far East. Since Salisbury's unsuccessful projects in the nineties for a partition of Turkey, British policy had become much less hostile to Russian aims in the Straits and in the Balkans. The German interest in Turkey and the Baghdad Railway plan had much to do with this change.[1] In the Far East Russia was no longer able to threaten British interests. There remained the Indian frontier. Here three countries were concerned—Persia, Afghanistan and Tibet. These were the subject of the discussions between Britain and Russia,

[1] See below, p. 332.

which began in the summer of 1906 between the new Russian Foreign Minister Izvolski[1] and the new British ambassador in St. Petersburg and former British delegate at Algeciras, Sir Arthur Nicolson.[2]

In Persia, Izvolski was alarmed by German penetration, and especially by a project to found a German bank in Teheran. He expressed his fears openly to Bülow during a visit to Berlin in September 1906. Bülow assured him that the bank, if it ever came into existence, would be concerned only with financing German-Persian trade and would not invest in any railway, telegraph or other construction in Persia, nor make loans to the Persian government. Bülow also told Izvolski that he had no objection to an Anglo-Russian agreement, which Izvolski had said was now essential to Russia in her weakness and would not be directed against Germany.[3] Izvolski was not entirely satisfied with Bülow's assurances, for he pressed the British to grant a loan to the Persian government in order to forestall possible German loans, as Russia was herself not in a position to make any foreign loans. The British were mainly concerned with a delimitation of zones of influence which would ensure British supremacy in the area nearest to India. They would also have liked an agreement on the Persian Gulf. This however the Russians refused, on the grounds that the Gulf was not of immediate interest to Russia but was of interest to Germany. Russian support to British policy in the Gulf would be interpreted in Berlin as a sign of Russian hostility to Germany, which Izvolski was determined to avoid.

Russia had declared her intention of establishing direct relations with Afghanistan in 1900, but British enquiries had failed to elicit an explanation of the type of relations required. In May 1903 the Russian Governor-General of Transcaspia had entered into contact with the Afghan Governor of Herat in connection with a frontier incident, and in October 1903 the Russian government had informed the British once more of its intention to handle frontier problems directly with the Afghan government and if necessary to send its own agents into Afghanistan. But the war with Japan had postponed this problem. In 1904 a British mission had gone to

[1] Before his appointment as Minister of Foreign Affairs Izvolski had been Russian Minister in Copenhagen from 1903 to 1906, and had previously served in the Russian missions at the Vatican, Belgrade, Munich and Tokyo.

[2] For the Anglo-Russian negotiations, see *B.D.*, Vol. IV. Special studies are R. P. Churchill, *The Anglo-Russian Convention* (Iowa, 1939); and Polst, *Die anglo-russische Entente* (Hamburg, 1932). There is some material in Harold Nicolson's life of his father, *Lord Carnock* (London, 1930).

[3] For Izvolski's conversations in Berlin, see *B.D.*, Vol. IV, pp. 248, 251-2; *G.P.*, Vol. XXII, pp. 38-41.

Kabul, and on 21st March 1905 an Anglo-Afghan treaty had been signed. Britain was to give the Emir of Afghanistan a subsidy and to defend Afghanistan against any foreign Power. In return, Afghanistan undertook to deal with foreign Powers only through British diplomatic channels. Thus Russia, fully occupied in Japan, had lost a round in the struggle for Afghanistan.

Britain's relations with Tibet had been settled by the Anglo-Chinese treaties of 1890 and 1893. The two Powers were to prevent aggression in Tibet, and to settle matters relating to trade and to rights of pasture for herdsmen who habitually crossed the border between Tibet and India. But the Tibetan authorities in practice showed little respect for Chinese authority, and ignored the treaty. The Viceroy, Lord Curzon, suspected that Tibetan hostility on the border and refusal to reach a clear agreement with the government of India were a result of Russian intrigue. This does seem in fact to have been the case, although there is evidence that Nicholas II himself had ideas for future Russian penetration into Tibet.[1] Curzon however decided to send a mission to Lhasa, the Tibetan capital, with instructions only to obtain satisfaction concerning the repeated incidents on the Tibet-Indian frontier. Colonel Young-husband, in command of the mission, exceeded his instructions, and signed in Lhasa a convention on 7th September 1904 which provided for a Tibetan indemnity of £500,000 and temporary occupation by British troops of a Tibetan valley, and at the same time pledged Tibet to give no concessions on her territory, and admit no agents or representatives of a third Power. Official protests in London by the Russian government, that these terms exceeded the original instructions, as summarised in a British note to St. Petersburg of June 1904, led only to a reduction to one-third of the sum of the indemnity. In April 1906 the Chinese government recognised the Anglo-Tibetan convention. In Tibet, too, Russia's war with Japan had enabled Britain to strengthen her position.

During the negotiations of 1906-7 on Persia, Afghanistan and Tibet, both the Russian and the British governments were subject to pressure at home. The Russian army leaders were unwilling to renounce all influence in areas which could be used, if not as bases for serious attack on British territory, at least as means of pressure on the British. At the same time, as the Right triumphed in Russia during the summer of 1907, so hostility to the two Western Powers,

[1] On 1st/14th January 1906 the Tsar recorded in his diary that he had given an audience to two Buddhist Kalmyks, an officer Ulanov and a lama of the same name, who were on their way to Tibet (*Dnevnik*, p. 128). Badmaev (see above, p. 201) was also interested in schemes for Tibet.

regarded as the patrons of the hated and defeated liberalism, became an important factor. Though Stolypin and his colleagues wished agreement with Britain, they could not ignore the opinions of their supporters. In Britain, the Foreign Office was under constant pressure from the India Office, and from Curzon in Delhi, not to make any concessions which might weaken Britain's position in India. At the same time, liberal opinion in Britain, to whose wishes the Asquith government was of course sensitive, distrusted Russia as a reactionary and autocratic Power, and objected to any policy based on an imperialist division of "spheres of influence".

Despite these difficulties, the two governments were able to reach agreement, and the convention was signed on 31st August 1907. Persia was divided into three spheres. In the Russian sphere, which included Teheran and Ispahan and reached the Turkish frontier at a point north-east of Baghdad, no concessions were to be asked on behalf of British subjects. In the British sphere, which ran from the port of Bandar Abbas on the Gulf to the meeting-point of the Persian, Afghan and Indian frontiers, no concessions were to go to Russian subjects. The area between the two spheres, which included the western part of the coast of the Gulf, was to be a neutral zone, in which subjects of either Power might obtain concessions. The agreement also laid down the conditions in which Persian tariff revenue might be used as a guarantee for the amortisation and interest on loans made to the Persian government by the Russian-controlled Discount and Loans Bank of Persia or the British-controlled Imperial Bank of Persia. A British statement published at the same time declared that it had not been felt necessary to make any reference to the Persian Gulf, in which Britain had interests more than one hundred years old. Britain would continue to maintain the *status quo* in the Gulf and to protect British commerce, without excluding the legitimate trade of any other Power.

In Afghanistan Britain undertook to make no change, and neither to take, nor to encourage Afghanistan to take, any measures which would threaten Russia. The Russian government stated that Afghanistan was outside the Russian sphere of interest, and that Russia would not maintain political relations with Afghanistan except through British channels. Local Russian and Afghan authorities might have direct contacts for settling matters of local and non-political nature. Both Powers would have equal opportunities of trade, and should it be necessary to send trading agents into the country they would consult each other.

The sovereignty of China over Tibet was recognised by both Powers, which also stressed Britain's special interest owing to her geographical position in the maintenance of the present state of Tibet's foreign relations. Negotiations with Tibet would be conducted only through the Chinese authorities, with the two reservations that British commercial agents might have direct contact with the Tibetan authorities and that Buddhist subjects of either Britain or Russia might have direct contact with the Dalai Lama in strictly religious affairs. Neither government would have representatives in Lhasa. No concessions in mines or means of communication in Tibet might be granted, and no Tibetan revenues might be pledged, to the governments or to subjects of Britain or Russia. An additional protocol provided that the British occupation of the Chumbri valley, undertaken after the Younghusband Mission, would be terminated after three years unless the Tibetan authorities failed to fulfil their obligations; and in this case the British and Russian governments would consult each other.

The convention was criticised by the more fervent nationalists on both sides. It was however of real value to both countries, and appreciably reduced friction. But it did not finally solve even the limited problems with which it dealt.

In Persia, Britain and Russia sympathised with rival factions. During the Persian revolution of 1908–9 and the subsequent disorders, public opinion and diplomacy in Britain were on the whole on the side of the reformers, while Russia favoured the Shah or the reactionaries. In 1911 the American adviser, Morgan Shuster, whom the Persian Assembly had invited to reform the national finances, was involved in a quarrel with Russian consular officials. The Russian government demanded Shuster's dismissal and moved troops towards Teheran. The Assembly capitulated, to the indignation of public opinion in the United States and to the embarrassment of the British government.[1]

In Tibet, the Chinese government profited from the Anglo-Russian agreement to restore its authority. In 1910 it sent troops to Lhasa and deposed the Dalai Lama. The Chinese revolution of 1911 however gave the Tibetans a chance to recover their independence. Now, instead of treating the British as enemies, as in the past, they sought their support as a counterweight to Chinese pretensions. Russia, which with the consent of Japan, was estab-

[1] For events in Persia up to 1909, see Browne, *The Persian Revolution* (Cambridge, 1910). For a general survey of Persian affairs throughout our period, see Brockelmann, *Geschicte der islamischen Völker* (Berlin, 1939). For the Shuster affair, BD Vol. x. Part I, pp. 812–900.

lishing her predominance in Mongolia by encouraging a revolt against the Chinese,[1] was hardly in a position to object to British encouragement to the Tibetans. The British government at first tried to mediate between Tibetans and Chinese, and proposed the division of Tibet into an "inner zone" in which the Chinese should be allowed to have officials and garrisons, and an "outer zone" with Lhasa as its capital which should be completely independent. When the Chinese government refused these proposals, Britain made, in July 1914, a separate agreement with Tibet by which British military instructors and mining prospectors were to be accepted in Lhasa and Britain was to treat Tibet as independent in all but name.[2]

.   .   .   .   .

The assurances of Russian statesmen that the agreement with Britain was in no way directed against Germany were received in Berlin with politeness but increasing scepticism. But the evidence is that they were sincere on the Russian side. In fact, though from the Bosnian crisis of 1909 Russo-German relations deteriorated, two concrete agreements were reached between the two Powers.

The first concerned the Baltic. The Paris treaty of 1856 had provided for the demilitarisation of the Åland Islands, which control the entrance to the Gulf of Finland. The Russian nationalism of Stolypin, which required an end to Finnish autonomy, also required the reassertion of full sovereignty over all Russian territory in the Baltic. The occasion for a change was provided by the separation of Norway from Sweden in 1905. The Great Powers agreed to guarantee Norway, and were prepared to guarantee Sweden. The Swedes however resented this suggestion as implying international tutelage incompatible with their prestige. Instead it was suggested that a multilateral agreement should guarantee the *status quo* in the Baltic. It was therefore essential that Russia should not miss this opportunity to obtain the modification of the 1856 treaty with regard to the Åland Islands.

In August 1907, when William II and Nicholas II met at Swinemünde, Izvolski suggested to Bülow the signature of a German-Russian secret protocol, guaranteeing the *status quo* in the Baltic and ending the demilitarisation of the Åland Islands. Denmark and Sweden were to be later invited to associate themselves. After some minor changes, the German government accepted the Russian draft, and the protocol was signed in October in St.

---

[1] See below, pp. 337–9.   [2] Renouvin, *op. cit*, pp. 281–4.

Petersburg. The British and French governments however learned of the protocol through the indiscretion of the Russian ambassador in London, Count Benckendorff. In order to allay their suspicions of Russo-German intrigue, Izvolski decided to substitute for a secret bilateral protocol a public agreement between Russia, Germany, Sweden and Denmark. This was not easily obtained owing to the opposition of Swedish public opinion to the remilitar-isation of the Åland Islands. Ultimately however the document was signed on 23rd April 1908. The additional protocol on the Åland Islands was modified at the last moment as a result of a personal appeal by King Gustav of Sweden to Nicholas II. The phrase finally adopted was interpreted by the Russians as justifying the exercise of full sovereignty over the islands, and by the Swedes as an assurance that there would be no change.[1] In practice there were no difficulties in the following years between Russia and Sweden. In the summer of 1912, when King Gustav visited the Tsar in his yacht in the Finnish archipelago, Sazonov, then Russian Foreign Minister, assured the Swedish Foreign Minister, Count Ehrens;ärd, that Russia would do nothing to "transform the Åland archipelago into an offensive base against Sweden". According to the subse-quent testimony of Sazonov, though there was always a strong pro-German element in Sweden, up to 1914 Russia and Sweden were good neighbours, and their relations were "troubled by no political misunderstanding or frontier discussion".[2]

It may seem surprising that the narrows of the Baltic, which were as much a door closed against Russia as were the Black Sea Straits, played so small a part in Russian foreign policy before 1914. It is the more surprising since a large part of her growing imports of raw materials for industry came by this route. Part of the explanation lies of course in the fact that the Baltic narrows were only a strategic and economic problem, while the Straits question had religious, racial and sentimental aspects of equal importance. There were no Slavs near the Danish Belt and Sounds. But St. Petersburg did not even treat the Baltic narrows as an important strategic problem, above all because it was clear that in case of war there was nothing that Russia could do about it. If Russia

[1] The relevant phrases were: "The principle of the maintenance of the *status quo* affects only the territorial integrity of the present possessions, continental and insular, of the High Contracting Powers in the Baltic region, and consequently the said arrangement can in no way be invoked when it is a question of the free exercise of the rights of sovereignty of the High Contracting Powers on their above-mentioned respective possessions." For a discussion of the whole question, and an account of the negotiations, see Taube, *op. cit.*, chapter 2.
[2] Sazonov, *Les années fatales* (Paris, 1927), p. 71.

were at war with Britain with Germany as an ally, Germany
would look after the narrows. If Russia were at war with Germany
with Britain as an ally, she might or might not hope that Britain
would force the narrows, but it was clear that her own naval
strength would not suffice. In the Black Sea, Russia might hope in
favourable conditions to seize and hold the Straits. In the Baltic
area she could have no such hope. As this was clear in both St.
Petersburg and Berlin, the two governments could afford to be
friendly and polite in Baltic questions. The improvement in the
position of the German minority in the Baltic provinces of Russia
which followed the events of 1905 perhaps also contributed to this
friendliness.[1]

The second problem on which German-Russian agreement was
reached was the Baghdad Railway. This enterprise had been
approved by the Sultan in March 1903. The main financial interest
concerned was German.[2] The French and British governments had
for some time wavered in their attitude to it, but by the end of 1903
were opposed. Russia regarded the affair with suspicion from the
beginning. The Young Turk revolution of 1908[3] was at first
a setback to German influence, but this did not last long. Germany
granted the loan which the new government had not been able to
raise in Paris or London. Germany showed much less sympathy
for the Balkan Christians than did the Entente Powers or Russia.
Germany had no objection to Turkish nationalism or to Panislamism, both of which had their champions among the Young Turks,
and both of which were suspect to the three Great Powers which
had the largest number of Moslem subjects. By 1910 the Young
Turks were as pro-German as Abdul Hamid had been, and consented to the Baghdad Railway.

Russian dislike was not diminished, but the Russian government
was keen to show Berlin that it was not anti-German, and that
the Anglo-Russian convention was not directed against German
interests in the Middle East. So keen was it to prove this that it
signed a convention at Potsdam in November 1910 which dealt with
the two Powers' positions in Persia. Germany recognised Russian
supremacy in the zone of Persia defined by the Anglo-Russian
convention. Russia withdrew all diplomatic opposition to the
Baghdad Railway project. Russia undertook to obtain from the
Persian government a concession for a railway from Teheran to

[1] See above, p. 305.
[2] For further details, see Earle, *Turkey, the Powers and the Baghdad Railway*
(London, 1923).
[3] See below p. 341.

Khanikin on the Perso-Turkish frontier. This would link up Persia with the Baghdad line, and greatly assist German trade in the Persian market. If Russia should not succeed in building this connecting railway, German subjects might later apply for the concession. The principle of equal trade opportunities for both Powers was asserted. In practice, the superior competitive power of German goods ensured German predominance. The intention to conclude the agreement had been communicated beforehand by the Russian to the French and British governments, and their consent obtained. Its terms were however criticised in both France and Britain.[1]

Right up to 1914 Russo-German friendship was strongly urged in Russian government circles and in the Duma. A good example of the arguments used is a memorandum written in February 1914 by P. N. Durnovo.[2] It stated that the central factor in international relations was now Anglo-German rivalry. It was not to Russia's interest to support Britain. In the past Germany had held back Austria in the Balkans: it was only since Russia had come closer to Britain that Germany had been obliged to back Austrian aims. "The vital interests of Russia and Germany are nowhere in conflict. . . . The future of Germany is on the seas, where for Russia, essentially the most continental of all the Great Powers, there are no interests at all."

This reasoning is interesting, but in the light of subsequent events it is not convincing. As long as Germany was a mere extension of Prussia, it was true that Russo-German vital interests did not conflict. But Germany was now no longer Prussia. The relative decline of the power of the Prussian landlords and officer class, and the relative growth of power of the German (whether west or east, north or south) middle class (industrial, bureaucratic, professional and academic), had made the Reich's foreign policy no longer Prussian but German. The interest of Berlin in south-east Europe and the Middle East, which brought Germany inevitably into conflict with Russia, was due not to the Anglo-Russian agreement of 1907 but to the social and political changes in Germany and in German Austria. The aristocratic monarchy of William I and Bismarck could maintain friendship with Russia.

[1] The British attitude to the Potsdam Meeting can be studied in BD, Vol. x, Part I, pp. 549–723.
[2] The full text of the memorandum is given in English in F. A. Golder, *Documents on Russian History, 1914–17* (New York, 1927), pp. 3–24. P. N. Durnovo was Minister of Interior in Witte's government, and is not to be confused with I. N. Durnovo, who held the same office from 1889 to 1895. See above pp. 136–7, 252–3.

The demagogic monarchy of William II had to support Austria. Public opinion had become a factor in German foreign policy. Public opinion was more, not less, bellicose than the Prussian Junkers. Public opinion would never sacrifice Germandom to Slavdom in south-east Europe.

And even if some great statesman in Berlin had somehow kept the Reich from binding itself to Austrian imperialism, one may doubt whether Russo-German friendship could long have survived. If Germany had not supported Austria, Austria would have collapsed as a result of internal conflicts. The Danubian heritage would have had to be divided. Could Russia and Germany have partitioned the domains of the Habsburgs as they and the Habsburgs once partitioned Poland? Russia would no doubt gladly have abandoned to Germany, not only German Austria but also the Czech lands. The Czech people could adore the Russia which they so little understood: the fate of Western schismatic quasi-Slavs was of small interest to the Orthodox Tsar of all the Russias or the nationalist deputies of the Third and Fourth Dumas. For their part the Germans would gladly have abandoned to Russia Galicia, and might have abandoned Roumania and Transylvania. But a German government whose frontiers extended to the Julian Alps could hardly have permitted Russian domination, through the South Slavs, of the whole eastern coast of the Adriatic. And the Hungarians would not have allowed any Power to decide their fate for them. Partition of Austria would have brought violent conflicts, which must soon have brought Germany and Russia to blows. A partnership of Germany with Russia at the expense of Austria, was as impracticable as a partnership of Russia with Austria at the expense of Germany, such as the Neoslavs had urged. There remained only the third combination—Germany and Austria, joint champions of *Deutschtum* against Russia.

The Far East

The defeat of 1905 did not end Russian interest in the Far East. Having failed to impose her will on Japan, Russia sought expansion in a more limited field, with the co-operation of Japan. It was clear that Japan would control Korea, and dominate southern Manchuria. In northern Manchuria and Mongolia however Russia might hope to develop her influence. Thus Russian policy was forced by defeat on to the basis earlier favoured by Kuropatkin and opposed by the Bezobrazov clique.[1]

[1] See above, pp. 210-1.

The Anglo-Japanese treaty was renewed on 12th August 1905, on a wider basis. It now applied not only to the Far East but also to India, and it came into force if either ally were attacked by only one Power. This did not make Russo-Japanese reconciliation easier. But French diplomacy made efforts on behalf of Russia. Japan as well as Russia was economically exhausted. Like her defeated rival, she applied to France for a loan. In March 1907 a sum of 300 million francs was agreed. The French government asked, as a condition of approving the loan, that a political treaty should be made between France and Japan.[1] This was done on 10th July 1907. The treaty guaranteed the territories of both Powers in Asia and the maintenance of peace and security in the provinces of the Chinese Empire bordering on these possessions. A simultaneous exchange of secret letters recognised Japanese predominance in southern Manchuria and part of Mongolia and "special interest" in Fukien province opposite Formosa, and a French "special interest" in the three provinces bordering Indo-China. At the same time the French government pressed the Japanese to work for an "era not only of peace but of confidence" in their relations with Russia.[2]

French diplomatic efforts achieved some success in the series of Russo-Japanese agreements signed during the summer of 1907. The first was an agreement on the Manchurian railways of 13th June. It was followed by a settlement of the rights to fisheries off the Siberian coast. This agreement was considered extremely hard in St. Petersburg. The terms were regarded as giving Japan in effect the indemnity which Russian diplomacy had succeeded at Portsmouth in avoiding. Finally on 30th July a political treaty was signed. The published portion merely affirmed the will of both Powers to maintain the *status quo* and to consult each other should events threaten to disturb it. A secret annex however recognised Japanese "special interests" in Korea and southern Manchuria and Russian "special interests" in northern Manchuria and outer Mongolia. It laid down a line of demarcation between the two spheres in eastern Manchuria.

In the following years both Powers went ahead with their plans in agreement. On 26th October 1909 Marquess Ito was assassinated by a Korean during a visit to Harbin to confer with Kokovtsov, who was making a Far Eastern tour. This was used as a pretext to abolish the remnants of Korean independence. On 23rd August 1910 Korea was incorporated in the Japanese Empire. On 4th

---

[1] Renouvin, *op. cit.*, p. 236. [2] Ibid., p. 237.

July 1910 a further Russo-Japanese secret convention had been signed. It interpreted the "special interests" of the two Powers in a positive instead of a negative sense. It recognised the right of each Power "within its sphere freely to take all measures necessary for the safeguarding and defence" of its interests. It also provided that the two governments would communicate with each other on any "matters affecting in common their special interests in Manchuria". Yet another secret convention, signed on 8th July 1912, extended the line of demarcation of the 1907 treaty annex to western Manchuria and Mongolia.[1]

The Power against which Russia and Japan acted in common was the United States, whose demands for the open door in trade and for equal opportunities of investment conflicted with the aims of both states. Suspicion of Japan was growing rapidly in America. President Roosevelt had fears for the security of the Philippines, and on the west coast of the United States racial agitation against Japanese immigrants created bad feeling between the two countries. The Root-Takahira exchange of notes of 30th November 1908 did not greatly improve the situation, as it was differently interpreted on each side.[2]

In 1909 the American industrialist Harriman obtained a concession for a new railway across Manchuria, from Chinchow on the Gulf of Liaotung to Aigun on the Amur, thus crossing and competing with the Russo-Japanese railway system. The American Secretary of State Knox then proposed that all Manchurian railways should be "neutralised" and placed under an international syndicate. Russia and Japan strongly opposed the project, with reluctant support from Britain. Russo-Japanese pressure on the Chinese government caused the latter to postpone its signature of the Chinchow-Aigun concession.[3]

In the following year a group of American, French, British and German banks combined to offer a credit to the Chinese government for industrial development in Manchuria. Russia and Japan demanded to be included in the group. Although neither Russia nor Japan was in a position to make foreign loans, their demands were supported, for reasons of international policy, by France and

---

[1] These agreements are discussed, and their texts are given, in E. B. Price, *The Russo-Japanese Treaties of 1907–16* (Baltimore, 1933).

[2] Renouvin, *op. cit.*, pp. 231–4.

[3] The negotiations are described and analysed in detail by Zabriskie, *op. cit.*, chapter 6. This excellent work clearly shows how American diplomacy failed to make use of the pro-American trend which did exist in the Russian Government and Foreign Office, and instead drove Russia, in spite of her distrust of Japanese intentions, into closer co-operation with Japan.

Britain. A Six-Power "Consortium" was thus created. Its operations were postponed by the Chinese revolution of 1911. The new government, however, though hostile to all foreign domination in China, needed loans as much as had the overthrown Manchu dynasty. The Consortium decided to negotiate with the conservative politician Yuan-shih-kai, who seemed to them more likely to ensure order in China for foreign business than the enthusiastic republican idealists of the Kuomintang movement led by Sun-yat-sen. The conclusion of the loan agreement enabled Yuan to set up his own dictatorship in the greater part of China. Russo-Japanese pressure was however able to limit the powers of the Consortium by excluding all revenues from Manchuria, Mongolia or Turkestan from the securities offered for the loan. The election of Woodrow Wilson to the presidency of the United States brought a change in American policy. On 18th March 1913 the new president withdrew governmental support from the American banks participating in the Consortium on the ground that the terms of the agreement were incompatible with Chinese independence. The American banks therefore left the Consortium, which broke up in the autumn of the same year.[1]

The conflict between the Russo-Japanese combination and the United States was an even greater source of embarrassment to British policy, which valued American friendship, than was the Russo-American conflict in Persia.[2] Britain's relations with Japan cooled during these years. In July 1911 the Anglo-Japanese alliance was renewed, but its scope was reduced. It no longer applied to India.

The disorder which followed the Chinese revolution of 1911 gave Russia her opportunity in Mongolia. The Mongols, numbering some 3,000,000, differed from the Chinese in language, social structure and religion. Their society was pastoral, semi-feudal and theocratic. They were organised in tribal units under hereditary princes, at whose head was the Buddhist religious leader or *hutuhta*. They disliked the Chinese traders and moneylenders who lived in the few towns of Mongolia, strongly objected to colonisation of Mongolian land by Chinese peasants, and feared the prospect of tighter Chinese political control resulting from the extension of the Chinese railway system to Mongolia which was being prepared by the Chinese government. Russia had taken some

---

[1] Zabriskie, *op. cit.*, pp. 144–8, 185–9. For a survey of Russia's policy in China after 1905, and its effect on the relations with the other Great Powers, see D. J. Dallin, *The Rise of Russia in Asia*, chapter 4.

[2] See above, p. 329.

interest in Mongolia since the nineties. The trade of Russia with Mongolia was extremely small until 1909, when Moscow trading firms began to interest themselves in what had been the concern only of small local merchants. The Ministry of Commerce in St. Petersburg began to study the Mongolian market. The prospect of a railway link with China alarmed the Russians, who foresaw that their trade would be faced with the competition not only of Chinese but of West European goods from the south. Russians in Mongolia encouraged the Mongol leaders to seek the support of the Russian government in their struggle with Peking.[1]

In July 1911 a Mongol delegation came to St. Petersburg to ask for a Russian protectorate and the despatch of Russian troops to the Mongolian capital Urga. It was received by Kokovtsov and Stolypin, against the advice of the Foreign Ministry. Sazonov opposed a forward policy, but was forced by the events in China to act. He gave his consent to the delivery of Russian arms from the Irkutsk military district to the Mongols. In November 1911 the Mongols decided to revolt. With the overthrow of the Manchu dynasty, to which they had felt some loyalty, the last link with China was broken. The Chinese were able to hold Inner Mongolia, south of the Gobi Desert, but they were forced to give up Outer Mongolia. In December 1912 the *hutuhta* proclaimed himself independent Khan of Mongolia.[2]

Russia now established a protectorate in all but name. Russian military and financial advisers were sent to Urga, a Russo-Mongolian Bank was founded, and a Russian loan was granted, with the revenue from mines as security. Russian subjects were allowed to acquire land in Mongolia. Imports from Siberia were given preferential treatment. These privileges were sanctioned by a Russo-Mongolian treaty signed in November 1912. The treaty also provided for Russian armed assistance in the event of Chinese attempts at reconquest or immigration, and pledged the Mongols to conclude no treaty with a foreign Power without Russian approval. The Chinese government protested but could do nothing. In November 1913 Yuan-shih-kai signed an agreement

[1] On the situation in ·Mongolia and Russian policy, see documents and introductory article by Popov, in *Krasny Arkhiv*, XXXVII, pp. 3–68. Popov makes the usual Marxist assumption that the commercial factor was the cause of Russian policy. In fact it would seem to have been one of several contributory causes—the others being both military and political. There is an excellent survey in Dallin, *op. cit.*, chapter 5, of Russia's policy in all the Chinese borderlands from Turkestan to Manchuria.
[2] For these events see Korostovets, *Von Cingis Khan zur Sowjetrepublik*, *Geschichte der Mongolei* (Berlin, 1926); *Krasny Arkhiv, loc. cit.*

with Russia. China recognised the autonomy of Outer Mongolia, but the principle of Chinese sovereignty was reasserted. China was to be represented in Urga by a resident, Russia only by a consul. Both China and Russia undertook not to interfere with Mongolia's internal affairs, and not to send officials, soldiers or colonists. In practice however Outer Mongolia became a vassal of Russia. The Mongols had exchanged the rule of King Log for that of King Stork.

The Balkans, 1903–14.

The replacement of the Obrenović by the Karadjordjević dynasty in May 1903 was not at first expected to bind Serbia more closely to Russia. Since Alexander's marriage with Draga Mashin in 1900, Serbian policy had been pro-Russian, and Vienna had come to regard the young king as an enemy. Peter Karadjordjević on the other hand was not considered to be anti-Austrian. Though hardly able to approve the means by which the change had been made, the Austrian statesmen hoped that it would turn to their advantage.[1] Francis Joseph was the first European monarch to communicate with the new king. His example was followed by Russia, Italy and Germany. The French attitude was reserved, while the British government recalled its minister, and did not replace him until 1907.

Unfortunately for Austria, Peter was no Milan Obrenović. He had no wish to be a despot, and firmly believed in constitutional monarchy. He would accept whatever government the Serbian people elected. The Serbian people were not pro-Austrian. In the elections of October 1903 the strongest parties were the Radicals led by Pašić and the Independent Radicals, who stood to their left. Discussion of the Serbian cause in Bosnia and Hungary in Press and speech became freer and fiercer than before. The first dispute between Serbia and Austria came when the Serbian government gave a contract for army supplies to the French firm of Creusot instead of the Austrian firm of Skoda. When negotiations began for a new Austro-Serbian trade treaty, the Austrian negotiators tried to force the cancellation of the Creusot contract. Meanwhile, with the blessing of Russian diplomacy, Serbia was seeking better relations with Bulgaria. In April 1904 provisional agreements were reached on commercial and military collaboration and on a common policy towards Turkey. In July 1905 a commercial treaty was

---

[1] On Serbian policy, see V. M. Markov, *Serbien zwischen Osterreich und Russland, 1897–1908* (Stuttgart, 1934); Boghitschewitsch, *Die auswärtige Politik Serbiens, 1903–1914*(Berlin, 1928). Both are hostile studies.

signed, to go into effect in March 1906, and to prepare the way for ultimate customs union between the two countries. The last point was to be achieved by March 1917, and meanwhile the intention was to be kept secret. At the end of 1905 however an indiscretion in the Bulgarian parliament revealed its existence. In January 1906 the Austrian Foreign Minister, Baron Aehrenthal, threatened to break off all trade negotiations unless Serbia refused to ratify the treaty with Bulgaria. When the Serbs refused, Austria boycotted all Serbian goods. In February the Serbian government agreed not to ratify the Bulgarian treaty, but this was no longer sufficient for Austria. Further demands were put forward for preferential treatment for Austrian goods. When these were rejected, the breach became complete.

There followed what has become known as the "Pig War", pigs and pork products being Serbia's most important export. Its motives on the Austrian side were mainly political, but an economic motive was also provided by the landowning interest in Hungary, which had long disliked competition from Serbian pigs, and had been mainly responsible for the earlier and shorter tariff war of 1896-7.[1] Serbia was hard hit by the "Pig War", but she did not yield. It was fortunate for her that Germany did not follow the example of her ally. The Serbs were able to export their goods to Germany, Britain and other countries through Salonica and through Bulgaria. In February 1907 a new trade treaty was made with Bulgaria, but the political co-operation, which had made a promising beginning in 1904, was not carried further. In 1908 the Bulgarian elections brought a marked swing to the Left. Alexander Malinov, leader of the Democrat Party, the most radical of the middle class democratic parties in Bulgaria, became Premier. His main interest was in internal reform, and a forward foreign policy, together with Serbia against Turkey or Austria, did not greatly interest him.

Baron Aehrenthal, who became Austrian Foreign Minister in 1906, had previously served as ambassador in St. Petersburg, and had a reputation for Russophile sympathy. During his first year in office he seemed to favour close co-operation with Russia. In October 1907 he even spoke to the Council of Ministers in Vienna in favour of a new commercial treaty with Serbia and a new policy towards the South Slav subjects of the empire calculated to win the goodwill of Serbia.[2] His attitude seems to have changed early in

---

[1] See above, pp. 192-3.
[2] Baernreither, *Fragments of a Political Diary* (London, 1930).

1908 as a result of a diplomatic blunder. In January 1908 he proposed to the Delegations[1] that Austria should build a railway
through the Sandjak of Novi Bazar, to link Austrian-occupied
Bosnia with Turkish Macedonia and Salonica, by-passing the
territory of Serbia. Already in 1902 this plan had been suggested
by his predecessor, Gołuchowski, to the German government and
to Count Lamsdorff. When Lamsdorff did not reply, it was
dropped. Now however Aehrenthal asked and received the approval
of the Sultan, but did not consult St. Petersburg, When the concession became known, Izvolski protested, and refused Russian
co-operation in the judicial reforms for Macedonia which had been
worked out in accordance with the Mürzsteg agreement of 1903.[2]
In the end nothing was done about the Sandjak railway, but the
incident infuriated both the Serbian and the Russian government,
and may have contributed to turning Aehrenthal against both.[3]

The condition of Bosnia and Hercegovina was now seriously
worrying the Austrian government. Serb nationalist agitation was
a growing nuisance, and as long as the two provinces legally formed
part of the Ottoman Empire it was possible for the Serbs to hope
that they would ultimately pass to Serbia. At the same time
economic reforms were badly needed, and could hardly be carried
out with the existing constitution. The Austro-Hungarian
administrators felt that annexation to the empire was an essential
precondition to reform and to political stability. The issue was
made urgent by the Young Turkish Revolution of 25th July 1908.
It was probable that the Turkish reformers, who were nationalists
as well as radicals, would argue that the whole Ottoman Empire
now had a progressive government and that the provinces which
had been placed under Austrian supervision in the days of the bad
old regime should now be restored to a regime capable of ensuring
their inhabitants' welfare. At the same time Prince Ferdinand of
Bulgaria was faced with the possibility that the new Turkish rulers
would try to make effective the theoretical suzerainty over Bulgaria

[1] There were two bodies, of sixty members each, chosen by the parliaments of
Austria and of Hungary, which heard statements from the common Minister of
Foreign Affairs of the Monarchy. The Hungarian delegation, chosen by majority
vote in a parliament elected on a restricted franchise, represented the Hungarian
ruling class, not the Hungarian masses or the non-Magyar nationalities. The
Austrian delegation, elected in a more complicated manner, represented a variety of
classes and nationalities. Thus the Hungarian delegation, whose opinion was
united, imposed its will on the Austrian, whose opinions were divided. For details
see Louis Eisenmann, *Le Compromis austro-hongrois* (Paris, 1904); A. J. P. Taylor,
op. cit.

[2] See above, p. 197.

[3] There is a thorough study of the Sandjak railway affair in an article by A. J.
May in *Journal of Modern History* (1938).

which had been left to the Sultan by the Berlin treaty of 1878. The time had come to proclaim Bulgaria's formal independence and to assume for himself the royal title.

Aehrenthal now favoured close co-operation with Bulgaria not only against Turkey, but also against Serbia. After consulting Burian, the Governor of Bosnia and Hercegovina, on 6th August, Aehrenthal decided to annex the provinces. In a memorandum of 9th August he recommended Austrian support to Bulgarian claims in Macedonia. He was prepared to let the Sandjak of Novi Bazar go, though the Hungarian leader Andrássy[1] wished to retain it. Aehrenthal argued that the aims of Austrian policy could best be secured "not through Novi Bazar but through Belgrade", and that the best way to this was by an Austro-Bulgarian pincer movement on Serbia.

At the same time he wished to consult the Russian government before acting. On 15th–16th September took place the famous meeting between Aehrenthal and Izvolski at the castle of Buchlau in Moravia. Subsequent disagreement between the two statesmen as to the nature of the agreement that was then reached between them—which concerned Russian consent to the annexation of Bosnia and Austrian consent to a revision of the Straits convention to the advantage of Russia—was an important factor in the Austro-Russian tension of the following year.[2]

On 23rd and 24th September Aehrenthal met Ferdinand of Bulgaria in Budapest. According to Aehrenthal's account, they agreed to respect the territorial *status quo* of Turkey, but "that Bulgaria should not neglect an opportunity which was perhaps favourable to realise her legitimate wishes". Four days later Aehrenthal told the German ambassador in Vienna that he had the impression that Bulgaria would proceed to declare her independence, and added that he "needed the Bulgarians". Meanwhile Malinov was pressing Ferdinand to declare independence, and Bulgarian public opinion was clamouring for it. On 5th October Bulgarian independence was announced, and was followed next day by the annexation of Bosnia and Hercegovina.

The ensuing international crisis can be briefly summarised as follows. Russia asked for a formal conference of the Great Powers which had signed the Berlin treaty of 1878. Britain agreed that there should be a conference, but did not wish to weaken Turkey,

---

[1] Son of the former Foreign Minister (pp. 98–106 above).
[2] For the annexation crisis, see B. Schmitt, *The Annexation of Bosnia* (Cambridge, 1937); M. Ninčić, *La crise bosniaque (1908–9) et les Puissances européennes* (Paris, 1937).

which she expected to be more friendly towards her under the Young Turk regime than under the rule of the Germanophile and Panislamist Sultan Abdul Hamid. For this reason Britain opposed Russia's desire for a modification of the Straits convention. Austria declared herself willing to take part in a conference provided that all problems between herself and Turkey had been settled bilaterally before the conference opened. Izvolski thus found that Austria's consent to a change in the Straits was valueless since Britain, with whom he had taken so much trouble to reach an agreement on Asiatic problems in the previous year, was against change. At the same time, he could only obtain Austrian consent to a conference, which for reasons of his own and his country's prestige seemed essential, at the cost of accepting an Austro-Turkish agreement which would involve the abandonment of Serbia. Among the Powers there was a vague agreement in principle that Serbia had some sort of right to compensation, but Britain insisted that the compensation should not be at the expense of Turkey, while Germany insisted with even greater emphasis that it should not be at the expense of Austria.

Serbia at first attempted common diplomatic action with Turkey against Austria. Britain and Russia to some extent favoured this, but did not wish such action to have an anti-Bulgarian character. This however was precisely what the Turks were looking for. When they found that Serbia, on British and Russian advice, hesitated about committing herself to alliance with Turkey against Bulgaria, co-operation with Serbia ceased to interest them, and they came to terms with Austria on 26th February 1909. Austria returned the Sandjak of Novi Bazar to Turkey, and paid money compensation for the annexation of Bosnia and Hercegovina. On 15th April 1909 a Turco-Bulgarian agreement was signed. Bulgaria also agreed to pay a sum in compensation for her independence. During April Ferdinand was recognised as King by the Powers.

The climax of the crisis came during March, over Serbia's claim for compensation. Austria categorically refused the claim, and had full German support. Russia advised Serbia, on 27th February, to give up territorial claims and to take no military measures on her frontier with Austria-Hungary. On 10th March a Serbian note addressed to all the Powers placed Serbia's fate in their hands and renounced any compensation from Austria, "territorial, political or economic". But this was not enough for Aehrenthal. He required a direct undertaking from Serbia that she had renounced com-

BOUNDARIES OF TREATY OF BERLIN - - - -
  "   "   "   " BUCHAREST - · - · -
MIDYE – ENOS LINE · · · · · · · ·
TURKISH TERRITORY ACQUIRED
                    BY SERBIA
  "   "   " " GREECE
  "   "   " " BULGARIA
SERBIA – BULGARIA CONTESTED ZONE
         (BY 1912 ALLIANCE)

8. THE

RUSSIA

R. Dneistr

BESSARABIA

R. Prut

Odessa

MOLDAVIA

TRANSYLVANIA

ROUMANIA

HUNGARY

WALLACHIA

•Bucarest

Constantza

IA

R. Danube

Silistra

Nish•

BULGARIA

Varna

•Sofia

R. Maritza

Kumanovo

•Plovdiv

Skoplje

Adrianople

Midye

•Veles

Lule Burgaz

Prilep

Constantinople

Bitolj•

Kavalla

T H R A C E

San Stefano

•Florina

Salonika

Dedeagatch

Enos

THESSALY

G R E E C E

pensation and "had decided for the future to fulfil her obligations as a good neighbour towards the Monarchy". The German government, which supported Aehrenthal in declaring the Serbian note to the Powers unsatisfactory, now proposed that all the Powers should exchange formal notes with Austria recognising the annexation, and that Russia should then put pressure on Serbia to fulfil the Austrian demand. On 13th and 20th March the Russian Council of Ministers discussed the crisis, in the presence of the chiefs of the armed services and with the Tsar presiding. The opinion of all was that Russia could not go to war. Izvolski on 20th March gave a vague reply to the German note, stressing the "goodwill displayed by Serbia" and the bellicose attitude of Vienna, and arguing that acceptance of the procedure suggested by the German government "does not exclude the necessity of a European conference". The German reply came the next day. It demanded "a precise answer, yes or no". Any "evasive, conditional or unclear answer" would be considered a refusal. In this case, "things would take their course", and the Russian government would be solely responsible for the result. On 23rd March Izvolski surrendered. If the Austrian government should make a request to the Powers for an exchange of notes recognising the annexation, "Russia will not fail to give her unconditional assent". On 31st March the Serbian government, abandoned to its own devices, gave the assurance required by Austria.

Aehrenthal had won a diplomatic victory. He had humiliated Serbia, and Germany had humiliated Russia. But the gain was more apparent than real. Serbia had been made an irreconcilable enemy but had not been destroyed. The South Slavs inside the empire had been more antagonised than ever. The Zagreb treason trial of 1909, and the Friedjung libel case of the following year, at which it was shown that senior Austro-Hungarian diplomats had forged documents in order to justify their anti-Serbian and anti-South Slav policy at home and abroad, turned still more subjects of the Habsburgs into enemies, and lowered Austria's international repute.[1] If Austrian statesmen had made up their minds that only force could settle the issue between them and the South Slavs, then they should have struck while Russia was hopelessly weak. The fact that they did not strike proves that they were not warmongering monsters, but does not show them to have been good statesmen. Conrad von Hötzendorff, the Austrian Chief of Staff, felt that

[1] R. W. Seton-Watson, *The South Slav Question* (London, 1911), chapters 10-12.

Austria's best opportunity was lost in 1909.[1] From the point of view of long-term Great Power politics, there can be little doubt that he was right. If however moral considerations are introduced, and preventive wars are to be regarded as inadmissible, then Austria should have chosen the opposite path, and sought understanding and friendship with the South Slavs, with the Kingdom of Serbia, and with Russia. Aehrenthal did neither. He did not go to war in 1909, but his action made war a few years later more probable. And every year made Russia less weak, and a European war less easy for the German Powers to win.

Russian diplomacy at once made efforts to repair the losses. In April 1909 Russia agreed to pay a part of Bulgaria's compensation to Turkey. This action at once reduced the strength of the Austrophiles in Sofia. In October 1909 Nicholas II met King Victor Emanuel of Italy at Racconigi. Discussions between Izvolski and the Italian Foreign Minister Tittoni were followed by an exchange of notes. These stated that both Powers accepted the *status quo* in the Balkan peninsula, but that if there were a change both would support the application of the principle of nationality, to the exclusion of any single Power from a dominant position. Neither Power would conclude any new agreement on the Balkans with a third Power without the other's participation. Russia promised "benevolent consideration" to Italian aims in Libya, and Italy to Russian aims in the Straits. This agreement reflected the disappointment of Italy at failure to receive any compensation from Austria, her ally, for the latter's gains in an area of obvious geographical interest to Italy. Austria claimed that by restoring the Sandjak she had compensated for the annexation of Bosnia and Hercegovina, and so was under no obligation to compensate Italy territorially. Though the Austrian argument was legally compatible with the terms of the Triple Alliance, Tittoni had hoped that Austria would at least make some gesture to Italy as an ally. He had hoped for gains in Albania, or a cession of territory in the Giulian region, or the foundation of an Italian university in Trieste or Trento. But Aehrenthal offered nothing. In December 1909 an Austro-Italian convention was signed concerning the Sandjak. If Austria should later wish to reoccupy it, she would consult Italy before hand and grant her compensation. No further agreement would be made with a third Power on Balkan affairs without the participation of the other on terms of complete

[1] Conrad, *Aus meiner Dienstzeit* (Vienna, 1921), pp. 113–275, esp. 173–4, 203, 271.

equality. Each Power would communicate to the other any proposal received from any third Power which would modify the Balkan *status quo*. The last two points of course did not affect the secret Racconigi agreement, which had preceded this convention by two months.

The following two years were devoted to an intense diplomatic effort by Russia to create a barrier in the Balkan peninsula against Austrian influence. The ideal combination was an alliance between Serbia, Bulgaria and Turkey. This was strongly urged by Charykov, the Russian ambassador in Constantinople, during 1909–11. But the conflict of interest between the two Slav states and Turkey could not be bridged, and German influence in Constantinople, though shaken by the Young Turk revolution, soon recovered. The most that could reasonably be hoped was a Serbo-Bulgarian alliance, and co-operation between it and Greece. From the beginning there was a difference between the aim of the Balkan states—dismemberment of Turkey in Europe—and the aim of Russia—an anti-Austrian block. But it was hoped in St. Petersburg that any collaboration between the Balkan states under Russian auspices would be of advantage to Russia. Russian policy was helped by the change of government in Sofia in 1911 and by the outbreak of the Italo-Turkish war in the same year. Geshov, who succeeded Malinov as Premier of Bulgaria, was an ardent Russophile, and so was his Foreign Minister, Danev. The Italian attack made the collapse of the Ottoman Empire seem a real possibility, and so provided an urgent incentive to Serbia and Bulgaria to agree on the future of Macedonia.

The negotiations began in earnest with a conversation between Danev and the Serbian Premier, Milovanović, in Belgrade in October 1911. Serbian proposals were then communicated to Sofia, and in November two Bulgarian authorised negotiators had a further talk with Milovanović in Paris. Throughout the discussions the common interest in clearing the Turks out of the Balkans conflicted with the incompatible claims of the two countries on Macedonian territory. The Russian ministers in Belgrade and Sofia, Hartvig and Neklyudov, were kept fully informed by both governments. Hartvig, a keen Panslav, was especially active. In a long memorandum to his government of 5th November 1911 Hartvig argued that agreement between the Balkan Slav states and Turkey was incompatible with Russia's interests, which he assumed to be assistance to the Slav nations in the attainment of their immemorial ideals, the division between them of the Ottoman territories in Europe, and the achievement of Russia's own historic task, "to stand with firm foot on the shores of the Bosphorus, at the gate of entry to the Russian Lake".[1] In St. Petersburg there was less enthusiasm. Both the new Foreign Minister, Sazonov, and his deputy, Neratov, were alarmed by the draft Serbo-Bulgarian agreement, which clearly assumed common military action against Turkey. Sazonov wished to avoid war in the Balkans. But Hartvig pointed out that, shorn of its military provisions, the alliance would be of no interest to either party, and that this would "open a wide field for subterranean agitation from outside to the detriment of Slav, and consequently of Russian, interests".[2] The contrast between the caution of Sazonov and the forward policy of Hartvig recalls the similar contrast in 1876 between the attitudes of Gorchakov in St. Petersburg and Kartsov in Belgrade.[3]

Russian influence was consistently used to make each government moderate its Macedonian aims sufficiently to secure agreement. At the same time, fear that Russia would come to terms with Turkey at their expense was an important incentive for the governments to achieve a compromise. The Serbo-Bulgarian treaty was finally signed on 14th March 1912. A Serbian zone (north and west of the Shar mountains) and a Bulgarian zone (east of the Struma) were defined. With regard to the area lying between—the greater part of Macedonia—both governments agreed that if it were not found possible to create an autonomous Macedonia—a project long favoured by Bulgarian opinion, and one which in practice would have secured Bulgarian domination of the province—then it should be divided between the two allies. In this event Serbia agreed to claim nothing beyond a stated line. Somewhere between this line and the boundary of the agreed Serbian zone, the frontier would be drawn, and if necessary the Russian Tsar would be invited to arbitrate.[4] Attached to this treaty was a military convention which provided that Serbia would assist Bulgaria against Turkey or Roumania, while Bulgaria would assist Serbia against Turkey, Roumania or Austria-Hungary.[5]

On 29th May 1912 a Greek-Bulgarian treaty was signed. Greece had officially proposed a treaty of alliance in October 1911. Russia approved of Bulgarian-Greek co-operation, but as in the case of Bulgarian-Serb negotiations, insisted that there must be no aggression against Turkey. The Bulgarian government argued in reply

---

[1] *Krasny Arkhiv*, VIII, pp. 45–8.
[2] Ibid., IX, p. 5 (despatch of 14th/27th November).   [3] See above, p. 98.
[4] The contested zone, between the two lines, is marked in the map on pp. 344–5.
[5] Texts in Geshov, *The Balkan Alliance* (London, 1915), pp. 112–27.

that if Greece were discouraged by Bulgaria she might join an anti-Slav combination under Austrian leadership. This argument impressed the Russian minister in Sofia. As eventually signed, the Bulgarian-Greek alliance did not contain detailed territorial provisions. It promised mutual assistance in the event that either state were attacked by Turkey on her own territory or were threatened by systematic disregard by Turkey of treaty obligations. The two governments would act together to ensure respect for privileges conceded by Turkey in the past, by treaty or otherwise, to the Greek and Bulgarian nationalities on Ottoman territory. There was also a military convention, which laid down the number of troops to be furnished by Greece against Turkey, and the number of Bulgarian or Serbian troops to act against the Turks in the provinces of Kosovo, Monastir and Salonica, which lay to the north of Greece.[1]

In May 1912 Danev visited the Tsar at Livadia, and officially informed him of the contents of the treaty with Serbia. Nicholas expressed his approval. Sazonov, whom Danev saw in St. Petersburg some days later, approved of the treaty but again impressed on his visitor that Russia did not wish war. In June Pašić visited the Tsar in Moscow. In July discussions for an alliance began between Bulgaria and Montenegro.

The Russian government did not inform its French ally of the terms of the treaties. In July the Franco-Russian alliance had been extended by the conclusion of a naval convention. On 9th-11th August Poincaré visited St. Petersburg. He asked for information on the Balkan alliances. After an evasive reply, Sazonov showed him the texts. He was alarmed at their warlike implications, and was not reassured by Sazonov's belief that the Balkan allies would not declare war, or even mobilise, without Russian approval. Poincaré decided not to support a French loan to Bulgaria, for which Sazonov had earlier asked him. Throughout the crisis of 1912 the French government pressed the Russians to be cautious. "We shall fulfil the obligations of our alliance, but we shall not go beyond them".[2]

The crisis came in the autumn. Turkey was weakened not only by the war with Italy but also by revolts in Albania. When even the Albanians, a mainly Moslem people and hitherto loyal subjects of the Sultan, became disaffected, the days of Ottoman rule in Europe were numbered. In September the Balkan allies made

---

[1] Texts in Geshov, *op. cit.*, pp. 127-33.
[2] Poincaré, *Au service de la France* (Paris, 1926), Vol. II, pp. 114-17.

military preparations, and at the same time publicly denounced the inability of the Turks to keep order and protect their Christian subjects. On 8th October a joint Austro-Russian diplomatic intervention was made in the Balkan capitals in favour of peace. But now friendly or restraining words from Great Powers no longer sufficed to hold back the Balkan states. On 8th October Montenegro declared war on Turkey, and on 18th Bulgaria, Serbia and Greece did the same.

The allied armies were rapidly victorious. On 22nd–23rd October the Bulgarian armies in Thrace defeated the Turks at Kirk Kilise, and on 24th October the Serbs won a big victory at Kumanovo. On 8th November the Greeks were in Salonica. At the end of November the Turks were driven back to the Tchataldja lines outside Constantinople. Otherwise only three Turkish garrisons still held out—Scutari in north Albania, Yanina in Epirus and Adrianople in Thrace. On 3rd December, after intervention by the Great Powers, an armistice was signed. In the same month a conference of ambassadors of the Powers met in London to discuss the political results of the war.

Four main political questions had to be considered. They were the attempts of Serbia and Montenegro to obtain ports on the Adriatic, the future of Albania, the claim of Roumania for compensation for Bulgaria's gains, and the Serbo-Bulgarian rivalry for Macedonia.[1]

Austria was absolutely determined to prevent Serbia from acquiring an Adriatic port. She was supported by both Germany and Italy. During November tension between Russia and Austria reached a dangerous point. Conscripts due for release in the Russian army were kept on, thus increasing the numbers under arms by nearly 400,000 men. During the month Austrian forces were increased by about 220,000. The Corps in eastern Galicia was substantially increased. After some hesitation Russia decided that she could not support Serbia on the Adriatic issue, and Sazonov advised the Serbs to yield. French pressure for moderation was largely responsible for the decision. The London conference agreed that Serbia should be offered facilities for commerce in an Albanian port, to be linked with her territory by a railway under international control. With the settlement of this problem the most critical moment of the Balkan crisis was passed.

---

[1] For the events of 1912–13, see R. W. Seton-Watson, *The Rise of Nationality in the Balkans* (London, 1917); E. Helmreich, *The Diplomacy of the Balkan Wars* (Harvard, 1939).

In March 1913 Russia and Austria both declared their intention to demobilise.

The conference accepted Austria's proposal that there should be an independent Albanian state. When this state's frontiers came to be discussed however tension between the Great Powers revived. Russia wished to give Montenegro as much territory as possible, and so push her vassal southwards. Austria insisted on frontiers that would include the whole Albanian nation, and so push her vassal northwards and eastwards. In the south, Albania's claims conflicted with those of Greece. Here too Austria supported the Albanians, but the Greek cause was defended by Germany, for dynastic reasons,[1] and by France and Britain, the traditional friends of Greece. In the end a compromise was reached. The only serious incident was the refusal of King Nicholas of Montenegro, though ordered by all the Powers, to raise the siege of Scutari. A naval demonstration by the Powers at the fishing village of Bar on 5th April 1913 was ignored. On 21st April the Turkish commander surrendered to Nicholas, and Sazonov showed signs of reverting to his original pro-Montenegrin position. Largely as a result of British mediation, Austro-Russian tension was again overcome, and on 5th May Nicholas surrendered the town to the Powers. It was included in the Albanian state.

The war was not finished by the armistice of 3rd December 1912. On 23rd January 1913 the war party in Turkey, under Enver Bey, overthrew the government and resumed hostilities. The main scene of fighting was Adrianople, which held out until 26th March. The Bulgarian army had to ask for Serbian assistance to capture the city. This was the end of Turkish hopes of a recovery.

The London conference ended with the signature of a treaty on 30th May, between Turkey and the victors. All European territory beyond the Enos-Midia line—which left a small strip of land outside Constantinople along the shore of the Marmara and the two Straits—was renounced by the Turks. The division of the ceded territories among the victors however remained to be settled.

The Roumanian claim for compensation from Bulgaria concerned the city of Silistria, a Turkish fortress on the Danube, which it had been expected would be given to Roumania after the Berlin settlement of 1878, but had remained in Bulgarian hands. The right of Roumania to receive the city now, at a time when Bulgaria had greatly increased her territory, was accepted by all the Powers. But

[1] King Constantine was married to William II's sister.

the Roumanian government, not content with Silistria, now claimed a much larger strip of territory, the so-called "quadrilateral", consisting of all land lying to the north of a line drawn almost due east from Silistria to the Black Sea coast. This would have given Roumania the whole territory of the Dobrudja, which lies between the Black Sea and the last stretch of the Danube, which near Silistria turns north and runs parallel with the sea until its delta. The Berlin settlement had given Roumania northern Dobrudja: the territory now in dispute has become well known in the diplomatic history of the last thirty years as "southern Dobrudja." Roumanian compensation was discussed by the representatives of the Powers in St. Petersburg. Austria and Germany supported large compensation for Roumania. Austria however also wished to give Bulgaria further compensation for any cession to Roumania, and proposed that she should annex Salonica. This was opposed by all the other Powers, and especially by Germany and France, as an injustice towards Greece. In the end Roumania was given only Silistria. Bulgaria undertook to build no fortifications between Silistria and the sea, and to give fair treatment to the Roumanian minority in the area, while Roumania was obliged to pay compensation to any Bulgarian inhabitants of Silistria who should wish to leave the city. The convention was signed in St. Petersburg on 8th May.

The Macedonian problem proved too much for the diplomats. When the war ended, the Serbs and Greeks were in occupation of the greater part of Macedonia. The Serbs claimed that they should receive Macedonian territory even beyond the line which, in the Serbo-Bulgarian treaty, had been stated as their maximum demand. Their arguments were, that as Bulgaria had sent no troops to the Vardar area to fight the Turks the whole brunt of fighting in this sector had been borne by Serbs: that Serbia had made a much larger contribution to the seige of Adrianople than the military convention had provided for; that Bulgarian gains in Thrace were larger than had been expected; and that as Serbia had been prevented by Austria from achieving her aims towards the Adriatic, and Bulgaria had not been called upon to give her the support against Austria to which she was pledged in the military convention to the treaty, Serbia should be compensated by a larger share of Macedonia.[1] Already in January 1913 Serbia began secret negotiations with Greece. On 5th May a Serbo-Greek protocol was signed which divided between the two states all territory west of the Vardar.

[1] See Seton-Watson, *op. cit.*, Geshov, *op. cit.*

On 1st June this was followed by a treaty of allaince with a military convention.

Meanwhile the Russian government invoked the provision of the Serbo-Bulgarian treaty that the Tsar should arbitrate in case of disagreement on the division of territory. In the continued exchange of messages which took place during May, both Balkan governments were evasive in their dealings with Russia. On 19th June Sazonov asked for unconditional acceptance by Serbia of the Tsar's arbitration, but a week later no definite acceptance had been received. On 22nd June Bulgaria accepted, with the proviso that, for reasons connected with technical problems of demobilisation of the Bulgarian army, the Tsar must decide within seven days. This reply enraged Sazonov, who accused the Bulgarians of acting on Austrian advice and of giving an "ultimatium" to the Russian emperor. He formally repudiated all Russian engagements towards Bulgaria, including the convention of 1902.[1] On 28th June the Bulgarian commander, General Savov, with the approval of King Ferdinand, ordered his forces to attack the Serbs. An attack was also made on the Greeks, which Ferdinand later claimed that he had not approved.

The evidence does not show whether Ferdinand was encouraged to this action by the Austrian government, but it is obvious that the latter was delighted to see Russia's two protégés at each other's throats.[2] The Bulgarian leaders appear to have believed that their action would be treated as a "demonstration" which would increase their bargaining power during the discussions connected with the intended arbitration by the Tsar. But both Serbia and Greece formally declared war. Bulgaria still did not wish to antagonise Russia, and the Russophile Danev (who had succeeded Geshov as Premier on 30th May) was still in power. Bulgaria therefore avoided any commitment towards Austria, and ignored Austrian advice to offer larger compensation to Roumania. The result was that Roumania declared war on Bulgaria on 11th July. An attempt by Sazonov to mediate failed. On 12th July Turkey also attacked and on the 22nd the Turks recaptured Adrianople. On 16th July Danev resigned, and the Austrophile Radoslavov became Premier. By the end of July Bulgaria was incapable of resistance.

[1] See above, p. 194.
[2] Helmreich, *op. cit.*, pp. 362-3, points out that Ferdinand did not see the Austrian Minister between August 1912 and July 1913, and that there is no positive evidence of Austrian influence on Bulgarian policy. It would however be rash to assume from this that there was no such influence.

On the proposal of Austria, a new peace conference was held in Bucarest. It opened on 30th July. Bulgaria ceded all south Dobrudja (the "quadrilateral") to Roumania. Serbia and Greece took the greater part of Macedonia, both states extending their territory well to the east of the Vardar and leaving Bulgaria only some small gains to the south-west of Sofia. Western Thrace, with the port of Kavala, was given to Greece, despite the efforts of Austria to keep it for Bulgaria. An outlet to the Aegean at Dedeagach was left to Bulgaria. The treaty was signed on 10th August 1913. The Bulgarians still hoped for some support from the Great Powers with regard to Adrianople. But though Russia was anxious not to lose Bulgaria, and Austria was anxious to win her, neither was prepared to put effective pressure on the Turks. On 29th August Bulgaria was obliged to send envoys to Constantinople to discuss directly with the Turkish government. Adrianople was formally restored to the Ottoman Empire.

As in 1909, Austria had gained something but had lost an opportunity. She had enforced her will on Serbia in the Adriatic area, but had not been able to prevent her hated small neighbour from coming out of the war with great gains. The Second Balkan War was an opportunity for Austria to finish Serbia off altogether, but she had been unable to do so owing to the attitudes of Roumania and Germany. Roumania was Austria's formal ally. She could not fight against Roumania's associate in favour of a state with which Roumania was at war, without definitely throwing over Roumania's alliance. But this Germany was determined not to allow. William II attached great importance to Roumania as an ally, and insisted that Austria must not antagonise her. He was also strongly pro-Greek, which was another reason against helping Bulgaria. In fact, in the months between the Second Balkan War and the outbreak of the World War, William II urged Austria to abandon Bulgaria and to come to terms with Serbia, in order to form under German-Austrian leadership a Balkan block of Roumania, Greece, Turkey and Serbia. King Carol I of Roumania, whose sympathies for Germany remained extremely strong, also did his best to reconcile Austria and Serbia. This however was unthinkable in Vienna, where the main aim was on the contrary to reconcile Roumania with Bulgaria, and make them a block against Serbia.

Austria was at least successful in consolidating her influence in Bulgaria. The new Premier, Radoslavov, was eager to base his policy on the Central Powers. He was helped by the unwillingness of French banks, on Russian advice, to give Bulgaria the loan she so urgently needed for reconstruction. This was provided instead by a group of German banks.[1]

Germany was also successful in Turkey. Abandoned by the Western Powers and fearful as ever of Russia, the Young Turks turned to the same Power which had protected Abdul Hamid. In October 1913 an international crisis was caused by the appointment of the German general, Liman von Sanders, as head of a military mission in Turkey, and commander of the Turkish military district of Constantinople. Sazonov felt extremely strongly about this, which he interpreted as a German threat to Russia's Straits interest. The Turkish government pointed out that a British admiral was advising the Turkish navy, and a French general the Turkish gendarmerie, but this argument did not appease the Russian government. Eventually the crisis was solved in January 1914 by relieving von Sanders of the command of the Constantinople Army Corps, on the ground that his rank in the German army was too high for such a command, and leaving him as head of a military mission.[2] The prestige of the Russian government was thus saved, but resentment was not removed. That Germany, which had traditionally approved Russia's special interests in the Straits, should establish herself there, could not be forgiven in St. Petersburg.

Roumania, on the other hand, moved away from the German Powers. Hungarian policy towards the Roumanians of Transylvania had in no way improved. The Independence Party, which had come to power in Budapest after the crisis of 1906, was no more tolerant than had been the Hungarian Liberals. The 1907 Education Bill introduced by Count Apponyi was a further blow to the Transylvanian Roumanians. While official Hungarian policy grew no better, the number of Roumanians both in Hungary and in Roumania who objected to it notably increased. The more liberal tendency in politics, and the growth of education, in the Kingdom of Roumania, made it impossible for Roumanian governments to ignore public opinion, and public opinion was above all against Austria-Hungary. The pro-Austrian policy of Bulgaria showed the Roumanians that their southern neighbour could be used against them in a pincer movement directed from Vienna as well as from St. Petersburg. At the same time, though there was little love for Russia in Roumania, hostility was diminish-

[1] Radoslawow, *Bulgarien und die Weltkrise* (Berlin, 1923), pp. 87–101. The most important participant was the Berlin Discontogesellschaft. The Russophiles in the Bulgarian parliament bitterly opposed the loan, but it was carried by a majority.
[2] Taube, *op. cit.*, pp. 281–5; Sazonov, *op. cit.*, pp. 125–32. The incident is thoroughly discussed in three articles by R. J. Kerner in *Slavonic Review*, 1927–8, Nos. 16, 17 and 18.

ing. One reason for this was the close association of Russia with France, which all educated Roumanians loved, and with Britain, which they trusted.

The parallel with Italy, mentioned above in connection with the making of Roumania's alliance with the German Powers,[1] applies also to the dissolution of that alliance. Like Italy, Roumania found that Germany was either unable or unwilling to restrain Austria from pursuing a hostile policy. At the same time, just as France grew less alarming to Italy by her association with Italy's friend Britain, so Russia grew less alarming to Roumania through her association with Roumania's friend France.

It must also be added that Russia made efforts to win the friendship of Roumania. Sazonov was especially keen. A first step was the mission of the Grand Duke Nicholas to Bucarest in December 1912 with a Russian field marshal's baton for King Carol on the occasion of the twenty-fifth anniversary of the fall of Pleven. During the diplomatic negotiations of 1913 Russia had shown marked consideration to Roumanian wishes. A further step was the visit of Nicholas II in his yacht to Constantsa on 1st June 1914. He was accompanied by Sazonov, who proceeded to Bucarest and to the royal palace of Sinaia. On 3rd June Sazonov went for a motor ride with the Roumanian Premier Brătianu from Sinaia across the Hungarian frontier into Transylvania. This incident was greeted with fierce protests in the Budapest Press, and strikingly illustrated the movement of Roumania away from the German Powers.[2]

During the first six months of 1914 nothing occurred to change the basic hostility between Austria and Russia in the Balkans or to appease the national hatreds within the Habsburg Empire. Vienna still faced the same choice. Either the South Slavs must be given what they asked for, or Serbia must be destroyed. The South Slavs would certainly ask for more in 1914 than in 1900 or even in 1909, and if concessions were made to them, others—Roumanians, Italians, Czechs, Slovaks—would put forward their demands. The destruction of Serbia could have been accomplished in 1909 with fairly small risk. In 1913 it would have been more dangerous. Every year that passed, and so gave time for Russia's military recovery, increased the danger. When on 28th June 1914 the Archduke Francis Ferdinand was assassinated by a Bosnian Serb in Sarajevo,[3] Austria had an excuse for action. Her leaders decided to take it.

[1] See above, pp. 171–2.   [2] Sazonov describes his visit in *op. cit.*, pp. 118–23.
[3] For the assassination and its background, see R. W. Seton-Watson, *Sarajevo* (London, 1925).

The mass of documents published after the war makes it possible to follow almost from hour to hour the thoughts and emotions of the principle figures of European diplomacy in the fateful days between 23rd July, when the Austrian ultimatum was handed to the Serbs, and 1st August, when Germany declared war on Russia. The events have been so often and so minutely analysed that there is no purpose in repeating them here.[1] Nor is there any need to discuss the old question of "war-guilt". It is true that Austria was determined, at any cost, to smash Serbia. It is true that the pace was quickened by the Russian general mobilisation, which the Tsar and his Foreign Minister reluctantly accepted when their military advisers had convinced them that for technical reasons the partial mobilisation which they had first preferred would endanger the defence of Russia.[2] It is true that in the decision of German policy the General Staff played an important part, and that its influence was on the side of war. But war was not caused by sinister and clear-headed warmongers. There were probably few people in any of the great states of Europe who desired war, and it is unlikely that these few had much effect on events. War was the result of an insoluble crisis, which diplomacy had postponed in 1909 and 1913 and could postpone no longer.

Austrian and Russian ambitions in the Balkans were not compatible. Both governments were driven onwards by the ever more acute national and social problems within their own borders. The forces of national and social revolution, the result of the impact of the West on the semi-medieval domains of Romanov, Habsburg and Ottoman, could not be understood, still less controlled, by Francis Joseph and Nicholas II, by Berchtold or Sazonov. And weak and ignorant though these men may sometimes seem, it is hard to imagine that others in their place would have done much better.

It is often pointed out that Germany, isolated by the mistakes of the preceding decade, had no ally left but Austria, and so was obliged to support her. The opposite is also true. If Austria failed in this crisis, when the prestige of her imperial house was directly affected, to behave as a Great Power, she might well fear that Germany would no longer regard her as *bündnisfähig* (worth having as an ally), and would come to terms with Russia at her expense. If

---

[1] Apart from the mass of "coloured books" and the collections of British, French, German, Austrian and Russian documents, mention should be made of Schmitt, *The Coming of the War* (New York, 1930); Renouvin, *Les causes immédiates de la guerre* (Paris, 1925); Albertini, *Le origini della guerra del 1914* (Milano, 1942), (3 vols.).

[2] See M. T. Florinsky, "The Russian Mobilisation of 1914," *Political Science Quarterly*, Vol. XLII, June 1927.

Germany needed her, she also needed Germany. Her need for Germany was an inducement to go ahead against Serbia, come what might. To a lesser extent the same is true of the Franco-Russian alliance. The Balkans were not of direct interest to France, but if Russia regarded them as vital, she must support her ally. To lose Russia would put France in future at the mercy of Germany, and Germany's attitude to her since 1905 had given her no ground to expect friendly treatment from that quarter. For Russia, a third surrender in the Balkans, following those of 1909 and 1912, would have been a fatal blow to prestige. It might even—though this is less likely—have raised doubts in Paris as to whether Russia was worth having as an ally, whether France should not try to fall back on her friendship with Britain, and keep out of Continental affairs. Here too the question of *Bündnisfähigkeit* played its part. As for Britain, it was a question of whether to allow the Power which had emerged as her most dangerous rival to dominate the Continent in general and the Low Countries in particular. The Anglo-German naval rivalry of the preceding decade did not cause the war: it ensured that when war had broken out, Britain would be on the side of Germany's enemies.

So Europe entered the catastrophe from which she has not yet recovered, and from which the greatest sufferer has been the Russian people.

EPILOGUE

THE respite of the Stolypin regime was too short to save Imperial Russia. The war smashed it to pieces. The story of collapse, revolution and civil war has often been told, and the regime which emerged from the ruins provides a quite different subject of study. All that will here be attempted is to relate those events and that regime to the period that has formed the subject of this volume; to show very briefly what problems the new regime inherited from the old and how it approached them; and to draw some conclusions from the history of the last decades of Imperial Russia which may be relevant to other periods and other lands.

Though the military reforms of 1909–14 had made the Russian army a more formidable force than it had been during the war with Japan, they had not raised it to the standard of the German army. This indeed was more than any purely military reformer could have achieved, for Russia's military weaknesses had political, social and cultural causes with which no War Minister or General Staff could deal. The highest commanders in the Russian army were not impressive, and the manpower at all levels was of primitive quality, possessing, it is true, the virtues of the primitive—courage and endurance. Russia's greatest strength, her numbers, was wastefully used by her leaders. In the Russian offensives great masses of soldiers were hurled against strong enemy positions. That Russian losses were so greatly in excess of those on the Western Front was at least largely due to the commanders' recklessness with human lives. It was also due to poor supplies of arms and munitions, to poor communications and to poor hospital services. The substantial improvement in supplies and medical care which was achieved by 1916—when the effects of the earlier massacres on military and civilian morale had already made themselves felt—was largely due to the energy of unofficial patriotic bodies. The most important of these were the Red Cross organised by the zemstvos and the city councils ("Zemgor") and the War Industries Committee organised by the congress of industrialists, which also contained delegates elected by the workers. Both these bodies were regarded with suspicion by the authorities, and their activities hampered, though the army welcomed their co-operation. Despite all defects and difficulties, the Russian army fought heroically, and made a decisive contribution to the course of the war. The Russian offensive in East Prussia at the end of August 1914, though defeated by the Germans at Tannenberg, caused German forces to be removed from the Western Front and so made possible the Battle of the Marne. In the autumn of 1914 the Russian offensive into Galicia was a notable victory over the Austrians. In the summer of 1915 the Russians were faced with a great German and Austrian offensive. Even the large surrender of territory and immense loss of lives which this caused did not break them. In the spring of 1916 they undertook a costly but unsuccessful attack near Vilna, and in the summer Brusilov's brilliant offensive gained considerable territory in Galicia. Throughout 1917 the Russian army was still in the field. The vast efforts of the Russians had made it possible for the French to hold out in the West, for Britain to create and to put in the field a great army, and for the Western Powers, with American help, ultimately to defeat Germany. Even in so brief a summary as this it is necessary to mention these things, for both civil and military historians, both in the West and even in Russia after 1918 showed an astonishing ignorance of Russia's contribution to the Allied war effort, an ignorance which cost the West dear in 1939–40 and cost the Russian people dearer still in 1941–4.

The Russian authorities completely failed to understand the need for economic planning of the war. At first the economic effects were not unfavourable. Heavy industry profited from increased demand, and workers employed in it did well. The army's great demand for food benefited the farmers, and gave them an alternative market to that which they had lost through the interruption of exports of grain by Turkey's entry into the war. Sons of poor peasant or worker families were better fed in the army than at home. But before long shortages became serious. Workers were mobilised without regard to the best use of their labour. Industries not working directly for the war effort were ruined. Most consumer goods became very scarce. Mobilisation of agricultural labourers disorganised the big landed estates, which in normal times produced the best crops. The peasant smallholdings were less adversely affected by mobilisation, since there had long been a large surplus of labour in peasant agriculture. But as it became ever more difficult to buy anything with the money paid to them, the peasants lost much of their incentive to produce. Thus the total output of Russian agriculture declined though total consumption, owing to the needs of the army, was rising. By the autumn of 1916 the food supply in the main cities had become dangerously small.

More important even than military and economic deficiencies was the lack of competent political leadership. The feeble Goremykin would not stand up to the Empress and the Rasputin clique.[1] When in August 1915 Nicholas II himself assumed the supreme command of the armed forces, government in Petrograd[2] fell completely into the clique's hands. Sturmer, appointed Premier in February 1916, and Protopopov, appointed Minister of Interior in September 1916, were creatures of "Our Friend". Loyal advice from friends and moderate criticism in the Duma were alike regarded by the Empress as sedition. The belief spread—though there is no solid evidence to support it—that the Empress and Rasputin were betraying the country to the Germans. The assassination of Rasputin on 17th/30th December 1916 came too late.

In the summer of 1915 there was formed in the Duma a Progressive Block, consisting of members of the Cadet and Octobrist parties together with some smaller groups of the moderate Left and Right. The Block asked for various political and civil liberties, and for a government "with the confidence of the nation". During 1916 the attacks of its spokesmen, especially of the Cadet leader Milyukov, on the policy of the government and the "dark forces" behind it, became extremely bitter. On 25th February/10th March 1917 the Tsar decided to prorogue the Duma. The Progressive Block members appointed a permanent committee, which remained in the Taurid Palace. On the morning of 27th February/12th March the troops in the capital began to come over to its side. The revolution had come. On 2nd/15th March a Provisional Government was formed, mainly of Octobrists and Cadets, with Prince Lvov as Premier. The same day the Tsar abdicated, and when his brother Michael refused the Crown, Russia became in effect a republic.[3]

The main problem before the Provisional Government was the question of war or peace. The people were utterly sick of the slaughter. The new leaders knew this, and on the whole shared its feeling. But they also knew that defeat and occupation by the

---

[1] The best work in English on the Court and Rasputin in the war years is Pares, *Fall of the Russian Monarchy*. An excellent treatment of the political and economic situation up to the collapse is M. T. Florinsky, *The End of the Russian Empire* (Yale, 1931).

[2] The name of the capital had been officially changed, on outbreak of war with the German Powers, from the German-sounding Petersburg to the "pure Slav" Petrograd.

[3] The republic was formally proclaimed in the autumn by Kerenski's goverment.

EPILOGUE 363

German army would be a deadly blow to the revolution. Though they earned much abuse for their attempt to continue to defend Russia—abuse which has been accepted as justified by many writers in the West who are far from followers of the Bolsheviks—it does not seem, after thirty years, that there was anything ridiculous or ignoble about their attitude. As long as the government was dominated by the bourgeois parties, the socialists in opposition pressed, with varying degrees of urgency, for peace. On 6th/18th May a new government was formed. Milyukov and Guchkov, who had held the posts of Foreign Affairs and War in the first government, and had made themselves unpopular with the masses by their insistence that Russia would fulfil her obligations to her allies, were left out of the second, in which the Socialist Revolutionaries and Mensheviks were represented. A Socialist Revolutionary lawyer, Alexander Kerenski, became Minister of War. But the new government also wished to continue the defence of Russia. Its attempts to win the confidence of the troops by "democratising" the army contributed to the further disintegration of discipline. But by this time morale was so low, and defeatist propaganda so active, that it is doubtful whether much could have been done.[1] In July a last Russian offensive was attempted in Galicia. After a few days of success it collapsed when whole units began to abandon their positions.

The two other most important problems—the land and the nationalities—depended on the problem of peace and war. Even the Octobrists were prepared to make considerable concessions to the nationalities and to make a redistribution of land, while the parties to their left supported very radical programmes. But as long as Russia was defending herself against the German armies it was not felt possible to carry out land reform or to introduce autonomy, let alone a federal relationship, for the non-Russians. Thus the Cadets and even the moderate Socialists, all of whom insisted that the land and nationalities' questions must be decided by the Constituent Assembly, which was due to meet in the autumn, appeared to the masses to be postponing indefinitely the changes which their propaganda had long promised them.

The attitude of the Marxist parties was at first far from clear.

---

[1] The question whether the Russian army was destroyed by the blows it had suffered before the Revolution, or by the defeatist propaganda of agitators sent to the Front by the Soviet of Workers' and Soldiers' Deputies, is the central controversy in the history of the Russian Revolution. Both factors clearly played their part. But this is no place, nor do I feel myself qualified, to assess their relative importance. The reader is warned, that the question is still, after 35 years, an open one.

A part of the Mensheviks supported national defence, and so also the postponement of land reform and self-determination of the nationalities. Their left wing however wished for immediate peace. The Bolsheviks too were divided. Of the three main Bolshevik leaders who returned from Siberia at the end of March, Kamenev supported national defence, while Stalin and Muranov, though not going so far as this, at least urged qualified support to the provisional government. On 3rd/16th April 1917 Lenin arrived in Petrograd from Sweden, having crossed Germany from Switzerland with the consent of the German General Staff. He at once came out against the provisional government, and in the following months urged immediate peace, immediate land reform, and immediate self-determination for the nationalities. He accused the other parties, who wished to postpone reforms and continue defence, of deliberate betrayal. Lenin cared nothing for the defence of Russia, and nothing for Russia's allies. He completely discounted the threat of the German army to the Russian revolution, as he expected "the German workers" to save Russia by making a revolution against their own leaders—a revolution which, as Germany was a more advanced country, would be a more important victory for international socialism than the revolution in Russia. Caring nothing for defence, Lenin was able to promise the Russian masses at once everything for which the other parties asked them patiently to wait. The uninhibited demagogy of the Bolsheviks brought them quick results.

In his campaign Lenin gave great importance to the Soviets of Workers' and Soldiers' Deputies. These, the successors of the Soviets of 1905, were spontaneous and representative bodies, which truly reflected the feelings of the Russian city workers and of at least a part of the army. In 1905 Lenin had paid little attention to the Soviets. In the last weeks of his exile in Switzerland, however, he had been impressed by the coexistence of two authorities in Petrograd—the bourgeois Provisional Government and the proletarian Soviets. In the Soviets Lenin now professed to see a new form of government which would make possible the immediate transition from the bourgeois revolution initiated by the overthrow of Tsardom, to a socialist revolution. The Provisional Government, he argued, was the organ of the bourgeois revolution, while the soviets were organs of the socialist revolution. The "Dual Power" could not last: one or the other must triumph. Lenin believed that the Soviets could triumph, and the socialist revolution be achieved. The gap between the two revolutions, which had formed so important a subject in Marxist discussions before 1917, and about which Lenin had formulated his ideas in his *Two Tactics* in 1905,[1] was to be reduced to a few months.

In April 1917 the Bolsheviks were not only unrepresented in the government, but were also in a minority in the Soviets. The enthusiasm of Lenin for the Soviets, and his insistence that they were a political form superior to the parliamentary, may at first seem curiously doctrinaire. But Lenin had a good practical reason for his view. The essential feature of the Soviets was that they represented the primitive, politically inexperienced masses. In the Petrograd Soviet, it is true, and still more in the Central Executive Committee elected by the All-Russian Congress of Soviets, the best known socialist leaders of Russia—such as the Socialist Revolutionaries Gotz and Chernov and the Social Democrats Martov, Dan, Chheidze and Tseretelli—played an important part. But the mass of members even of these high organs, and much more in the local Soviets, were persons of no fixed programme, easily swayed by the events of the moment and by the most attractive of the slogans put before them. In any parliament, the parties would be represented by experienced politicians, already possessing clearly defined political convictions. If the Bolsheviks took part in parliamentary politics, they would have to bargain and make concessions to other parties. But if they could capture the Soviets, they would make themselves the leaders of the masses. Lenin's plan was a partnership between the politically trained and well-disciplined Bolsheviks and the politically ignorant and gullible masses. This partnership would give the Bolsheviks a monopoly of political leadership. The other parties might have brilliant and civilised leaders, but their mass support would be undermined. In a parliament composed of educated men they would prevail, therefore this forum must be denied them. In the Soviets, if Bolshevik infiltration were successful, they would be powerless.

The method by which Lenin set out to capture the Soviets was uninhibited demagogy. He was greatly helped by the Kornilov rebellion of September, which enabled the Bolsheviks to appear as the most resolute defenders of the revolution. He was also greatly helped by the mistaken democratic loyalty of the Socialist

---

[1] See above, p. ooo. Probably the best single work on the whole period of revolution and civil war is W. H. Chamberlin, *The Russian Revolution* (London, 1935). Two invaluable works in Russian on the period from March to November are P. N. Milyukov *Istoriya vtoroy russkoy revolyutsii* (Sofia 1921) and N. Suhanov, *Zapiski o revolyutsii* (Moscow 1923).

Revolutionaries and Menshevik leaders. Ever suspicious of every word or action by "bourgeois" politicians or army generals, they showed extraordinary tolerance to the Bolsheviks. Regarding Lenin as essentially "one of themselves", a good revolutionary even if a misguided one, they were unable to take resolute repressive action against him. Kornilov was denied, Lenin granted, the benefit of every possible doubt. After the "July days" Lenin was allowed to escape, In September not only was Kornilov treated as an enemy before he began to revolt, but after his defeat the General Staff was drastically purged, thus depriving the army of what little leadership it still possessed.

But Lenin had no scruples of loyalty towards his socialist rivals. All who did not take orders from him were his enemies, and were to be treated as such. By the end of September the Bolsheviks had won a majority in the Soviets of Petrograd and Moscow, and during October they won over the troops in the capital. On 25th October/7th November 1917 the Bolsheviks seized power and a new government was formed with Lenin as Premier.[1] There followed the forcible dissolution in January 1918 of the Constituent Assembly (in which out of about 707 seats the Bolsheviks had 175 and the Socialist Revolutionaries 410); the signature of a separate peace with Germany at Brest-Litovsk in March 1918; the loss of Poland, Finland and the Baltic States; and more than two years of civil war, accompanied by atrocities on both sides, and enormous casualties from battle, disease and famine. By the end of 1920 the Bolsheviks were supreme but Russia was prostrate.

. . . . .

Before 1917 Russian Marxists, in so far as they had envisaged the possibility of a socialist revolution in Russia, had agreed that it would be doomed to failure unless socialist revolutions also took place in advanced industrial countries. Lenin himself expected a revolution in Germany. But he was disappointed. He was saved from the vengeance of William II and Ludendorff not by the German proletariat but by Marshal Foch.[2] When the civil war was over, though the Bolsheviks were in power in Russia, there were no socialist revolutions in industrial Europe. The Bolshevik

[1] For the political action of the Bolsheviks in the first years of power, see the brilliant and independent work of E. H. Carr, *The Bolshevik Revolution* (Macmillan, 1950).
[2] The help which—of course unintentionally—the Western Powers thus rendered to the Bolsheviks completely dwarfs the small-scale and unimportant activity of the "interventionist" Western forces which spent a short time on Russian soil during the civil war.

invasion of Poland, the armed struggle of the Finnish workers, the Communist revolution in Hungary in 1919, and the pathetic attempts at armed rising by Communists in Germany between 1919 and 1923 and in Bulgaria in 1923 were all defeated. What then was to happen in Russia? Were the Russian workers to wait, before they could build socialism, for the victory of incompetent and probably cowardly comrades in the West?

An answer to this question gratifying to the pride of Russian Bolsheviks was provided by Stalin when he launched the slogan "Socialism in one country". In the past the belief of the Bolshevik leaders that socialism could not exist in Russia if there were no socialist revolutions in Europe had been based on their conviction that Russia was economically too backward to build a socialist economy. It was not only the threat of armed attack by the "capitalist world", but still more the internal economic weakness of the country which would doom Russian socialism to collapse unless it had victorious allies in more advanced countries. Stalin however stressed the special features of Russia which were favourable to her development—her vastness, the great numbers of her people and the great wealth of her soil and subsoil. If these could be effectively exploited, Russia could build a great industry which would form the foundation of an advanced socialist economy. Industrialisation in other countries had required three factors—resources, manpower and skill. The first two Russia had in abundance, only the third was inadequate. For it a substitute must be found. Stalin's substitute was force. The men and the materials must be fused together by force. Managers and workers must be given production targets and ordered to achieve them. If they failed, examples must be made. The essential points of the new policy were mass direction of labour, exceptional powers for the security police, and sabotage trials for the unsuccessful manager.

When Stalin's policy was launched, Russian agriculture was based on small peasant holdings. Having received the land during the revolution, and having been freed in 1921, under the New Economic Policy (N.E.P.), from most of the burdens imposed while the civil war was on, the Russian peasants had been able to do what for most of them had been impossible under the old regime— eat enough. It was no longer possible to export the vast amounts of grain which in imperial days had brought profits to big landlords, raw materials to industrialists and empty bellies to peasants. What had been exported was now eaten. The peasants were not inclined to work harder in order to supply the towns with food. There were however important differences among the peasants. The class differentiation anticipated by Lenin was in fact taking place. Some peasants (*kulaks*) were growing wealthy. They had enough land and animals, employed labour, and sold their surplus to the towns. Others were poor, had little land and lived miserably. Rural over-population, the basic illness of Russian society in the last decades of the empire, could not be legislated out of existence.

The new policy of rapid industrialisation would greatly increase the number of those who would work outside agriculture—not only in factories but also in the many public-works schemes essential to the new plans. These would have to be fed by the peasants. The number would increase the more rapidly because, with the great scarcity of skilled labour and machinery, the desired aims could only be achieved by an unusually large number of unskilled labourers. What could be done by one skilled man with the right equipment might have to be done by two, or five, or ten unskilled men with their bare hands. Thus the food supply would become an acute problem. On the other hand the existence of a surplus of labour in the over-populated villages would be an advantage. It was from this source that the new labour army must be recruited. It was necessary however to create a centralised bureaucracy which would control the peasants, and obtain from them the required amounts of food and the required numbers of industrial recruits. This bureaucracy was the collective farm. Its first task was to ensure that the towns did not go short of food or workers. If someone had to starve in consequence it must be the peasant. Its second task was to raise the output of agriculture, so that ultimately there would be enough to eat for all.

The collectivisation of agriculture and the industrial Five Year Plans, whose cost in human wastage and suffering this is no place to discuss, created a new regime in Russia, as different from the regime at the death of Lenin as the latter had been from the regime of Stolypin. Lenin's Bolshevik party, renamed Communist Party in 1918, strictly disciplined and much more thoroughly controlled from above than it had been in its earlier years, controlled the political, industrial and agricultural machines. It controlled the political machine through the party members holding key positions in central and local government institutions, in the judiciary, in the army and in the police. It controlled the industrial machine through the party members holding key positions in factory managements and in the hierarchy of trade unions, whose function was no longer to defend the workers against the boss but to ensure obedience by the workers to the employer-state and to extract the maximum labour from them. It controlled the agricultural machine through the party members who served as chairmen or secretaries of the managing committees of collective farms or in the "machine tractor stations" which ploughed the farms' lands for them. Of these three pyramids of command by the Communist Party, the last was certainly the least efficient. In the years after the Second World War there were far-reaching re-organisations of Soviet agriculture, whose results are as yet uncertain. But the political, social and economic pattern was clear enough.

The pattern was in fact repeated, with some variations, in the countries which were bolshevised after the Second World War. The technique of infiltrating local popular organs of government, of the partnership between disciplined Bolshevik conspirators and inexperienced masses, first adopted by Lenin in 1917, was closely copied elsewhere. It was successful in Yugoslavia, Albania and China, and temporarily successful in Greece and Indo-China. Elements of the technique could be observed in Communist tactics in the other countries of Eastern Europe in 1944–7, but their job was made so much easier for them by the presence of the "liberating" Soviet army that comparison is not fair.[1] Once power was monopolised by Communists, the pattern of the Stalinist stage of revolution was quickly adopted. By the end of 1950 the political and industrial pyramids were firmly established in the European "popular democracies", and the agricultural pyramid was being constructed. In China only the political pyramid had been built, but there seemed little doubt that the other two were being planned.

The Soviet leaders, it was clear from the statements of their authorised spokesmen, considered that they had found a scientific formula for all political, social, and economic problems. With minor variations, Stalin's socialism-in-one-country was exportable and applicable to any country in the world. Only the Soviet Union and its satellites had created socialism. Nothing created by persons independent of the Soviet Union could ever be called socialism. World revolution was still both desirable and necessary. Until it was achieved there could be no security for the socialist fatherland, surrounded by "capitalist encirclement". But both the reason for, and the content of, "world revolution" had now changed

---

[1] The process is described in some detail in my book, *The East European Revolution* (Methuen, 1950).

Trotski had believed the threat to the Soviet Union, should world revolution not take place, to be largely internal, arising from Russia's basic economic weakness: Stalin now claimed that Russia possessed the strongest and soundest social and economic system in the world, and was threatened only from without. Trotski had imagined world revolution as the result of victorious revolutions in other countries: Stalin imagined it as the extension of the Soviet system to other countries with or without or against their peoples' wishes.

This attitude to the rest of the world, this belief in the superiority of Russian institutions and methods, recalls views which we have encountered earlier in this volume. It is of course ridiculous to say, as some Western popular writers have sometimes said, that the Stalinists are Slavophiles. It is, however, true that both Slavophiles and Stalinists belong to a tradition of opposition to Western Europe and belief in the superior ability of Russia to solve the great problems of the human race. The controversy on the relationship between Russia and the West has four times split Russian political thought since the mid-nineteenth century. The first stage of the split was between Slavophiles and Westernisers, the second between Populists and Marxists, the third between Bolsheviks and Mensheviks, and the fourth between Stalinists and Trotskists.

.   .   .   .   .

The Soviet regime[1] is obviously very different from the regime of Imperial Russia, but the simple identification of the former with "Progress" and the latter with "Reaction" is not tenable.

To the credit of the Soviet regime must certainly be placed a sense of purpose. The leaders have clear aims for the future of Russia, and have made great efforts by a skilful and omnipresent propaganda to enthuse the people with these aims. How successful they have been can hardly be ascertained. But there is no doubt of the contrast with the drift and pessimism of Imperial Russia in its last years. To the new regime's credit must also be placed the thousands of new factories and other material enterprises. Huge new mining and manufacturing centres have been created in the

[1] The Soviets in fact lost all significance soon after the Bolshevik victory. Having been used, for the tactical reasons described above, to get power for the Bolsheviks, they were then made into docile servants of the Bolshevik party. The supposed importance of the Soviets is a myth, which the Bolshevik rulers have found it convenient to perpetuate. Instead of "Soviet regime" one should say "Bolshevik regime". The phrase "Soviet regime" has however become universal, and I have therefore used it here.

Urals, in Siberia and in Central Asia, whose resources were barely touched under the Tsars. It is however only fair to add that their construction would have been much harder if the foundations of a Russian industry and of a Russian skilled working class had not been laid in the earlier period, with the help of the loans, investments and engineers from the West which Bolshevik propaganda delights to revile.

The "solution" by the Bolsheviks of the overpopulation problem must be accepted with some reserve. The surplus was to a very large extent removed by starvation of millions resulting from official policy. To massacre one's subjects is a course open to any absolute ruler, but one which, until the mid-twentieth century was not regarded as a mark of statesmanship. Moreover it is likely that concealed overpopulation and unemployment persist in the enormously inflated ranks of the many parallel bureaucracies— party, trade union, police, machine-tractor-station—and in the huge numbers of clerks, of whom the book-keepers in collective farms are the largest single category. Soviet statistics do not however make possible a definite answer to this question.

Comparisons of standards of living are notoriously difficult. It is clear that there are millions in the Soviet Union who enjoy better material conditions that they or their parents had in Imperial days. Many skilled workers, technicians and bureaucrats—of State, party or trade union—are to-day relatively prosperous. So are the leading officials of many collective farms and machine-tractor stations, at least in regions of fertile soil and within reach of a large urban market. Millions of others—not "just a few ex-bourgeois"—now fare incomparably worse that they did. But to compare the material lot of the scores of millions of unskilled workers and peasants in remoter areas with that of their predecessors in the age of Stolypin, a greater volume of reliable evidence would be needed than is at present available. And material conditions in any case no more make the whole of the life of a worker or peasant in Russia than in Western Europe.

In political freedom there has been retrogression. The Soviet regime was imposed, and is maintained, by force and terror. The comfortable dogma that the Russian people neither understands nor desires representative institutions, is not justified by the election campaigns of 1906, 1907 or 1917, in which not only townsmen but also peasants clearly showed the desire and ability to choose who should represent them. Still more groundless is the assertion that the Russian people does not value personal liberty. Of this there has of course been far less under the Soviet than the Imperial regime. The construction of new industries and the impressive reduction of rural unemployment have been achieved by a regimentation of labour such as neither Pleve nor Stolypin in their most ruthless moments could have conceived. The hardships suffered by colonists in Siberia before 1914, for whom the authorities who had encouraged emigration had failed to provide accommodation, were far surpassed by the horrors of housing conditions in the new industrial centres of the Soviet Union. The prisons and penal labour camps hold scores of times more people than were imprisoned or exiled under the Tsar, and their living conditions are far worse. The Imperial Ohranka was a children's party compared to the Cheka-M.V.D.-M.G.B. The best historical parallel to the latter is the Oprichnina of Ivan the Terrible, which directly ruled large territories handed to it by its master. But with its private army, private aerodromes, private railways, private factories, vast "special areas" and hosts of penal labour the modern Oprichnina dwarfs the old.

The Soviet censorship puts its Imperial predecessor to shame. Control of Press, radio, book publication, and—by no means least—the public libraries in which works published before 1917 are still available, efficiently shackles the minds of young and old. It is said that Pleve once remarked to N. K. Mihailovski, "Why do you want freedom of the Press when even without it you are such a master of saying between the lines all that you wish to say?"[1] Such a conversation would be meaningless in the Soviet Union. The Bolshevik leaders, having made skilful use of all loopholes in the old censorship, know well how to stop such loopholes in their own. They also pay great attention to literature, of whose vital role under the old regime, as a means of spreading a revolutionary frame of mind, they are well aware. To-day it is not enough to refrain from criticising the regime: the writer or artist must devote himself to its praise. He receives not only negative but also positive directives from the Agitprop department of the party. This is a perversion, but a recognisable perversion, of the revolutionary utilitarian puritanism of Dobrolyubov and Pisarev. The belief that literature and art must be judged by their utility to the revolution, and the dogma that science is always superior to the humanities, have, as we have seen, dominated Russian intellectual life from the seventies onwards. In a free atmosphere they would have been killed by ridicule: they were saved by the educational policy of

[1] Gardenin (Chernov), *op. cit.*, p. 49.

Dmitri Tolstoy and the obscurantism of Pobedonostsev. Only after 1906 did they begin to lose their hold on the intelligentsia. The failure of the "Liberation Movement" caused much heart-searching, and the somewhat better conditions of work for intellectuals reduced the direct incentive to revolutionary action. The writers of the last years before 1914 were less interested in "social themes" Philosophy began to be regarded as a subject in itself, rather than an instrument of political propaganda. The former Marxist intellectuals Berdyaev and Bulgakov were converted to Orthodoxy, the latter becoming a priest. The influence of Leo Tolstoy spread far beyond the circle of his own religious sect. Poets and novelists were seeking new values and new directions. For all its extravagance and decadence, it was a healthy reaction against the ealier dogma. But the war and the revolution arrested the process. "Socialist realism" became in the age of Stalin the compulsory outlook for Soviet writers. The difference between the "socialist realism" of Stalin and of Dobrolyubov is that the latter was intended to undermine, while the former is designed to enforce autocracy. The official ideologists, led until recently by the late A. A. Zhdanov, are thus in one sense heirs to Dobrolyubov but in another sense also heirs to Pobedonostsev.[1]

The effects of Bolshevik anti-religious policy are extremely difficult to judge. The revival of the Church during the Second World War seems to bear the marks of a new form of Zubatovism, an attempt by the M.V.D. to canalise discontent in harmless channels. Religious influence may yet be strong among the peasants. But there are certainly millions from whom it has been entirely removed. This is clear from the evidence of those who have been in contact with the Soviet armies in Europe. The removal of the influence of the Church, which for all its faults did represent a certain freely accepted moral discipline, explains to some extent why the Soviet troops in Central Europe in 1944-5 behaved so immeasurably worse than the Russian troops in Galicia in 1914-16. But to form an opinion of the religious life of the Russian people, as of its material standard of living, far more evidence is needed.

[1] Berdyaev and Bulgakov were responsible for an important collection of essays entitled *Vyehi* (*Landmarks*) (SPB, 1909). Struve was also a contributor. This attack on the whole outlook of the intelligentsia of the preceding decades provoked fierce replies from the revolutionaries, among them from Lenin. For a general survey of the literary trends of the last years before the Revolution, see D. S. Mirski, *A History of Russian Literature* (revised and abridged edition, London ,1949). The speeches of the late A. A. Zhdanov of 1947-8 have been published in English under the title, *On Literature, Music and Philosophy*, by Lawrence and Wishart (London, 1950).

The Bolsheviks are proud of their treatment of the nationalities. Lenin himself paid great attention to the theory of national self-determination. The Austrian Marxist leaders Otto Bauer and Karl Renner had advocated national cultural autonomy on a personal basis. Lenin considered this both too much and too little. He considered that the Russian socialist republic must be a centralised state, and the Russian party of the proletariat a single centralised party for the whole state. But any nationality that did not wish to remain in the Russian state must be free to secede and form its own state, within which again the party of the proletariat would be centralised. After 1917 there was much discussion as to the application of these principles. Distinctions were made between national movements in colonial and semi-colonial countries; in backward European countries; and in advanced European countries. The first were allies of the proletarian revolution, the second might be made into allies, the third were, owing to the class structure of advanced European countries, essentially bourgeois, and therefore reactionary. But there remained a difficult question. When the claim for self-determination was put forward by non-Marxists who were engaged in struggle with their own proletariat, which side should the Bolsheviks support? To whom should they recognise the right of self-determination? At the third congress of the Soviets in 1918 Stalin, who since his theoritical articles of 1913 had become the party expert on the question, declared that one must "interpret the principle of self-determination as a right not of the bourgeoisie but of the working masses of a given nation". Lenin however disapproved of this view, and insisted that, even at the risk of giving power to non-Russian bourgeois nationalists, the Russian proletariat must show itself innocent of the charge of "Great Russian chauvinism masked under the name of Communism". The official decision of the party in 1919 was a vaguely-worded compromise, capable of interpretation according to circumstances: "On the question of who is to express the nation's will to secede, the Russian Communist Party adopts the class-historical viewpoint, taking into consideration the stage of historical development of the given nation, whether it is evolving from medievalism to bourgeois democracy or from bourgeois democracy to Soviet or proletarian democracy."

These theoretical controversies are interesting, but they should not be given too much importance.[1] The fate of the non-Russian

[1] The brilliant analysis of Bolshevik nationalities' policy in E. H. Carr, *op. cit.*, errs perhaps in taking this policy too much according to the theories, and in underestimating the purely opportunist element.

peoples of the empire between 1917 and 1921 was decided not by such abstract criteria but by blood and iron. The Poles, Finns and Balts established their independence because their greogaphical position and the support of the Great Powers made it possible. The Bolsheviks attempted in 1920 to instal in Białystok a Polish Communist government, led by Dzierżinski and Feliks Kon. They were defeated by Piłsudski: it was not until 1944 that the Bierut government could be installed in Lublin. The Bolsheviks also made a treaty with a Finnish Workers' Socialist Government in 1918, but this government was defeated, with German help, by the former Russian Imperial General Mannerheim. Their second attempt in Finland, the treaty signed with the puppet government of Kuusinen in 1939, was defeated by the same general. The Ukrainians and White Russians were less successful in their attempts to achieve independence. They were partitioned between the Soviet Union and Piłsudski's Poland. In the Caucasus three independent republics of Armenia, Azerbaidjan and Georgia existed for a time. But placed between the Bolsheviks and a hostile Turkey and abandoned by the Western Powers, they fell in turn before Soviet force. The Menshevik regime in Georgia, strongly based on popular support of twenty years' standing, was simply conquered in February 1921. The efforts of the Tatars to establish some sort of Volga-Ural state were crushed by both the Russian Whites and the Bolsheviks. In Central Asia the backward, disunited and isolated Turkish, Iranian and Mongol tribes were brought under control by 1922. In the Far East a serious threat appeared in the Japanese army, but diplomatic pressure from the United States forced it to retire.

The Soviet Union was thus the old Russia without Finland, the Baltic provinces, Poland and a part of the Ukrainian and White Russian borderlands. It was reorganised in a number of constituent Soviet republics, some of which in turn contained "autonomous republics", "autonomous regions" and "autonomous provinces". In all these various territorial units, the languages of the inhabitants may be freely used, and jobs are on the whole given to local people. Systematic discrimination on grounds of national origin has been removed.[1] This linguistic toleration is combined

---

[1] Even this can be said only with reserve. Russians play a disproportionate role in the Ukrainian SSR, and in the Central Asian SSR's the preponderance of Slav names among the holders of responsible administrative posts is striking. Since the Second World War there have been such striking acts of discrimination as the deportation of the Crimean Tatars and the North Caucasian Ingush, and the increasing russification of Esthonia and Latvia.

with the most rigid centralism in political, economic and cultural life. The Votyak Communist organisations, like the Russian, are controlled by the Central Committee in Moscow. Those books or articles which the Soviet censor considers suitable for the Soviet public, may be published in Votyak as well as in Russian. There are no Votyaks or Russians, but Votyak-speaking and Russian-speaking Soviet citizens. This solution too is more ingenious and more ruthless than any which Pleve or Stolypin could have devised.

.   .   .   .   .

Is Russia a part of Europe? This controversy, beloved especially of Russian and Polish historians, embraces the whole of Russia's history.[1] It exceeds the scope of the present work. Within the period with which this work has been concerned, Russia certainly appeared a European state. For a thousand years the Russians had been bound to Europe by the two powerful bonds of religion and language. Since the eighteenth century, the political administration and economy of Russia grew ever nearer to those of European countries. If there were features of Russian life that seemed un-European, there was little that suggested Asia. The word "Asiatic" should not be used as a term of abuse. It is not a pejorative but a descriptive adjective, and it is one which during this period does not describe Russia.

Russia during these decades was a part of Europe, but a backward part. In Russia different Europes coexisted. The principle of autocracy, which formed in theory the whole, and in practice a large part, of the foundation of policy, derived from the Europe of Byzantium. The organisation of peasant society owed something to feudal Europe. The methods, procedure and hierarchy of the administration came from the Europe of enlightened despotism.[2] The economy was transforming itself into a nineteenth-century capitalist economy. Cultural life, at its highest level, was that of twentieth-century Europe and America.

In Russia the sixteenth, eighteenth and twentieth centuries lived side by side. But this phenomenon was not specifically Russian. In Poland, Hungary and the Balkans the educated class and the masses belonged to different centuries. In North America and north-western Europe, though differences in wealth created grave

---

[1] Recent works which discuss this issue are O. Halecki, *The Limits and Divisions of European History* (Sheed and Ward, 1950); G. de Reynold, *Le monde russe* (Paris, 1950); and W. Weidle, *La Russie, absente et présente* (Paris, 1949).

[2] On this point see Sumner, "Russia and Europe," *Oxford Slavonic Papers*, Vol. II, June 1951.

problems, everyone lived in the same century. But south of the Pyrenees and the Apennines, and east of Elbe, March and Leitha (if not already further to north and west), the gap of centuries between the classes grew wider. Thus Poland was "less Western" than Germany, Russia than Poland. To draw a line at Poland's eastern frontier—or perhaps a little further east, in order to include all that part of the Ukraine where Polish influence was once strong —and then declare that all to its west is completely Europe, and all to its east completely outside Europe, is gratifying to Polish national feeling, but is both unhistorical and meaningless. To declare that all to the west of such a line belonged, in the period under discussion, to twentieth-century Europe, and that all to its east lay outside, at least means something, but is still not true. The gap between the centuries existed far to the west and south-west of Russia's frontiers, though in most places it was not so wide as in Russia.

Though during our period this gap was wide in Russia, the unmistakable trend of the period was to narrow it. Industry, as we have seen, had made great strides. It had taken advantage of the technical experience of Western countries. The best Russian factories could stand comparison with modern enterprises in the United States, Germany or Britain. The business class by 1914 was an important factor in Russian life. It included modern-minded industrialists, traders and bankers as well as the older types of merchant and usurer. Among the factory workers the skilled were becoming numerous. The professional class was larger, more influential and less dissatisfied. Education showed astonishing progress. Even the peasant masses were going to school in great numbers. Civil liberties were by no means fully secured. But the citizen's opportunity to speak and write his opinion, and to associate with others of like mind, compared not unfavourably with those enjoyed by a citizen of Western Europe forty years earlier.

These positive developments should not be underrated. Too much has been said of the "futility" of the Russian bourgeoisie, of the liberals and the democratic socialists. Their basic weaknesses— small numbers and mental isolation from the masses—were diminishing with every year that passed. Education and economic progress were drawing the masses nearer to them. The political framework of the Stolypin regime, reactionary though it was, gave them some opportunity of action. To blame them for "cowardice" and "treason" in 1905–6 is also foolish. It is true that the promises of the October Manifesto attracted the liberals. It is true that they felt that the new regime might form a basis for democratic government, and that they did not insist on the acceptance of all the demands of the workers, less than one-tenth of the population. But it is hard to see why they should have insisted, or whom they betrayed. The St. Petersburg soviet can hardly be equated with the Russian nation.

The liberals and the democratic socialists had their errors, their illusions and their timidities, like their opponents on the Right and the Left. But it is not these faults, nor even the basic social and economic structure, that explain the tragedy of Russia. The democrats were learning, and the social and economic reality was changing, but one factor remained immutable and decisive throughout this period—the dogma of autocracy. Each of the three Tsars of the period defended the dogma, and relied principally on advisers who defended it. Alexander II had the chance to lay the foundations of a parliamentary Russia in the early sixties and rejected it. Nicholas II had the chance to make a democratic system work in 1906. Conditions were less favourable than in the sixties, and more radical reforms were required. But the men of the First Duma showed no lack of intelligence, courage, patriotism or realism. Their policies were rejected by Nicholas without consideration. The Tsar would not give up the absolute powers which he was so manifestly incompetent to wield. He was resolved to maintain a regime based on police rule, the supremacy of the landowner in the village, and Great Russian chauvinism. It is probable that the refusals of 1858–61 and 1905–6 doomed Russia. But perhaps all might yet have been saved. A constitutional regime might have worked under Witte, if Nicholas had let him govern. Stolypin was a loyal and able minister, Kokovtsov had high qualities. There were other men, conservative yet enlightened, able and willing to serve. Had Nicholas looked for such men he would have found them. Instead, he surrounded himself with abject creatures, and gratified every whim of "Our Friend". First among the grave-diggers of Russia comes her last emperor.

One argument used by defenders of the old Russia, which is not convincing, is that "all would have been well but for the war". The war was not something which suddenly happened to Russia. It was a result of the policy of Russia and her two German neighbours. Certainly it is not fair to throw the whole blame for the war on Russian "Panslavist imperialism". But it is hard to see how Russian and Austrian aims—or if Austria had dissolved, Russian and German aims—could have been reconciled. Nor does it help to suggest that both Powers should simply have refrained from imperialism, should have "left the Balkans alone". The Balkans would not leave them alone. The problems of the Balkans, and the national conflicts within Austria-Hungary, were not inventions of politicians or diplomats. They were real human problems, the results of national and social tensions caused by the impact of twentieth-century Europe on more backward lands. The governments of Russia and Austria had to take note of their existence, and adopt an attitude towards them. If Russia had yielded in 1914 as she had yielded in 1912 and 1909 there would have been peace. But nothing would have remained of Russia's status as a Great Power. She would have become a vassal of Germany, and France would have been delivered into German hands. There were perhaps some Russians who would have accepted this situation, seeing in the power of the German Reich a guarantee against revolution. But it is difficult to persuade oneself that this situation would have been compatible with Russia's interests. To the Russian Foreign Office, and to those elements of public opinion on which in 1914 the Russian regime relied, it was quite unacceptable. Nor is it easy to accuse Russia's diplomats of not preparing their country for the crisis. The Franco-Russian alliance saved both Russia and France in 1914. Russia entered the war with reasonable hope of victory. Her armies did their duty honourably. With better leadership the result might have been different. In the military as in the political field Nicholas II dug Russia's grave.

The last sixty years of Imperial Russia are not only in themselves a period of great historical interest: they are significant for other countries and other periods. The pattern of this period in Russia has repeated and is repeating itself elsewhere. It is not only in Russia, and not only in Europe, that the impact of the nineteenth- or twentieth-century West on a backward country has caused distortions and frustrations, has released revolutionary forces. New countries have been drawn into the world capitalist economy, into the rapid exchange of goods and ideas. The loss of centuries has to be made up in a few years. Improved communications, public order and sanitation increase population faster than output. The impoverished masses become more impoverished. The new ways create a new intelligentsia. The shrieking contrasts between the old and the new drive a part of the intelligentsia to revolutionary ideas, and if political conditions make this necessary, to conspiratorial organisation. The force which keeps such societies together is the bureaucracy. It holds the power, the privileges and the means of repression. From it and through it come such reforms as are permitted. It is outwardly impressive. It weighs heavily on the backs of the people. But like cast iron, though heavy it is also brittle. A strong blow can shatter it to pieces. When it is destroyed there is anarchy. Then is the moment for a determined group of conspiratorial revolutionary intellectuals to seize power. Having seized power, and having created their own repressive machine, they can, like their predecessors, rule a backward people accustomed to obedience until in turn their machine is shattered by another blow from outside.

Overpopulation and mass misery, a revolutionary intelligentsia, a conspiratorial party, and anarchy following the destruction from without of a hitherto all-powerful state machine—these were the four conditions which gave Lenin his opportunity. Only the third was of his making, and without the fourth nothing could have been done. Lenin himself did not fully understand how the fourth condition operated. He wildly underestimated the threat to the revolution from a German victory, wildly overestimated the chances of a German revolution. But luck was on his side. The Western Powers saved him by beating Germany, and the Western parliamentary system which he so deeply despised saved him by forcing the politicians of victorious France and Britain to promise their electors the return of their troops to their homes. Instead of sending their armies to destroy Bolshevism they demobilised.

Lenin made some stupid mistakes, and he had luck, but he was still a great leader. History does not produce many Lenins. But the four conditions which made possible his victory, have occurred several times in recent years. They occurred in China from the time of the Japanese invasion until the triumph of the Communists. They occurred in Yugoslavia from 1941 to 1944. In both these countries the same four conditions made possible a Communist victory. In Spain from 1936 to 1938, in Greece from 1943 to 1949, and in Burma and Malaya at the end of the Second World War these conditions existed to some extent, but the forces against the revolutionaries proved too powerful.

The fourth condition—the destruction of the State machine by an external blow—has hitherto proved decisive for the victory of Communist revolutionaries. But this condition would not have decisive effect in a society in which the first conditions were not also permanently present. These three conditions—mass poverty and ignorance, intellectual frustration and revolutionary conspiracy—exist to-day in varying degrees in large parts of southern

Europe, Asia, Africa and South America. These conditions do not necessarily produce revolutionaries of the extreme left: they may instead produce reactionary movements in which social discontent is mixed with nationalism and worship of past traditions, but which use a revolutionary technique of conspiracy. Examples of this are the Japanese military groups of the 1930's, or the Roumanian Iron Guard, which was to some extent the offspring of the Russian "black hundreds".

To-day when these conditions are giving birth to various types of national and social revolutionary movements in many parts of the world, from Peru to Nigeria and from the Lebanon to the Philippines, the history of the last decades of Imperial Russia is of more than academic interest. It throws light on some of the problems that most urgently beset the statesmen of our own day, and provides an impressive array of mistakes which they would do well to avoid.

BIBLIOGRAPHICAL NOTE

THE following list does not contain every work that I have consulted, but those which have been of some use to me, or may be of use to those who wish to pursue the study of the subject. In the case of books published in a Latin alphabet, the authors' names and titles are spelt as in the works themselves—this includes in certain cases transliteration of Slav names into French or German. In the case of books published in Cyrillic alphabet, the names and titles are transliterated as described in the Introduction. The place of publication is given for books not published in the United Kingdom. SPB means St. Petersburg.

GENERAL SURVEYS OF RUSSIAN HISTORY

V. O. Klyuchevski. *Kurs russkoy istorii* ("A Course of Russian History"), 5 vols. Published in Russian, 1904–21. Republished Moscow, 1936. English translation, 1911–31.

K. Stählin. *Geschichte Russlands*, 4 vols. Berlin, completed 1939

B. H. Sumner. *Survey of Russian History*. 2nd edition, 1948.

P. N. Milyukov. *Ocherki po istorii russkoy kultury* ("Outline History of Russian Culture"), 3 vols. SPB, 5th edition, 1904.

P. N. Milyukov, C. Seignobos and L. Eisenmann. *Histoire de Russie*, 3 vols. Paris, 1933.

S. F. Platonov. *History of Russia*. New York, 1925.

S. R. Tompkins. *Russia through the Ages*. New York, 1940.

G. Vernadsky. *A History of Russia*. Newhaven, 1943.

Sir B. Pares. *History of Russia*. 2nd edition, 1937.

E. Lo Gatto. *Storia della Russia*. Milano, 1948.

SURVEYS OF NINETEENTH- AND TWENTIETH-CENTURY RUSSIA

A. A. Kornilov. *Modern Russian History*. New York, 1924.

A. Leroy-Beaulieu. *L'Empire des Tsars et les Russes*, 3 vols. Paris, 1881–9.

M. Karpovich. *Imperial Russia*. New York, 1932.

A. von Hedenström. *Geschichte Russlands, 1878–1918*. Berlin, 1922.

Sir D. Mackenzie Wallace. *Russia*. 1877. Enlarged new edition, 1905.

O. Hoetzsch. *Russland*. Berlin, 1913.

H. Williams. *Russia of the Russians*. 1914.

PEASANT QUESTION

G. T. Robinson. *Rural Russia under the Old Regime*. 1932.

A. A. Kornilov. *Krestyanskaya reforma* ("The Peasant Reform"). SPB, 1905.

P. P. Maslov. *Agrarnii vopros v Rossii* ("The Agrarian Question in Russia"). SPB, 1908.

Sir J. Maynard. *The Russian Peasant*. 1942.

L. Owen. *The Russian Peasant Movement*. 1937.

Robinson is a thorough survey of the problem, and contains a comprehensive bibliography, most of the works in which are however not available in this country. Kornilov and Maslov are classic studies of the subject, written respectively from a Liberal and a Menshevik standpoint. Maynard is a useful introduction to the subject, Owen a special analysis of Lenin's agrarian policy.

ECONOMIC DEVELOPMENT

P. I. Lyashchenko. *Istoriya narodnovo hozyaistva SSSR* ("History of the National Economy of the U.S.S.R."), vol. 2. Moscow, 1948. An American translation was published 1950.

M. Tugan-Baranovski. *Geschichte der russischen Fabrik*. Berlin, 1900.

P. B. Struve. *Kriticheskie zametki k voprosu ob ekonomicheskom razvitiyu Rossii* ("Critical Observations on the Question of the Economic Development of Russia"). SPB, 1894.

N. Danielson (N.–on). *Ocherki nashevo poreformennovo hozyaistva* ("Outline of our Post-Reform Economy"). SPB, 1893.

Lenin. *Development of Capitalism in Russia*. First published, SPB, 1899. Forms vol. 3 of the 3rd Russian edition of his Works. Moscow, 1931.

Von Schulze-Gävernitz. *Volkswirtschaftliche Studien aus Russland*. Leipzig, 1899.

V. I. Kovalevski (ed.). *Rossiya v kontse 19-ovo veka* ("Russia at the end of the Nineteenth Century"). SPB, 1900.

P. P. Migulin. *Reforma denezhnovo obrashchenia v Rossii i promyshlenny krizis 1893–1902 godov* ("Reform of the Circulation of Money in Russia and the Industrial Crisis, 1893–1902"). Harkov, 1902.

Raffalovich. *Russia: its Trade and Commerce*. 1918.

M. Miller. *The Economic Development of Russia, 1905–1914*. 1926.

Ischtschanian. *Die ausländischen Elemente in der russischen Volkswirtschaft*. Berlin, 1913.

P. A. Berlin. *Russkaya burzhuaziya v staroe i novoe vremya* ("The Russian Bourgeoisie in Old and Modern Times"). Moscow, 1922.

I. H. Ozerov. *Politika po rabochemu voprosu* ("Policy in the Labour Question"). Moscow, 1906.

V. Grinevich. *Professionalnoe dvizhenie rabochih* ("The Trade Union Movement"). SPB, 1908.

S. N. Prokopovich. *Kooperativnoe dvizhenie v Rossii* ("The Co-operative Movement in Russia"). Moscow, 1913.

All these are useful sources. The four works by Tugan-Baranovski, Struve, Danielson and Lenin are essential for the Populist-Marxist economic controversies of the '90's, but were all based on inadequate material, covering only certain regions. The works relating to the period after 1905 are based on much fuller material.

MACHINERY OF GOVERNMENT

Polievktov. *Nikolay I, biografiya i obzor tsarstvovaniya*, Moscow, 1918 ("Nicholas I, Biography and Survey of His Reign").

Ministerstvo Vnutrennih Dyel, istoricheskii ocherk, 1802–1902 ("Ministry of Interior, a Historical Outline"). SPB, 1902.

Ministerstvo Finansov, 1802–1902 ("Minister of Finance"). SPB, 1902.

Ministerstvo Inostrannih Dyel, 1802–1902 ("Ministry of Foreign Affairs"). SPB, 1902.

Ministerstvo Morskoe, 1802–1902 ("Ministry of the Navy"). SPB, 1902.

Stoletie Voennovo Ministerstva ("A Century of the War Ministry"). SPB, 1902–11.

Ministerstvo Narodnovo Prosveshchenia ("Ministry of National Education"). SPB, 1902.

Obshchestvennoe dvizhenie v Rossii v nachale 20-vo veka ("Public Opinion and Society in Russia at the Beginning of the Twentieth Century"). SPB, 1908–11.

Djanshiev. *Epoha velikih reform* ("The Age of the Great Reforms"). Moscow, 1900.

A. A. Kornilov. *Obshchestvennoe dvizhenie pri Aleksandre II* ("Public Opinion and Society in the Reign of Alexander II"). Moscow, 1909.

B. Veselovski. *Istoriya zemstv za sorok let* ("History of the Zemstvos during Forty Years"). SPB, 1909.

P. B. Struve. *Materialy po universitetskom voprosu* ("Material on the University Question"). Stuttgart, 1903.

P. B. Struve. *Usilenie gubernatorskoy vlasti* ("The Strengthening of the Power of the Governor"). Stuttgart, 1903.

S. Yu. Witte. *Samoderzhavie i zemstvo* ("Autocracy and the Zemstvo"). Stuttgart, 1901.

Prince S. D. Urussov. *Memoirs of a Russian Governor*. 1908.

M. Lemke. *Nikolaevskie zhandarmy i literatura* ("Nicholas I's Gendarmes and Literature").

M. Laporte. *Histoire de l'Okhrana, 1880–1917*. Paris, 1935.

P. Zavarzin. *Rabota tainoy politsii* ("The Work of the Secret Police"). Paris, 1924.

P. Zavarzin. *Zhandarmy i revolyutsionery* ("Gendarmes and Revolutionaries"). Paris, 1930.

G. Kennan. *Siberia and the Exile System.* 1891.

M. Gernet. *Istoriya tsarskoy tyurmy* ("History of the Prison in Imperial Russia"). Moscow, 1946.

A. Sliozberg. *Dorevolyutsionny stroy Rossii* ("The Pre-Revolutionary System of Russia"). Paris, 1933.

A. F. Koni. *Na zhiznennom puti* ("From my Life"). SPB, 1914.

N. Hans. *History of Russian Educational Policy.* 1931.

K. P. *Pobedonostsev i yevo korrespondenty* ("Correspondence of K. P. Pobedonostsev"). Moscow, 1926.

Polievktov's book is a useful survey of the reign of Nicholas I. The next six works are official histories of the Ministries of Interior, Finance, Foreign Affairs, Navy, War and Education, prepared in their centenary year 1902. *Obshchestvennoe dvizhenie* is a four-volume symposium by Menshevik writers, edited by Martov, Potresov and Maslov, surveying the social and political structure, political movements and parties, nationalities and foreign policy on the eve of the 1905 revolution, during it and after it. The first volume is extremely useful as an analysis of Russia at the turn of the century, the second deals with the events of 1905 and the behaviour of the social classes during them, the third with political parties, the fourth with the results of the revolutionary period. This, though of course written from a Menshevik point of view, is one of the most valuable sources of information on Russia during the period. Of the other works quoted above, Kornilov's is a useful account of public opinion and political activity during the reign of Alexander II, Veselovski's a factual survey of forty years of zemstvo activity, Sliozberg's a competent summary of the political structure of Russia in the early twentieth century, Koni's a revealing work of memoirs of a judge. Dr. Hans competently summarises official educational policy from Alexander I to the eve of 1917. The two volumes of Pobedonostsev's correspondence published by the Soviet authorities throw light on the apparatus of state under Alexander III.

THE CHURCH

Ammann. *Abriss der ostslawischen Kirchengeschichte.* Vienna, 1950.

Curtiss. *Church and State in Russia.* Columbia, 1940.

Conybeare. *Russian Dissenters.* Cambridge (Mass.), 1921.

There is also much material on Church questions in Milyukov, *Ocherki*, and in Leroy-Beaulieu, *op. cit.*

POLITICAL IDEAS

The essential sources are the works of the political thinkers themselves, especially of Herzen, Chernyshevski, Dobrolyubov, Pisarev, Lavrov and N. K. Mihailovski. The following works of comment are of value.

N. Berdyaev. *The Origins of Russian Communism.* 1937.

N. Berdyaev. *The Russian Idea.* 1947.

T. G. Masaryk. *The Spirit of Russia.* 1918.

R. Hare. *Pioneers of Russian Social Thought.* 1951.

A. Coquart. *Dmitri Pisarev et l'idéologie du nihilisme russe.* Paris, 1946.

V. P. Vorontsov ("V.V."). *Nashi napravleniya.* SPB, 1893.

Vyehi. SPB, 1909.

Vyehi, a symposium whose contributors included Berdyaev, Bulgakov and Struve, is a most penetrating analysis of the Russian intelligentsia after the 1905 revolution.

THE POPULIST MOVEMENT

E. H. Carr. *The Romantic Exiles.* 1933.

E. H. Carr. *Bakunin.* 1937.

M. Lemke. *Ocherki osvoboditelnovo dvizhenia 60-h godov* ("Outline of the Liberation Movement of the '60's"). SPB, 1908.

Aptekman. *Obshchestvo Zemlya i Volya* ("The Society 'Land and Liberty'"). Moscow, 1919.

D. Footman. *Red Prelude.* 1944.

Stepnyak. *Underground Russia.* 1883.

Figner and Pribyleva-Korba. *A. D. Mihailov.* Moscow, 1925.

Materialy dlya biografii A. I. Zhelyabova ("Material for a Biography of A. I. Zhelyabov"). Moscow, 1930.

A. Thun. *Geschichte der revolutionären Bewegung in Russland.* Leipzig, 1883.

Figner. *Zapechatlyonny trud.* ("A life's work completed") Moscow, 1920.

P. B. Akselrod. *Perezhitoe i peredumannoe* ("Experiences and Reflections"). Berlin, 1923.

Debogori-Mokrievich. *Vospominania* ("Memoirs"). SPB, 1906.

Spiridovich. *Histoire du terrorisme russe 1886–1917.* Paris, 1930.

V. M. Chernov. *Zapiski sotsialista-revolyutsionera* ("Notes of a Socialist-Revolutionary"). Berlin, 1922.

Gershuni. *Iz nedavnevo proshlovo* ("From the Recent Past"). Paris, 1908.

V. Burtsev. *Borba za svobodnuyu Rossiyu* ("The Struggle for a Free Russia"). Berlin, 1923.

B. Nikolaevski. *Azeff, the Russian Judas.* 1934.

Protokoly 1-oy obshchepartiinoy konferentsii P.S.R. ("Minutes of the First All-Party Conference of the S.R. Party"). Paris, 1908.

E. E. Kluge. *Die russische revolutionäre Presse, 1855–1905.* Zürich, 1948.

The two brilliant works by E. H. Carr deal with the period before the emergence of Populism, but throw light on its origins. The most useful single work on the revolutionaries of 1877–1881 is Aptekman. The short study of Zhelyabov by Footman may be strongly recommended. Spiridovich was a high officer in the political police. Despite its limitations, his book gives a more thorough survey of the Socialist-Revolutionary movement before 1917 than any other work that I have been able to find. Chernov's memoirs are interesting but end before the formation of the party.

THE MARXIST MOVEMENT

Yu. O. Martov and F. Dan. *Geschichte der russischen Sozialdemokratie.* Berlin, 1926.

Lenin. Complete works in Russian. 3rd edition, Moscow, 1930–33, begun under the direction of Kamenev and completed by Adoratski, Molotov and Savelyev, 30 vols. 4th edition, Moscow, 1941–50, published anonymously by the Marx-Engels-Lenin Institute, 35 vols. English abridged edition, *Lenin Selected Works,* 1936–1939, 12 vols.

The most important of his individual political pamphlets in this period are *Who are the Friends of the People?* (written 1894); *What is to be Done?* (1900); *One Step Forward, Two Steps Back* (1904); and *Two Tactics of Social Democracy* (1905).

G. V. Plehanov. *Nashi raznoglasiya* ("Our Differences"). Geneva, 1884.

G. V. Plehanov. *Sotsializm i politicheskaya borba* ("Socialism and the Political Struggle"). Geneva, 1885.

G. V. Plehanov. *Russkii rabochii v revolyutsionnom dvizhenii* ("The Russian Worker in the Revolutionary Movement"). Geneva, 1892.

Tahtarev ("Peterburzhets"). *Ocherki peterburzhskovo rabochevo dvizhenia 90-h godov* ("Outline of the Petersburg Workers' Movement of the '90's"). London, 1902.

Yu. O. Martov. *Zapiski sotsial-demokrata* ("Notes of a Social Democrat"). Berlin, 1922.

Yu. O. Martov. *Spasiteli ili uprazdniteli* ("Saviours or"). Paris, 1911.

Pisma P. B. Akselroda k Yu. O. Martovu ("Letters of P. B. Akselrod to Yu. O. Martov"). Berlin, 1924.

N. Krupskaya. *Memories of Lenin.* 1942.

L. D. Trotski. *1905.* Milano, 1948.

P. A. Garvi. *Vospominaniya* ("Memoirs"). New York, 1946.

F. Dan. *Proiz'hozhdenie bolshevizma* ("The Origin of Bolshevism"). New York, 1946.

E. H. Carr. *The Bolshevik Revolution.* 1950.

B. D. Wolfe. *Three who made a Revolution.* New York, 1949.

D. Shub. *Lenin.* New York, 1948.

Lyubov Krassin. *Leonid Krassin, his Life and Work.* 1929.

Badaev. *The Bolsheviks in the Tsarist Duma.* 1929.

2-oy s'yezd R.S.D.R.P. ("2nd Congress"). London, 1903.

Protokoly ob'yedinitelnovo s'yezda R.S.D.R.P. ("Minutes of the Unifying Congress"). Moscow, 1926, ed. Varentsova.

5-y s'yezd R.S.D.R.P. ("5th Congress"). Moscow, 1935, ed. E. Yaroslavski.

Vserossiiskaya konferentsiya 1912 goda ("The All-Russian Conference of 1912"). Paris, 1912.

Martov's history of the party, from a Menshevik standpoint, and Lenins' Works, are essential reading. So also are the first two pamphlets of

Plehanov, Trotski's *1905*, and the proceedings of the Congresses of the party. I have quoted above the editions which I have personally used. There are others. E. H. Carr's brilliant book contains a valuabe summary, in its introductory section, of the views of the Marxist fractions before 1917. Dan's posthumous work is also of considerable interest. I have not included in the list the contemporary official Stalinist version, *Short History of the C.P.S.U.(b)*, as I cannot honestly recommend it to readers. Its value lies not in its relevance to the history of this period but in its influence in the last decade as a sacred writing of Stalinism. As such it is of course an essential document.

POLITICS AFTER 1905

Gosudarstvennaya Duma, stenograficheskie otchoty, 1906–1914 ("The Imperial Duma, Stenographic Record").

Obshchestvennoe dvizhenie, vol. 4.

Sir B. Pares. *Russia and Reform*. 1907.

Sir B. Pares. *My Russian Memoirs*. 1931.

Sir B. Pares. *The Fall of the Russian Monarchy*. 1939.

Sir J. Maynard. *Russia in Flux*. 1941.

Kizevetter. *Na rubezhe dvuh stoletii* ("On the Border Line of Two Centuries"). Prague, 1929.

Witte. *Mémoires du comte Witte*. Paris, 1921.

Kokovstov. *Out of my Past*. Stanford, 1935.

Dnevnik Imperatora Nikolaya II ("Diary of Emperor Nicholas II"). Berlin, 1923.

Letters of Tsar Nicholas and Empress Marie. 1937.

Suchomlinow. *Erinnerungen*. Berlin, 1924.

Polivanov. *Memuary* ("Memoirs"). Moscow, 1924.

Danilov. *Velikii knyaz Nikolay Nikolayevich* ("Grand Duke Nicholas Nicholaevich"). Paris, 1930.

THE NATIONALITIES

Cambridge History of Poland, vol. 2. 1941.

W. J. Rose. *The Rise of Polish Democracy*. 1944.

J. Feldman. *Geschichte der politischen Ideen in Polen seit dessen Teilungen*. Munich, 1917.

R. Dmowski. *Mysli nowoczesnego Polaka* ("Thoughts of a Modern Pole"). Lwow, 1903.

R. Dmowski. *La question polonaise*. Paris, 1909.

F. Perl ("Res"). *Dzieje ruchu socjalistycznego w zaborze rosyskim* ("History of the Socialist Movement in the Russian Partition"). Warsaw, 1910.

F. Perl ("Res"). *Koordynacya czy utożsamienie?* ("Co-ordination or Identification?"). Cracow, 1906.

R. Luxemburg. *Kwestya polska a ruch socjalistyczny* ("The Polish Question and the Socialist Movement"). Cracow, 1905.

R. Luxemburg. *Die industrielle Entwicklung Polens*. Berlin, 1898.

Chałasinski. *Genealogja społeczna inteligencji polskiej* ("The Social Genealogy of the Polish Intelligentsia"). Warsaw, 1946.

Hrushevski. *Abrégé de l'histoire de l'Ukraine*. Paris, 1920.

Ed. Doroshenko and others. *Velika Istoriya Ukrainy* ("Big History of the Ukraine)". Winnipeg, 1948.

Krupnyckyj. *Geschichte der Ukraine*. Leipzig, 1943.

Academy of Sciences of Ukrainian S.S.R. *Narys istorii Ukrainy* ("Sketch of the History of the Ukraine"). Kiev, 1942.

I. Mazepa. *Pidstavy nashoho vidrozhdennya* ("Foundations of our Rebirth"). Augsburg, 1946.

Greenberg. *The Jews in Russia*. Newhaven, 1944.

Dubnow. *History of the Jews in Russia and Poland*. Philadelphia, 1916–20.

Ames (ed). *The Revolution in the Baltic Provinces*. 1907.

Hampden Jackson. *Esthonia*. 1941.

Villecourt. *L'Esthonie*. Paris, 1932.

Segreste. *La Lettonie*. Paris, 1930.

Bossin. *La Lithuanie*. Paris, 1933.

B. Kalnins. *De baltiska Staternas Frihetskamp*. ("The Baltic States' Fight for Freedom"). Stockholm, 1950.

Schwabe. *Agrarian History of Latvia*. Riga, 1930.

Dalton. *Offenes Sendschreiben an den Oberprokuror des heiligen Synods, K. P. Pobedonostsev*. 1889.

Schybergson. *Geschichte Finnlands*. Gotha, 1926.

Wuorinen. *Nationalism in Modern Finland*. New York, 1931.

Von Törne. *Finland under hundra trettio år* ("Finland During 130 Years"). Stockholm, 1943.

Paasivirta. *Arbetarrörelsen i Finland* ("The Workers' Movement in Finland"). Stockholm, 1948.

Hampden Jackson. *Finland*. 1940.

Pasdermadjian. *Histoire de l'Arménie*. Paris, 1949.

Allen. *History of the Georgian People*. 1932.

Azerbaijan Soviet Republic, Ministry of Foreign Affairs. *Dokumenty po russkoy politike v Zakavkazi* ("Documents on Russian Policy in Transcaucasia"). Baku, 1920.

G. von Mende. *Der nationale Kampf der Russlandtürken*. Berlin, 1936.

Revue du monde musulman.

Obshchestvennoe dvizhenie, vols. 1, 3 and 4.

P. I. Kovalevski. *Russkii natsionalizm i natsionalnoe vospitanie* ("Russian Nationalism and National Education"). SPB, 1912.

The best single work is *Obshchestvennoe dvizhenie*. Of the others, Feldman, Krupnyckyj, Schybergson, Törne and von Mende are competent summaries. The polemical works of Dmowski, Luxemburg and

Perl are of great interest. The other works in the list all contain some material of use. Thorough surveys of the position of most of the individual nationalities have still to be made. This is still more true of the Russian nationality problem as a whole. For Bolshevik views of the problem, see Lenin's works and Stalin's *Marxism and the National and Colonial Question*.

FOREIGN RELATIONS

DIPLOMATIC DOCUMENTS

British Documents on the Origins of the War.
Documents diplomatiques français.
Die Grosse Politik der europäischen Kabinette.
Krasny Arhiv.
Österreich-Ungarns Aussenpolitik.

RUSSIA AND THE GREAT POWERS

Eyck. *Bismarck*. Zürich, 1944.
Bismarck. *Gedanken und Erinnerungen*. Berlin, 1898.
W. L. Langer. *European Alliances and Alignments*. New York, 1931.
Pribram. *Secret Treaties of Austria-Hungary*. Harvard, 1920.
Simpson. *The Saburov Memoirs*. 1929.
Skazkin. *Konets russko-avstro-germanskovo soyuza* ("The End of the Russo-Austro-German Alliance"). Moscow, 1928.
Schweinitz. *Denkwürdigkeiten*. Berlin, 1927.
Baron Boris Nolde. *L'alliance franco-russe*. Paris, 1936.
Michon. *L'alliance franco-russe*. Paris, 1927.
W. L. Langer. *The Franco-Russian Alliance*. Harvard, 1929.
W. L. Langer. *The Diplomacy of Imperialism*, 2 vols. New York, 1935.
William II. *Briefe Wilhelms II an den Zaren, 1894–1914*. Berlin, 1920.
Anderson. *The First Moroccan Crisis*. Chicago, 1930.
Klein. *Der Vertrag von Björkö*. Berlin, 1931.
Trubetskoy. *Russland als Grossmacht*. Stuttgart, 1913.
Baron Taube. *Der grossen Katastrofe entgegen*. Leipzig, 1937.
Sazonov. *Les années fatales*. Paris, 1927.

RUSSIA, AUSTRIA AND SLAV PROBLEMS

Eisenmann. *Le compromis austro-hongrois*. Paris, 1904.
A. J. P. Taylor. *The Habsburg Monarchy*. 1948.
Wickham Steed. *The Habsburg Monarchy*. 1913.
R. W. Seton-Watson. *Racial Problems in Hungary*. 1908.
R. W. Seton-Watson. *The South Slav Question*. 1911.
R. W. Seton-Watson. *History of the Czechs and Slovaks*. 1944.
Baernreither. *Fragments of a Political Diary*. 1930.
Aurel Popovici. *Die Vereinigten Staaten von Gross-Österreich*. Leipzig, 1906.

Von Chlumecky. *Erzherzog Franz Ferdinand.* Berlin, 1929.

Otto Bauer. *Die Nationalitätenfrage und die Sozialdemokratie.* Vienna, 1924.

Fischel. *Der Panslawismus bis zum Weltkriege.* Berlin, 1918.

Werner. *Der alldeutsche Verband.* Berlin, 1935.

Molisch. *Geschichte der deutsch-nationalen Bewegung in Österreich.* Jena, 1926.

BALKAN PROBLEMS AND CRISES

Sir Charles Eliot. *Turkey in Europe.* 1900.

Goriainow. *Le Bosphore et les Dardanelles.* Paris, 1910.

Anchieri. *Constantinopoli e gli Stretti.* Milano, 1948.

Sumner. *Russia and the Balkans, 1870–1880.* 1937.

R. W. Seton-Watson. *Disraeli, Gladstone and the Eastern Question.* 1935.

Rupp. *A Wavering Friendship: Russia and Austria.* Harvard, 1941.

Stojanović. *The Great Powers and the Balkans.* 1939.

Ćubrilović. *Bosanski ustanak, 1875–8* ("The Bosnian Rising"). Belgrade, 1930.

S. Jovanović. *Vlada Milana Obrenovića* ("The Government of Milan Obrenović"), 3 vols. Belgrade, 1934.

S. Jovanović. *Vlada Aleksandra Obrenovića* ("The Government of Alexander Obrenović"). Belgrade, 1935.

S. Novaković. *Dvadeset godina ustavne politike u Srbiji* ("Twenty Years of Constitutional Policy in Serbia"). Belgrade, 1912.

Svetozar Marković. *Srbija na istoku* ("Serbia in the East"). Republished Belgrade, 1946.

Hajek. *Bulgarien unter der Türkenherrschaft.* Berlin, 1925.

Black. *The Establishment of Constitutional Government in Bulgaria.* Princeton, 1943.

S. Radev. *Stroitelite na s'vremena B'lgariya* ("Builders of Contemporary Bulgaria"). Sofia, 1911.

Y. S'kazov. *B'lgarite v svoyata istoriya* ("The Bulgarians in their History"). Sofia, 1922.

D. Blagoyev. *Prinos k'm istoriyata na sotsializma v B'lgariya* ("A Contribution to the History of Socialism in Bulgaria"). First published Sofia, 1906 republished Sofia 1948.

N. Todorov. *Politička istorija savremene Bugarske* ("Political History of Contemporary Bulgaria"). Belgrade, 1938.

T. Pavlov. *Botev, Levski i Markovich.* Sofia, 1946.

H. Madol. *King Ferdinand of Bulgaria.* 1933.

H. N. Brailsford. *Macedonia.* 1906.

R. Swire. *Bulgarian Conspiracy.* 1939.

V. M. Markov. *Serbien zwischen Österreich und Russland, 1897–1908.* Stuttgart, 1934.

Boghitschewitsch. *Die auswärtige Politik Serbiens, 1903–1914.* Berlin, 1928.

B. Schmitt. *The Annexation of Bosnia.* 1937.

M. Nintchitch. *La crise bosniaque (1908–1914) et les puissances européennes.* Paris, 1937.

Conrad von Hötzendorff. *Aus meiner Dienstzeit.* Vienna, 1921.

R. W. Seton-Watson. *The Rise of Nationality in the Balkans.* 1917.

Geshov. *The Balkan Alliance.* 1915.

Radoslawow. *Bulgarien und die Weltkrise.* Berlin, 1923.

E. C. Helmreich. *The Diplomacy of the Balkan Wars.* Harvard, 1939.

RUSSIA AND ASIA

Sumner. *Tsarism and Imperialism in the Middle and Far East.* 1940.

Krausse. *Russia in Asia.* 1899.

Meyendorff (ed.). *Correspondance diplomatiqne du baron de Staal.* Paris, 1929.

I. Zarubin. *Spisok narodnostei turkestanskovo kraya* ("List of the Naticnalities of the Turkestan Region"). Leningrad, 1925.

W. Jochelson. *Peoples of Asiatic Russia.* American Museum of Natural History, 1928.

Brockelmann. *Geschichte der islamischen Völker.* Berlin, 1939.

Browne. *The Persian Revolution.* 1910.

R. P. Churchill. *The Anglo-Russian Convention.* Iowa, 1939.

Polst. *Die anglo-russische Entente.* Hamburg, 1932.

G. F. Hudson. *The Far East in World Politics.* 1939.

P. Renouvin. *L'Extrême-Orient, 1840–1940.* Paris, 1940.

Franke. *Die Grossmächte in Ostasien.* Brunswick, 1923.

D. J. Dallin. *The Rise of Russia in Asia.* 1950.

B. D. Romanov. *Rossiya v Manchzhurii* ("Russia in Manchuria"). Leningrad, 1928.

B. D. Romanov. *Diplomaticheskii ocherk russko-yaponskoy voiny* ("Diplomatic Outline of the Russo-Japanese War"). Moscow, 1947.

B. Glinski. *Prolog russko-yaponskoy voiny* ("Prologue to the Russo-Japanese War"). SPB, 1915.

Rosen. *Forty Years of Diplomacy.* 1922.

Hayashi. *The Secret Memoirs of Count Hayashi* (ed. Pooley). 1915.

Takeuchi. *War and Diplomacy in the Japanese Empire.* Chicago, 1935.

Price. *The Russo-Japanese Treaties of 1907–1916.* Baltimore, 1933.

Korostovets. *Von Cingis Khan zur Sowjetrepublik: Geschichte der Mongolei.* Berlin, 1926.

Tyler Dennett. *John Hay.* 1933.

Tyler Dennet. *Roosevelt and the Russo-Japanese War.* 1925.

S. Bemis. *Diplomatic History of the United States.* 1937.

Zabriskie. *American-Russian Rivalry in the Far East.* Philadelphia, 1946.

Sumner's lecture is a brilliant brief survey of Russia's Asia policy. The works of Hudson and Renouvin are excellent summaries of Far Eastern affairs during the period. Dallin's book is the most convenient summary of

Russian policy. Romanov's first book is a valuable contribution to historical knowledge, his second is perverted by the needs of Soviet propaganda. Glinski's publication of Witte's papers is an invaluable source. Zabriskie's study of Russo-American relations after 1905 is also of great value.

INDEX

INDEX OF PERSONS